American Dictionaries
of the English Language
Before 1861

by

EVA MAE BURKETT

The Scarecrow Press, Inc.
Metuchen, N.J. & London
1979

To the Memory of

Dr. Charles S. Pendleton

and

Dr. Fremont P. Wirth

Library of Congress Cataloging in Publication Data

Burkett, Eva Mae.
    American dictionaries of the English language before
1861.

    Originally presented as the author's thesis, George
Peabody College for Teachers, 1936 under title: A study
of American dictionaries of the English language before
1861.
    Bibliography: p.
    Includes index.
    1. English language--Lexicography. 2. Lexicographers
--United States--Biography. I. Title.
PE1611.B7 1978   423'.028   78-11677
ISBN 0-8108-1179-0

PREFACE

A study of American dictionaries is a phase of the history
of the social, cultural, and educational development of the American people. The addition of new words and new uses of old words
coincide with the changes that occur in social life; the record of
the pronunciation and definition of words is an index to the stages
of cultural evolution; while the ideas of dictionary making are determined to some degree by the educational theories of the time.

The topic for investigation as a doctoral dissertation was
suggested by Dr. Charles S. Pendleton, to whom the writer is indebted for his interest and guidance in the compilation and organ-
ization of the data and for his careful criticism of the manuscript.
Dr. Fremont P. Wirth aided much in suggesting sources for
material and by his unfailing interest in the work. Many other people and many libraries have been helpful in the lending of books
and material, in replying to inquiries, and in making suggestions
for further research. Included in the list are the following persons
and libraries: Mrs. Roswell Skeel, Jr. , a great-granddaughter of
Webster; Elizabeth G. Davis, Guilford, Connecticut, who aided in
collecting material about Samuel Johnson, Jr. , of whom she is a
collateral descendant; Frank Chapman Leete, Guilford, Connecticut,
and Frederick C. Norton, Guilford, Connecticut, both of whom
helped in securing information about Johnson; Dr. Walter R. Steiner,
Hartford, Connecticut; Allen Walker Read, University of Chicago;
Ellsworth Eliot, Jr. , a relative of John Elliott; Mrs. J. J. Didcoct,
Librarian, Peabody College; Isa Lee Sherrod, Librarian, State
Teachers College, Murfreesboro; R. W. G. Vail and Clarence S.
Brigham, American Antiquarian Society, who have been generous in
lending material and in allowing the examination of the collection of
dictionaries in their library; the libraries of Yale University, Har-
vard University, and the Public Library of the City of Boston; the
New York Public Library, which allowed the use of the Webster
manuscript material; the G. & C. Merriam Company; the Connecti-
cut Historical Library; the Kent Memorial Library, Suffield, Connecticut; the Massachusetts Historical Society; the New York State
Library, Albany; the New Jersey Historical Society; the Middlesex
County Historical Society; University of Pennsylvania Library; His-
torical Society of Pennsylvania Library; State Library, Boston;
Iowa State Library; Onondaga Historical Association; the Carnegie
Library, Nashville; Vanderbilt Library; Y.M.C.A. Graduate School
Library; and the Tennessee State Library. The Library of Con-

gress permitted the examination of several rare books and newspapers.

The study was written as a doctoral dissertation at George Peabody College for Teachers, August 1936.

CONTENTS

ILLUSTRATIONS

PART ONE

AMERICAN DICTIONARIES EXCLUSIVE OF WEBSTER AND WORCESTER

CHAPTER I

THE BEGINNINGS OF AMERICAN LEXICOGRAPHY

This study of dictionaries of the English language is a survey of the volumes compiled by Americans prior to 1861. The period thus covered begins with the publication of A School Dictionary by Samuel Johnson, Jr. in 1798, and closes with the publication of A Dictionary of the English Language by Joseph Emerson Worcester in 1860. The works of thirty-four compilers are treated in chronological order.

The study is divided into two parts. Part One concerns the dictionaries published by Americans before 1861, exclusive of Webster and Worcester. Part Two deals with the dictionaries of Webster and Worcester and the conflict that arose over the rival publications of these two men.

Chapter I is a discussion of the men and their dictionaries which constitute the beginning of lexical work in America. The eight men whose works are treated in this chapter are Samuel Johnson, Jr., John Elliott, Caleb Alexander, William Woodbridge, Henry Priest, Daniel Jaudon, Thomas Watson, and Stephen Addington. John Elliott collaborated with Samuel Johnson, Jr. on the second dictionary, while Jaudon, Watson, and Addington worked together on one dictionary. Although these early dictionaries made little contribution to the science of dictionary making, they were beneficial in the prevention of the formation of dialects.

Chapter II presents a description of the work of twenty compilers, two of whom worked together on one dictionary. These men were interested chiefly in the publication of dictionaries for school and for handy reference work. In the order of their treatment, these compilers and their works are as follows:

Abel Flint, A Spelling, Pronouncing and Parsing Dictionary, 1806.

Susanna Rowson, A Spelling Dictionary, 1807.

Richard Wiggins, The New York Expositor, 1811.

Richard S. Coxe, The New Critical Pronouncing Dictionary of the English Language, 1813.

3

Burgess Allison, The American Standard of Orthography and Pronunciation, 1815.

William Grimshaw, An Etymological Dictionary of Analysis of the English Language, 1821; The Ladies' Lexicon and The Gentlemen's Lexicon, 1829.

J. Kingsbury, A New Improved Dictionary for Children, 1822.

Hezekiah Burhans, The Nomenclature and Expositor of the English Language, 1826.

Eliza Robbins, Primary Dictionary, 1828.

E. Hazen, The Speller and Definer, 1829.

William W. Turner, The School Dictionary, 1829.

Noah J. T. George, The Gentlemen and Ladies' Pocket Dictionary, 1831.

D. J. Browne, The Etymological Encyclopedia of Technical Terms and Phrases, 1832.

Rufus Claggett, The American Expositor, or Intellectual Definer, 1836.

Lyman Cobb, abridged edition of Walker's Critical Pronouncing Dictionary, 1828; Expositor or Sequel to the Spelling-Book, 1833; A New Dictionary of the English Language, 1832; and The Ladies' Reticule Companion, or Little Lexicon of the English Language, 1834.

Thomas Hopkins Gallaudet and Horace Hooker, The School and Family Dictionary, 1841.

James H. Martin, The Orthoepist, 1851.

"A Public School Teacher," The Public School Dictionary, 1855.

Alexander H. Laidlaw, An American Pronouncing Dictionary, 1859.

Chapter III is divided into two parts. The first part deals with the dictionaries of Americanisms. They are three in number:

John Pickering, A Vocabulary, or Collection of Words and Phrases Which Have Been Supposed to be Peculiar to the United States of America, 1816.

John Russell Bartlett, A Dictionary of Americanisms, A Glossary of Phrases, Usually Regarded as Peculiar to the United States, 1848.

Alfred L. Elwyn, Glossary of Supposed Americanisms, 1859.

The second part of Chapter III contains a description of the two phonetic dictionaries:

William Bolles, An Explanatory and Phonographic Pronouncing Dictionary of the English Language, 1845.

Daniel S. Smalley, The American Phonetic Dictionary of the English Language, 1855.

In Chapter IV the dictionaries of Noah Webster before 1860 are described and the facts of Webster's life as have a bearing on the production of his dictionaries are presented. The principal dictionaries included in this chapter are as follows:

A Compendious Dictionary of the English Language, 1806.

A Dictionary of the English Language; Compiled for the Use of Common Schools in the United States, 1807.

An American Dictionary of the English Language, 2 volumes, 1828.

An American Dictionary of the English Language, Joseph Emerson Worcester, abridged edition, 1829.

An American Dictionary of the English Language, Webster's revision, 1841.

An American Dictionary of the English Language, Chauncey A. Goodrich's revision, 1847.

An American Dictionary of the English Language, Chauncey A. Goodrich, Pictorial Quarto unabridged edition, 1859.

Joseph Emerson Worcester and his dictionaries are discussed in Chapter V. Arranged in chronological order, his dictionaries are as follows:

An edition of Johnson's Dictionary as improved by Todd, and abridged by Chalmers, 1828.

Abridgment of Webster's An American Dictionary, 1829.

A Comprehensive, Pronouncing and Explanatory Dictionary of the English Language, 1830.

Elementary Dictionary, 1835.

A Universal and Critical Dictionary of the English Language, 1846.

Primary Dictionary, 1850.

A Pronouncing, Explanatory, and Synonymous Dictionary of the
    English Language, 1855.

A Dictionary of the English Language, 1860.

Chapter VI presents an account of the struggle that arose between Webster and Worcester and their publishers and friends as to
the merits of their respective dictionaries.

*   *   *

The eight men who wrote dictionaries during the period covered in this first chapter probably felt the need, at the time when the
Americans were wavering in their allegiance between France and England, not only politically but also as regards language, to try to sta-
bilize our language and to make it a unifying force in the new government.   Their efforts are another example of the pioneering spirit of
the New England people.

The early dictionaries made very little contribution to the science of lexicography, but by recording the words that had come into
use as a result of life in a new environment, they serve as historical guides to the growth and development of our language.   By setting up a standard they aided in preventing the formation of dialects
and helped the foreigner acquire the language of his adopted country.
Based as they were on English dictionaries, they follow, in the main,
the principles of dictionary making laid down by such men as Perry
and Johnson, but sufficient original material was added to mark them
as distinctly new productions.

In the order of their treatment, the compilers and their six
dictionaries discussed in this chapter are as follows:

Samuel Johnson, Jr., A School Dictionary, [1798].

Samuel Johnson, Jr. and John Elliott, A Selected, Pronouncing
    and Accented Dictionary, 1800.

Caleb Alexander, The Columbian Dictionary, 1800.

William Woodbridge, A Key to the English Language, 1801.

Henry Priest, The Young Ladies' Pocket Companion, 1801.

Daniel Jaudon, Thomas Watson, and Stephen Addington, An English
    Orthographical Expositor, [1804].

A

School Dictionary,

Being a *COMPENDIUM* of the L
and *mostImproved*

DICTIONARIES,

Comprising an Easy and Concise Method
of teaching Children the true meaning and pronunciation of the
most useful words in the

ENGLISH LANGUAGE,

Not attainable by *common School Books* :
In which the *parts of Speech are distinguished*
and explained, and a general rule is given for
spelling derivative, and compound words.

BY SAMUEL JOHNSON, JUN'R.

Published according to Act of Congress.

NEW-HAVEN:

Printed and sold by *Edward O'Brien*, who
holds the copy-right for the states
of *Connecticut* and *New-York*.

1798 ?

Title page of the first American Dictionary.

A School Dictionary
by
Samuel Johnson, Junior

The first dictionary compiled by an American was A School
Dictionary, printed and sold in New Haven by Edward O'Brien, who
held the copyright for the states of Connecticut and New York. Although no date is given on the title page, the year 1798 is without
doubt the correct one, [1] for in the Connecticut Journal, a newspaper
published in New Haven and continuing as the New Haven Journal
Courier, appeared an announcement on November 8, 1798, (page 4,
column 1) as

>   Just published, and for sale by several Merchants in
> this and the adjacent towns, A School Dictionary; Being a
> Compendium of the latest and most improved Dictionaries;
> but principally of the Royal Standard English Dictionary:
> Comprising an easy and concise method of teaching chil-
> dren the true meaning and pronunciation of the most use-
> ful words in the English language, not attainable by common
> school books.
>   In which the words are divided agreeable to the Gram-
> matical Institute; and the sound of the accented vowel
> pointed out, by a particular character placed over it, which
> also marks the accented syllable: The parts of speech are
> distinguished and explained in an easy and familiar manner;
> and a general rule is given for spelling derivative and
> compound words.
>
>   By SAMUEL JOHNSON, jun.

The advertisement continues:

>   The difficulty which attended the printing a book of this
> kind from manuscript, and the ill state of health of the
> printer, while a part of the book was printed, has subject-
> ed the mechanical part of this edition to some inaccuracies,
> but the plan is honored with the following Recommendation:-
>   We, the subscribers have examined a small Dictionary,
> designed for children and common Schools, by Samuel John-
> son, jun. which we with pleasure recommend to the use of
> Instructors, as being well calculated to facilitate the means
> of improvement in the minds of their pupils
>
>   The Rev'd Benjamin Trumbull, D. D.
>   The Rev'd Athbel Baldwin
>   The Rev'd Lynde Huntington
>   Noah Webster, jun. Esq. - - Simeon Baldwin, Esq.
>   - - - Nathaniel Raffeter, Esq. - . - Jeremiah
>   Atwater, Dan Huntington, Tutors of Y. College.

The advertisement explains the purpose of the book by quoting from the Preface:

The design of the Author has been to furnish schools
with a book, which will enable youth more easily to acquire
a knowledge of the meaning of words in our language: - - -
Should it answer this purpose, his design will be accomplished, and his ruling passion (that of being serviceable to
youth) highly gratified.

The greater part of words in common Dictionaries, are
either so familiar, or so obsolete, that the time spent by
children in studying them and their definitions, is unprofit-
able.   They are, also, by this multiplicity of words rendered too voluminous to be advantageous, and too expensive
to be generally afforded as school books.

In addition to those familiar and obsolete, there are
others really useful, and such as are not easily and generally understood by children; a knowledge of which is
necessary in order to read good authors to advantage, and
without which no person can either write or speak our language with purity or elegance.

To select these from the huge mass of words with which
our language abounds, and to bring them into the compass
of a sizeable and cheap schoolbook, so that the spelling,
pronunciation, and definition of them may be easily obtained,
has been the object of the Author.

Of this first American dictionary, a 24mo., 12 1/2 cm., of
198 pages and near 4,100 words arranged in single columns, there
was but one edition, [2] of which, as far as has been determined in
this study, only four copies are now in existence.   In the British
Museum there is a copy presumably perfect; Yale College Library
has Sally Stanton's copy, with its nibbled edges, and from which
pages 89-92 inclusive, 101-104 inclusive, 149-152 inclusive, and 157-
168 inclusive are missing, which came from the sale of George Brin-
ley's library in 1886;[4] Harvard University owns a copy; and the
Library of Congress has a copy in the original binding.

The Preface asserts that:

> The Author, from long experience as an Instructor, hav-
> ing found the want of a sizeable School Dictionary has been
> stimulated to compile, and now offers to the public the
> following performance.   It is not calculated or intended to
> afford either entertainment or instruction to persons of
> Education.

Pages 5-11 of the Dictionary offer a few grammatical hints
"as a necessary appendage to the work," for it

> ... is difficult to implant clear and distinct ideas of the
> several parts of speech in the minds of youth.   In order
> therefore to effect this, they are here described in as
> plain and familiar a manner as possible; which with the
> assistance of able instructors, it is presumed will have
> the desired effect. [5]

The remarks on grammar are followed by an explanation of the symbols used to indicate the vowel sounds and pronunciation. The modesty of the author causes him to add that the

> ... different sounds of the vowels are not as accurately pointed out in the following work as they are in the Grammatical Institute by the ingenious Mr. Webster; nor can it be expected: but the author has endeavored to place them in such order as to prevent any material error in pronunciation.[6]

The character over a vowel in each word, marks the accented syllable and the sound of the vowels. The macron (ˉ) marks the first or natural sound of the vowels, as abāsement; the breve (˘), the second or short sound of the vowels, as abăndon; while the "circumflex is a more direct character denoting a sound different from either of the former. It represents the natural sound of the diphthongs, ôi, ôu, or ôw, as chôice, sôund, fôwl, the sound of au or aw as câuse, lâw, the sound of u made by e, i, and o, as hêr, stîr, sôme, pronounced hur, stur, sum. The sound of a made by e and i, as their, reign, pronounced thare, rane. "[7]

On page 61, beginning with the word enhance, the "want of a supply of accented Types, obliges the printer to omit the accent in such words as are safely pronounced by the division only. " There is no attempt at etymology. The words are divided into syllables by spacing.

Although it is stated that the School Dictionary met with a favorable reception,[8] "certain Guilford folk, not lovers of language, laughed at the new dictionary. "[9] The following words are interesting examples of what might have caused a knowing smile to play upon the faces of the intelligentsia of Guilford:

> bemused, overcome with musing
> chymistry, act of separating bodies with fire
> lout, to bow awkwardly
> mizzy, a quagmire, a shaking meadow
> mome, a dull, stupid person
> mouth-honor, insincere civility [Cf. Macbeth V, iii, 27]
> night-foundered, lost in the night time
> nustle, to fondle, to cherish
> tongue-pad, a very great talker
> yard-wand, measure of a yard

In the main, however, the definitions are good, although brief. They consist usually of two or three words which convey only one meaning.

As is seen in the Preface, Johnson makes no claim to originality in his work; his dictionary was intended chiefly to supplement the common school books, a fact that caused it to have somewhat the character of a dictionary of hard words. The spelling is not consistent. The simplified form is used in arbor, fervor, and author, but humour, odour, and candour follow the English spelling.

But who was the author of this first American dictionary? The New York Times Saturday Review, October 15, 1898, page 683, column 2, lamented the fact that very little was known "about this worthy man, whose pioneer work in American lexicography was well conceived and carefully executed." Contrary to a statement made in the same article and to others of a similar nature,[10] Samuel Johnson, Jr. was not the son but the great nephew of the learned Dr. Samuel Johnson, the first president of King's College.[11] Dr. Samuel Johnson had a younger brother, Nathaniel,[12] who, in 1744, was warden of the Episcopal Church in Guilford. Nathaniel married Mary Morgan, granddaughter of Governor William Jones and great-granddaughter of Theophilus Eaton of New Haven. Nathaniel's son Samuel married Margaret Collins, great-great-granddaughter of Governor William Leete of Guilford, and it was their son Samuel Johnson, Jr. who compiled the first American dictionary.[13]

The Johnson homestead was on Fair Street,[14] Guilford, and it was here that Samuel Johnson, Jr. was born March 10, 1757.[15] Nothing is known about his early life except that he attended Yale College.[16] On May 24, 1780, he married Huldah Hill of Guilford.[17] They moved to Bethlehem (presumably Connecticut) in May, 1783, and returned to Guilford in May, 1786.[18] According to the town records,[19] he and his wife owned, from 1786 to 1800, another house on Fair Street, next to his father's house, but whether or not he lived there is not known. Of their three sons and one daughter, only one son, Samuel Collins, married and lived to an advanced age.[20] The family is now extinct.[21] Johnson died June 20, 1836, in Guilford, where he was

> ... remembered ... by a few patriarchs who recall from childhood a tall, spare, old gentleman with piercing eyes and rounded shoulders who moved briskly between the home on Fair Street and the fulling mill on the upland meadow.[22]

The Johnsons were Tories during the American Revolution and were among those cited in 1781 as "inimical and dangerous persons."[23] They were both teachers and clothiers or fullers of cloth, their establishment being the first in the state.

> A site for clothiers' works on West river, northwest of the borough, one of the first in the state, was granted to Samuel Johnson, 1707. The most that this establishment could do was to full the cloth sent to it, 'a large proportion of which was worn without shearing or pressing.' Cloth dressing at this establishment was carried on by the family of Samuel Johnson for many years, being even prosecuted by a great grandson of the same name within the memory of the present inhabitants.[24]

Teaching was the profession inherited for generations, and, possibly for most of the time from 1750 to 1810, Samuel Johnson, Sr. and Samuel Johnson, Jr. taught in the Academy on Guilford Green.[25]

> A school house was built as early as 1645, repaired
> 1671 and a new one built in its stead in 1677. Mr. Jos-
> eph Dudley was chosen schoolmaster in 1705, Mr. James
> Elliott in 1706, Doct. William Johnson about 1720 for a
> year or two, and the school was afterwards kept in the
> family of Samuel Johnson for seventy or eighty years.[26]

The Johnson Academy was probably typical of the American
academies of its period.

> ... Men and women of that day have told of the old
> academy with its cobwebbed hall and two chimneys with
> open fireplaces built out into the room, and the 'corder'
> outside, where the wood was thrown between the posts and
> measured; and the red-cloak and foolscap, hung in the ward-
> robe of punishment, kept to shame the village dunce.[27]

It was in this academy that our first lexicographer doled out
the three R's, supplemented by grammar, geography, and the birch
rod. Here he filled his place as the "Luminary of learning to the
region around,"[28] and here one day when the country seemed to be
going over to France, he set the urchins this copy, "Demons, Dem-
agogues, Democrats, and Devils,"[29] for Johnson was a "real 'Blue
Light Federalist,' such as could be found only in Massachusetts,
Connecticut, and Delaware."[30] It was here also that he taught Fitz-
Greene Halleck, the poet, one of his favorite pupils,[31] to whom he
gave a copy of Campbell's "Pleasures of Hope" and with whom he
took many a pleasant walk after school hours, "the gentle and dif-
fident boy drinking in with eagerness the teacher's conversation
about poetry and other literary topics."[32]

Johnson was one of the first in his section to propagate fruit
trees, and he grafted apple and pear trees for the farmers around.

> ... He was a student of genealogy, a skillful calligra-
> phist and given to writing down choice English extracts
> from classic authors. Being rather spare of limb, one
> day a peddler accosted him and despite his protestations
> that he wanted nothing insisted like a good peddler upon
> selling something, until the master, in sheer desperation
> cried out: 'Well have you a pair of tin boots?' 'I
> have,' said the peddler, 'and they will just suit you.'
> Out went the man of tin and brought in a pair of candle-
> moulds saying, 'there, I guess those will fit you.'[33]

But what caused Johnson to compile a dictionary? Steger
concludes that:

> ... This dictionary shows no innovations and no improv-
> ements on previous English works. It is nothing more
> than a synopsis, a compendium of existing works, minus a
> number of their merits, lacking in individuality and follow-
> ing the beaten path of lexicography....[34]

✓   During the Revolution, the idea was started in the colonies
that they would revenge themselves on England by rejecting its language and adopting that of France. [35] Robinson explains the making
of the dictionary as an attempt on the part of the compiler to stem
the tide of interest in other languages--Hebrew, French, Latin--
that was then at a great height in Connecticut, and to establish a
guide for the English language, not only for children in the schools
but also for foreigners.

> Now mending the accent has been a favorite pastime of
> our Guilford schoolmasters. Remnants of such disorderly
> words as pompoddlers (strange visitors), pantopound (for-
> est), Gillkicker, furzino (as far as I know), nip, sling,
> winkum, stun, portin; with Scran, Grissel, Guttridge for
> Scranton, Griswold, Goodrich, appearing about that day in
> our Guilford, show a dangerous disorder of palate and
> cartilaginous tongue. There was even a tendency among
> the young to wander from the native vernacular and take
> to fine foreign language. Miss Roxana Foote (the mother
> of the Beechers) became so infatuated with French as to
> tie it in books to her spinning wheel and study it while
> spinning out the flax....
> The danger that Guilford would turn about and talk
> Hebrew, out of respect for the Jews, has once loomed up
> here when that earlier Samuel Johnson introduced his lit-
> tle Hebrew grammar, which he believed to be the first
> and original language, taught by God to mankind. And it
> was much beloved by all old-fashioned and looking-back-
> ward people as the supposed parent of all tongues and
> mothers used Hebrew to call their children: and Aaron,
> Reuben, Ichabod, Zebulon, Abigail, Mehitabel, all back to
> Noah's flood, handicapped the urchins and jarganized [sic]
> the household.
> But further, at that day some chose to talk like the
> Romans. In a decision on the question, 'is the study of
> the learned languages beneficial?' President Dwight said:
> 'When I was tutor and had occasion to introduce foreigners
> into the library, I could converse with them in Latin. ' ...
> Against these dangers and alarms Master Johnson fought,
> not with empty trumpets like Joshua at Jericho but he si-
> lently resolved a sober little book that should mayhap show
> mothers how to call their children and give mongrel folks
> from Europe something to be guided by.... [36]

Fifteen years after the Revolution the expansion that was taking place in material things was also causing a renewal of interest
in learning, and attention began to be paid to the lack of genteelness
in speech. The spirit of independence dominant a few years earlier
was manifesting itself in the literature and language. Emerson was
not the first American to set forth the doctrine of intellectual independence. In 1789, Noah Webster made a plea for establishing a
national language.

We have therefore the fairest opportunity of establishing
a national language, and of giving it uniformity and perspi-
cacity, in North America that ever presented itself to man-
kind. Now is the time to begin the plan. The minds of
the Americans are roused by the events of a revolution;
the necessity of organizing the political body and of forming constitutions of government that shall secure freedom
and property, has called all the faculties of the mind into
exertion; and the danger of losing the benefits of independence, has disposed every man to embrace any scheme
that shall tend, in its future operation, to reconcile the
people of America to each other, and weaken the prejudices which oppose a cordial union.

. . .

But America is in a situation the most favorable for
great reformation; and the present time is, in a singular
degree, auspicious. The minds of men in this country
have been awakened. New scenes have been, for many
years, presenting new occasions for exertion; unexpected
distresses have called forth the powers of invention; and
the application of new expedients has demanded every possible exercise of wisdom and talents. Attention is roused;
the mind expanded; and the intellectual faculties invigorated.
Here men are prepared to receive improvements, which
would be rejected by nations, whose habits have not been
shaken by similar events.

. . .

Let us then seize the moment, and establish a national
language, as well as a national government. Let us remember that there is a certain respect due to the opinions
of other nations. As an independent people, our reputation abroad demands that, in all things, we should be federal; be national; for if we do not respect ourselves, we
may be assured that other nations will not respect us. In
short, let it be impressed upon the mind of every American, that to neglect the means of commanding respect
abroad, is treason against the character and dignity of a
brave independent people. [37]

Toward the close of the century a reading or spelling mania
swept over the country and "Webster's spelling books, with the im-
mortal boy in the apple tree and the romantic milkmaid, began to
fall like leaves in autumn upon the land. "[38] Webster was also trying to effect reforms in speech through his Grammar and Reader.
Johnson's dictionary was therefore not an isolated phenomenon, but
was merely an expression of the interest in the language that was
characteristic of the time, and was the attempt of one more schoolmaster "to be serviceable to youth. "

Robinson characterizes the contribution of Johnson in the following words:

> Without exaggerating the merit of the special work
> Master Johnson performed, it was fundamental and unique,
> far more significant then than it could be now. The lan-
> guage had few watchmen and warders. That it was not
> abandoned by maddened patriots, nor degraded by local
> looseness, nor mongrelized by mixed European influences
> already enumerated, has been due in a measure to the
> sagacity and vigilance of such men as Webster, Pickering,
> Elliott and Johnson, who defended it and beat back the He-
> brew and fought its other enemies with spelling-book and
> lexicon.
> So Samuel Johnson, Jr. accomplished that triad of a-
> chievements, which Sterne has declared warrants a man
> in living; he planted trees and wrote a book and handed
> down his name to posterity. [39]

The following verses include most of the known facts about
the life and work of Johnson.

Samuel Johnson, Jr.

March 10, 1757-June 20, 1836

A ripe old man with shoulders round and eyes[40]
That peering, pierce and hidden stars surprise.
A teacher and yet lover of our rising race,
We cannot slight him with any grace.

Indeed, he is recalled by not a few
To whom he had imparted all he knew,
Or would have, had Fortune to him brought them
And in other ways this teacher taught them;
A lexicon, for instance, once he made
This rare remembered present passing shade.

He reared and disciplined into their letters,
That generation past, so much our betters,
Our very sires; and watched their scanty speech
And taught them, not the words, to overreach.

He ruled and copy wrote and 'corder' used,
Then fulled the cloth no gentleman refused.
To mill he strides in cloak and double cape;
All this, his life and form, to toil must shape.

But now, his lexicon is rare as he.
Sall Stanton's kept at Yale, is sad to see;
The cover boards have lost their paste through fraud,
For Sally was a bookworm, there she gnawed.

He stocked the town with Eden's apple fair,
The Bristol and the Pippin, pledged to bear.
Those lustrous eyes, that form remembered yet,
Prove him a man, not easy to forget.
Those choice Colonials in Johnson meet,
Eaton, Theophilus and Jones and Leete. [41]

A Selected, Pronouncing, and Accented Dictionary
by
John Elliott and Samuel Johnson, Jr.

Johnson's first lexicon, declared to be tentative and introductory to a future edition, [42] was disposed of so quickly[43] that the author set about a new and larger work. This time he had as collaborator the Reverend John Elliott of East Guilford, Connecticut.

The title of the second American dictionary is as follows:
A Selected, Pronouncing, and Accented Dictionary, comprising a
selection of the choicest words found in the best English authors.
Being an abridgement [sic] of the most useful Dictionaries now extant: together with the addition of a number of words now in vogue
not found in any Dictionary, in which the definitions are concisely
given, the words so divided as to lead to the present mode of pronunciation and by a typographical character, the sound of the vowels
and accented syllables are distinctly pointed out; and the parts of
speech noted and explained. The whole made easy and familiar to
children and youth, and designed for the use of schools in America.
By John Elliott, pastor of the church in East Guilford and Samuel
Johnson, Jr., author of the "School Dictionary." In addition to the
above the work contains some general observations on the derivations of words, and an explanation of the inseparable prepositions,
together with a table correcting common errors in spelling and pronunciation. Published according to Act of Congress: Suffield; Printed by Edward Gray for Oliver D. and I. Cook, and sold by them in
sheets or bound at their Book Store, Hartford, MDCCC, 16mo. oblong, sheep, pp. 223.

The title was registered in the office of the District of Connecticut in June, 1799; the book was published in 1800, the Connecticut Journal advertising it in its issues for January 30, February 6, and February 13, 1800. [44]
Of this second American dictionary, an oblong 16mo., 10 1/2
x 12 1/2 cm., there were two editions, both in 1800. The first
edition has sixteen pages of introduction, 223 pages of text, and
nearly nine thousand words;[45] the second, 32 pages of introduction
and 203 pages of text, printed two columns to a page with no spacing between the lines. There are approximately 9,500 words. Yale
University has a copy of the first edition, lacking the last two
pages of introduction; there is a copy in the library of the New York
Historical Society, one in the New York Public Library, and another
in the library of Ellsworth Eliot, Jr., a relative of Reverend John

Elliott.[46] Of the second edition there are copies in the Lenox and New York Historical Society libraries; Mr. Albert C. Bates, Worcester, Massachusetts, has a copy; as have also Harvard University Library and the Library of Congress. The Kent Memorial Library, Suffield, Connecticut, in its Hezekiah S. Sheldon Collection, has copies of both editions.

As was the custom at this time, the book contains several recommendatory letters, pages 2-4 inclusive, which are prefixed "as a kind of invitation hung out to the purchaser." The list contains many names of respectability in the state of Connecticut. A representative selection from the letters is given here. The first is an extract of a letter from one of the Justices of the Court of Common Pleas for the County of Berkshire, Massachusetts.

> The learner who takes in hand a full Dictionary, finds himself in a field too spacious for his views, and shrinks at the undertaking; but will be pleased with the prospect of making himself master of one so limited as this; and it appears to me your omission of words, the import of which is obvious to every one, and those which are seldom used, is a useful improvement, and, as far as I can judge, am satisfied, that it contains such a selection of words as will be applicable to the use of common schools.

> Nathaniel Bishop

It is interesting to note a scathing comment on this letter made by a reviewer a short while after the publication of the Dictionary.

> What the judge means by the undertaking, to make oneself master of a dictionary, we are at a loss to determine, unless it be committing it to memory, a kind of labour we never yet knew anyone attempt; and what there is so very frightful to a learner, in taking up a full dictionary, which will afford him the word he is in search of, we are equally unable to comprehend. Had the learned judge sought for reasons to support his recommendations, where 'reasons were as plenty as blackberries,' he could not probably have discovered a more singular one than this, that the value of the dictionary is in direct proportion to its smallness. His letter reminds us of a couplet of the duke of Buckingham's, which may be thus parodied:

> > 'The work is great, because it is so small; If it were greater, 'twould be none at all.'[47]

Noah Webster takes time to endorse the Dictionary.

> Mr. Eliot, I have not time to examine every sheet of your manuscript, but have read many sheets in different parts of it; your general plan and execution I approve of,

and can sincerely wish you success in your labors, I am.
Sir, with much respect, your obedient servant.

Noah Webster, Junr.

At a meeting of the association of the Eastern district of New
Haven County, Connecticut, May 3, 1799,

The Rev'd John Elliott presented to them a selected,
accented and pronouncing Dictionary, compiled by him and
Mr. S. Johnson for their patronage, and said association,
having approved its design and general plan, appointed the
Rev'd Messrs John Foot, Matthew Noyes and Lynde
Huntington, more particularly to examine and recommend
said Dictionary, if to them it should appear meritoriously
executed.
We the subscribers having attended to the business of
our appointment, with pleasure, approve its execution, and
hereby recommend it to the public, and particularly to
overseers and instructors of schools, as a work happily
calculated for the improvement of youth in the knowledge
of the English language.

John Foot
Matthew Noyes   Committee of
Lynde Huntington   Association

The Preface, given on pages five and six, is indicative of
the aim and purpose of the book.

The Education of youth, in a free republic, is a matter
of the highest importance. The increasing attention which
has been paid to this interesting subject in our country,
for several years, affords just grounds of congratulation,
and joy, among the friends of order, virtue, and religion.
Great improvements have already been made upon former
systems, but to complete the circle of useful School-
Books, a Dictionary of suitable size, seem'd very requisite.

The authors object to the extant dictionaries, both because of
their size and cost and because of their lack of delicacy and chastity
in language.

Serious objections lie against those in common use,
arising from their price, but more especially from their
want of delicacy, and chastity of language. Many words,
there found are highly offensive to the modest ear, and
cannot be read without a blush. To inspire youth with
sentiments of modesty, and delicacy is one of the principal objects of early instructions; and this object is totally
defeated by the indisciminate use of vulgar and indecent
words.

These objections we have endeavored to remove, and to combine as much as possible, cheapness with utility.

With this object in view, we have carefully chosen the most valuable words, whilst many of those which are rarely used or easily understood, are excluded.

We trust the learner will here find a selection of those most commonly used in the purest, and best writers in our language.

The moral idea expressed here was due undoubtedly to the influence of Elliott. However, attention was called, in the review mentioned above, to a definition that was evidently not in accord with the ideas of Elliott. After commenting on the new words in the Dictionary, the reviewer continues:

... There is another word, to which, at first, we thought these gentlemen had the exclusive right. We can-not soil our pages with the transcription of it; it is to be found under the letter F, and is called French, but we are sure no French dictionary would admit a word so shock-ingly indecent and so vulgar.

There is, indeed, a work in that language, called Dictionaire Comique, in which this, among a curious col-lection of words and phrases, is inserted, with the follow-ing observation preceding the definition:- 'Mot sole and indécent, qui n'est proféré d'ordinaire que par des personnes mal eleves, par des bruteaux, des polissons, des libertins et des gens sans maeurs.' Nor did we think it possible that it should find its way into any English dictionary; but turning to Ash, whose purpose it seems to have been to insert every word written or spoken in our language, we there found it. We hope, however, that neither the authority of the reverend pastor, nor even of his learned colleague, will be sufficient to give it currency. Observing, from the definition of this word in Ash, which they have literally copied, that he does not understand the meaning of the term, we sincerely hope that they may have the same apology; for ignorance would here afford some excuse, as men of decency and piety, though none as lex-icographers. [48]

In order to conserve space the authors have varied the parts of speech, taking at times the verb, the noun, and the adjective. Participles and adverbs ending in ly are generally omitted. The explanation of some words that are not given is found in the defini-tions of others. In the division of syllables and the pronunciation of words the standard has been 'the practice of men of letters, and Gentlemen of the first abilities, and experience in school education in modern times. '[49] According to the authors, many new words have been added, the choice of which was determined, 'partly by the advice of others, and partly by our own judgment. '[50] One reviewer took the trouble to examine the book to ascertain the number of new words. He concludes that

... The sum total of words, not to be found in any other
dictionary, which we have looked into, amounts to ten.
Chouan, Ci devant, De pot, Sans cu lotte, Hau ter, In
fluen za, Sa mi el, Tom a hawk, Wampum, Composuist.
Of these ten words, we may observe, that the first four
are pure French, and are to be found in any French dictionary, where only they should still be sought for; the
fifth, which they call French, is not so, nor does it
belong to any language; the sixth, seventh, eighth, and
ninth, are very properly adopted, and only want correct
explanation to make their insertion valuable; the tenth is
nothing more than a provincialism; and as it conveys no
new idea, nor supplies the place of any circumlocution,
ought not to be legitimated, by being introduced into any
English dictionary.... [51]

On page 32 the key to pronunciation is given. As in A
School Dictionary, the typographical character, over a vowel marks
the sound of the vowel and the accented syllable. The first or long
sound is indicated by the grave accent, as abàtement; the second or
short sound by the acute accent as abándon; while the circumflex
marks various sounds, as â in there. Diphthongs ôi, ôy, ôa, âu,
âw, ôu, ôw are marked with a circumflex when they have their
diphthongal sounds as in bôil, and are printed in Roman letters.
Otherwise one of them is in italics and is silent as in quack. "In
such words as cannot be comprised in the foregoing rules, the word
is spelled as it should be pronounced and included in brackets; as
sugar [shu gar]."[52] Here, as suggested by Steger, [53] is the beginning of phonetic respelling in American lexicography. Concerning
the problem of pronunciation as exhibited in this dictionary the
reviewer quoted above says:

It is called a 'selected, pronouncing and accented dictionary.' That it is a 'selected and accented,' and, if the
editors please, syllabical, we are not disposed to deny;
but its claim to the title of a pronouncing dictionary rests
on very slender pretensions. To render a pronouncing
dictionary in any degree complete, it is indispensible, not
only that the different sounds of the vowels should be indicated by proper signs placed over them, but that the
syllables, of which the words are composed, should, in a
word annexed, be spelt in the manner they are to be pronounced. In both these particulars, the dictionary under
review is deficient. It is true, that a sort of key is
given, containing certain typographical characters to be
placed over the vowels, so as to mark 'the sound of the
vowel and of the accented syllable.' But how very imperfect the plan is, may be readily discovered, in almost
every page of the book; for instance, the vowel a, in the
words affráy, agást, báth, and báttery, is marked with
the same typographical character; and the like error
prevails, in numberless other instances....

The plan being thus faulty, we might rationally expect that the execution would be no less so; and the examination of any single page will show that such an expectation is not without foundation; though, as will be seen, there are imperfections, which are not owing to this cause only. Let us take, for example, the first letter of the alphabet, and we shall find many words, in which the compilers have adapted an accent, or given a sound to the vowel, which is not warranted by the established usage of good speakers. We observe the word ad-mi-ra-ble, with the accent placed on the second syllable, and the i marked long; agriculture, with the accent on the third syllable; but this, we believe, is a typographical error; an-cient, with the a marked short, as in anguish, and the same fault in the words ar-range, chamber, dan-ge-rous, and many others; ... an-ti-po-des; ap-a-thy, with the first a marked long; ap-pre-hend, with the accent placed on the first syllable, instead of the last; a-re-a, with the accent on the second syllable instead of the first; as-so-ci-a-tion, where c ought to become aspirated, and the ci pronounced as if written she.... [54]

Pages seven to thirty-two give a short "Introduction to English Grammar." There are definitions and examples of parts of speech, general observations on the derivations of words, some general rules for the derivation of words, a list of words (nearly twelve pages, three columns to a page) the meaning of which might be confusing, such as accept, except, and a list of vulgar errors in pronunciation with their corrections. A survey of this list of one hundred sixty-five words shows the kinds of errors in pronunciation then prevalent. The list includes chimbly, cowcumber, ketch, cairds (for cards), hisen and housen for his and houses, larnin', vige for voyage and inion for onion.

The definitions are similar to those in Johnson's dictionary and for the same words are copied. They are always brief and in some cases incomplete. Except ile (aisle) no serious departure is made from the accepted spelling. The English form is followed in arbour, colour, favour, honour, labour, valour, vigour, and in theatre, metre, spectre, fibre. Ct is used instead of x in deflection, inflection, reflection, but connection is spelled connexion. A few words ending in ck have dropped the k. There is no attempt at etymology, and no pictorial illustrations are given. Aside from the improvement in pronunciation by phonetic respelling and by syllabication, this dictionary adds very little to the development of American lexicography.

John Elliott belonged to a line of respectable and pious ancestors, among whom was the apostolic John Eliot. He was the grandson of Dr. Jared Eliot (1685-1763), a minister of Killingworth (now Clinton, Connecticut), as well as a botanist and a scientific and practical agriculturist. His father was Deacon George Elliott, a farmer of Killingworth; his mother, Hannah, eldest daughter of Captain Samuel and Hannah (Marsh) Ely, of North Lyme, Connecticut. [55]

Elliott prepared for college with Reverend Achilles Mansfield. He then attended Yale, from which he graduated in 1786, after which time he spent several years in teaching and in the study of theology.

> From the period of his leaving college [1786] to that of his taking the pastoral charge of his people in 1791, he was employed principally in the business of instruction, and in the prosecution of his theological studies. During the interval he united with the church in Schenectady, in 1789. [56]

Licensed by the Middlesex (Connecticut) Association of Ministers, on August 23, 1791 he preached for the first time in the Congregational church in East Guilford, and on November 2, 1791 was ordained and installed as its third pastor, at the age of twenty-three.

> The Society voted to give him 'as a settlement, £ 200 lawful money,' to be paid, 'one-third in cash, one-third in neat cattle, and one-third in produce at the current market price.' ... 'the sd. sum of two hundred pound, to be paid in three years from the time he settles, one-third part of each payment to be made annually.' His salary was fixed at '£ 80 lawful money per annum, and 20 cords of merchantable oak wood.' This was subsequently increased to '£ 85, and 25 cords of wood. '[57]

Elliott retained the same pastorate until his death on December 17, 1824, a period of thirty-three years. During the time of his pastorate Elliott took into the church 335 members. Concerning this fact Fitch makes the following statement:

> ... Eighty were admitted into the church as the fruits of the first revival in 1802; about fifty, of a revival in 1809; and about one hundred, of a revival in 1821. He admitted into the church during his ministry, in all, 335 members; leaving at the period of his death a church consisting of 243. [58]

In September, 1812, Elliott was elected a Fellow of the Corporation of Yale College, and in 1816 a member of the Prudential Committee of the body. [59] In recognition of his services he was awarded the honorary degree of Doctor of Divinity by Yale in 1822. [60] In the reports of the Treasurer of Yale College, theological department, is listed the "Elliott" fund which in 1888 was $1,564.75. The origin of this fund is as follows: Rev. John Elliott bequeathed to the college the "Neck lot" subject to the conditions that the lot should be sold and the proceeds used for the benefit of the theological department; that the interest should be spent for books except one per cent which should be added to the permanent fund. Three hundred sixty dollars was realized from the sale of the lot in 1825. [61] In 1901 this fund amounted to $1,780.80. [62]

Another instance of the wise foresight of Elliott was the es_
tablishment of the Ministerial Fund in Madison, Connecticut. Prior
to 1818 the institutions of the Gospel were supported by taxing all
the inhabitants within the bounds of a society. By a provision of the
constitution then adopted, the support of religion was made entirely
voluntary. Elliott was so apprehensive of the failure of this plan
that he determined that a ministerial fund should be raised for the
benefit of the church and society, and kept at interest until it
amounted to $10,000. The fund became available in 1855. In 1901
it amounted to about $12,000.[63]

In his autobiographical sketches, Dr. John Todd gives his
impression of Elliott received when as a boy he lived with his uncle,
Jonathan Todd, in East Guilford. He says:

He was a tall, very thin and slim man. His legs,
always draped in black stockings and small clothes, seemed
too slender to hold him up. How neatly he was always
draped, not a spot or wrinkle on his garments! What a
broad-brimmed hat he wore, renewed just once in two
years. His manners and bearing were most gentlemanly.
He was a fine scholar, a genuine lover of study, a capital
preacher, a wise and shrewd man, never trying to be rich
or known, but well known and all his life long he received
the enormous salary of $400 a year. He was the life and
soul of the village library, and ready for every good work.
How we boys and girls were wont to look upon him with
awe and reverence, unable to believe that the common frail_
ties of human nature hung about him. I never dared enter
his front door until I had been in college a year or two.
I have never met the minister who to me was so great.[64]

William C. Fowler says of Elliott:

He was dignified, deferential to others, and yet very
cordial and polite in his manners. His enunciation was
distinct but slow, and very impressive. In his public
services he never seemed to hesitate for a word or
thought. His style was transparent, and his sermons
written out in a clear, handsome hand, ready for the
press. He was a good classical scholar, a daily reader
of the Hebrew Bible.[65]

In the sermon preached at Elliott's funeral, Fitch says that
he was a man of distinguished prudence, of cool judgment, of up_
right constancy, affectionate kindness, of peculiar sedateness and
solemnity and of pious devotion.[66]

Dr. Elliott was an able preacher, and it was under his
ministry that the half-way Covenant Plan of church membership died
out.[67] It was also during his pastorate that one of the first records
of a Sunday School occurs.[68] It is as follows:

At a church meeting in May, 1820, William Hart, Deacon Meigs, Deacon Holt, Timothy Dudley, Amos Bishop,
Benjamin Hart and Ezra Smith were appointed a committee
to organize the Sabbath School and superintend the school
when organized. [69]

On November 3, 1792, in Canaan, Connecticut, Dr. Elliott
married Sarah Norton, daughter of Lot and Esther Norton, of Salisbury, Connecticut, who survived him and who later married General
Elisha Sterling. They had no children. [70] Dr. Elliott's health began
to decline in 1823, and he died in East Guilford, very suddenly,
from disease of the heart on December 17, 1824, in his fifty-seventh
year. [71]

The Columbian Dictionary
by
Caleb Alexander

The year 1800 saw the publication of another dictionary--one
by Caleb Alexander, a preacher and school teacher who had already
published several textbooks on the English, Greek, and Latin languages. It was the first dictionary to boast of its Americanisms on
the title page. The Columbian Dictionary of the English Language
in which many new words, peculiar to the United States, and many
words of general use, not found in any other English dictionary, are
inserted. The words are divided as they are pronounced, and each
word is accented according to the most approved authors and speakers; with abbreviations used to denote each part of speech; all the
irregular verbs are properly arranged, and made plain to the reader. The whole is calculated to assist foreigners in acquiring a just
pronunciation of the English language; and to be used as a school
book, by any who wish to study the language grammatically. To
which is prefixed, A Prosodial Grammar, containing, a short dissertation on vowels and consonants. To the whole is added Heathen
Mythology: or, A Classical Pronouncing Dictionary. By Caleb
Alexander, A. M., author of "Virgil's Works translated into literal
English Prose," etc., and Teacher of the English Language. Published according to Act of Congress, Printed at Boston by Isaiah
Thomas and Ebenezer T. Andrews. Sold by them and the other
booksellers in Boston, by I. Thomas, in Worcester; by Thomas,
Andrews and Penniman, in Albany; and by Thomas, Andrews and
Butler, in Baltimore August, 1800.

The publication of the Dictionary was greeted by one reviewer
as follows:

One Alexander, a presbyterian preacher, at a little
village in Massachusetts-Bay [Mendon] has published a
ridiculous book which he calls 'A Columbian Dictionary.'
This work, a disgrace to letters, is a disgusting collection of every vicious word or phrase, chosen by the absurd
misapprehension, or coined by the boors of each local

jurisdiction in the United States. It is a record of our imbecility. A map and journal of our tottering and imperfect step in the walks of literature. God forbid that any man who has the memory of his ancestors in his heart, or a spark of English spirit, glowing in his veins, or one trace of English style in his memory, should ever recur to this blind Columbian guide! Possessing Johnson's and Walker's Dictionaries, the first filling the mind with the most energetic, and elegant words, and the second filing the tongue to the most accurate and courtly pronunciation, scholars will hardly consult the sectary Alexander, nor on his authority adopt wigwam words, or pronounce coquette, kokwet, according to the new-dangle gibberish of this village schoolmaster. 72

The Dictionary is a 16mo., 14 x 13 1/2 cm., and contains 556 pages. The first four pages are introductory; the Advertisement, which serves as the preface, is given on pages three to four inclusive. It is given here in full.

This Dictionary is not offered to the public, with an expectation of fixing an uniform and permanent standard of pronunciation. If a Roman Emperor, at the head of his legions, could not introduce one letter into the alphabet, much less an obscure individual persuade, or compel men to pronounce alike. Could any means be used, or any plan devised, to alter and unite Americans, in giving similar sounds to all the vowels and consonants, and their various combinations, the event would be happy. In doing this, a man would have to encounter prejudice, ignorance, malice and pedantry, four powerful enemies. In spite of the most learned dissertation and the best rules, some would pronounce tūne, others tshône; some tuesday, others tshôsday; some vŏl'um, others vôl'yum; some pic'-ture, others pic'tshur; some vĕndue, and others wĕn'due; and each would have his admirers and followers.

Not despairing, however, of doing a little to fix an uniform and permanent standard of pronunciation, no pains have been spared in dividing and accenting the words according to the practice of the most approved and polite speakers.

Johnson's, Sheridan's, Perry's, and Walker's dictionaries have been deemed the best standards in America. And yet, no one implicitly follows any of them. No one pronounces jū'ni-or, according to Perry; and but a very few, tune, tshôn, according to Sheridan. To avoid their peculiarities has been my intention, and yet to adopt their pronunciation, so far as it appeared to be just.

To the accentuation and orthography the greatest care has been paid: and as to the explanation of words, the most natural has been preferred as the most easy, and the most simple as the most elegant. 'As to words esteemed synonimous, when the slightest shade of difference arises, it is marked by the most delicate distinction.'

> Sensible of the difficulties under which youth and common people labor, in acquiring a just pronunciation, I have written, the second time, each word with the letter used, in giving it the right sound. And, of course, no one, who can sound the letters properly, can fail of giving every word its due pronunciation. To persons of inexperience, this plan is easy and familiar; and I am persuaded they will find this dictionary very useful, not only in giving them a just definition of every word, but in assisting them to pronounce with elegance and propriety.
>
> To the candid and benevolent this work is humbly inscribed. As I have nothing to hope, and but little to fear, from the ill-natured and captious, so I have no favor to ask of them.

Mendon, July, 1800   The Author

The Dictionary proper covers 514 pages and includes approximately 25,700 words, counting fifty to a page. The increase in the number of words as compared with the preceding American dictionaries is due in a large measure to the same word being repeated each time a different meaning is given. The author states that in order to make the work both concise and cheap he has omitted all the obsolete words, many nouns ending in ness and nearly all the adverbs ending in ly.

> ... Instead of injuring, this omission will be of service to our language. For elegance, in diction or writing, forbids the use of obsolete words and phrases; authenticity is a more easy and polite word than authenticalness, and a small degree of attention and practice will teach how to form adverbs from adjectives or participles, by the addition of ly; as just, justly; pious, piously; obliging, obligingly; feigned, feignedly; holy, holily. [73]

Although the title states that "many words not found in any other English dictionary, are inserted," one reviewer concludes that after "due research," only the following new words have been discovered: lengthy, antifederalism, booties, caucus, ratiability, sophomore, lintar, Yanky, accordingto, and composuist. [74] An interesting note is given as to the word lengthy.

> The word lengthy has here, for the first time, the honour of being publicly adopted by the lexicographer. As this word has been frequently tried and condemned by several writers among us, as of base coinage, we may be excused if we examine the grounds of their verdict. It must be admitted, that if its definition is precisely that of long, as given by Mr. Alexander, it is at best but a useless synonym, and ought, perhaps, to be expelled; but if it is intended to be used as a diminutive, and to mean approaching too long, it may possibly, though we do not mean to say it, be supported by fair analogy. But, at any

rate, it seems to be entitled to a fairer trial than it has
yet undergone. The first person who formally attacked its
legitimacy gave as a reason that it was as ridiculous to say
lengthy as it would be to say breadthy or depthy, and this
has been repeated by every critic since who has sat in
judgment upon it in our ephemeral prints; but ridicule is
not the test of truth. [75]

Another writer comments in a very critical manner on many
barbarous American words and phrases, among which he includes the
word lengthy. Of lengthy, he declares that it can be found in no
English dictionary and in no English author. "It is undoubtedly the
growth of the wigwam; and is a vicious, fugitive, scoundrel and True
American word. It should be hooted by every elegant English scholar,
and proscribed from every page. Spry, caucus, Illy, etc. are likewise fairly tried and justly condemned. It is pleasant to remark the
hardihood of American sciolists, men who never saw the fair pro-
portions of graceful English, and whose leathern ears never listened
to aught, but to the rumbling of July orations, and the provincial
whine of a whiggish reader of the declaration."[76]

Krapp agrees with the reviewer above as to the number of
new words.

> ... Practically all the words are in Perry and Walker,
> even picturesque words like widow-hunter, one who hunts
> up widows with jointures, sneak-up, one who creeps up,
> etc. But telegraph is in Alexander, though not in Perry
> or Walker, and ducape, a kind of silk, is in Perry and
> Alexander, but not in Walker. On the whole, Alexander
> seems to stand somewhat closer to Perry than to Walker.
> Only a few distinctively American words are given, e.g.
> dime, ten cents; dollar, one hundred cents; Yanky, a New
> Englander. Alexander gives freshet in the American
> sense of a sudden rise of water due to rainfall, and also
> a fresh-water pool, as Perry and Walker do.... [77]

The problem of accentuation and pronunciation is dealt with
in A Prosodial Grammar, pages 5-24 inclusive. Here are exhibited
a complete scheme of the vowels, an elaborate one of diphthongs and
triphthongs, as well as a discussion of consonants, syllables, terminations, articulation, accent, and emphasis, to assist in the proper
pronunciation. The macron, grave accent, broad accent, the breve,
and the acute accent are used to distinguish the long, broad, short,
long broad, and short broad vowel sounds. The scheme of the
vowels is given below. The figures over the vowels denote the
number of sounds each one has, and those under, the number of
vocal sounds there are. The same figures under the vowels
indicate those that have the same sound. Thus the vowels a, e, i, o,
u, y, in the words liar, her, mirth, dove, cub, martyr have a
similar sound.

1	2	3	4	5	6	7	8	9
bâll	băt	bāte	wăs	pàrt	liăr	bāre	villăge	măny
1	2	3	10	4	13	5	9	7

1	2	3	4	5	6	7
mēte	mĕt	thére	hĕr	lēeward	yĕs	clèrk
6	7	5	13	15	9	4

1	2	3	4	5
clīme	dĭn	píque	mĭrth	sĭrrah
8	9	6	13	2

1	2	3	4	5	6	7
dōte	dŏt	dŏff	mōve	rŏŏk	dŏve	wŏmen
11	10	1	12	14	13	9

1	2	3	4	5
cūbe	cŭb	pŭsh	bŭry	bŭsy
15	13	14	7	9

1	2
view	nŏw
16	17

1	2	3	4
mȳ	glōrў	hўmn	martȳr
8	7	9	13

Pronunciation is indicated after each word by the markings which have just been given and by spelling of the word to indicate the sound, as ache, āke, fulfil, fŏŏl fĭl, neighbor, na˙bŭr. The key to pronunciation is given at the top of each page. There is no attempt at etymology and no use of synonyms except as assisting in defining. The definitions are very brief, usually only a short phrase.

The last eighteen pages provide a Heathen Mythology, or Classical Pronouncing Dictionary, a list of men of learning and genius, and a list of fifty-six important men of England. In including the Heathen Mythology Alexander is following in the footsteps of John Walker, who included a "Key to the Pronunciation of Greek, Latin, and Scripture Proper Names" in his Critical Pronouncing Dictionary.

Caleb Alexander, the author of the third American dictionary, was born in Northfield, Massachusetts, July 22, 1775. He was the great-grandson of John Alexander, who, in the early days of New

England, emigrated from Scotland and made a settlement on the Connecticut River. [78] It was John Alexander who, with twelve others, first purchased from the Indians the land on which was built the old town of Northfield. [79]

Caleb was the second son and the fifth child of Simeon Alexander, a farmer of Northfield, and of Margaret (Willard) Howe, also of Northfield. [80] He spent his youth on his father's farm but he early determined to get a liberal education. After spending three years at Dartmouth, he was recommended in 1776 by President Wheelock for senior standing at Yale. The following is an abstract from Wheelock's letter:

> He is another of that number of which I have sent you already, who was, in the judgment of Christian charity, the subject of God's saving mercy, in that special season of the outpouring of his Spirit here, the winter before last. The change appearing in the youth was very great, as, before it, he was considerably of the wild order; but ever since, as far as I have seen or heard, he has adorned his Christian profession by a truly religious and exemplary conversation. He has been a diligent student and a good scholar. [81]

Alexander was graduated from Yale in 1777. He took his second degree at Brown University in 1789. Soon after leaving college he began the study of theology with the Reverend Ephraim Judson, of Norwich, Connecticut, and on October 14, 1778 was licensed to preach by the Eastern Association of Ministers of New London County, at Groton. [82]

In 1780 he married Lucina Strong, whose father, the Reverend Thomas Strong, was the pastor of the town of New Marlborough, Massachusetts. On September 4, 1780, Alexander was called to fill the pastorate made vacant by the death of Strong. He accepted after he had secured the renunciation of "the half-way covenant" and was ordained and installed on February 28, 1781. According to a grant of the proprietors, he was entitled to the second ministerial lot, or a quantity of land equal in value. [83]

Alexander retained this office only sixteen months because of his position on the half-way covenant and because of the directness and pungency of his preaching, which was strongly Calvinistic. [84] He was then employed for the greater part of a year in the neighboring town of Great Berrington. [85]

In 1784 and 1785 Alexander supplied the vacant pulpit in Harwinton, Connecticut. From there he went to Mendon, Worcester County, Massachusetts, where he was installed as pastor on April 12, 1786. The sermon for the occasion was preached by the Reverend Nathaniel Emmons. In 1801, under the appointment of the Massachusetts Missionary Society, he spent three or four months visiting the churches and Indians in the western part of New York.

After returning to Mendon, he asked for and obtained dismissal
(December 7, 1802) from his congregation because of insufficient
support and because of other plans. When he returned to New York,
he served the three churches of Salisbury, Norway, and Fairfield.
In May, 1803, he removed to Fairfield with this family and became
preceptor of the Fairfield Academy, which had been incorporated the
preceding March. [86]

Under his supervision the Academy became prominent but did
not, as he had hoped, grow into a college. In 1807 he gave up his
church in Norway because of the inability of the members to pay his
salary. Later he discontinued his work at Salisbury and Fairfield
for the same reason. The same cause forced him to resign his
position in the Academy in January, 1812, for he found it impossible
to build up as liberal an institution at Fairfield as he had hoped for.
He next helped, through his solicitation of funds, to advance the
Academy at Chilton, Oneida County, to the rank of a college, and on
July 22, 1812 he was unanimously elected president of the new institution, called Hamilton College. [87] He declined the place, however,
and the following autumn moved to Onondaga Hollow, in Onondaga
County, where he was instrumental in the establishment of an academy. He also preached at Selina (which became a part of Syracuse
in 1848), and in 1816 organized a Sunday School there. [88] He served
as principal of the academy for four years, after which time he
resigned and retired to a farm in the neighborhood. He then became
interested in the founding of a theological seminary, at first in Onondaga, but finally in Auburn, Cayuga County. In September, 1820, he
accepted an appointment to solicit gifts for the endowment of profes-
sorships. In 1822 the Connecticut Missionary Society appointed him
missionary to the destitute churches within the bounds of the Onondaga
Presbytery, and he remained at this work for nine months. [89] During
the next five years much of his time was devoted to writing for religious newspapers, and to the advancement of education. He continued to preach, as opportunity offered, until the close of his life.
He died at Onondaga, April 12, 1828. [90] His wife survived him until
October 25, 1847. Their children were seven daughters and one son.
One daughter died in infancy, and one married the Reverend Dirck
C. Lansing. [91]

Oliver R. Strong describes Alexander as follows:

In form, Mr. Alexander was thick set, and about five
feet, nine or ten inches in height. He was slightly lame,
and walked in a manner that would indicate that one leg
was shorter than the other. His face was full: broad, of
rather florid complexion, and expressive of reflection and
intelligence. His manners evidenced a benevolent spirit,
and yet he was distinguished for strength of purpose. I
well remember that his tenacity and perseverence used to
be indicated by his being called, 'the old Scotchman,'--
with reference to his Scotch descent. Though I cannot
say he was reserved in conversation, yet neither was he
particularly communicative, except on some special

occasions; and then he would make himself highly interest_
ing. He was exceedingly amiable and exemplary in his
private relations, and was preeminently a loved and loving
husband and father.[92]

A Key to the English Language
by
William Woodbridge

Another one of the early dictionaries is that compiled by
William Woodbridge, the first preceptor of the Phillips Exeter Acad-
emy, and the father of William Channing Woodbridge, the geographer.
It has as its title-page A Key to the English Language, or a Spelling,
Parsing, Derivative, and Defining Dictionary: Selected from the most
approved authors, --viz. Johnson, Bailey, Entick, Perry, Sheridan,
Jones, Kendrick, Peacock and others, by William Woodbridge. A.M.
First Preceptor of the Phillips-Exeter Academy, and Principal of
the Young Ladies' Academy in Medford, Middletown: Printed by T.
& J. B. Dunning, 1801.

The work, intended for "schools and polite readers," and
therefore containing "no low or indecent word," is a small book
5 1/2 x 3 1/2 x 1 inches in size. It consists of 348 pages (not
numbered) which contain "one with another, more than a hundred
words each so that the number amounts to thirty-five or thirty-six
thousand. Of these words, some again occur once, and some twice
in the definition of others, so that the real number defined and spelt,
does not, perhaps, exceed twenty thousand."[93]

The object of the Dictionary, as stated in the Preface, is to
render the study of language easy, and to provide for schools and
for general use the plainest and most useful dictionary at half the
usual price of any work of the kind. The author states that the
plan and arrangement are new, concise, and plain, that the book
contains a competent selection of the most useful and elegant words
in the English language, and that no valuable words that occur in
good authors are designedly omitted. One critic, writing the next
year after the book was published, calls attention to the fact that
such words as description, accompaniment, interference, indecision,
inefficient, frivolity, circuitous, valuable words that occur in good
authors, are not found in this dictionary. The secret, he says, is
that they had not found their way into Johnson.[94]

The words are arranged one column to a page, with letters
in front of each line to point out the part of speech of each word.
Two other columns of words follow as definitions and synonymous
words. Examples are as follows:

| v. | aban`don | desert | renounce |
| n. | abase`ment | depres`sion | humilia`tion |

In the main the words are defined by a word of the same part of speech. There are, however, three exceptions: 1) where the word is defined by a phrase, as <u>amphibious</u>, living in air and water; 2) where the adjective is defined by a participle; 3) where the noun and the verb are the same.

Words that are used as more than one part of speech are given twice, as,

v.	answer	reply	confute
n.	answer	reply	confut'ation

Where the noun and verb are the same, n. v. is placed before the word. When the definition is continued through more than one line, the following line begins this definition and the part of speech is the same as the first word. Long and very plain words are not accented. Italic <u>g</u> is like <u>j</u> and <u>s</u> is like <u>z</u>.

The accent is placed after the accented syllable as <u>aban'don.</u> Words accented on the last syllable are not marked. Where the derivative is not marked, it has the same accent as the primitive. Since the book is based on English dictionaries, conservative spelling is followed.

An examination of the Dictionary leads one to agree with the critic referred to above when he says:

> We must risque the imputation of a want of judgment, when we refuse our concurrence with the opinion expressed in the 'preface and introduction.' We do not think that the acquisition of the English language will be at all facilitated by this publication.
>
> ...
>
> If 'this little and elaborate work' was intended merely as a substitute for more 'voluminous and costly diction-aries,' the labour of the compiler might have been spared, as Entick, Perry, Jones, Peacock, etc., have furnished dictionaries equally convenient in point of size. It is a real burden to the public, and an injury to literature, when books are multiplied without improvement, and distract the judgment without adding to the knowledge of the readers.[95]

William Woodbridge, the youngest son of Reverend Ashbel Woodbridge, was born in Glastonbury, Connecticut, September 14, 1755.[96] The family was poor, and the early death of the father seemed to destine Woodbridge to a life on the farm or to some trade. However, the desire to become a minister, probably inherited from a line of dissenting ministers in England extending back to the time of Edward the Sixth, when one of his ancestors, a clergyman in the Church of England, refused to wear the ecclesiastical vestments, caused Woodbridge to determine to obtain a college education.[97]

While preparing for college, Woodbridge taught school, served as a clerk in his brother's store, and at one time did an excellent business in the commercial line, until the vessel which he had bought and fitted out was wrecked.[98] In 1776 he entered Yale College, where, though hampered by poverty, he became a leader in the religious life of the students.[99] He paid his way by teaching and in the summer of 1779 began his life work by conducting a school for young ladies at Worthington Society, now Berlin, Connecticut.[100] The next year he held an evening school of a more advanced character for girls in New Haven, where he imparted instruction in grammar, rhetoric, and geography. Woodbridge was always inclined to date this as the beginning of superior education for women in New England.[101] He later called himself "The Columbus of Female Education."[102] He founded a similar school at Ripton Parish, now Huntington, Connecticut.[103]

In July, 1780, after finishing his course at Yale, Woodbridge took charge of a grammar school at Newburyport, Massachusetts, from which place he was called, in 1783, on a salary of £100 6s 8d, to be the first preceptor of Phillips Exeter Academy, in Exeter, New Hampshire, which had been opened on May 1 of that year.[104] Of the beginning of his work in the Academy, Woodbridge writes thus in his diary:

> Exeter Academy was opened in April, 1783. During the war few men could be educated. A crowd of such were ready to fill up the Academy. By charter, no boarders in a family where morning and evening prayers were not maintained should be admitted to the privileges of the Academy. Such a prohibition would break up the Academy at once. One expedient only remained: I must make them my family, as in college. In order to do this, the students were called to the Academy at one half after five in summer, and before sunrise in winter. Prayers were attended, and morning lessons recited before breakfast. The other six hours as usual were attended. Wednesday P. M. was recess, also Saturday P. M., yet prayers always attended. Saturday and Sabbath mornings and evenings was a moral or pious lecture. Five years and a half--with the exception of about six weeks--this course was attended in term time. The number of scholars in languages, figures, geography, composition, speaking, was from 45 to 64, who gave in their account of their studies Wednesday and Saturday noon.[105]

Woodbridge continued with the Academy until 1788. His health was not good, and the numbers of pupils had gradually decreased.

After leaving Exeter, Woodbridge preached, taught, wrote, and edited textbooks. He studied a year at Harvard and then opened a private school at Medford.[106] This school, to which boys were admitted, continued for seven years and then the building in which it was held was sold. In 1790 he began another school for girls in New Haven. [107] From 1797 to 1800 he taught in Middletown, Connecticut, and preached in the vicinity. [108] In June, 1800, he opened a school for both boys and girls in Norwich, Connecticut, but after a few years the school had to be closed because of lack of students. [109] From 1802 to 1809 he taught in the public academy in Newark, New Jersey. [110] He spent the next few years in New York City, where he was taken under the care of the Presbytery of New York as a licentiate, and in Philadelphia, where he taught for two years, later serving as home missionary in the destitute churches of Pennsylvania and elsewhere. In 1822 he was teaching in Cincinnati. From 1827 to 1828 he was stationed in Wayne County, Pennsylvania, as a missionary. The next year he was in Blakeslee, Monroe County, and for the two or three years following he was in Utica and in Roxbury. Much of his time in his old age he lived as a boarder in the family of his friend Dr. Nott in Franklin, Connecticut. He began teaching a class of young women in Franklin in 1835, and had just finished the first quarter's service when he was stricken with apoplexy, which caused his death on February 27, 1836. He outlived four wives. [111]

An amusing picture of Woodbridge as he appeared late in life is found in the diary of C. C. Baldwin, former librarian of the American Antiquarian Society, Worcester, Massachusetts, under the date of February 20, 1834.

> I was visited at the Antiquarian Hall this morning by the venerable William Woodbridge, now at Utica, N. Y. He is in his 80th year.... He had the airs and dry humor of an old pedagogue about him. I laughed heartily to hear him complain of the innovations that have been introduced into the system of education. 'When,' said he, 'will people be done trying experiments? There are several conceited fops now at work attempting to palm off upon the community their crude and impracticable schemes in the work of instruction. There's Noah Webster, old as he is, is as full of changes as the moon. Do but look at his productions! I have been striving for more than half a century to put down his spelling book. But cui bono? It is in use everywhere. And there is his great dictionary, which he calls his opus magnum. What is it but a great evil, mega biblon, mega kakon. But, alas, tempora mutantur et nos mutamur in illus. We can make no progress in the great work of education until we return to the point from which we have diverged, but hic labor, hoc opus est, and I fear it is now too late to accomplish so desirable an object. He introduced his Latin so thickly that I could not remember half of it. '[112]

The Young Ladies' Pocket Companion
by
Henry Priest

The second school dictionary published in 1801 is The Young Ladies' Pocket Companion, Being a Short Dictionary of Arts, Sciences, Geography, Heathen Mythology, etc., Intended for the Senior Classes of Young Ladies' Academies, by Henry Priest, New York, and printed by Isaac Collins. The book is 5 1/2 x 3 1/2 x 1 inches in size, and contains 260 pages with approximately 2,600 words. As the dedication indicates, it was prepared for the use of the young ladies in Mr. and Mrs. Priest's Academy in New York. The dedication is as follows:

Young Ladies,

As the following little work was compiled solely with a view to your instruction, it cannot with so much propriety be dedicated to any one else, as to you; and it is with the greatest pleasure and satisfaction, I thus publicly declare that, from the many specimens already given of your great diligence, and unwearied attention to the several branches of education I have had the honour to instruct you in, this small tribute of my labours will not be neglected, but on the contrary will contribute to your improvement, and my pleasure and profit.

With my best wishes for your present improvement, and future welfare,

I have the Honor to be,
Young Ladies,
Your Sincere Friend, and
New York   Humble Servant
June 1st, 1801   Henry Priest[113]

The book seems to be mainly a list of hard words and geographical names. Since this is true, no statement can be made concerning the orthography, but in the dedication honor is spelled both ways and labors is spelled with a u. No attention is given to etymology, pronunciation, division of words into syllables, etc. The nine words given on the first page are typical of the entire number.

A, the first letter in the Alphabet, in all the known languages in the world, except the Ethiopic.
AA, a river in Germany, which empties into the Embs.
AAR, a river in Switzerland, which falls into the Rhine.
ABBEVILLE, a town in France.
ABERRATION, in astronomy, a small apparent motion of the fixed stars.
ABERDEEN, a town in Scotland.
ABBREVIATURE, a mark used for the sake of shortening.
ABINGDON, a town in Maryland, on Bush River.
ABINGDON, a town in Virginia, capital of Washington County.

An English Orthographical Expositor
by
Jaudon, Watson, and Addington

Another small school dictionary, copyrighted in the District
of Pennsylvania on the "first day of June, in the twenty-eighth year
of the Independence of the United States of America,"[114] is An
English Orthographical Expositor: Being a Compendious Selection of
the Most Useful Words in the English Language, Alphabetically Arranged; Divided, Accented, and Explained According to the Most
Approved Modern Authorities. Also, a list of more than eight hundred words, similar, or nearly similar in sound, but of different
spelling and import. By Daniel Jaudon, Thomas Watson, and Stephen
Addington. Four editions of this dictionary were printed. The third,
examined for this study, was published and sold at Philadelphia by
D. Hagan, 1809, with Stiles as the printer.

The Expositor is 7 1/2 x 4 1/2 x 1/2 inches, and contains
223 pages and over 7,000 words. There are also ten pages which
include more than eight hundred words that are similar in sound but
different in spelling and signification. The words are arranged two
columns to a page and divided into syllables by spacing. The part
of speech is indicated after each word. The definitions are very
simple.

The object of the compilers as stated in the Preface is to
make "a compendious and useful spelling book, rather than a minute
explaining dictionary," so that children may be provided with a list
of words not as deficient as is usually found in the common spelling
books, nor filled with as many useless words as are found in a
dictionary. The compilers have attempted to keep a middle ground
between these two extremes, and have provided what they believe "to
be as good a selection of English words as can easily be made; and
they hope, the orthography, division, accentuation, and explanations
will be found correct, and sanctioned by the best modern authorities."[115]

In spelling, the Expositor follows Johnson almost exclusively,
while Walker has been made the standard for accentuation and division. Short words of easy spelling and of obvious meaning, technical terms, and derivatives have been omitted where the attain-
ment of correct spelling or useful information did not require their
insertion.

No information concerning Watson and Addington has been
found. Daniel Jaudon, the eldest son of Peter Jaudon, was born
July 7, 1767, at Mount Pleasant, Bucks County (Pennsylvania?). He
was descended from the Huguenots of France, who were forced to
leave their country in 1685. His early education was obtained in
Philadelphia and Germantown. He engaged in the study of medicine
for a while and taught school for two or three years. The Rev.
Ashbel Green assisted him in the acquisition of classical learning

He married Anna McNeil on December 24, 1793, and in 1794 taught in the English Department in the College and Academy of Philadelphia. In 1796 he established a Seminary for Young Ladies which he superintended until his death in 1826.

American lexicography had its beginning in the publication of A School Dictionary by Samuel Johnson, Jr. in 1798. This dictionary was followed within the next two years by the publication of A Selected, Pronouncing, and Accented Dictionary in the compilation of which Johnson collaborated with John Elliott. During the next four years dictionaries were compiled by Caleb Alexander, William Woodbridge, Henry Priest, Daniel Jaudon, Thomas Watson, and Stephen Addington. The last three worked together on one dictionary. All of the dictionaries compiled by these men were for school use and were little more than small editions of some of the English dictionaries. Although they introduced no new ideas in dictionary making, nevertheless, their recording of new words and new uses of old words, as well as their setting a sort of standard for the English language in America, makes them of significance in an interpretation of the changes and development of our language.

Notes

1. As is pointed out by Stewart Archer Steger, American Dictionaries (Baltimore: J. H. Furst, 1913), p. 19, in the Preface to Johnson and Elliott's dictionary, dated January 1, 1800, mention is made of "the favourable reception with which the School Dictionary met, the last year." Since the Preface was probably written prior to January 1, 1800, "last year" would refer to 1798. For a detailed discussion of Johnson and his dictionaries, see Martha Jane Gibson, "America's First Lexicographer, Samuel Johnson, Jr., 1757-1836," American Speech, XI (December, 1936), 283-292; XII (February, 1937), 19-30.
2. Cf. "Besides various augmented editions of his [Johnson's] dictionary he published a Grammar of the English Tongue and a History of the English Language," W. S. Monroe, "Samuel Johnson," in Paul Monroe, Cyclopedia of Education (New York: Macmillan, 1914), III, 537. No other reference to "various augmented editions" nor to the Grammar and History has been located. The fact that Johnson collaborated with John Elliott in compiling a dictionary, the title of which was registered in the Office of the District of Connecticut in June, 1799, and which was published in 1800, perhaps indicates that no other edition was made available.
3. "Johnson's Dictionary," The New York Times Saturday Review, October 15, 1898, p. 683, column 1.
4. Henry Pynchon Robinson, "Samuel Johnson, Jr., of Guilford and His Dictionaries," The Connecticut Magazine, V (October, 1899), 526; and Stewart Archer Steger, op. cit., p. 18.

5. Samuel Johnson, Jun'r. A School Dictionary, New Haven: Edward O'Brien, p. 5.

6. Ibid., p. 11.

7. Ibid., p. 12.

8. Preface to John Elliott and Samuel Johnson, Junior. A Selected, Pronouncing, and Accented Dictionary. Suffield, Connecticut: Printed by Edward Gray, publishers, Oliver D. and Increase Cook, Hartford, 1800.

9. Robinson, op. cit., p. 529.

10. Cambridge History of American Literature, IV, 475; George Philip Krapp. English Language in America. New York: The Century Company, 1925, I, 356; and Yale University Gazette, III (1929), 65.

11. The son of the first president of King's College was William Samuel Johnson (October 7, 1727-November 14, 1819). He was born in Stratford, Connecticut, where he spent most of his life. He was graduated from Yale in 1744 and three years later received the degree of M.A. from Harvard. Evarts B. Greene. "William Samuel Johnson," Dictionary of American Biography, New York: Charles Scribner's Sons, X, 131-134. Cf. also the statement of Dr. Samuel Johnson: "My son W. Samuel was born at Stratford, Connecticut Oct. 7, 1727, and christened Nov. 5, following...." Herbert and Carol Schneider. Samuel Johnson President of King's College, His Career and Writings. New York: Columbia University Press, 1929, I, 60.

12. James Savage. Genealogical Dictionary of the First Settlers of New England. Boston: Little, Brown and Company, 1860, II, 557.

13. Robinson, op. cit., p. 527 and material taken from the fly leaves of a New Testament which belonged to Samuel Johnson, Jr., and is now in the possession of Mrs. George S. Davis, Guilford, Connecticut, whose husband was a descendant of Nathaniel Johnson, Jr. Personal letter from Elizabeth G. Davis, September 5, 1935.

14. "The oldest house now standing on this Johnson plot was built not earlier than 1730 by Nathaniel, a grandfather of Samuel Johnson, Jr. The elder man lived to be eighty-eight years of age and prudently retained title to the place until 1793. Then it passed to his son, Samuel, Jr., and from our Samuel Jr. to his son Samuel Collins Johnson who sold it out of the family in 1868." Personal letter from Elizabeth G. Davis, September 16, 1935.

15. Robinson, op. cit., p. 527. That it was Samuel Johnson, Jr. who compiled A School Dictionary is shown by the name given on the title page, "By Samuel Johnson, Jun'r," and also that of A Selected, Pronouncing, and Accented Dictionary by John Elliott and "Samuel Johnson, Jun'r, Author of A School Dictionary."

16. James Grant Wilson. The Life and Letters of Fitz-Greene Halleck. New York: D. Appleton and Company, 1869, p. 52.

17. Robinson, op. cit., p. 527.

18. Fly leaves of New Testament formerly owned by Samuel John-
    son, Jr. and now in the possession of Mrs. George S.
    Davis, Guilford, Connecticut.
19. Personal letter, September 16, 1935, from Elizabeth G. Davis
    who had examined the town records.
20. Robinson, op. cit., p. 527.
21. Personal letter from Frederick Calvin Norton, Guilford, Con-
    necticut, June 22, 1935.
22. Robinson, op. cit., p. 526.
23. Personal letter from Elizabeth G. Davis, September 16, 1935.
24. Ralph D. Smith. The History of Guilford, Connecticut, from
    Its First Settlement in 1639. Albany: J. Munsell, 1877,
    p. 9.
25. Robinson, op. cit., p. 526.
26. Smith, op. cit., p. 81.
27. Robinson, op. cit., p. 527. "The house was removed to
    Church Street a century or so ago (around 1834) and con-
    verted into a house owned now by Mrs. Levi Odell Chit-
    tenden. Nothing remains but the framework of what was
    once the town's academy." Personal letter from Frederick
    Calvin Norton, Guilford, Connecticut, June 22, 1935.
28. Robinson, op. cit., p. 527.
29. Henry Pynchon Robinson. "Country Sketches," No. 10, New
    Haven (weekly) Palladium, January 15, 1880, quoted in
    Charles H. Levermore, "Two Centuries and a Half in
    Guilford, Connecticut," New England Magazine, I (n. s.),
    (December, 1889), 421.
30. Levermore, op. cit., p. 421.
31. Nelson Frederick Adkins. Fitz-Greene Halleck. New Haven:
    Yale University Press, 1930, p. 16. Cf. also: "It is
    said he [Halleck] was the favorite pupil of Master Samuel
    Johnson of the Guilford Johnson blood, a teacher who
    would be likely to write in characters deep and large upon
    the boy's impressionable imagination." Levermore, op.
    cit., p. 421.
32. Wilson, op. cit., p. 52.
33. Robinson. "Samuel Johnson, Jr. of Guilford and His Dic-
    tionaries," The Connecticut Magazine, V (October, 1889),
    527.
34. American Dictionaries, p. 23.
35. Sir Herbert Croft, Letter to the Princess Royal of England
    on the English and German Languages, 1797, quoted by E.
    H. Barker in a letter to Noah Webster, June 27, 1831,
    Webster's Letters, New York Public Library.
36. Robinson, op. cit., pp. 528-529.
37. Dissertations on the English Language: with Notes, Historical
    and Critical. To which is added, by way of Appendix, an
    Essay on a Reformed Mode of Spelling, with Dr. Franklin's
    Arguments on that subject. Boston: Isaiah Thomas and
    Company, 1789, pp. 36 and 405.
38. Robinson, op. cit., p. 530.
39. Robinson, op. cit., p. 531.

40. Cf. " ... The Johnson physiognomy and physique from one generation to another, have preserved the courtliness of their magisterial descent and it has been the peculiar property of the family to transmit eyes of rare and lustrous beauty. " Robinson, op. cit., p. 527.

41. Henry Pynchon Robinson. Guilford Portraits. New Haven: The Pease-Lewis Company, 1907, p. 208.

42. Preface to A School Dictionary, p. 4.

43. Robinson, op. cit., p. 530.

44. "Johnson's Dictionary, " New York Times Saturday Review, October 15, 1898, p. 683, column 1.

45. Steger, op. cit., p. 23, and Robinson, op. cit., p. 531. The copy examined for this study was of the second edition.

46. "Wyllys Elliot doubled the '1', and Andrew Elliott doubled both '1' and 't'. " National Cyclopedia of American Biography. New York: James T. White and Company, 1904, XII, 39.

47. "A Selected, Pronouncing, and Accented Dictionary, " American Review and Literary Journal, I (1801), 216-217.

48. Ibid., pp. 215-216. For a discussion of the word mentioned by the reviewer, see Allen Walker Read, "An Obscenity Symbol, " American Speech, IX (1934), 264-278. Read, however, does not mention the word.

49. Preface, pp. 5-6.

50. Ibid., p. 6.

51. "A Selected, Pronouncing, and Accented Dictionary, " American Review and Literary Journal, I (1801), 215.

52. A Selected, Pronouncing, and Accented Dictionary, p. 32.

53. American Dictionaries, p. 28.

54. "A Selected, Pronouncing, and Accented Dictionary, " American Review and Literary Journal, I (1801), 212-213.

55. William B. Sprague. Annals of the American Pulpit. New York: Robert Carter and Brothers, 1866, II, 321, and James A. Gallup, "Historical Discourse, " Proceedings at the Celebration of the 250th Anniversary of the Settlement of Guilford, Connecticut. New Haven: The Stafford Printing Company, 1889, p. 29.

56. Eleazar T. Fitch. A Sermon Preached at the Funeral of the Reverend John Elliott, D.D.; Late Pastor of the Church in East Guilford. New Haven: Printed by Nathan Whiting, 1825, p. 12.

57. Gallup, op. cit., p. 29.

58. Fitch, op. cit., p. 13.

59. Franklin Bowditch Dexter. Biographical Sketches of the Graduates of Yale College with Annals of the College History, 1701-1815. New Haven: Yale University Press, 1907, IV, 463.

60. Ibid.

61. John Todd. John Todd, The Story of His Life, Told Mainly by Himself. New York: Harper and Brothers, 1877, p. 114.

62. Genealogy of the Descendants of John Eliot, "Apostle to the Indians, " 1598-1905. A New Edition, 1905, Prepared and Published by the Committee Appointed at the Meeting of His Descendants, at South Natick, Massachusetts, June 3, 1901, p. 113.

63. Ibid.
64. James A. Gallup, op. cit. , p. 30.
65. Ibid.
66. Op. cit. , pp. 15-16.
67. Ibid. , p. 31.
68. Ibid. , pp. 31-32.
69. Ibid. , p. 32.
70. Dexter, op. cit. , p. 465.
71. Ibid.
72. The Portfolio, I (1801), 347.
73. The Columbian Dictionary of the English Language, p. 23.
74. The American Review and Literary Journal, I (1801), 219.
75. Ibid. , Footnote, p. 219.
76. The Portfolio, I (1801), 247.
77. George Philip Krapp, op. cit. , p. 358.
78. Sprague, op. cit. , III, 405.
79. Ibid.
80. Dexter, op. cit. , III, 644.
81. Sprague, op. cit. , III, 405.
82. Ibid.
83. Harley Goodwin. "History of the Town of New Marlborough,"
    in David D. Field, editor, History of the County of Berk-
    shire. Pittsfield: S. W. Bush, 1829, p. 289.
84. Sprague, op. cit. , III, 405.
85. Dexter, op. cit. , III, 644.
86. Ibid.
87. Ibid. , p. 648.
88. Dwight H. Bruce, editor. Onondaga's Centennial. Boston:
    The Boston Huston Company, 1894, I, 512.
89. Dexter, op. cit. , III, 648.
90. Ibid. , pp. 648-649.
91. Ibid.
92. Sprague, op. cit. , III, 408.
93. Preface, p. iii.
94. The American Review and Literary Journal, II (1802), 226.
95. Ibid.
96. Dexter, op. cit. , IV, 170.
97. Laurence M. Crosbie. The Phillips Exeter Academy, a His-
    tory. Printed for the Academy, 1923, p. 48.
98. Ibid. , pp. 48-49.
99. Dexter, op. cit. , IV, 170.
100. Ibid.
101. Ibid.
102. Thomas Woody. A History of Women's Education in the
    United States. New York: The Science Press, 1929, I,
    154.
103. Crosbie, op. cit. , p. 49.
104. National Cyclopedia of American Biography. New York:
    James T. White and Company, 1900, X, 104.
105. Exeter News Letter, July 5, 1895, quoted in Crosbie, op.
    cit. , pp. 49-50.
106. Dexter, op. cit. , IV, 170.
107. Woody, op. cit. , p. 154.

108. Dexter, op. cit., IV, 170.
109. Ibid.
110. Ibid., p. 171.
111. Ibid., p. 174.
112. Quoted by Crosbie, op. cit., p. 52.
113. The Young Ladies' Pocket Companion, pp. iii-iv.
114. The date is assumed to be 1804.
115. Preface, p. iv.
116. Edwin Jaquett Sellers. An Account of the Jaudon Family. Philadelphia: J. B. Lippincott, 1890, p. 10.

CHAPTER II

SCHOOL AND POCKET DICTIONARIES

The number of school dictionaries published in America during the first half of the nineteenth century indicates that there was a decided belief in the educational world that children should not only learn how to spell the words as given in their spelling books, but that it would be profitable for them to acquire the meaning of the words along with the spelling and pronunciation. Many spelling and pronouncing dictionaries, containing the "most useful words in the English Language," as well as some grammatical information, such as plurals of nouns, declensions of pronouns, participles of verbs, and comparisons of adjectives and adverbs, were published in cheap and convenient form for children. They were prepared with the idea that they would serve both as spelling books and as substitutes for the larger and more expensive dictionaries. Several of these dictionaries were compiled by persons who were themselves authors of spelling books, and the dictionaries provided another step in their series of textbook publications. In these dictionaries, too, there came to be added, beginning with Webster's Compendious Dictionary (1806), much encyclopedic information, such as lists of names of distinguished persons of antiquity, mythological data, chronological tables of remarkable occurrences, tables of money, weights, and measures, etc.

Some of the dictionary makers felt the necessity of giving the child etymological information. William Grimshaw claims the distinction of being the author of the first etymological dictionary (published 1821) "of any language founded on a minute and regular system of analysis." In a few of the school dictionaries stress is laid on elegant and polite orthoepy as opposed to the barbarous and vulgar, and lists of words that contrast the two are given. A few of the dictionaries are devoted almost exclusively to orthoepy.

To fit in with the theory of formal discipline, some of the compilers stress the fact that the proper study of words trains the mind in the habits of thinking, and a few of them give directions to the teachers as to the best methods of using the dictionary for this purpose

A Spelling, Pronouncing and Parsing Dictionary
by
Abel Flint

Little is known about Abel Flint, a compiler of one of the
early American dictionaries. The fourth son of James Flint, he was
born in Hampton [Connecticut?], August 6, 1766, and died March 7,
1825. [1] He was graduated from Yale College in 1785; was tutor at
Brown University from 1786 to 1790; and was ordained April 20,
1791 in Hartford, Connecticut. He married Amelia, the daughter of
Hezekiah Bissel, of East Windsor, Connecticut. [2] In addition to his
dictionary, he published a geometry and trigonometry with a treatise
on surveying, 1806, and a translation of some of the sermons of
Massilon and Bourdaloue. [3]

The dictionary by Flint, copyrighted in the District of Connecticut, July 18, 1806, is A Spelling, Pronouncing and Parsing
Dictionary: Containing all the most common and useful words in the
English Language, Divided into syllables, and accented so as to
lead to their pronunciation: with the parts of speech pointed out at
the end of each word. Designed for the Use of Schools, Hartford,
printed by Hudson and Goodwin, 1806.

The author states in the Preface that the work is designed to
furnish schools with a convenient and cheap book, from which children may learn to spell and pronounce all the common words in the
English language. Spelling books, he says, do not contain all the
words that children should know, and dictionaries are too expensive
for general use in the schools. Furthermore, since they do not
have their words divided into syllables nor properly accented, it is
difficult for children to learn to spell from them.

The Dictionary is 6 1/2 x 4 1/2 x 1/2 inch and is bound
in boards. There are nearly twenty thousand words, arranged
three columns to a page, divided into syllables, and accented according to their pronunciation. Definitions are omitted, so that the book
may be kept small enough to sell for a low price. The author says
that in the division and accent of words he has endeavored to lead
to that pronunciation which appears to him most universally adopted
in New England; and in orthography he has followed the most approved modern dictionaries. [4]

The author thinks that a great number of rules and directions
for pronunciation only perplex the learner, and many words can be
learned only by the ear. However, he gives a rather elaborate list
of explanations and directions. The accented syllable is designated
by an acute accent placed over the vowel in the syllable, or by an
apostrophe at the end of the syllable. When the accent is on a
vowel, the vowel has its long sound except in the following cases:
1) In those diphthongs which have an appropriate sound. The accent
then shows that the stress of the voice is upon that diphthongal
sound, as in the word ac cloy.´ 2) When the accent is over italic
e final, in syllables in which there is another vowel. In such

syllables the final e is silent, and the accent is upon the preceding consonant, as in ac qui escé, lové ly. 3) When otherwise directed at the end of the word.

The vowels are also long when they form a syllable by themselves, when they end a syllable, or when they occur in a syllable terminated by Roman e. When the accent is on a consonant, the preceding vowel has its short sound, except when otherwise directed at the end of the word. Unaccented vowels are also generally short when the syllable in which they occur is terminated by a consonant, or when the consonant is followed by italic e. In some cases monosyllables are accented to show that the vowel has its long sound. An apostrophe placed at the end of a vowel denotes that the accent is upon that syllable, but the vowel is short; and in pronouncing the word, the sound of the succeeding consonant is joined to that vowel; as in a'cid, illi'cit, lo'gic, pronounced assid, illissit, lodgic. A great many other directions are given that pertain to the pronunciation of vowels under certain conditions, of consonants, and of diphthongs.

In words where there are both an apostrophe and an accent, the apostrophe shows the sound of the preceding letter; and the accent shows on which syllable the principal stress of the voice is to be placed. When the pronunciation of a word differs much from its spelling, it is printed in italics, at the end of the word, in such letters as will show its pronunciation.

Certain classes of words are omitted in this dictionary: adverbs ending in ly, which are formed immediately from adjectives, the comparative and superlative degrees of regular adjectives, the past tense and participles of regular verbs and the second and third person singular of verbs, nouns ending in er, which are formed directly from verbs, and the plural number of regular nouns.

The one hundred sixty-two pages of the vocabulary are followed by four pages of words alike in sound but different in meaning, as weak, week, terse, tierce.

A Spelling Dictionary
by
Susanna Rowson

That there is no monopoly by any one profession on the making of dictionaries is shown by the fact that one of the early school dictionaries was compiled by Susanna Rowson, a teacher, an actress, and the author of Charlotte Temple, the first American "best seller." The title is as follows: A Spelling Dictionary Divided into Short Lessons, For the Easier Committing to memory by Children and Young Persons; and Calculated to Assist Youth in Comprehending what they read; Selected from Johnson's Dictionary, for the use of her pupils by Susanna Rowson, Portland: Published and for

sale by Isaac Adams, No. 7, Exchange Street, and West and Richardson, No. 75, Cornhill, Boston, 1815. A. and J. Shirley, Printers, Copyrighted, 1807, District of Massachusetts. [5]

Before any idea of compiling a dictionary presented itself, Mrs. Rowson had enjoyed a very colorful career. She was born in Portsmouth, England, in 1762. When about five years of age, she came to America with her father, Lieutenant William Haswell, who was stationed in Boston as a collector of Royal Customs. The long and perilous voyage was ended by a shipwreck on Lovell's Island, memories of which Mrs. Rowson later recorded in her novel Rebecca. Her girlhood was spent at her father's home in Nantasket, Massachusetts, where at ten years of age she won many praises from her summer neighbor, James Otis, because of her familiarity with Spenser, Shakespeare, and Homer and Virgil in Pope's and Dryden's translations. [6]

When the Revolutionary War broke out, Lieutenant Haswell, as an officer of the Crown, could not take the oath of allegiance to the colonies, and his property was seized and confiscated. His family was removed to Hingham, thence to Abington, and finally, in 1778, to Halifax. Later they returned in poverty to England, where Susanna became governess in the family of the Duchess of Devonshire. [7]

In 1786 Miss Haswell published her first novel, Victoria, and in the same year married William Rowson, who was in the hardware business in London and was a trumpeter in the Royal House Guards. In 1793 she came with her husband to America where, for four years, they engaged in acting both in Philadelphia and in Boston. In the last year they were in the Federal Street theatre, Boston. [8]

On leaving the stage in the spring of 1797, Mrs. Rowson, under the patronage of Mrs. Samuel Smith, opened a "Young Ladies' Academy" in Federal Street, Boston, with a single pupil, Mrs. Smith's adopted daughter, and continued it thus for a whole term. [9] The staid Bostonians could not trust their children to the care of one who had been both a writer of novels and an actress. However, it was not long before her school became very popular.

In the spring of 1799, Mrs. Rowson created a sensation in the musical world of Boston by introducing a piano into her school room. A Mr. Laumont was employed as the teacher, and many young ladies from different parts of the country began to abandon their study of the spinet and harpsichord for that of the newer instrument. Mrs. Rowson's popularity with her students is shown in a letter written by Eliza Southgate to her father.

Boston, February 13, 1789
Hon. Father:

I am again placed at school under the tuition of an amiable lady, so mild, so good, no one can help loving her; she treats all her scholars with such tenderness as would win the affection of the most savage brute, tho' scarcely able to receive an impression of the kind. I learn Embroidery and Geography at present and wish your permission to learn Musick.... [10]

In 1800, Mrs. Rowson transferred her school to Medford, where she drew pupils not only from Massachusetts but from other states and even from the British provinces. [11] Later the school was moved to Newton, and in 1807, with the assistance of her sister-in-law, Mrs. Mary Cordia Haswell, she established her school on Washington Street, near Roxbury. In 1811 it was again moved to what became its permanent location in Hollis Street, Boston. Here she continued her work until failing health caused her to withdraw in 1822.

During the twenty-five years spent in conducting one of the most famous girls' schools in America, Mrs. Rowson engaged in many other activities. She edited one magazine (The Boston Weekly Magazine), contributed to several others, wrote poetry, songs, essays, novels and textbooks, and interested herself in a number of charitable enterprises. [12]

This study is concerned with Mrs. Rowson mainly as the compiler of A Spelling Dictionary, the publication of which, like Webster's Spelling Book, was the result of teaching. She explains in the Preface the reasons for publishing the book. It is interesting to note in it her ideas on the methods of education.

> Engaged as I have been, for some years past, in the important task of Education, it has ever appeared to me a most essential object, to store the young mind with ideas. Almost every child of a tolerably good capacity has its tender memory burthened with vast store of words; but as they are in general ignorant of the meaning of more than two-thirds of these words, how is it possible any ideas can arise, or associate themselves in their minds, from reading, study, or recitation? I have myself witnessed young people who have read with precision and even elegance; every stop was scrupulously observed, every mark, every pause attended to, and the voice modulated to the sense of the subject; yet I have been convinced by subsequent questions, that they have attached no idea whatever to what they have read, but that any string of words with the same capitals, breaks and points, would have been read exactly in the same manner. To this mechanical kind of reading I was a perfect stranger, till repeated instances assured me it really did exist; it then appeared to me a very serious evil; but how was it to be remedied? To set a child to study the Dictionary, even the smallest of Johnson's or the common one of Perry's, appeared so laborious a task, that they were wearied before they got through the letter A; and spelling-books afforded little or no assistance in the increasing a child's stock of ideas. I frequently wrote short lessons of ten or twelve words, with the definitions, these the children would study with avidity; and from that circumstance I formed the resolution of printing the selection of Spelling Lessons, which I now offer to the public, flattering myself the book will be found serviceable in the instruction of youth, either in schools or private families. Children study with more cheerfulness, when the lesson is short and determined, and if they are early habituated to connect ideas with words as they advance in life this pleasing association continues, their minds being informed, their studies and readings are pleasures, for they afford some degree of amusement. I do not say all these good consequences will arise from the study of my little book; but if it in the least contributes to the advancement of so desirable an end, I shall have attained my purpose; for it is my fixed opinion, that it is better to give the young pupil one rational idea, than fatigue them by obliging them to commit to memory a thousand mere words.

The first edition, a square 12 mo., with four pages of introduction and 132 pages of words, double columns, was published and sold by John West, Cornhill, Boston. David Carlisle was the printer.

Copies of the first edition, considered quite rare by collectors of
early American textbooks, are in the library of the American Antiquarian Society, the Boston Public Library, the Watkinson Library,
and Harvard College Library. The Harvard copy was presented by
Charles Sumner. The second edition is 14 1/2 x 13 cm. and contains four pages of introduction and one hundred fifty-two pages of
words--approximately 5, 300--arranged in double columns. The
words, divided into 413 lessons of about 13 words each, are carefully separated into syllables and defined in simple language. Since
the book is based on Johnson's dictionary, the spelling is conservative. It is printed on coarse brown paper with poor type and ink
and is bound in boards. The last four pages present "A Concise
Account of the Heathen Deities, and Other Fabulous Persons; with
the Heroes and Heroines of Antiquity." There are approximately
one hundred such names. The second edition contains an advertisement signed by the compiler and dated at Hollis-Street, Boston,
1815. The advertisement is as follows:

> That this little Book should become of consequence
> enough to demand a second Edition, is extremely grati-
> fying to my best feelings. It has been my study for
> eighteen years past, to render the little talent with which
> I have been entrusted, beneficial to society: and I can
> truly say, that the happiest moments of my life have been
> those, in which I have been employed in the instruction of
> the young, and uninformed - Should it please God to con-
> tinue my life and indulge me with a moderate portion of
> health, I hope in a short time, to give unquestionable
> proofs, that the permanent good of the rising generation
> is the object nearest my heart.
> I should be wanting in gratitude were I to omit, on
> this occasion, to offer my acknowledgment to that generous
> public, who hold my school at this moment in as high, if
> not higher estimation than in the first years of my appeal
> to their favour.

> Hollis-Street, Boston, 1815   S. Rowson

There are copies of the second edition in the library of the
American Antiquarian Society, the Boston Public Library, Harvard
College Library, the Hispanic Society of America, the Library of
Congress (two copies), the New York Historical Society, and Watkin-
son Library.

That the Spelling Dictionary enjoyed a popularity between 1811
and 1820 in Boston, Bridgeport, Philadelphia, and Salem is testified
by the number of booksellers and libraries offering it: Isaiah Thomas, Jr. , Boston, 1811; Lambert Lockwood, Bridgeport, 1813; Auction
Stock of Late Ebenezer Larkin, Boston, March 15, 1814; Matthew
Carey, Philadelphia, 1816; Cushing and Appelton, Salem, 1818; Samuel T. Armstrong, Boston, 1820. [13]

The New York Expositor
by
Richard Wiggins

Another of the American dictionaries prepared primarily for schools is The New York Expositor or Fifth Book; Being a Collection of the Most Useful Words in the English Language by Richard Wiggins, to which is added A Vocabulary of Scientific Terms by John Griscom, The Whole Selected, Divided, Accentuated, and Explained, with References to a Key For Their Pronunciation; Chiefly on the Authorities of Johnson and Walker, For the Use of Schools, printed and sold by Samuel Wood, New York, 1811. It is 5 1/2 x 3 1/2 x 1 inch in size and contains 285 pages and approximately nine thousand words arranged in two columns to a page. The words are divided into syllables and a few have their pronunciation indicated by respelling. Accented syllables are marked and silent letters are in italics.

The last thirty-five pages contain the Vocabulary of Scientific Terms prepared by John Griscom (1774-1852), who had achieved some prominence as a teacher of chemistry.[14] There are approximately five hundred words in the list.

The New Critical Pronouncing Dictionary
of the English Language
by
Richard S. Coxe

The New Critical Pronouncing Dictionary of the English Language, by an American Gentleman, published at Burlington, New Jersey, 1813, by D. Allinson and Company, was the work of Richard S. Coxe, a member of a distinguished New Jersey family. At the time of the publication of the dictionary the real author was not known. On the title page of a copy in the Library of Congress the name of Robert Walsh was written in pencil, but it was later crossed out and the name of Coxe substituted. Sidney Willard wrote in 1813:

> No responsibility appears to be attached to any name except to that of the publisher, Allinson, who, with his partner or partners in trade, has associated the names of the various booksellers that are to deliver and vend his book. Report has sometimes fixed on Dr. Wharton, as having the principal concern in the compilement, as it is facetiously called in the preface; and the publisher, when he came here to solicit subscriptions, held out certain vague promises concerning the share Mr. Walsh was to have in the superintendence of the work. He also mentioned a young man of great learning and industry, who was to be the principal drudge in filling up and correcting the work.... All we know with certainty is, that the dictionary

RICHARD S. COXE

purports to be the work of "An American Gentleman." We
do not think this the fairest way of introducing a book of
this kind to the public.... And this is the first instance
that we recollect of a dictionary, so imposing in many
respects, coming into the world, without a father to acknowledge it, or answer for any of its defects. [15]

Richard S. Coxe was the second son of William Coxe, famous
in New Jersey for his interest in horticulture. The Coxe family had
been long settled in New Jersey and had for more than a century
filled an important place in its history. Dr. Daniel Coxe, of London,
was the physician to the Queen of Charles II, and subsequently to
Queen Anne, and was also a governor of St. Bartholomew's Hospital
in London. [16] He was the owner of twenty-two shares of proprietary
rights in West Jersey and was governor of the province from 1687 to
1690. He resided at Burlington, where he built a dwelling house
and a pottery, probably the first in the State. [17] The extent of his
property is seen by the fact that in 1691 he sold to the "West New
Jersey Society," of London, with certain reservations of surveys in
old Salem County, his twenty-two shares of rights in West Jersey,
and two hundred thousand acres contiguous to West Jersey, two
shares of property in East Jersey, three whole shares in Merrimac,
New England, ten thousand acres in Pennsylvania, town lots at Perth
Amboy, Gloucester and Egg Harbor, and his dwelling house and
pottery house, with all the tools, in Burlington. [18]

William's son Daniel was an able lawyer who succeeded to
his father's possessions in America, and in 1734 was appointed one
of the associate justices of the Supreme Court of New Jersey. [19]
William, the second son of Daniel Coxe, spent most of his life in
Philadelphia, where he married the daughter of Tench Francis. [20]
Of this gentleman, Richard Smith Coxe was the grandson.

At seven years of age, Richard was placed under the charge
of the Reverend Mr. Staughton at the academy in Burlington, where
he remained until he was thirteen. From that time until 1805, when
he was admitted to Princeton, he was aided in his studies by the
Reverend Mr. Wharton, rector of St. Mary's Church, in Burlington,
who prepared him for matriculation. When he enrolled in Princeton,
he was the youngest student in the institution, but throughout his
three years of college work maintained a conspicuous position. [21]

After leaving college on his graduation as bachelor of arts at
the age of sixteen, Coxe entered as a student of law in the office of
Judge William Griffith, at Burlington, where he remained for three
years, after which time he studied with Horace Binney in Philadelphia. In 1812 he was admitted to the bar of the Supreme Court in
Pennsylvania and began the practice of his profession in Philadelphia,
making a special study of real property law. In 1816 he married
Susan B. Griffith and returned to Burlington where he was admitted
to the bar of New Jersey in May 1817. In 1822 he established himself in Washington, D.C. and was admitted to the bar of the circuit
court of the District of Columbia. His knowledge of real property

law won him a reputation as a leader of the Supreme Court because of his skill in handling suits in connection with the cession of Florida, and Louisiana. [22] In 1849 he married as his second wife Mrs. Susan R. Wheeler. He died in Washington in 1865.

The title of the dictionary by Coxe is quite promising in its fullness: A New Critical Pronouncing Dictionary of the English Language, containing all the words in general use, with their significance accurately explained, and the sound of each syllable clearly expressed: among which will be found several hundred terms, with their acceptions and derivations, which appear to have been hitherto omitted by the best lexicographers: also, a variety of the technical terms of medicine, law, commerce, arts, and general science: the whole interspersed with critical and philological observations, and references to the respective authorities. To which will be prefixed, Mr. Walker's Principles of English Pronunciation: a nomenclature of the names of distinguished persons and places of antiquity: comprising a sketch of the mythology, history, and biography of the ancients, from the most authentick sources: a chronological table of remarkable occurrences, from the earliest ages to the present time: containing whatever is worthy of record as discoveries, inventions, &c, &c. Compiled from authors of the most approved reputation: with considerable additions by An American Gentleman.

Very little of critical value is to be found in the Preface. "It begins with a lofty march of mock-majesty, that seems to betray the aspirations of an ambitious youth to reach the real dignity and grandeur of the great English lexicographer. It is forced and artificial; it violates constantly all rules of symmetry and proportion, and despises the shackles of rhetoric."[23] An example of its flowery leftiness is exhibited in the following quotation:

> ... But as the Sun is the only source of that light, by which we are enabled to perceive the spots upon its surface; so it is solely by adhering with the utmost inflexibility to the plan proposed, and in a considerable degree executed by this profound Lexicographer Dr. Johnson, that we have ventured to assume upon ourselves the responsibility of endeavouring to repair his faults, and to supply his deficiencies. [24]

Johnson's dictionary was taken as the basis of the vocabulary of Coxe's volume, and many words, together with the explanation attached to them, were added from the works of Mason, Ash, Mavor, Dyche, Brown, and Walker. Others were supplied from authors of reputation. Scientific and technical words were also admitted, but the compiler is not explicit as to his plan of rejecting or admitting words, nor has he told in what respect he has deviated from the orthoepy of Walker whom he acknowledges to have followed. It is upon this combination of Johnson and Walker that the author hopes his work will receive the sanction and authority that will entitle it to respect and to lay claim to a "precedency before any other work of the same description in the language."

The Dictionary is a quarto of 941 pages, with an introduction of 85 pages devoted to Walker's principles of English pronunciation. Six hundred thirty-seven pages of the Dictionary are devoted to the vocabulary; 276 to a Classical Dictionary; and 28 pages to a Chronological Table of Remarkable Events, Discoveries, and Inventions, from the Creation to the year 1807. The Classical Dictionary is a mixture of classical and biblical names.

There are approximately 54,000 words in the Dictionary, arranged in two columns to a page. The foreign words from which each word is derived are given after each word. The compiler acknowledges that some errors in etymology may occur, but adds, "the inaccuracies having, however, been found in general to be no otherwise interesting than merely as matters of curiosity, have, except in a few instances, been suffered to remain uncorrected."[25] The pronunciation is indicated after each word by means of superior letters. A key at the top of each page furnishes suggestions for the sound of vowels. An example of how a very simple word is defined in this dictionary in a very elaborate manner is seen in the following word:

> To take, tàke, v. n. preterite took, part, pass. taken, sometimes took [taka Islandick]. To receive what is offered; to seize what is not given; to receive; to receive with good or ill will; to lay hold on, to catch by surprise or artifice; to snatch, to seize; to make prisoner; to captivate with pleasure, to delight, to engage; to surprise, to catch; to entrap, to catch in a snare; to understand in any particular sense or manner; to exact; to get, to have, to appropriate; to use, to employ; to blast, to infect; to judge in favour of; to admit any thing bad from without; to get, to procure; to turn to, to practice; to close in with, to comply with; to form, to fix; to catch in the hand, to seize; to admit, to suffer; to perform any action; to receive with the mind; to go into; to go along; to follow, to pursue; to swallow, to receive; to swallow as a medicine; to choose one or more; to copy; to convey, to carry, to transport; to fasten on; not to refuse, to accept, to adopt; to change with respect to place; to separate; to go in; to receive any temper or disposition of mind; to endure, to bear; to draw, to derive; to leap, to jump over; to assume, to allow, to admit; to receive with fondness; to carry out for use; to suppose, to receive in thought, to entertain in opinion; to direct; to separate for one's self from any quantity; not to leave, not to omit; to receive payments; to obtain by mensuration; to withdraw; to seize with a transitory impulse; to comprise, to comprehend; to have recourse to; to produce, or suffer to be produced; to catch in the mind; to hire, to rent; to engage in; to be active in; to suffer, to support; to admit in capulation; to catch eagerly; to use as an oath or expression; to seize as a disease; to take away, to deprive of; to set aside, to remove; to take care, to be careful, to be solicitous for, to superintend;

to take course, to have recourse to measures; to take down, to crush, to reduce, to suppress, to swallow, to take by the mouth; to take from, to derogate, to detract; to deprive of; to take heed, to be cautious, to beware, to take heed to, to attend; to take in, to comprise, to comprehend, to admit, to win, to receive, to receive mentally; to take oath, to swear; to take off, in invalidate, to destroy, to remove; to withhold, to withdraw; to swallow; to purchase, to copy, to find place for; to remove; to take order with, to check, to take course with; to take out, to remove from within any place; to take part, to share; to take place, to prevail, to have effect; to take up, to borrow upon credit or interest, to be ready for, to engage with, to apply to the use of, to begin; to fasten with a ligature passed under; to engross, to engage, to have final recourse to, to seize, to catch, to arrest; to admit, to answer by reproving, to reprimand; to begin where the former left off, to lift, to occupy; to accommodate, to adjust, to comprise, to adopt, to assume; to collect, to exact a tax; to take upon, to appropriate to, to assume, to admit to be imputed to, to claim authority.

Willard says that the Dictionary was compiled in too much haste, as is evidenced by its inconsistencies. He calls attention to the fact that in the list of words beginning with the letter A, not a single word is marked as obsolete or not used, but as the work progresses there is a deviation from this plan. Other faults he mentions are the fact that there is no way of distinguishing the new words added to the vocabulary and that Coxe copied the errors found in Johnson. Willard concludes that

> ....when we find such evident marks of a want of a consistent, preconceived plan, and of carelessness, and haste in execution, we cannot think that learning has gained much by this addition to the number of dictionaries; and do not believe that any scholar, who has much reputation to lose, will avow himself willingly to be the person entirely, or principally responsible for the Compilement, or coacervation, or heaping up, as the word is explained in the dictionary. 26

The American Standard of Orthography
and Pronunciation
by
Burgess Allison

Another dictionary designed for the use of schools which made little contribution to the development of lexicography in America is The American Standard of Orthography and Pronunciation and Improved Dictionary of the English Language, abridged for the Use of Schools, by Burgess Allison, D. D., Burlington, New Jersey.

Printed by John S. Mechan, for D. Allinson, et al. iv 5 -16, 390
p. , 17 cm. , 1815. It was based on Johnson, Ash, Walker, and
Allinson's big dictionary, Walker's pronunciation with few exceptions having been adopted. 27 It contains approximately 23,400
words, arranged in two columns to a page, with the pronunciation
indicated after each word by respelling and by the use of superior
letters to indicate the sound of vowels, which are marked according to the directions given in "A Table of the Simple and Diphthongal Vowel Sounds" on page sixteen of the Introduction. The words
are divided into syllables by hyphens where the accent does not
fall. There is no attempt at etymology, and the definitions are very
simple and brief.

The author says in the Preface that he has been very careful to banish vulgarisms, low cant words, obsolete terms, expressions peculiar to other countries, and especially those words that
require "unchaste definitions. " Care has also been exercised to
render the work as perfect as possible. "The definitions have been
compared with those of other lexicographers, the most appropriate
terms have been adopted, new ones have been substituted where the
old were deficient or unapplicable, such as were redundant have
been expunged, the pronunciation of each word has been introduced,
and the essence of lexicography so concentrated as to form a useful book of reference, and at the same time a convenient manual to
all classes of society. "28

In the first edition of the Dictionary the author promises to
furnish the same work in a common octavo without abridgment, and
in an advertisement at the beginning the proprietor, David Allinson,
solicits suggestions for improvements for future editions, but no
other editions appeared. Krapp calls attention to the fact that both
Coxe's and Allison's dictionaries are considerably larger than the
earlier school dictionaries, thereby indicating that the making of
school dictionaries in America was growing in dignity at least as a
commercial undertaking. 29

The author of The American Standard of Orthography and Pronunciation was the son of Richard and Ruth Allison. He was born
in Bordentown, New Jersey, August 17, 1753. His father was very
pious and Allison early became a convert to the Baptist faith and
began to preach when he was sixteen years of age. 30 In 1777, he
studied a session at Rhode Island College (now Brown University)
and subsequently became pastor of a small congregation at Bordentown. He opened a classical boarding school, with his mother as
matron, to eke out his salary as a pastor. The school rose rapidly
in reputation and in numbers and ultimately brought him a small
fortune. His pupils, numbering generally about a hundred, came
from almost every state in the Union, from Lisbon, the West Indies,
the Azores, and South America. The Revolutionary War prevented
his importing apparatus and he constructed most of the instruments
needed for experiments. An electrical machine and an orrery were
of his own construction. 31

In December, 1783, Allison married Mrs. Rhoda Stout, who aided him in his school work by assisting in his new plan of discipline without a rod. They had seven children--four sons and three daughters. In 1796, having become economically independent, he rented his school buildings and spent his time in the invention and improvement of various machines. Among these were a machine for taking profiles, a polygraph in which steel pens were used, and the steam engine. These, however, wasted his money, as did heavy losses by endorsements, and the discovery of a flaw in the title to twenty thousand acres of land in Kentucky. In 1801, he again took charge of his academy and resumed his pastorate, but his health soon compelled him to give up both of these labors.

For some years Allison gave his attention to theological studies. In 1816, he was elected Chaplain of the House of Representatives, in which office he continued for several years. He was then appointed Chaplain at the Navy Yard in Washington. In this office he died, February 20, 1827. Howard Malcom characterizes the work of Allison in the following words:

> As a preacher, Dr. Allison may be said to have lacked fluency, though his discourses always indicated good sense, a well furnished mind, and an evangelical spirit. He was an eminently wise man, and this rendered him a most acceptable and useful counsellor. In all ecclesiastical meetings, he was honoured and trusted, and his influence ever tended to love and zeal. As a teacher of youth, he had few, if any, superiors. His reputation in this respect procured him invitation to the Presidency of three several Colleges, all of which he declined. He possessed great mechanical ingenuity, and was no mean connoisseur in some of the fine arts. He was adept particularly in music and painting, in both which he took great delight as recreations and spent some hours almost daily. At an early period, he was elected a member of the American Philosophical Society, and was long one of its Secretaries. He kept up an extensive foreign correspondence, and wrote much for magazines and newspapers. On the formation of the Baptist Board of Foreign Missions, he was chosen one of its Vice Presidents. Indeed, I may safely say that few men have lived a longer, better, happier and holier life than Burgess Allison. [32]

The following notice of Allison was written by Morgan Edwards in 1789:

> Mr. Allison is a slender built man, and neither tall nor of firm constitution, yet approaches towards an universal genius beyond any of my acquaintance. His stated preaching shows his skill in Divinity. The Academy he opened in 1778 gives him daily opportunities of displaying mastership in the liberal arts and sciences, and ancient and modern languages; several foreign youths deem his

seminary their Alma Mater: foreigners prefer him for a
tutor, because of his acquaintance with the French, Spanish, Portuguese, etc. The Academy is well furnished
with books, globes, glasses, and other pieces of apparatus for experiments in Natural Philosophy, Astronomy,
Geography, Optics, Hydrostatics, etc. Some of the said
pieces are of his own fabrication. He is now preparing
materials for an Orrery, on an improved plan. He is
not a stranger to the Muses and Graces: for he is an
adept in Music, Drawing, Painting, Katoptrics, &c. He
has two curious and well finished chandeliers in his parlour, which show the maker, whenever he stands before
them. He is as remarkable a mechanic as he is an
artist and the philosopher: the lathe, the plane, the hammer,
the chisel, the graver, &c., have displayed his skill in
the use of tools. His accomplishments have given him a
name and a place in our Philological Society, and in that
distinguished by the name of Rumsey, and in the Society
for promoting Agriculture and Home Manufactures. [33]

Grimshaw's Dictionaries

William Grimshaw was born in Greencastle, near Belfast,
Ireland, November 22, 1782. [34] He emigrated to America in 1815,
and lived for many years in Philadelphia and its vicinity. [35] He
wrote a number of books, among which are histories of England,
France, Greece, Napoleon, Rome, South America, Mexico, and
the United States; and the Merchant's Law Book, as well as his
dictionaries. [36] He died in 1852.

His first dictionary was An Etymological Dictionary or Analysis of the English Language, Containing the Radicals and Definitions of Words Derived from the Greek, Latin, and French and all
the Generally Used Technical and Polite Phrases Adopted from the
French and Latin, Philadelphia: Printed for the Author by Lydia
R. Bailey, 1821. It is a 12mo., 18 1/2 cm., and contains eight
pages of introduction and 328 pages (not numbered) of the dictionary
proper.

The author states in the Preface that few sciences are more
worthy of acquirement than etymology. "If the terms of scientific
instruction be not clearly understood by the pupil, his perception
will at first be imperfect, and in the end abortive; if not fully comprehended by the teacher, his manner will betray his ignorance;
and, in place of developing his subject, he will involve it; instead
of delighting, he will fatigue."[37] He compliments himself on the
fact that his is the first etymological dictionary that has ever
appeared, of any language, founded on a minute and regular system
of analysis. [38]

The words are arranged one column to a page and are written in capitals. The definitions are followed by the etymological data, for example: "logomachy, s. A contest in, or about, words. G. logomachia; com. of logos, a word, and mache, a battle." Sycophant, s. A deceitful parasite; a designing flatterer; a mean insinuating fellow. L. sycophanta; G. sukophantes; suke, a fig, and phac, to tell. 'By a law of Sonon,' says Plutarch, 'no production of the Attican lands, except oil, was allowed to be sold to strangers, - and, therefore, it is not improbable, what some affirm, that the exportation of figs was formerly forbidden, and that the informer against the delinquents was called a sycophant.'" There are nearly six thousand words in the Dictionary. Foreign words are inserted in their regular order. There are no diacritical marks, and no attempt is made to indicate pronunciation. The words are not divided into syllables.

There were two other editions of An Etymological Dictionary in 1826 and in 1848. Very few changes were made in the later editions except in the number of words, the two editions together adding about a thousand words. In the last edition the accented syllables are indicated. The price of the Etymological Dictionary was 84 cents. [39]

In 1829 another of Grimshaw's dictionaries was published under two titles, the material in each being the same. The titles are The Ladies' Lexicon, and Parlour Companion, Containing Nearly Every Word in the English Language, and Exhibiting the Plurals of Nouns and the Participles of Verbs; Being also Particularly Adapted to the Use of Academies and Schools, Philadelphia: Grigg, Elliott and Company, and The Gentleman's Lexicon, or Pocket Dictionary ...(the remainder of the title is the same). These were also published under the title of The Handy Dictionary.

The Ladies' Lexicon is a 16mo. and contains 407 pages. It professes to supply the deficiencies of all preceding dictionaries, and therefore to contain, already formed, "every word in the English language, that may be necessary in the composition of a Letter."[40] The main feature stressed in the Preface is that it contains the plurals of all nouns which are not formed by the mere addition of the letter s, and the participles of every verb that are generally used. The rules on which the spelling of the plurals and participles are based are taken from the grammar of Lindley Murray. [41]

The words are written in capitals and are not divided except where the accent falls. The definitions are short and no etymological data are given. There are over fourteen thousand words which have been selected primarily for their use in letter writing or in conversation. No especial contribution to lexicography is exhibited.

A New Improved Dictionary for Children
by
J. Kingsbury

A work designed as a simple definition book for children is
A New, Improved Dictionary for Children; or Definition Book, for
the Use of Schools. Being a Selection of the most Important and
Necessary English Terms, with Plain, Simple Explanations. By J.
Kingsbury. Boston: Published by Munroe and Francis, 1822. It is
a small book, 6 x 5 1/2 x 1 inch, and is dedicated "To All Good
Children, Who Love Their Books." The dedication, in part, is as
follows:

My Dear Little Friends,

For you this little book has been written, and to you it
is dedicated. Offered to your particular notice and accept-
ance; not dedicated to you, to tell you, or tell the world,
how wise and good you are ; but devoted to your special
use, that it may help you to become wise; since it is well
known, all little folks wish to be men and women. If you
learn to know a great deal, you will be like men, though
you are little; but it would be sad, indeed, to grow large
as men, yet be ignorant and illiterate, like little children!

The author then gives advice as to the best way of acquiring
knowledge and direction as to the use of his dictionary as an aid in
the learning of new words.

The compiler says that although the book appears to contain
but a small selection of words, it probably embraces all the important terms likely to occur in general miscellaneous reading except words in familiar, domestic use, the definition of which is
considered unnecessary. Vulgar words, obsolete and technical
words, except those relating to the arts and professions, are omitted. These last are included because of their frequent occurrence
in European history and in all travels. Many derivative words,
participles, and adverbs have been omitted.

The word which seemed nearest primitive, or the most
natural root, has usually been placed first. In this way it was
hoped to give children some idea of the etymology of the words, and
to show where to refer any derivatives not inserted. Words of the
same derivative are included in brackets. Foreign primitives are
annexed where sufficient space is allowed. Abstract terms are explained in connection with some subject or object already familiar.
Many ideas foreign to the mere definition of words have been introduced, particularly on the subject of superstitious fancies, such as
those that relate to charms, enchantments, fascinations, elves, fair-
ies, ghosts, goblins, etc. These have been considered as mere crea-
tures of superstition, ignorance, or the invention of poets and fabulists.

The Dictionary proper contains 282 pages. The last four
pages include a sketch of mythology and a list of abbreviations.

The Nomenclature and Expositor
of the English Language
by
Hezekiah Burhans

Among the school dictionaries published around the first quar-
ter of the nineteenth century in America is The Nomenclature and
Expositor of the English Language; in which the meaning of each
word is clearly explained, and the orthoepy of every syllable accur-
ately pointed out, according to John Walker's Pronouncing Dictionary.
Compiled for Use of Schools in the United States, and Great Britain,
By Hezekiah Burhans, Counsellor at Law; and Author of the Critical
Pronouncing Spelling Book.   Philadelphia: Printed and Sold by Uriah
Hunt, Philadelphia, William Williams, Utica, John Montgomery, New
York, and Armstrong and Plaskett, Baltimore.   The copyright was
presented in the Eastern District of Pennsylvania, January 11, 1826.
A copy of the title page appeared in The Saturday Evening Post from
February 4 to March 11, 1826.   The copyright was signed, May 15,
1826, by Henry Clay as Secretary of State.   The title is followed on
the title page by four lines by the author.

> Without our words are sounded as they ought,
> Reading nor Elocution can be taught:
> Whilst all we learn unhappily may tend
> To Babylon's confusion in the end.

The Dictionary was adapted to succeed the author's Spelling
Book, "so as to form a complete system of useful and exceptionable
language."[42] The book is 3 3/4 x 6 x 3/4 inch in size, and
contains 212 pages and approximately 7,500 words.   A Table of the
Simple and Diphthongal Vowels is given on page 5.   The sounds of
the vowels are indicated by the use of superior letters, and the
parts of speech are shown by numbers following each word.   The
key to the vowels and the numbers representing each part of speech
are given at the top of each page.   The words are divided into syllables by spacing and the accented syllable is marked by an apostrophe.   Each word is respelled to indicate the pronunciation.   The
definitions are very simple.   The way in which the data concerning
each word is given is shown in the following examples: "A ban don
(a ban dun, 5) to forsake." "Ac cessi on (ak, sesh, un, 2)." (Note the
division of sion.)   A word used as more than one part of speech is
given only once, as "truss (trus, 2) a bundle of hay or straw, (5)
to pack close."

The vocabulary is followed by a section on the "Principles of
English Pronunciation," which contains eight tables of the sound
vowels, diphthongs, triphthongs, consonants of one, two, and three
or four letters, and of syllabication.   In the discussion of syllabication the author says that the object of syllabication is two-fold: 1)
To show the exact pronunciation of each word, as the-ol-o-gy.   2)
To point out the parts of which it is composed, as theo-logy.   Since
this last embraces some foreign and dead languages, it is absurd

to teach it to a child. Such a division is constantly at variance with the true orthoepy and leads the child from the analogy of his mother tongue.

A table of words similar in pronunciation, but dissimilar in spelling follows the section on syllabication. A Chronological Table enables years to be determined as well as the Dominical or Sunday letter. A list of abbreviations is given on page 184, while pages 185-205 contain six tables of correct and corrupt pronunciation, which the author hopes will be effective at least in improving the rising generation. He realizes, he says, that the vernacular errors are of so long standing that it is not easy to eradicate them but that the one mode of orthoepy is elegant and polite and the other is barbarous and vulgar, it would eventually produce the proper uniform pronunciation. Examples of the tables of correct and incorrect pronunciation follow.

Orthography	Orthoepy	Barbarisms
are	$\overset{2}{a}$r	$\overset{1}{a}$re
ask	$\overset{4}{a}$sk	$\overset{4}{a}$ks
boil	b$\overset{3}{o}\overset{2}{i}$l	b$\overset{1}{i}$le
catch	k$\overset{4}{a}$tsh	k$\overset{2}{i}$tsh
caught	k$\overset{4}{a}$wt	k$\overset{3}{o}$tsh
deaf	d$\overset{3}{e}$f	d$\overset{1}{e}$fe
fetch	f$\overset{2}{e}$tch	f$\overset{2}{i}$tsh
first	f$\overset{2}{u}$rst	f$\overset{2}{u}$st
guide	g$\overset{1}{y}$ide	g$\overset{1}{i}$de
haunt	h$\overset{2}{a}$nt	h$\overset{3}{a}$wnt
sauce	s$\overset{3}{a}$wse	s$\overset{4}{a}$s
took	t$\overset{2}{o}\overset{2}{o}$k	t$\overset{2}{u}$k
whole	h$\overset{1}{o}$le	h$\overset{2}{u}$ll
year	y$\overset{2}{e}$re	y$\overset{1}{a}$re

Pages 206-212 contain the author's address to the teachers of the United States.

The author states in the Preface that among the early writers on the subject of pronunciation are Elphinston, Kendrick, Sheridan, and Nares, all of whom have peculiar excellencies, but Walker, he thinks, has combined the advantages of all into one complete system. Walker's system has been followed in this dictionary which, the author thinks, is particularly fitted for the young since it omits all obsolete and indelicate terms, thereby reducing the vocabulary to about one-third of what is usually comprised in a dictionary. It also simplifies the definitions, and keeps them restrained to primary meaning.

Primary Dictionary
by
Eliza Robbins

Eliza Robbins (1786-1853), author of several elementary textbooks and a teacher in Boston for many years, [43] was the author of the Primary Dictionary, or Rational Vocabulary, Consisting of Nearly Four Thousand Words Adapted to the Comprehension of Children, and Designed for the Younger Classes in Schools. [44] She objects to the custom of giving a certain number of words, with definitions annexed, to be committed to memory, and thinks that when words without application and of meaning wholly remote from the knowledge of children are forced upon their memory, the language becomes dead rather than an instrument for expressing what is known and for acquiring what is unknown. She thinks, however, that a selection of words suited to their understanding and intelligently explained is useful to children. [45] With this idea in mind she has constructed her dictionary.

The Dictionary is 16 cm. in size and contains 257 pages. The definitions are usually a word or a phrase and the meaning of a great many of the words is shown by illustrative sentences. An example of the explanations may be seen from the following word: "Con - di - tion. Condition, rank, station in life; a man who is very poor, and who is forced to work hard for others, in a low condition; one who is not forced to labor with his hands, but who is engaged in some profession which employs his mind, is in a higher station, or condition. Whatever looks well, and is not broken, or torn, or hurt, or thin, or sick, or poor, is said to be in good condition; a fine horse is in a good condition; this old coat of yours is in a bad condition. " The words are divided into syllables by hyphens, but no other aid to pronunciation is given. A few illustrations are given of such things as angles, horizontal lines, etc. The spelling is conservative.

The Speller and Definer
by
E. Hazen

In The Speller and Definer; or Class-Book No. 2, Designed to Answer the Purpose of a Spelling-Book, and to Supersede the Necessity of the Use of a Dictionary as a Class-Book, New York: Printed and Published by M'Elrath and Banks, and Sold by all the principal booksellers

and country merchants in the United States and Canadas [sic], 1829, E.
Hazen, author of The Symbolical Spelling Book, A Practical English
Grammar and several other popular school books, [46] attempted to prepare a book that would serve the place of both the spelling book and the
dictionary in the schools. The book is 15 cm. in size and contains 215
pages and between seven and eight thousand words classed according to
their parts of speech and to the number of letters or syllables of which
they are composed. The pronunciation is indicated by diacritical marks,
and the words, divided into syllables, are in large print. The definitions, usually of one word, are printed in smaller type. The author
states in the Preface that in fixing the orthography and pronunciation no
authority has been implicitly followed, but that in most cases the Boston
stereotype edition of Johnson and Walker has served as the basis for
his work. Most of the words are primitive ones, given with the idea
that the student will form the derivatives. To assist the student in this
respect, a list of prefixes and affixes is included in the Appendix.

Several reprints were made of The Speller and Definer and a
revised edition containing 312 pages was published in Philadelphia by
Lippincott, Grambo and Company, in 1851. [47]

The School Dictionary
by
William W. Turner

There seems to have been a decided interest in the preparation
of school dictionaries during the first quarter of the nineteenth century.
Among those produced at this time is The School Dictionary, Designed
for the use of Academies and Common Schools, in the United States.
By William W. Turner, A. M. Instructor in the American Asylum,
Hartford: H. and F. J. Huntington, P. Canfield, Printer, 1829. The
object of the Dictionary is to select from the English dictionaries those
words which are used in conversation and which occur in common
school books, and to define each word in as concise and simple a manner
as possible, noting the accent and part of speech. [48] The author states
in the Preface that the dictionaries generally introduced into the schools
are encumbered with many hundred obsolete words, uncommon words
never found in school books or in other books adapted to the capacities
of children, and vulgar words. The uncommon words include technical
terms with which, the author thinks, the minds of children should not be
perplexed until they become acquainted with them in their textbooks.

The author complains in the Preface that the study of the dictionary has been much neglected in the schools mainly because the system
of teaching is fundamentally wrong, the sole object being to communicate
the art of pronouncing a certain combination of letters, or of expressing
a certain sound of letters without stopping to inquire whether the child
understands the meaning of these combinations. "There must, and there
will be," he says, "a change in the mood of instructing; and the sooner
it is effected the better. Let the instructer [sic] teach ideas as well as
words; let the dictionary be reinstated, and be made the textbook of all

the upper classes; and much will be done towards accomplishing an object so desirable. "[49]

The School Dictionary is 14 1/2 x 9 cm. and contains 234 pages
and approximately ten thousand words arranged two columns to a page.
The accent is the only direction given for the pronunciation of words.
The author believes that it is useless to perplex children with marks and
figures when these can be learned more easily from their teacher. The
accent is placed over the vowel in the accented syllable, but the consonants are not always joined to the proper vowel, one of the faults Webster
attempted to remedy in his first dictionary. Examples of words of this
kind are a'dvocate, a'lgebra, a'ncestor, i'vory, o'rphan. Distinction
is not always made in the pronunciation of a word that is used as more
than one part of speech, as "a'bsent, a, not present; inattentive - v. a.
to keep away"; "abuse, v. a. to make an ill use of; to revile - s. ill use;
injury." However, most words of this kind are distinguished, as "a'c-
cent, s, a mark on a syllable to show its pronunciation, accent, v. a. to
write or note the accent"; "i'nsult, s. contemptuous and unjust ill treatment, insult, v. a. to treat with insolence."

In the Preface the author objects to the general method
of defining as not calculated to benefit children. He favors the
use of examples to illustrate the meaning. His definitions are
not, however, all that one would like them to be. Examples of
the definitions are given. "Table, a flat surface supported with
feet, to eat on." "Tooth, a bone with which we chew." "Tub, a
vessel of wood to wash clothing in." "Waist, the smallest part of
the human body." "West, the region where the sun sets." "Negro,
a man with a black skin." "Syringe, a squirt-gun." "Bile, one of
the juices of the human body, a sore." "Button, that with which
men's clothes are fastened." "Humorist, one who habitually grati-
fies his own humour." "Hysterics, fits, particularly incident to
women." "Knocker, a thing on the door to knock with." "Sister,
a female born of the same parents." Turner criticizes Webster
for defining metal as "a hard body," yet he defines leaf as "what
grows on trees," and lily as "a beautiful flower."

The author states in the Preface that in settling the orthography
of this dictionary he has adopted the spelling of the standard English and
American dictionaries. Where they disagree, reference is had to common usage and to the practice of the best writers. In some cases two
forms are given, as odor, odour; almanac, almanack; bauble, bawble;
camphor, camphire. In all cases the our form is used in the definitions,
and in the main the conventional English spelling is used, as centre,
skilful. Words that are interchangeable are given together, as beside,
besides; between, betwixt; arbiter, arbitrator; judgment, judgement.

In order to condense the work the adverbs which are formed
from adjectives of the same significations by adding ly have been omitted, but at the end of the adjective a hyphen is placed to give notice of
the omission. The last four pages contain the principal parts of a list
of irregular verbs, as bid, bid, bade, bidden, bid; forget, forgot, forgotten, forgot; sing, sung, sang, sung.

The Gentlemen and Ladies' Pocket Dictionary
by
Noah J. T. George

In 1831 was published The Gentlemen and Ladies' Pocket Dictionary, To Which is Prefixed Tables Showing the Day of The Month For One Hundred Years by Noah J. T. George, author of the Vermont Geographical and Statistical Gazeteer and the Gentlemen's Pocket Companion.[50] The book was printed by Luther Roley at Concord. It is 2 1/2 x 4 1/2 x 1/2 inch in size, contains 128 pages and over four thousand words. The pronunciation of each word is indicated by respelling and by division of the words into syllables, as bibliographer, bib le og gra fur. The definitions are very simple and no etymological information is given. The spelling is conservative, but almanac is given without the k. Foreign words and expressions are included in the vocabulary.

The Etymological Encyclopedia of Technical
Terms and Phrases
by
D. J. Browne

A dictionary of special words was compiled by Daniel J. Browne for the purpose of providing etymological data and definitions for words used in the arts and sciences. The complete title is The Etymological Encyclopedia of Technical Words and Phrases Used in the Arts and Sciences and of Many Words in Common Use, with Popular Quotations From Foreign Languages and Their Translators. From the best authorities, Boston: William Hyde and Company, 1832.

The Dictionary is 6 x 3 1/2 x 3/4 inch, contains 258 pages and over five thousand words, and is arranged one column to a page. Enclosed in brackets after each word is the foreign word from which it is derived with its English meaning. This is followed by a simple definition, as, "abbot, s. [Syr. abba, father.] The chief of a convent or fellowship of canons." The words are not divided into syllables, nor is their pronunciation indicated. A great many foreign expressions are included.

Browne was born in Fremont, New Hampshire, December 4, 1804, the son of Isaac and Mary Browne.[51] It is not known what school he attended except that he took some courses at Harvard University. When twenty-six years old, he published a monthly journal called The Naturalist. He was also the author of Sylva Americana. During 1833-35 he traveled in the West Indies, Cuba, Canary Islands, Spain, France, Sicily, Madeira, Cape Verde Islands and South America. He served ten years as civil engineer on the public works of the United States and Prussia.[52] The remainder of his life was spent in working in agricultural projects. He was the first corresponding secretary of the American Agricultural Association and a member of the Board of Agriculture of the American Institute in New York. From 1845 to 1851 he was employed in the Agricultural Warehouse of R. L. Allen and Company,

New York, and helped in editing their paper The American Agriculturist.
For the next several years he worked in the agricultural department of
the United States Patent Office to obtain information on agricultural subjects and to arrange for procuring seeds and cuttings. His work in the
Patent Office in connection with his distribution of seeds became the subject of much controversy and caused the Agricultural Committee of the
House of Representatives to institute an investigation. Although Browne
was vindicated, the criticism of his administration continued and resulted in the termination of his appointment on October 10, 1859. He was
later appointed by the Patent Office to investigate the cultivation and
manufacture of flax. Besides his Etymological Encyclopedia he published
other books, among which are Trees of America (1846), The American
Bird Fancier (1850), American Poultry Yard (1850), and the American
Muck Book (1851).

The American Expositor
by
Rufus Claggett

Rufus Claggett, the author of The American Expositor or Intellectual Definer, designed for the use of schools, was the son of Wentworth
and Jane (McQuestion) Claggett. [53] He was born in February 28, 1803.
After graduating from Dartmouth College in 1826, he studied law with
William Claggett of Portsmouth and John Whipple of Providence, where
he was admitted to the bar. For a while he was principal of Central
High School in Providence. [54] He moved to New York City in 1843 and
remained there in the practice of law until his death in 1875. He married
Louisa J. King of Providence. They had seven children.

Claggett states in the Preface to The American Expositor that
his experience in teaching convinced him that the usual method of requir-
ing the pupils to commit to memory the definition of words was only a
burdensome tax upon the memory without exercising the "nobler powers
of the mind. " Finding no textbook prepared to render the study of
words in our language a matter of training the mind in the habits of
thinking, he has prepared this dictionary with the purpose in view that
the "minds of his pupils may be successfully disciplined, and a ready,
free, and correct use of words acquired. " Directions for the use of
the book so as to bring about these results are given at the close of the
Preface, but the precaution is also taken to call attention to the fact that
those teachers who want to follow the usual method will find this work
as advantageous as any. The plan of the work as given in the Preface is
as follows:

1. The words are arranged in syllabic order, and so far as
the classification of the vowel sounds admits, in alphabetical order.
2. The vowel sounds of the monosyllables and accented
syllables are indicated by a word instead of a figure
placed over each class. The sounds of the unaccented
syllables are left to the decision of the ear, which will

as accurately distinguish them without figures as with them.

3. The words are selected and defined with a special view to their being used in classes of various ages and capacities.

4. The orthography and pronunciation are in accordance with the best standard authors.

The first edition of the Expositor was published in 1836, in Boston by Perkins and Marvin, in Providence by George P. Daniels, and in Philadelphia by Henry Perkins. A second edition was published the same year by Gould, Kendall and Lincoln, Boston; a revised edition was published in 1845 in New York by Paine and Burgess; while Cody and Burgess, New York, brought out a new and revised edition in 1851. The price of the last edition was thirty cents. [55]

The first two editions were 24mos., 13 x 11 1/2 cm., containing two hundred pages and approximately seven thousand words. The words are capitalized and are arranged in groups according to certain similarities such as words of two syllables accented on the first, words with the same vowel sounds, words of three syllables accented on the first, etc. Pages of illustrative sentences consisting mainly of quotations from various authors show more fully the meaning of those words defined in the preceding pages. The illustrated word is printed in italics. The definitions are very simple, usually consisting of one word. The pronunciation is not shown except by division of words into syllables.

Cobb's Dictionaries

Lyman Cobb, the son of Elijah William Cobb and Sally (Whitney) Cobb, was born in Lennox, Massachusetts, September 18, 1800, lived chiefly in New York State, and died in Colesburg, Potter County, Pennsylvania, October 26, 1864. [56] Very little is known about his early life and education, but he began teaching at the age of sixteen and published his first spelling book a few years later. [57] He was very zealous in getting his spelling book before the public (the publication reached millions of copies), [58] and in order to do so attempted to disparage the school books of other people. His first attack was on the spelling books and dictionaries of Noah Webster. He tried to show the discrepancies existing between the orthography of the spelling books and the different editions of the dictionary. (For a discussion of this controversy see Chapter V.) In the early forties Cobb engaged in another controversy over spelling books with Charles W. Sanders. [59]

Besides his spelling books Cobb was the author of five reading books, an expositor or sequel to his spelling books, a primary arithmetic, a higher arithmetic, a book on the evils of corporal punishment, perhaps one of the most significant of his books, and sixty or seventy small juvenile books, as well as two dictionaries of his own and a revision of the dictionary of Walker. [60] At his death he left unfinished a concordance, a national dictionary, and a pronouncing Testament. [61]

A Just Standard for Pronouncing the English Language, published in Ithaca, New York, by Spencer and Stockton, 1821, contains many of the fundamental phases of a dictionary except the definitions. In 1828 Cobb edited an abridged edition of Walker's Critical Pronouncing Dictionary and it was reprinted in 1831 and 1837. Concerning this dictionary Noah Webster makes the following comment:

> Cobb's Dictionary has some peculiarities. He gives nouns, not only in the singular numbers, but in the plural, which is wholly unnecessary. The Spelling and pronunciation of regular nouns, plural are never mistaken. The participles of verbs are inserted, but not defined. This is a great defect; and the participles which become mere adjectives, of which there are more than two hundred, are very few of them noted at all. This is a defect in all the English dictionaries. [62]

Webster considers the principal defect in the book a lack of words. He lists nearly four hundred words under the first letter of the alphabet which are not included in Cobb's dictionary but are inserted in his own. In the same proportion he considers that the number wanting in the whole book must be four thousand and seven hundred words. He also says that many of the definitions are incorrect because they have not been defined to conform to the recent scientific knowledge. [63]

In his Expositor or Sequel to the Spelling-Book; Containing about Twelve Thousand of the Most Common Words of the Language; in which each word is accurately spelled, pronounced, divided, and explained, and the primary and secondary accents noted; to which are prefixed Concise Principles of Pronunciation, and Rules for the Accentuation and Division of Words, published in New York by Collins and Hannay, stereotyped by J. S. Redfield and Company, 1833, Cobb provides the definitions of the words included in the spelling book and others in common use so that children might be taught the definitions of words as soon as they learn the spelling and pronunciation. It is supposed to provide an easy step from the spelling book to the dictionary. The pronunciation is indicated after each word by superior figures representing the vowels, the scheme for which is given at the top of each page. The primary stress is distinguished by the acute accent, and the secondary by the grave accent. Cobb claims to be the inventor of this method of marking the secondary accent. In treating of the subject he says: "It is of the utmost importance that the secondary accent be properly placed. This is fixed with as much certainty as the place of the principal accent itself; and a wrong position of one would as much derange the sound of a word as a wrong position of the other." [65]

In the American edition of The Treasury of Knowledge and Library of Reference was included, as Part I, A New Dictionary of the English Language, Containing Many Words Not to be Found in Any Previous Work of the Kind and Also the Plurals of Nouns; the Present Tenses, the Participles and the Preterits of Verbs and a Systematick Division of Words into Syllables, with the Accentuation of Each Word Properly Noted, To Which are Prefixed a Compendious English Grammar, by Goold Brown; and English Verbal Distinctions, with Occasional Illustrations: A List of Abbreviations, Proverbs, Terms, and Phrases, in the Latin, Spanish, French, and Italian Languages, Translated: Scripture Proper Names, and Names of Males and Females, Sixth Edition, [66] by Lyman Cobb, New York, published by Conner and Cook.

The long title is perhaps sufficient explanation for the contents of the Dictionary. It was designed mainly as a handy reference book. The definitions are brief. Although Cobb admits his admiration for Johnson as a lexicographer, he says that the laws of language are changeable and the most that can be done is to consult analogy and etymological precision. [67] He compliments his own dictionary on the saving it will insure because only one spelling of words of disputed orthography is given, and because of the lack of discrepancies in the spelling of words in the vocabulary and in the definitions. He also thinks that the insertion of many primitive words and the plurals of nouns and the participles and preterits of verbs, which are not given in other dictionaries, is an improvement.

Although the work is not designed primarily as a pronouncing dictionary, it gives some assistance in this field. The syllables are divided and the one to be emphasized is accented. Hyphens are used to designate the division of syllables, while double hyphens indicate the division of compound words. Pages 37-74 contain lists of words, with occasional illustrations, which show certain distinctions. The words are grouped into six parts. Part I contains words differently spelled and defined, but pronounced alike; Part II, words differently spelled and defined, but pronounced nearly alike; Part III, words spelled alike, but differently pronounced and defined; Part IV, words spelled and pronounced alike, but differing widely in meaning; Part V, words spelled alike, but of which the part of speech is changed by change of accent; Part VI, words accented on the same syllable, but whose orthography and pronunciation are changed by change of the part of speech.

Cobb has the distinction of being the author of the smallest American dictionary of those that come within the period studied. It is The Ladies' Reticule Companion, or Little Lexicon of the English Language, published by Harper and Brothers, New York. The edition examined was a stereotype edition of 1841, but the book was copyrighted in 1834. It is designed, as the title indicates, as a convenient reference book in the matters of orthography, definition, and accentuation. The limits of the book prevent a long list of words or detailed definitions, yet it contains about twenty-five thousand words, divided into syllables by hyphens, the stressed syllables accented, the part of speech indicated, and short definitions attached. English spelling is followed.

The book contains 818 pages, the first 68 of which are devoted to the same word groups as are given in A New Dictionary. On each side of every page, beginning with the Preface, maxims

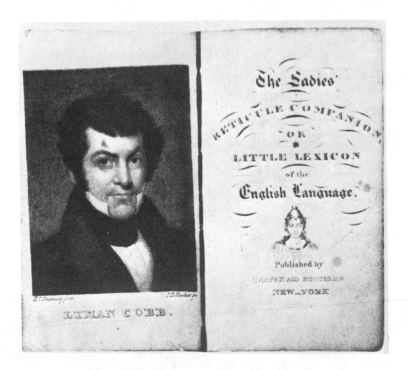

Frontispiece and title page of The Ladies' Reticule Companion, by Lyman S. Cobb.

and proverbs are printed. The Preface page contains the following statements: "Eloquence is the language of nature." "Rashness is the errour of youth." "Conversation is the music of the mind." "Applause is the end and aim of weak minds."

The School and Family Dictionary
by
T. H. Gallaudet and Horace Hooker

Thomas Hopkins Gallaudet (1787-1851) was the son of Peter Wallace Gallaudet, a merchant of Philadelphia, and Jane Hopkins Gallaudet of Hartford, Connecticut, who was a descendant of both John Hopkins and Thomas Hooker.[68] The first of the family to come to America was Peter Elisha Gallaudet who fled from France not long after the Revocation of the Edict of Nantes and settled at New Rochelle, New York. Thomas, a son of the emigrant, married Catharine Edgar and they became the parents of Peter Wallace Gallaudet.[69]

Little is known of the childhood of Thomas Hopkins Gallaudet except that he was of studious habits and was rather precocious. When he was thirteen years of age, his father moved the family from Philadelphia to Hartford. There Gallaudet completed his preparation for college and entered the sophomore class at Yale in the fall of 1802, the youngest member of the class. He distinguished himself in college by his studious habits and by his proficiency in mathematics and in English composition. He completed the course at Yale in 1805, one of six in a class of forty-two to graduate with the honor of an oration. [70]

Soon after graduation Gallaudet began the study of law in the office of Chauncey Goodrich of Hartford. The state of his health caused him to suspend his legal studies at the close of the first year. He spent the next year in an intensive study of English literature and in the practice of composition. From 1808 to 1810 he served as tutor at Yale but his health not having improved, he accepted a position with a large commercial house in New York, the prosecution of which took him mostly on horseback through the states of Ohio and Kentucky. On his return he became a clerk in a counting-house in New York City. [71]

In January, 1812, Gallaudet entered Andover Theological Seminary where he remained until his graduation in 1814. He was licensed to preach on June 14, 1814, and later received several invitations to take charge of vacant pulpits. During the winter of 1814-1815 he remained mostly at his father's home in Hartford. It was while he was there that he became interested in the case of Alice Cogswell, a deaf mute of about ten years of age, whose father, Dr. Mason F. Cogswell, lived nearby. As a result of his interest he was selected by a group of men in Hartford to undertake the establishment of a school for the deaf and dumb in Hartford and to go to Europe to qualify himself for the business of instruction. Not finding what he desired in England he went to Paris, March 19, 1816, where he was received by Abbé Sicard, whom he induced to allow his principal aid, Laurent Clerc, to come to America to become a teacher in the asylum in Connecticut. The institution was opened in April, 1817, and Gallaudet remained as its head until 1830. In 1821, he had married Sophia Fowler, one of his pupils in the school. [72]

The remainder of his life was spent in Hartford, mainly in the preparation of elementary school books and in helping in many phases of moral and religious education. From 1838 until his death on September 10, 1851 he was Chaplain to the Retreat for the Insane in Hartford. [73]

Gallaudet published several educational works, among which are the Child's Book on the Soul, which went through several editions in America and in England, and was translated into the French, Spanish, German, and Italian languages; the Mother's Primer, used in many schools; and the School and Family Dictionary and Practical Spelling Book, both of which were prepared in collaboration with the Rev. Horace Hooker, a clergyman and author of Hartford. [74] Henry Barnard lists the writings of Gallaudet as follows: 29 books and addresses, 9 Scripture biographies published by the American Tract Society, 13 articles to the American Annals of Education, 4 articles to the Connecticut School Journal, and 6 articles to Mother's Magazine. [75]

The School and Family Dictionary and Illustrative Definer, published by Robinson, Pratt, and Company, New York, 1841, with several reprints later, contains 221 pages and is 16 cm. in size. Its words are those of "middle range," since the words of daily use in the family and in the common intercourse of life which the child already knows, and the more difficult words, including the technical and scientific ones, have been omitted. It has as its aim, as stated

in the Preface, to furnish a convenient reference book to the English
language which will aid in forming "accuracy of thought, propriety
of diction, correctness of taste, and soundness of moral principles. "

The Dictionary contains approximately twenty-five hundred
words arranged two columns to a page. The definitions are usually
phrases followed by illustrative sentences selected "to communicate
valuable knowledge, to cultivate a correct taste, and to impress
moral truth. " The definitions are printed in a larger type than are
the illustrative sentences. Words of the same family are brought
together under the definition of one of them and are printed in
italics. Compound words whose meaning can be obtained from the
simple words have been omitted.

Diacritical markings and superior numbers are used to indicate the sounds of the vowels. The accented syllable is denoted by
the figure, or the mark of a long or short vowel placed over it, as
bår gain, cắp tive, except in a few cases where the acute accent
is used for this purpose. Silent letters are printed in italics.

The following letter from S. R. Brown, a missionary in
Morrison Hill, China, dated March 24, 1845, to Gallaudet shows the
extent to which the Dictionary was used.

> My dear Sir, - Your favor of Feb. 16, 1844, did not
> reach me till nearly a year after its date. I received it,
> with a copy of your "Spelling-book" and "Mother's Primer, "
> on the 7th of January, 1845. "The School and Family
> Dictionary" was also in the parcel. The two last mention-
> ed works I have had and made use of in our school for
> about two years. My brother-in-law, Mr. David E. Bart-
> lett, had the kindness to send me a number of copies of
> each, I think in 1843. The "Spelling-Book" I had also
> seen, though having but one copy I could not introduce it
> into the school. It is out of my power, therefore, to
> comply with your request, and give you my opinion of its
> adaptation to the wants of such a school. I can, however,
> speak of the other two - the primer and the dictionary.
> We have four classes, in a school of thirty-five boys, and
> one of them had made a fair trial of the primer....
> The older pupils in the school each have a copy of the
> dictionary, and think much of it. I dare say it needs no
> commendation among those who have tried it. I will only
> say that, so far as it goes, it is precisely what we require
> in our school. I could wish that you would extend it to
> about twice its present size, for the sake of those who are,
> like myself, laboring to teach English to foreigners. The
> enlargement would not make it less, but more useful in
> the United States. My boys are delighted when they can
> find their hard words explained in it. But their knowledge
> of English is so limited, that they have to suffer frequent
> disappointments.... 76

The Orthoepist
by
James H. Martin

James H. Martin was the author of The Orthoepist; Containing a Selection of All Those Words of the English Language Usually
Pronounced Improperly; with a Reading Exercise Following Each
Letter, Including in It All the Words to be Found in the Preceding
Vocabulary, New York: A. S. Barnes and Company, 1851. This
book contains a list of eighteen hundred and forty words usually pronounced improperly as well as a few of the Latin and French terms
most frequently used. The pronunciation and orthography follow those
of the 1848 Unabridged Edition of Webster's Dictionary. The definitions are very simple. Most of the words have been respelled to
indicate pronunciation. The words are written in capitals and the
syllables are marked by hyphens. The stressed syllable is marked
by an acute accent. An example of the treatment of the words in
this Dictionary is given. "A - MEL'- IOR - ATE, (A meal' yur
ate), v. t. to improve."

The Orthoepist is 1/2 x 4 1/2 x 7 inches in size and contains 151 pages. The last three pages are devoted to a list of 204
words believed to exhibit the orthography of Webster as laid down
in the rules for orthography in his Unabridged Dictionary of 1848,
page lxxxi. It should be remembered, however, that this dictionary
of Webster had been revised by Goodrich and that the orthography
does not truly represent Webster's ideas.

The Public School Dictionary

Protests were made by several compilers of dictionaries that
the usual method of teaching the meaning of words developed the
memory without aiding the other faculties. One dictionary maker who
signed himself "A Public School Teacher" thinks that this objection
is not well founded since he believes that the learning of definitions
is not a mere exercise of memory, but that while the child is committing the words and their definitions to memory he is also comparing the definitions with the words and both with the meaning which
he knows to be ordinarily attached to the words in conversation and
in the books which he reads. In this way he is developing the
faculty of comparison--the faculty on which the power of correct
reasoning depends. He therefore believes that the learning of definitions is one of the most important of school exercises. He compiled The Public School Dictionary, Designed for the Primary, Secondary, and the Lower Classes in Grammar Schools, published by
James H. Smith and Company, Philadelphia, 1855. It contains 288
pages and over eight thousand words, and is 15 1/2 cm. in size.
The definitions are very simple and the English spelling is followed.
It is merely another school dictionary.

An American Pronouncing Dictionary
by
Alexander H. Laidlaw

Probably the most imposing American dictionary, with the exception of those of Webster and Worcester, included in the period covered in this study, is one compiled by Alexander H. Laidlaw and published by Grissy and Markley, Philadelphia, 1859. The title is An American Pronouncing Dictionary of the English Language; in which variable, contested, and difficult spellings are designated; and irregular inflections, primary and secondary accents, appropriate prepositions, corresponding conjunctions and adverbs, and numerous references to writings of standard merit, are inserted: and to which are appended definitions of geographical names and proper names of persons, translations of foreign phrases, rules for spelling, lists contrasting the conservative and Websterian orthographies, and a collection of proverbs and maxims.

The author says in the Preface that the original plan of the work was to answer the demands in every phase of English lexicography, but that gradually he abandoned the idea of presenting information on obsolete words, technical terms, and etymology. Obsolete words were left out because it seemed more important that living words be learned first. Technical terms were omitted because of the limited benefits a knowledge of them would confer, while the department of etymology was abandoned as impracticable since the arrangement of etymological data is incompatible with alphabetical order. Vulgar words and those not used in polite intercourse have also been omitted.

The title American Pronouncing Dictionary signifies that preference is given, whenever there is a variation between British and American pronunciation, to the usual pronunciation in the United States; and whenever the pronunciation of the people of the Middle, Southern, and Western states differs from that of Webster and Worcester, preference is given to the first because the author believes that the voice of millions of people throughout the country should be followed rather than that of a few in New England. [77]

The Dictionary covers 600 pages, is 16 1/2 x 14 1/2 cm. in size, and contains nearly forty thousand words. No rules of orthography are followed but all words of variable orthography are given in every form in which they are accepted as correct by respectable authors. The asterisk is placed beside words of difficult, peculiar, or contested spellings. This, thinks the author, is a very desirable feature since teachers can stress the difficult words.

As far as the letter k, asterisks have been placed beside words which have been inflected or compounded by a regular and slight change in the primitive word. From page 290 to the end, asterisks are applied to words which are difficult, rare, or alien. The total number of starred words is ten thousand. [78] Compound words, except those which retain the meanings of the words of which they are composed, are separated by hyphens and the beginning letters of the simple words are capitalized.

The sounds of the vowels are indicated by superior numbers. All well authorized pronunciations of a word are indicated in the order of their acceptability. Words are divided into syllables and the primary and secondary accents noted. All plurals of nouns, declensions of pronouns, participles of verbs, and comparisons of adjectives are entered beside the words from which they are formed, and also in their alphabetical positions. The regular inflection is usually inserted when its spelling is worthy of note. The definitions are usually clauses. The appropriate prepositions, conjunctions, and adverbs are given in parentheses after the definition of the words they follow. Page references for illustrations are made to Hart's Class Book of Prose and Emerson's First Class Reader.

The main feature of the Appendix is lists of words selected from Webster's Unabridged Dictionary, published in 1853, and Worcester's Universal and Critical Dictionary, published in 1858, which show the contrast in the Websterian and the conservative spelling. The author says that he has presented the contrast without any display of partiality and with the hope that it may become "a bridge on which the advocates of both sides may meet to compromise, and to forget the bitter waters that now roll between."[79] (For an account of the Webster-Worcester controversy see Chapter VI.) The words are divided into three classes. Class A, contains 222 words in the spelling of which Worcester but not Webster doubles the final consonant in adding such formatives as ing, ed, er, etc., as leveled, levelled. Class B, containing approximately 200 words, is composed of all words which have one or more forms accepted in one system but rejected in the other, as peddler, pedlar; peddler, pedler, pedlar. Class C contains approximately a hundred words of which spelling is given preferred by Webster and not recognized by Worcester, or the contrary.

Laidlaw was assisted in the preparation of his dictionary by Edward Gideon, who aided in the construction of definitions; William Stirling, who helped in planning and completing the tables of the Appendix; and Thomas Shearer, who revised the medical terms and their definitions.[80]

Notes

1. John Flint and John H. Stone. Flint Genealogy. Andover: W. F. Draper, 1860, p. 59. Dictionary of American Biography, edited by Francis S. Drake. Boston: Houghton, Mifflin Company, 1879, p. 329, says that he was born in Windham, August 6, 1765.
2. Flint and Stone, op. cit., p. 59.
3. Drake, op. cit., p. 329.
4. Preface, p. iii.

5. The copy examined for this study was of the second edition.
6. Rufus Wilmot Griswold. Female Poets of America. New York: James Miller, 1893, p. 33.
7. R. W. G. Vail. Susanna Rowson, The Author of Charlotte Temple, A Bibliographical Study. Worcester, Massachusetts: The American Antiquarian Society, 1933, p. 6.
8. Ibid., p. 11.
9. Elias Nason. A Memoir of Mrs. Susanna Rowson, Albany: Joel Munsell, 1870, p. 90.
10. Eliza Southgate Bowne. A Girl's Life Eighty Years Ago. New York: Charles Scribner's Sons, 1887, p. 17.
11. Mary E. Sargent. "Susanna Rowson," The Medford Historical Register, VII (April, 1904), 30.
12. Vail, op. cit., p. 27.
13. Vail, op. cit., pp. 35-36.
14. Edgar W. Knight. Reports on European Education. New York: McGraw-Hill Book Company, 1930, p. 11.
15. "A New Critical Pronouncing Dictionary, etc.," General Repository and Review, IV (1813), 160.
16. John Livingston. Portraits of Eminent Americans Now Living. New York: Cornish, Lamport and Company, 1853, I, 247.
17. E. M. Woodward and John F. Hageman. History of Burlington and Mercer Counties, New Jersey, with Biographical Sketches of many of the Pioneers and Prominent Men. Philadelphia: Everts and Peck, 1883, p. 63.
18. Ibid.
19. Livingston, op. cit., p. 248; and John Clement. Sketches of the First Emigrant Settlers in Newton Township, Old Gloucester County, West New Jersey. Camden: Printed by Sinnickson Chew, 1877, p. 174.
20. Livingston, op. cit., p. 249.
21. Ibid., p. 250.
22. Ibid., pp. 251-252.
23. Willard, op. cit., p. 171.
24. Preface, p. iv.
25. Ibid., p. vi.
26. Op. cit., p. 173.
27. Preface, p. iv.
28. Ibid.
29. Op. cit., p. 370.
30. The biographical material is taken from an article by Howard Malcom in Sprague. Annals of American Pulpit, VI, 121-124.
31. Perhaps there is some connection between the basis of the poem by Francis Hopkinson, "The Battle of the Kegs," and Allison's experiments. The following statement is found in Sprague, op. cit., footnote, p. 123: "His [Burgess Allison's] ingenuity, as well as patriotism, was exerted, about this time, in preparing kegs containing explosive substances, which were floated down the Delaware, for the destruction of the British men-of-war, at anchor there."
32. Sprague, op. cit., VI, 124.
33. Ibid.

34. A. H. Grimshaw. Letter to Childs and Peterson. Original in the Historical Society of Pennsylvania Library.
35. S. Austin Allibone. A Critical Dictionary of English Literature and British and American Authors, etc. Philadelphia: J. B. Lippincott & Company, 1882, I, 743.
36. O. A. Roorbach. Bibliotheca Americana. Catalogue of American Publications, including Reprints and Original Works, from 1820 to 1852, inclusive. New York: Orville A. Roorbach, 1852, p. 234.
37. Preface, p. iv.
38. Ibid.
39. Roorbach, op. cit., p. 234. The edition is not indicated, but the publisher is Lippincott, G. & Company.
40. Preface, p. iv.
41. Ibid.
42. Preface, p. iv.
43. Encyclopedia of American Biography of the Nineteenth Century. Edited by Thomas William Herringhsaw. Chicago: American Publishers' Association, 1898, p. 793.
44. The Preface is dated April 28, 1828. The copy examined for this study was of the third edition, published by Roe Lockwood at his school-book depository, New York, 1842. Another edition was published in 1848 by A. W. Desilver of Philadelphia, and by Roe Lockwood and Son, New York.
45. Preface, p. iv.
46. Allibone, op. cit., p. 810.
47. Ibid.
48. Preface, p. i.
49. Ibid., p. iv.
50. Title-page.
51. Unless otherwise indicated, the biographical material is taken from The Dictionary of American Biography, edited by Allen Johnson et al. New York: Charles Scribner's Sons, 1929, III, 164.
52. Allibone, op. cit., p. 260.
53. Except where otherwise indicated, the biographical material is taken from Edmund Wheeler. History of Newport, New Hampshire. Concord: Republican Press Association, 1879, p. 343.
54. Title page of The American Expositor.
55. Roorbach, op. cit., p. 112.
56. Thomas Laurence. Historical Genealogy of the Laurence Family. New York: E. O. Laurence, 1858, p. 201, and Obituary in the Ithaca Journal and Advertiser, Ithaca, Wednesday, March 1, 1866, p. 4.
57. I. Thomas Scharf. History of Westchester County. Philadelphia: L. E. Preston and Company, 1886, I, Pt. 2, 638.
58. Obituary, op. cit., p. 4.
59. Dictionary of American Biography, 1930, IV, 244.
60. Obituary, op. cit., p. 4.
61. Scharf, op. cit., I, Pt. 2, 638.
62. To the Friends of American Literature, p. 4; bound with other pamphlets in a volume entitled English Language, publisher

and date of pamphlet not given. See also Webster's letter "To the Public," in Letters of Noah Webster. Edited by Harry R. Warfel. New York: Library Publishers, 1953, pp. 428-431.

63. Ibid. , p. 7.
65. Preface, p. iv.
66. The Preface is dated August, 1832.
67. Preface, p. xxxv.
68. Dexter, op. cit. , V, 7.
69. Edward Miner Gallaudet. Life of Thomas Hopkins Gallaudet. New York: Henry Holt and Company, 1888, p. 2.
70. Ibid. , pp. 18-23.
71. William B. Sprague, op. cit. , II, 609.
72. "The Life and Labors of Rev. T. H. Gallaudet, by Rev. Herman Humphrey," North American Review, LXXXVII (1858), 519-525.
73. Ibid.
74. Dexter, op. cit. , V, 19.
75. Tribute to Gallaudet, A Discourse in Commemoration of the Life, Character and Services, of the Rev. Thomas H. Gallaudet, LL. D. Delivered before the citizens of Hartford, January 7, 1852. Hartford: Brockett and Hutchinson, 1852, pp. 266-267.
76. Herman Humphrey. The Life and Labors of the Rev. T. H. Gallaudet. New York: Robert Carter and Brothers, 1857, p. 287.
77. Preface, p. v.
78. Ibid. , p. ix.
79. Ibid. , p. v.
80. Ibid. , p. vi.

CHAPTER III

DICTIONARIES OF AMERICANISMS AND
THE PHONETIC DICTIONARIES

This chapter contains accounts of the dictionaries of Americanisms and the phonetic dictionaries. To the first group belong
John Pickering, Vocabulary, or Collection of Words and Phrases
Which Have Been Supposed to Be Peculiar to the United States of
America, 1816; John Russell Bartlett, A Dictionary of Americanisms,
1848; and Alfred Langdon Elwyn, Glossary of Supposed Americanisms,
1859. The phonetic dictionaries are: An Explanatory and Phonographic Pronouncing Dictionary of the English Language, 1845, by William Bolles, and the American Phonetic Dictionary of the English
Language, 1855, designed by Nathaniel Storrs and compiled by Daniel
S. Smalley.

Dictionaries of Americanisms

The language of early America, like that of other countries
at certain periods of their history, was marked by a lack of uniformity among its different sections, and by the continual addition of
words indigenous to the new country. Whenever people are confront-
ed with new conditions for which their previous mode of existence
fails to supply them with the proper vocabulary, new words are
coined and new uses for old words spring up. Clapboard, in England signifying a thin board used by a barrel maker, was applied in
America to weatherboard. In the same way, in harvesting the
Indian corn a new use was made of the English husk. The word
creek, which in England meant an estuary, was used in America to
refer to small streams. 1 One writer says that new words naturally
grow upon our soil as a result of our institutions, habits, and customs, as the mullein grows on neglected ground, or as moss grows
on the trees in the swamps of the Mississippi. This writer includes
in his list of words: stump orators, stump speaking, camp meeting,
protracted meeting, basket meeting--even friends meeting. The words

> ... had their origin in the habits and customs of our
> people, and they are so familiar to us that they need no
> explanation. Other countries may have adopted these
> phrases, but they belong to our soil, and mark distinct
> eras in the history of the religious movements of our

people. They point to the time when our population was widely scattered and but few accommodations found for religious meetings: and they indicate the social condition which obtains among us, and the determined and resolute manner in which we prosecute any attempt to reform the world, or build up a party. [2]

H. L. Mencken says that the first Englishman to notice an Americanism was one Francis Moore, a ruffian who came to Georgia with Oglethorpe in 1735. [3] The word was bluff, in the sense of "a cliff or headland with a broad precipitous face." He did not deign to argue against it, says Mencken, but simply dismissed it as "barbarous." For nearly a century the word was not accepted by Englishmen, and when it was printed in England, it was set off by "sanitary" quotation marks. [4]

The term "Americanism" was first defined by John Witherspoon, a Scottish clergyman, educated in Edinburgh, who became the sixth president of the College of New Jersey in 1768, and served in that capacity until the Revolutionary War, when the college was dispersed. With the Scottish hatred of the English he became a leader in the struggle for independence. He signed the Declaration of Independence and was the only clergyman to sit in the Continental Congress. [5] In a series of essays entitled "The Druid," which appeared originally in a periodical publication of 1761, [6] Witherspoon devotes about twenty pages to Americanisms, perversions of language in the United States, cent phrases, etc. He defines Americanisms as the "use of phrases or terms, or a construction of sentences, even among persons of rank and education, different from the use of the same terms or phrases, or the construction of similar sentences, in Great Britain. It does not follow from a man's using these, that he is ignorant, or his discourse on the whole inelegant; nay, it does not follow in every case, that the terms or phrases used are wrong in themselves, but merely that they are of American and not of English growth. The word Americanism, which I have coined for this purpose, is exactly similar in its formation and signification to the word Scotticism." [7]

Witherspoon observed that gentlemen and scholars in Great Britain spoke as much with the vulgar in common discourse as did those in America, but there was a remarkable difference in their public and solemn discourses. In America we heard in public speeches and saw in articles from the press, errors in grammar, improprieties, and vulgarisms which hardly any person of the same class would have fallen into in Great Britain. He became interested in the unusual expressions and began to make a collection, which, as it became larger, easily grouped itself into several classes. These he presented to the public under the following heads: 1) Americanisms, or ways of speaking peculiar to this country. 2) Vulgarisms in England and America. 3) Vulgarisms in America only. 4) Local phrases or terms. 5) Common blunders arising from ignorance. 6) Cant phrases. 7) Personal blunders. 8) Technical terms introduced into the language. As examples of Americanisms he listed the following:

1. The United States or either of them.
2. This is to notify the public; or the people had been notified.
3. Fellow countrymen.
4. Things were ordered delivered to the army. (to be omitted)
5. I wish we could contrive it to Philadelphia. The words to carry, to have it carried, or some such are wanted.
6. We may hope the assistance of God. The word for or to receive is wanting.
7. I do not consider myself equal to this task. The word as is wanting.
8. Neither today or tomorrow. Should be nor.
9. A certain Thomas Benson. The word certain, as used in England, is an indefinite, the Name fixes it precisely, so there is a kind of contradiction in the expression.
10. Such bodies are incident to these evils. The evil is incident or ready to fall upon the person liable or subject to the evil.
11. He is a very clever man. She is a very clever woman. The Americans mean goodness of disposition, worthiness, integrity, without the least regard to capacity. But in Britain, clever means capacity.
12. I was quite mad at him. [8]

The attitude of the British magazines toward the American language is shown by the extract quoted below, taken from the Quarterly Review.

> Nor have there been wanting projects among them [the Americans] for getting rid of the English language, [9] not merely for barbarizing it--as when they progress a bill, jeopardize a ship, guess a probability, proceed by grades, hold a caucus, conglaciate a wave, etc., when the President of Yale College talks of a conflagrative brand, and President Jefferson of belittling the productions of nature-- but by abolishing the use of English altogether, and substituting a new language of their own. One person indeed had recommended the adoption of the Hebrew, as being ready made to their hands, and considering the Americans, no doubt, as the 'chosen people' of the new world. But a Scotchman of the name of Thornton had a project of a more Babylonish kind....
>
> This project consisted in a barbarous murder of English orthography, in turning the e topsy-turvy, dotting the i underneath, and adding a few pot-hooks and ladles, which we shall not attempt to imitate.... 'Mai diir kun-trim n,' says this Scotch Creole, have only to adopt this new language, and all the best English books will not only be reprinted in America, but 'all Europe will purchase American editions.' The American Philosophical Society was so delighted with this brilliant project, that they not only

published it in their 'Transactions,' but bestowed the Magellanic gold medal on the inventor. [10]

Vocabulary
by
John Pickering

The first attempt to make a collection of all such words as were supposed to be American peculiarities was that of John Pickering, who in 1814 presented to the American Academy of Arts and Sciences his memoir on the present state of the English language in America, together with a vocabulary. After having been published in the collections of the Academy, the vocabulary was reprinted in 1816, as A Vocabulary, or Collection of Words and Phrases Which Have Been Supposed to Be Peculiar to the United States of America. To Which is Prefixed an Essay on the Present State of the English Language in the United States, Boston: Cummings and Hilliard; Cambridge: Hilliard and Metcalf.

Pickering states in the Preface that he first began the practice of occasionally noting Americanisms and expressions of doubtful authority for his own use during his residence in London, 1799-1801, but that he did not attempt to make a collection of American peculiarities until some of his friends persuaded him that such a work would be acceptable. He then began to organize the materials that he already possessed and to make such additions as his leisure would permit. The Vocabulary is the result of his labor.

The author warns the reader that he has not made a dictionary of our language, but a glossary of provincialisms: that many words would be admitted into such a work which would be rejected from a dictionary; and that it seemed to be useful to insert all words, the legitimacy of which has been questioned, in order that their claims to a place in the language might be discussed and settled. [11]

In the Essay, which covers thirteen pages, Pickering exhibits very strongly his belief in English authority. He makes a plea for endeavoring to restore the language to the purity with which our ancestors brought it from England. He thinks that this can be affected by carefully noting every unauthorized word and phrase, or by "setting a discountenancing mark" upon such of them as are not rendered necessary by the peculiar circumstances of our country. He thinks we should undoubtedly avoid all those words which are noticed by English authors of reputation, "as expressions with which they are unacquainted; for although we might produce some English authority for such words, yet the very circumstance of their being thus noticed by well educated Englishmen, is a proof that they are not in use at this day in England, and, of course, ought not to be used elsewhere by those who would speak correct English. "[12]

JOHN PICKERING

Pickering states that in making the Vocabulary he has resorted to all sources in his power. He has given, under each word,
some authorities for and against the use of it. To some of the
words are also added the criticisms of Franklin, Witherspoon, and
others. In all cases where a word had been noticed by a writer it
is given upon his authority. All words inserted are not of American
origin, but some are words the legitimacy of which has been questioned.

Pickering states that several of the words in the Vocabulary
were obtained from British reviews of American publications, and he
adds that "it is to be regretted, that the reviewers have not pointed
out all the instances, which have come under their notice, of our
deviations from the English standards."[13] He quotes from a review
of Marshall's Life of Washington in the Annual Critic for 1818, which,
he says, would have been more favorably received in America if it
had been made in a manner somewhat different. "We have been
more particular in noticing these faults in Mr. Marshall's language,
because we are not at all certain that the Americans do not consider
them as beauties; and because we wish, if possible, to stem that
torrent of barbarous phraseology, with which the American writers
threaten to destroy the purity of the English Language."[14]

It was this worship of English opinion that caused Thomas R.
Lounsbury to say that the chief value of the Vocabulary is in the
picture it presents of the state of mind then prevailing in the country
--for the light it throws upon the way our forefathers thought and
felt. Pickering, he says, was in the fullest sense an exemplar of
the beliefs entertained by the men who considered themselves the
representatives of the highest culture to be found in America. At
the time of the appearance of the Vocabulary, there was, in the
matter of language, a deference paid by the best-informed American
to the least-informed Englishman, a servility which the political
independence only seemed to emphasize. "The minds of men varied
between boastful national self-laudation and fairly cringing linquistic
submissiveness."[15]

Sidney Willard says that the most remarkable thing about
Pickering's Vocabulary is that the very Americanisms which were
so ridiculed by British critics at the time of its publication and
before, have been, with few exceptions, adopted by them.[16]

The Vocabulary contains 520 words which might be grouped
as follows: 1) New words. 2) New significations annexed to old
words that were still in use in England. 3) Words of local use
which have long been obsolete in England. As an example of the way
Pickering discussed his so-called Americanisms, the explanations
of the word gouging are given:

> The following account of the word is given by an English
> traveller, upon the authority of an American: The General
> informed me, that the mode of fighting in Virginia and the
> other Southern states, is really of that description mentioned

by preceding travellers, the truth of which many persons
have doubted, and some even contradicted. ... Gouging
is performed by twisting the forefinger in a lock of hair,
near the temple, and turning the eye out of the socket
with the thumb nail, which is suffered to grow long for
the purpose. Lambert's Travels, Vol. ii, p. 300. "A
diabolical practice (says an English Review) which has
never disgraced Europe, and for which no other people
have even a name." Quarterly Review, Vol. ii, p. 333.
The practice itself and the name are both unknown in New
England; and from the following remarks of a well known
American author it will appear, that the practice is much
less general in the Southern States than it has been. "We
are told (says Dr. Morse) that a strange and very barbarous practice prevails among the lower class of people in
the back parts of Virginia, North and South Carolinas, and
Georgia; it is called Gouging.... We have lately been
told, that in a particular county, where at the quarterly
court twenty years ago, a day seldom passed without ten
or fifteen boxing matches, it is now a rare thing to hear
of a fight." Morse's American Univ. Geog., Vol. i, p.
676; edit. 1805.

Mary Orne Pickering writes thus about her father's work:

> In the summer and autumn of 1815 my father was occu-
> pied in preparing for the press the Vocabulary and Intro-
> ductory Essay originally communicated to the American
> Academy. As the first attempt to ascertain the compara-
> tive state of the language used here and in the mother-
> country, the subject had attracted much interest; and there
> was a call for the publication of the Memoir in an indepen-
> dent form for general use. His friends who had been
> travelling in the Southern and Western States, as well as
> others engaged in literary pursuits at home, had turned
> their attention to collecting peculiarities of language com-
> ing under their own notice, and suggesting them to him
> for consideration; and while revising the whole subject
> carefully himself, he had the benefit of the judicious cri-
> ticisms of two English friends thoroughly educated in Eng-
> land, but who had now for many years made their home in
> this country. [Benjamin Vaughan, of Hallowell, Maine,
> and Thomas Langdon Elwyn, of Portsmouth, New Hamp-
> shire][17]

On July 15, 1816, Pickering sent his friend Horace Binney a
copy of his Vocabulary along with a letter in which he says that the
compilation is only the beginning of a work which must be completed
by gentlemen in different parts of the country. He says that he
expects to encounter the displeasure of some of the American re-
formers who think we ought to throw off our native language as one
of the badges of English servitude and establish a new language for
ourselves. "But," he says, "I have the satisfaction to know that

the best scholars in our country treat such a scheme with derision; they, on the contrary, are solicitous to retain the peculiar advantage we derive from a language which is common to ourselves and the illustrious writers and orators of our mother country. "[18]

The publication of the Vocabulary called forth the criticisms of Noah Webster, in a pamphlet of sixty pages entitled A Letter to the Honorable John Pickering, on the Subject of His Vocabulary; or, Collection of Words and Phrases, Supposed to Be Peculiar to the United States of America. By Noah Webster, Boston, Published by West and Richardson, No. 75, Cornhill. T. W. White, Printer, 1817. Pickering wrote to his father, February 17, 1817:

> At the time I read my Memoir to the Academy, Judge Dawes (who, you will recollect, is Mr. Webster's brother-in-law) said to me in a very emphatic manner, as soon as I had finished: "There! that is what I have been trying to bring my brother Webster to agree to; but he won't do it." And this is the fact; Webster wants to make an American language, and will of course feel hostile to those who take the opposite ground. [19]

Webster criticizes Pickering's work mainly because of his English leanings:

> There is nothing which, in my opinion, so debases the genius and character of my countrymen, as the implicit confidence they place in English authors, and their unhesitating submission to their opinions, their derision, and their frowns. But I trust the time will come, when the English will be convinced that the intellectual faculties of their descendants have not degenerated in America; and that we can contend with them in Letters, with as much success, as upon the Ocean. [20]

Lindley Murray seems to have thought better of the Vocabulary than did Webster. In a letter acknowledging the receipt of a copy he writes to Pickering:

> ... I think the work is well adapted to promote the purity, propriety, and precision of the English language in the United States, and to discountenance every undue attempt to introduce innovations. It gives me pleasure to perceive that the author of this publication has been so solicitous to establish the American language on the foundation of the purest and best writers in the English tongue. This is a standard which it is the peculiar felicity of America now to possess, and from which it will probably be long before she can properly depart; though the period of a vernacular standard may indeed be allowably contemplated. I am of the opinion that this volume may be read with advantage in England as well as in America.... [21]

Sir William Scott, a professor of the University of Oxford, wrote to Judge Story of Salem about the Vocabulary:

> I am much amused with the Vocabulary you sent me. Pray thank Mr. Pickering for it. It is full of curious research and remarks. I will not deny that some of your deflections from our modes of speech are real additions and improvements, though I should think that the safest course is a cautious adherence to our purest modes of speaking and writing. If every man has a right to coin words, great corruption must follow, such a right ripening into a habit. [22]

In 1836 Harriet Martineau made a visit to this country and during her stay in Boston became well-acquainted with Pickering, who presented her a copy of his Vocabulary. He received the following note in reply:

> Dear Sir, - I thank you for your volume, which will be both useful and entertaining to me. I shall have no bad tales to tell in England about the peculiarities of American speech; for the truth is, it is quite a holiday treat to an unready ear like mine to meet with intelligible English all over this great country, after being perplexed with the provincialisms with which one is assailed as often as one takes a journey in England. I have hoped for the pleasure of meeting you much oftener than I have done; but my indisposition has prevented my seeing any of my friends of late. Believe me, with much respect, truly your obliged.
>
> H. Martineau [23]

T. H. Lounsbury says that in its remarks upon words and phrases, the Vocabulary was largely a failure, due mainly to the inability of its compiler to comprehend the nature and growth of language. Although Pickering was a man of distinct scholarship, he had no conception of the movements which take place in language, the influences which operate upon it, and the principles which regulate its development. He says that Pickering's chance of becoming intellectually independent was destroyed by his having spent two years in London. "The meekness," he says, "with which he [Pickering] accepted the strictures on language by the most ignorant English reviewers displays the intellectual servitude which existed in America during the early part of the nineteenth century but most of all in New England. "[24]

Lounsbury also criticizes Pickering for his worship of American magazines, especially the Monthly Anthology, published at Boston and "Edited by a society of gentlemen." One of the English magazines which Pickering accepted was the British Critic, published from 1793 to 1843. Says Lounsbury:

> ... To the readers of the present time there seems to have been an unavowed rivalry going on between these two

critical Dogberrys as to which of them could exhibit more
ignorance of language in general and of the English language in particular. The fact that Pickering looked upon their
remarks as worthy of serious consideration is one of the
gravest charges that can be brought against his own linguistic competence. [25]

Sidney Willard says that the Vocabulary is as comprehensive,
in respect to the words and phrases then supposed to be peculiar to
the United States, as could be expected in a first attempt to collect
them, and that the work will be useful in aiding our writers and
public speakers to correct errors of language already existing and in
exciting such attention to the subject as to prevent the accumulation
of local peculiarities.   He concludes that

> The whole number of new words, single and compounded,
> of American origin, contained in the Vocabulary, is about
> eighty; certainly less than a hundred, including the cant
> and vulgar words, not used by good writers in grave dis-
> course.   Of these, a few are words contained in English
> dictionaries, but not used by British writers. Several are
> such as had been used by a single American writer; namely,
> alienism, Americanize, anxietude, etc., which have not
> been adopted.   Joel Barlow was probably the greatest of-
> fender of this kind.   Another considerable portion consists
> of words analogically formed, which do not endanger the
> purity of language, and may be used or avoided according
> to the taste of the writer or speaker.   Of this class are
> accountability, christianization, constitutional, noticeable,
> profanity, educational. Our political and religious institu-
> tions, and peculiar local customs and usages, have given
> rise to a considerable number of such words, being, for
> the most part, old words revived, or verbs made from
> nouns without any change of form, --a process admitting,
> indeed, an indefinite addition to the English vocabulary, --
> the number censured as Americanisms is not large. [26]

Gilbert M. Tucker says that not more than about seventy of
the five hundred twenty words, or less than a seventh of the whole
number, are really of American origin.   The other six-sevenths
consist of mere vulgarisms, unauthorized expressions invented by
eccentric writers and never generally adopted, and words really
British in their origin but not current in good British Society. [27]

Beck calls attention to the fact that the word fall, meaning
autumn, is not an Americanism as Pickering so charges, and quotes
from Johnson a selection he gives from Dryden to prove it,

> What crowds of patients the town doctor kills,
> Or how last fall he raised the weekly bills. [28]

The work attracted attention in Germany, where portions of
it were translated and published. [29]

H. L. Mencken seems to think that injustice has been done to Pickering. He says that although he made the usual errors of the pioneer, his contributions to the subject are considerable. "He established firmly the native origin of a number of words now in universal use in America--e. g., backwoodsman, breadstuffs, caucus, clapboard, sleigh and squatter--and of such familiar derivatives as gubernatorial and dutiable, and he worked out the genesis of not a few loan-words, including prairie, scow, rapids, hominy and barbecue. "[30]

Pickering's ancestors were among the settlers of Salem, Massachusetts, who emigrated from England about the year 1615. [31] The first John Pickering in America married Elizabeth, whose surname and personal history are unknown. Their oldest son John married Alice Flint in 1657 and this couple became the great-great-grandparents of the John Pickering who compiled the first Vocabulary of Americanisms. [32]

John Pickering was born in Salem, Massachusetts, 1777, the son of Timothy and Rebecca (White) Pickering. [33] Timothy Pickering was one of the most notable characters of the Revolutionary period. He was a judge in Massachusetts at thirty, then colonel of volunteers, and afterwards adjutant-general and quartermaster-general during the war. He was Post-Master General, Secretary of War, and Secretary of State under Washington and Adams. He was also a member of the Constitutional Convention of Pennsylvania, negotiator of Indian treaties, and Representative in Congress. [34]

Pickering was a precocious child, for his father wrote of him when he was five years old: "John is a good boy, intelligent, careful, and with only the little attention his mother has been able to pay him since last mid-summer (for he has never been to school) can read easy lessons without spelling; and he rarely errs in spelling, without a book, a work he has once read, however little affinity the letters have to the sound. "[35] Daniel Appleton White calls him "the self-taught infant philologist, " for his "lively curiosity and love of knowledge had become remarkable before he was two years old, evidenced particularly by a continued attention and interest in his observation of things. Nearly at the same time he commenced his philological career. Of his own accord he took it into his head to learn to read and, at the age of two years, he could repeat the letters of the alphabet, and in speaking would readily join adjectives and verbs to his nouns. "[36]

When he was nine years of age, Pickering was sent to his uncle John Pickering in Salem (his father having moved several years before to Philadelphia). He lived with his uncle for several years, attending Grammar School in Salem, where he studied Clarke's Introduction to the Making of Latin and Eutropius. [37] His rank as a Latin scholar at the school must have been high, for when President Washington visited Salem in 1789, Pickering was placed at the head of the Latin school in the procession of that occasion. [38] That his father was interested in his son's welfare is shown by a letter to

him from Philadelphia, October 28, 1789, in which he tells him to
bear in mind that knowledge will always be the source of his purest
pleasure. "Write to me," he says, "just as you would speak. Ima-
gine that I am with you, asking questions about the books you read
and the most striking sentiments they contain about your master,
your schoolmates, your sports, your farming and gardening. Tell
me what you please about these things, and write down your thoughts
just as they occur. Remember 'tis an indulgent father you will be
writing, who will not laugh at errors, but kindly point them out,
and be pleased with your efforts to comply with his wishes."[39]

In 1792, when Pickering was fifteen years of age, he entered
Harvard, "having performed with great propriety the tasks appointed
him."[40] He had been fitted for college by Thomas Bancroft of
Salem.[41] The courses he pursued while in college, as given in a
letter to his father, January 26, 1793, were valuable in preparing
for his later work in languages. He writes:

> We attend the tutor who teaches Latin, and the tutor
> who teaches Greek, a fortnight each alternately; the Latin
> books are Horace in the morning, and Sallust at eleven
> o'clock and at four on Monday, Tuesday, Wednesday, and
> Thursday. The Greek are Homer in the morning, and
> Xenophon at eleven and four o'clock on the same days of
> the week. On Friday we have very little to do. In the
> morning when we first went to college we used to read in
> the Art of Reading or Speaking. On Friday afternoons we
> recite in Dr. Lowth's English Grammar. On Saturday
> morning we used to recite in rhetoric; but when we return
> we are to read "History, Ancient and Modern," by the
> Abbê Millot. At half after eight we attend the professor
> of mathematics, which I like very well; and at nine we
> attend the French instructor, which finishes the week.[42]

Pickering graduated from Harvard in 1796, and in October of
the same year entered the law office of Edward Tilghman of Philadelphia. To a relative in New England, in writing of his children,
Timothy Pickering says:

> John is closely studious; besides the law, refreshing
> his memory with the dead languages, and improving in
> the knowledge of them, he also occasionally reads French,
> and has made such progress in the Spanish as to translate
> it without much difficulty. His pretty extensive knowledge
> of the Latin and French I knew would render the Spanish
> as well as the Italian, easy to learn, and the knowledge
> of various languages facilitates the learning of others....[43]

In July, 1797, Pickering went with William Smith of Charle-
ston, South Carolina, who was Minister Plenipotentiary at Lisbon,
as his Secretary. He remained in Spain and Portugal two years,
after which time he went to England. After he had been sometime
in England, he became Rufus King's private secretary. Before

returning home he spent four months on the Continent. He arrived
in America October 8, 1801, and established himself at the home of
his uncle in Salem to study law in the office of Samuel Putnam. [44]
In March, 1804, he was admitted to the bar. [45]

Daniel Appleton White describes Pickering's physical appearance:

> The personal appearance of Mr. Pickering was striking;
> it was both dignified and attractive. His stature was tall,
> and his form rather slender than stout, but well-propor-
> tioned; yet it was the expression of his countenance and
> the fine intellectual cast of his features which were the dis-
> tinguishing characteristics of his person. The form of his
> face was oval, with a remarkably high and ample forehead.
> His mild, clear hazel eye was expressive of the gentleness
> of his nature and the vigor of his intellect; while a straight
> nose, slightly inclining to the Roman, and a finely formed
> mouth, added to the regularity of his features. The ex-
> pression of his countenance when in repose was grave and
> thoughtful; but his eye kindled benignantly, and a benevolent
> smile played upon his lips whenever any object of interest
> came before him. It was this peculiar benignity of ex-
> pression, joined to an entire freedom from the slightest
> assumption of superiority, in word, look, or manner, which
> attracted towards him the young and those who were seek-
> ing relief from poverty or distress; while the intellectual
> refinement and remarkable dignity of his personal appear-
> ance and manners commanded the interest and respect of
> persons in all conditions of life. [46]

While in Europe, when not absorbed by his duties Pickering
spent his time in various studies. He acquired the leading European
languages and enlarged his knowledge of the Oriental tongues. In
the June number of the Law Reporter, 1846, appeared an article
written by Charles Sumner a few weeks after Pickering's death. It
contains the following statement:

> He [Pickering] seems, indeed, to have run the whole
> round of knowledge. His studies in ancient learning had
> been profound; nor can we sufficiently admire the facility
> with which, amidst other cares, he assumed the task of
> the lexicographer, which Scaliger compares to the labor
> of the anvil and the mine. Unless some memorandum
> should be found among his papers specifying the language
> to which he had been devoted, it may be difficult to frame
> a list with entire accuracy. It is certain that he was
> familiar with at least nine, --the English, French, Portu-
> guese, Italian, Spanish, German, Romanic, Greek, and
> Latin; of these he spoke the first five. He was less
> familiar, though well acquainted, with the Dutch, Swedish,
> and Hebrew; and had explored, with various degrees of
> care, the Arabic, Turkish, Syriac, Persian, Coptic,

Sanscrit, Chinese, Cochin-Chinese, Russian, Egyptian hiero-
glyphics; the Malay in several dialects, and particularly
the Indian languages of America and of the Polynesian Islands. It is, however, as a friend of classical studies and
as a student of language, or a philologist, that he is entitled to be specially remembered. It is impossible to measure the influence which he has exerted upon the scholarship of the country.... His genius for language was profound. He saw with intuitive perception their structure and
affinities, and was delighted in the detection of their hidden
resemblances and relations.... [47]

Pickering was successful as a lawyer, but his philological
interests were not lessened by his law practice. He refused the pro-
fessorship of Hebrew and Oriental languages in Harvard in 1806, and
later that of Greek literature. In 1820 there was published in the
Memoirs of the American Academy an essay "On a Uniform Orthography for the Indian Languages of North America" which was received
with great approval and was made the basis of the system on which
nearly all the Indian and many of the Oceanic dialects have since
been reduced to writing. With the aid of an educated native, he prepared a grammar of the Cherokee language, which had been partly
printed when the famous invention of the syllabic alphabet of George
Guess put a stop to the work. He prepared for publication, by deci-
phering, copying, and editing, the "Manuscript Dictionary of the
Abnake Language" by Sebastian Rasle, the celebrated and unfortunate
Jesuit missionary who was killed in a battle between the Indians and
the English in 1724. [48]

In 1826 Pickering published a much needed Greek-English
lexicon that immediately superseded all other Greek lexicons in the
schools since at that time the only Greek dictionaries had their definitions in Latin. He also published his "Memoir on the Pronunciation of the Greek Language," which brought him in touch with
many eminent scholars both in America and in Europe. [49]

A Dictionary of Americanisms
by
John Russell Bartlett

In 1848 was published A Dictionary of Americanisms, A Glossary of Phrases, usually regarded as peculiar to the United States, by
John Russell Bartlett, Corresponding Secretary of the American Ethnological Society, and Foreign Corresponding Secretary of the New
York Historical Society, Published in New York by Bartlett and Welford, it is an octavo in cloth, which sold for two and one-half dollars. [50] It contains 27 pages of introduction and 412 pages in the
main part.

Bartlett says that he began the beginning of the collection of
words which resulted in this Dictionary while he was traveling in a

JOHN RUSSELL BARTLETT

canal boat from Utica, west, on the way to visit his father at Cape Vincent. He amused himself by reading a new work in which the vulgar language of the United States abounded. He noted strange words and expressions on the margin of the work and on his return to New York wrote them in an interleaved copy of Pickering's Vocabulary. About this time several books were published relating to David Crockett, and stories and adventures in the Southwestern states, the idioms and peculiar expressions in which he noted and transferred to his interleaved copy of Pickering. He now became so greatly interested in the collection of words that he prepared a large blank book into which he transferred all that he had collected. His idea then was to publish a supplement to Pickering's Vocabulary, but he soon found that he had already collected a sufficient number of words to make a volume larger than that of Pickering. He then came to the conclusion that he would prepare and print a work on an entirely different plan--that of a dictionary. He set vigorously to work, ran over the numerous books which contained the familiar and the vulgar or slang language of the country, and carefully examined them from beginning to end. When finished, the work was published by Bartlett and Welford and met with a ready sale. The edition consisted of but seven hundred and fifty copies. 51

In the Introduction to the Dictionary, Bartlett says that he began to make a list of words peculiar to the United States, not knowing whether they were of native growth or had been introduced from England. After he had expanded the list so as to include a large number of words used in familiar conversation among both the educated and the rural classes, he began to examine the dialects and provincialisms of those parts of England from which the early settlers had come. On comparing these familiar words with the provincial and colloquial language of the northern counties of England, he found a striking resemblance, not only in the words commonly regarded as peculiar to the New England, but in the dialectical pronunciation of certain words, and in the general tone and accent. [52] "In fact," he says, "it may be said, without exaggeration, that nine-tenths of the colloquial peculiarities of New England are derived directly from Great Britain; and that they are now provincial in those parts from which the early colonists emigrated, or are to be found in the writings of well accredited authors of the period when that emigration took place. Consequently, it is obvious that we have the best authority for the use of the words referred to."[53]

Bartlett says that the next thing he had to decide was whether to include only words of purely American origin, or all words, whatever their origin, that are usually called provincial or vulgar. He determined to adopt the latter plan. This plan embraced such words as are found in Johnson and Webster marked low or vulgar, words found in the provincial glossaries of England, and slang words not noticed by lexicographers but so much employed as to deserve a place in a glossary. In carrying out this plan he made the definitions as accurate as possible by citing authorities when they were available. [54]

Except for words of purely American origin, that is, those derived from the Indian language and from the Dutch, Bartlett has avoided etymologies and etymological discussions. The American words he has attempted to illustrate by extracts from American authors whose works relate to that class of people among which these words are chiefly found. These books contain descriptions of country life, scenes in the backwoods, popular tales, etc. Such are the writings of Judge Halliburton of Nova Scotia which give a tolerably correct specimen of the provincialism of New England, the letters of Major Downing, Judge Hall, Mrs. Kirkland, the author of the New Purchase, Charles F. Hoffman, and David Crockett, "who has unintentionally made us better acquainted with the colloquial language of the West than any other author."[55] Other works used in the preparation of the Dictionary are the series of books called the Library of Humorous American Works, which deal with the life in the West; Major Jones's Courtship and Sketches; Georgia Scenes; Sherwood's Gazetteer of Georgia; and newspapers, chiefly those from New York, viz., the Commercial Advertiser, the Tribune, and the Herald. [56]

The words of Dutch origin were furnished by Alexander J. Catheal. [57] A few other words were supplied by other people, but in the main the work was of Bartlett's own compilation. In letters to E. A. Duyckinck, of December 20, 1834 and January 7, 1837,

Bartlett asks Duyckinck to send him any examples he might find in American authors of words and illustrations for his Dictionary. [58] John Inman, editor of the New York Commercial Advertiser, aided in the definition of political terms, while William W. Turner assisted in checking the etymologies and in supervising the work. [59] Cant words, except those in general use, terms used in gaming houses, words known only to certain trades, and obscene or blasphemous words have been omitted. There are over twenty-five hundred words in the entire lot. The Introduction contains essays on the dialects of England and America.

The Dictionary became very popular, passed through four editions--1859, 1860, and 1877--and the first edition was translated into Dutch and German. The Dutch translation was published in Gorinchen, Holland, in 1854, with the title of Woodenback von Americanismen ... bewerkt door M. Keijzer, J. Noorduyn en zeen, xxx p., 1., 96p. 16 x 13 cm. The quotations which illustrate the use of words were omitted. It was hoped that this work would furnish assistance in settling the etymology and meaning of some of the old Dutch words still used in New York[60] but it proved of little use. The German translation was published at Leipzig, in 1866. [61]

Bartlett says in the Preface to the second edition that he began the preparation for a new edition before the first edition had barely left the press. For the next ten years he was busily engaged on this work. Nearly three years of this period were spent in the interior of the country as United States Commissioner on the Mexican boundary where he came in contact with the language of the frontier. He collected words occurring in prairie and frontier life, as well as those common to Texas, New Mexico, and California. A great many of these came from the Spanish.

A large number of new words were added to the second edition so that the collection was about doubled, although nearly eight hundred words included in the first edition were rejected as not being pure Americanisms. The examples or illustrations from authors, showing the use of words, were increased. The histories of words and their definitions were also corrected and improved. [62] In this edition Bartlett divides his Americanisms into nine classes:

1. Archaisms, i. e., old English words, obsolete, or nearly so, in England, but retained in use in this country.
2. English words used in a different sense from what they are in England. These include many names of natural objects differently applied.
3. Words which have retained their original meaning in the United States, though not in England.
4. English provincialisms adopted into general use in America.
5. Newly coined words, which owe their origin to the productions or to the circumstances of the country.
6. Words borrowed from European languages, especially the French, Spanish, Dutch and German.

7. Indian words.
8. Negroisms.
9. Peculiarities of pronunciation. [63]

The second edition was published by Little, Brown, and Company, of Boston. It contains 32 pages in the introduction and 524 pages in the main part of the work. At the close of the work is a collection of American similes and proverbs, together with the abbreviations of the names of the states, etc., which are inserted in the body of the first edition. The third edition is a reprint of the second edition without alteration. [64]

A reviewer in the Atlantic Monthly at the time the second edition appeared comments very favorably on the volume by saying that the large number of Americanisms indicate that our language is alive. "No language," he says, "after it has faded into diction, none that cannot suck up feeding juices from the mother-earth of a rich common-folk-talk, can bring forth a sound and lusty look. True vigor of expression does not pass from pages but from man to man, where the brain is kindled and the lips are limbered by downright living interests and by passions in the very three.... There is death in the Dictionary; and where language is limited by convention, the ground for expression to grow is straightened also, and we get a potted literature, Chinese dwarfs instead of healthy trees."[65]

A critic in the Blackwood's Magazine thinks the work is pleasant reading, but that any work of the kind, in order to have any chance of being really complete and accurate, ought to be under a double editorship since it is impossible for any one man to be acquainted thoroughly with the vocabulary and idioms of two countries.[67] Krapp calls the Dictionary "a classic example among books of this kind."[68] Richard Grant White characterizes it as "a very misleading and untrustworthy book--a book injurious in its effect both at home and abroad. Here was a large octavo volume, of more than five hundred pages, filled with so-called 'Americanisms,' which, compiled by an 'American,' was accepted as a sort of confession of the extent to which the English language had been corrupted, perverted, and overlaid with slang, by the English race in 'America.' I remember having seen it so referred to more than once by British critics, and, I think, not altogether without reason. They did not make any allowances for the caveat 'usually regarded' in the title; and they were the more excusable for this because of the passages quoted and the arguments presented in its pages in support of the charge of Americanisms, erroenously, as I believe that I shall show, in a large number of instances.... The large number of these so-called 'Americanisms' I found to be no more 'American' in their origin than 'Yankee Doodle' is itself."[69]

John Russell Bartlett was born at Providence, Rhode Island, October 23, 1805, the son of Smith and Mary (Russell) Bartlett. [70] He was educated at schools in Kingston and Montreal in Canada, and at Louisville Academy in New York. [71] After leaving school, he became a clerk in a mercantile house in Providence. [72] Soon after he became twenty-one, he entered the banking house of Cyrus Butler as book-keeper, and three years later became cashier of the Globe Bank in Providence, a position he held for six years. [73] During this period he became interested in literature and history. He became a member of the Franklin Society, founded for the purpose of studying the natural sciences; of the Rhode Island Historical Society; and, with the aid of Dr. F. A. Farley and Thomas H. Webb, was instrumental in founding the Providence Athenaeum. [74] In 1837 he moved to the city of New York where he engaged in mercantile business until 1849. The business was unsuccessful and he turned to another pursuit adapted to his literary inclinations. In conjunction with Charles Welford he established a bookstore for the importation and sale of choice English and foreign works. This bookstore became a literary resort for men in the city and for scholars from all parts of the country. [75] Bartlett was elected Corresponding Secretary of the New York Historical Society, a position which brought him in contact with Albert Gallatin. He and Gallatin projected the American Ethnological Society, the first meeting of which was held at Bartlett's home. [76] He was also a member of several other learned societies in America and Europe. [77]

After he had retired from business, he was appointed in 1850 by President Taylor as United States Commissioner to run the boundary line between the United States and Mexico, under the Treaty of Guadalupe Hidalgo. He was employed in this task until February, 1853. The explorations which he made at this time in Texas, New Mexico, Chihuahua, Sonora, California and what is now Arizona, were published in 1854 in two volumes under the title of Personal Narrative of Explorations and Incidents, etc., connected with the United States and the Mexican Boundary Commission. In 1855 Bartlett was elected Secretary of State of Rhode Island and held this office by annual reelection for seventeen years. In 1867 he visited Europe, having been made a representative of the American Antiquarian Society to the International Congress of Archaeology and a delegate from the American Ethnological Society to the International Congress of Anthropology and Prehistoric Archaeology at Paris. In 1872 when he again visited Europe he was one of the United States Commissioners to the International Prison Congress at London. [78]

For the last thirty years of his life Bartlett was associated with John Carter Brown in the collecting and care of his books. He compiled a number of bibliographies and published a number of books of historical interest. He collected 68 volumes of clippings pertaining to the Civil War from the first organized act of rebellion in 1860 to the final overthrow of the Confederate Government in 1865. [79] He died in Providence, May 30, 1886.

Glossary of Supposed Americanisms
by
Alfred L. Elwyn

In 1859 there appeared another attempt at a collection of

words peculiar to America: the Glossary of Supposed Americanisms, collected by Alfred L. Elwyn, M. D., Philadelphia, published by J. B. Lippincott & Company, containing 122 pages, and 19 1/4 cm. in size. The book was undertaken, says the compiler in the Preface, to show how much there yet remains in this country of languages and customs directly brought from our remotest ancestry. The English travelers and authors who have twitted us because of our peculiarities and oddities in speech have done so because they were ignorant of the language and early literature of their own people. The simple truth, he says, is that almost without exception, all the words and phrases that we have been ridiculed for using are good old English, many of them of Anglo-Saxon origin, and nearly all to be heard at this day in England. A difference of circumstance may have altered a little their application, but not enough to make our use of them absurd. Elwyn thinks that if one wished to know how English was spoken in England two hundred years ago, he would find it sooner by a visit to New England than to the Old England, for the New Englander preserves, to a great extent, the mode of speaking of his pilgrim parents. [80]

Elwyn attributes our various strange and odd modes of using language to the fact that we have no standard such as the Parliament of England, filled with many people of the best education, for we would hardly look to our national legislature for an example in the use of language or of national refinement. [81]

The Glossary contains about five hundred words arranged, one column to a page, with long explanations following the word, and including some historical explanations of the words. There is no attempt at a classification of terms. It is merely a glossary of the archaic English words surviving in America. Tucker says that the chief value of the book lies in the contribution it makes to our knowledge of Pennsylvania provincialisms, of which the author is evidently a careful observer. He says that a clear majority of the words would be as little understood in decent American society as in decent British society. [82] The book is carelessly written and not accurately alphabetized.

The compiler of the Glossary was a member of a prominent New England family, his maternal grandfather being John Langdon, governor of New Hampshire and presiding officer of the first United States Senate. [83] Elwyn was born July 9, 1804, in Portsmouth, New Hampshire. He attended Phillips Exeter Academy and Harvard from which he graduated in 1823. [84] He then studied medicine in Boston under Dr. Gorham. He spent the years 1826-1829 in Europe where he continued his study. [85] In 1831 he received his diploma as M. D. from the University of Pennsylvania. [86] He was married in 1832 to Mary Mease, by whom he had two children; one, Alfred Elwyn, became a clergyman, and the other the wife of S. Weir Mitchell. [87] He interested himself in various topics, especially history, philology, and botany. He originated the Pennsylvania Agriculture Society and Farm School, of which he became president in 1850. [88] He was president of the Pennsylvania Institution for Instruction of the Blind, the Training School for Feeble Minded Children, and the Society for Prevention of Cruelty to Animals. [89] He died in Philadelphia, March 15, 1884.

Phonetic Dictionaries

Near the middle of the nineteenth century appeared two works which occupy a unique place in the history of American dictionaries. The first was An Explanatory and Phonographic Pronouncing Dictionary of the English Language to which is added a vocabulary of Greek, Latin, Scripture, Christian, and Geographical Names with their pronunciation; together with a collection of words and phrases from foreign languages, often met with in the works of English writers, with their signification, edited by William Bolles, New London: Published by Bolles and Williams, 1845, Svo., price four dollars. [90]

The compiler states in the Preface that the purpose of the work is to meet the need for a complete vocabulary of the English language, having each word properly defined, and its pronunciation clearly and correctly exhibited. Walker's dictionary, although it has held its place in public estimation as a criterion of orthoepy, is too limited in its vocabulary. The advancing literature and science of the last half century have introduced many new words which, together with the many changes in the pronunciation in words, make necessary a work corresponding to the needs of the time. [91]

The author boasts that the work contains about eighty-five thousand words, exclusive of more than twenty thousand Greek, Latin, Scripture, Christian, and geographical proper names, or nearly twenty thousand more than were ever before offered to the American public in any one work. [92] The words are divided into syllables, with the "pronunciation of each scientifically and phonographically exhibited, as deduced from the most approved usage, where usage is uniform and settled, and from analogy and classical authority, where usage is uncertain. "[93] The chief merit of a pronouncing and defining dictionary, according to the author, is in its tendency to prevent and correct provincial dialects and to produce uniformity of diction throughout the extensive regions where the English language already prevails. [94]

The following rules of Sheridan have been made the basis of the phonographic orthography.

1. No character should be set down in any word which is not pronounced.
2. Every distinct simple sound should have a distinct character to mark it, for which it should uniformly stand.
3. The same character should never be set down as the representative of two different sounds.
4. All compound sounds should be marked only by such

characters as will naturally and necessarily produce those sounds, upon their being pronounced according to their names in the alphabet. [95]

In orthography, that of Johnson is followed, except in cases "where custom decidedly sanctioned a change for the better," as in the omission of u in the termination our, and of final k, preceded by c, in words derived from the "learned" languages, etc. in which the usual mode of spelling has been adopted. Neither Webster nor Worcester is mentioned in the work.

Obsolete words are admitted when they are found in authors not obsolete, or when they have "any beauty that may deserve revival. "

> ... Indeed, the vocabulary of an explanatory English diction-
> ary would be exceedingly defective, in which one should
> look in vain for words occurring in such authors as Bacon,
> Boyle, Shakespeare, Milton, etc., while their works con-
> stitute a portion of the standard literature of the language.
> And when it is considered that many words marked obso-
> lete by Johnson have since come into good use, and that
> words regarded as out of use by some writers are elegant-
> ly used by others, and that, if only the more obvious were
> marked, it might be construed into an approval of all others,
> the impropriety, as well as impracticability, of an attempt
> to designate them will be readily perceived, and little re-
> gretted, in a country where the general spread of infor-
> mation enables almost all speakers and writers to use
> sound judgment in the selection of words best suited to con-
> vey their ideas.... [96]

The words are arranged two columns to a page with pronunciation indicated after each word by superior figures. The work
attempts to give the pronunciation of all words, not merely those
which are difficult or concerning which there has been a difference
of opinion. Not only do words have their accented syllables, but
syllables and monosyllables have their accented letters and the accent is placed on the letter on which the stress is laid in pronunciation, as bite, bi´t. The key to pronunciation is given at the top
of each page. The perfect and present participles of verbs are
given, when they vary, either in spelling or pronunciation, from the
spelling and pronunciation of the verb. The preterits are given
when they differ from the perfect participles.

The definitions are short and simple. There is no attempt
at etymology. In addition to the dictionary of 630 pages, the work
contains A Vocabulary of Greek and Latin Proper Names, with their
Pronunciation; A Vocabulary of Scripture Proper Names, with their
Pronunciation; A Vocabulary of Christian or Given Names, with their
Pronunciation; Words or Phrases from Foreign Languages, with
their Signification; A List of Abbreviations with their Explanations;
Maxims and Proverbs, alphabetically arranged; Distinguished

Characters of Ancient Greece, arranged by centuries; Distinguished
Characters of Several European Nations; Distinguished Characters of
Great Britain; and a table of the Value of Money in Different Coun-
tries.

Other printings of the Phonographic Pronouncing Dictionary,
8vo. appeared in 1846, 1847, and 1850. As promised at the close
of the Preface to the first publication, an abridged edition appeared
in 1846. It is a 12mo. of 587 pages which sold for one dollar and
twenty-five cents. [97] The plan of the work is the same as for the
larger edition, but the only supplementary list is that of the pronunciation of geographical names.

An advertisement of the octavo edition of the Dictionary characterizes it as follows:

> This valuable work has met with the most favorable re-
> ception from the American public. It contains more words
> than the 8 vo. edition of Webster, and has the pronuncia-
> tion attached according to the best authorities, which is a
> very important addition, and renders the work such more
> desirable for general use and reference than any of the
> large dictionaries now in use. No man of business or
> family should be without this valuable Dictionary.
> The same work abridged in one volume, 12mo. we have
> just published also, which will be found an invaluable class
> book for academies, seminaries, and higher order of
> schools, as well as an important companion to the educa-
> tion of every young person. [98]

William Bolles was descended from Joseph Bolles, who came
to America from England and in 1640 was engaged in trade in Winter
Harbor, Maine. William was the son of Roswell and Lois Bolles,
and was born in Marlborough, Connecticut, August 10, 1800. He
graduated from Amherst College in 1828. He died in 1883. [99] He
published, besides his dictionaries, the New American Spelling Book;
Solitude and Society, with Other Poems; and The Complete Evangelist,
of which he was the editor. [100]

The other phonetic dictionary, claimed by the compiler to be
the first in the world, is the American Phonetic Dictionary of the
English Language, Adapted to the Present State of Literature and
Science; with Pronouncing Vocabularies of Classical, Scriptural, and
Geographical Names, designed by Nathaniel Storrs, and compiled by
Dan. S. Smalley, with a general introduction by A. J. Ellis, Cincinnati: Longley Brothers, Phonetic Publishers, 1855. The object
of the work is to represent correctly, by means of a phonetic alphabet, the pronunciation of the English language that is supported by
the greatest number of competent authorities, and to define and
explain the words as they are generally employed by standard writers. [101] Since, according to the author, the common alphabet does
not contain a sufficient number of letters to represent accurately
the pronunciation of the language, new letters have been added to

make up the deficiency. In this way each letter represents but one
sound and its power is always known when it is once learned.[102]
This method, thinks the author, is superior to the use of diacritical
marks, which are objectionable because of their obscurity and necessary multiplicity resulting from the use of different letters marked
to represent the same sound.[103]

In regard to pronunciation, the compiler consulted the writings
of Walker, Webster, Worcester, Smart, and Alexander Melville
Bell.[104] With respect to words variously pronounced, the pronunciation which is supported by the greatest number of authorities is
placed first.[105] This rule is also followed in regard to spelling.

The definitions have been selected from the dictionaries of
Johnson, Walker, Reid, Smart, Craig, Webster, and Worcester.[106]
Many technical and scientific terms have been introduced, as well as
many obsolete or antiquated words found in books that are still read,
local or provincial words, and a large number of words and phrases
from foreign languages. The obsolete, colloquial, or exceptional
words are carefully noted.

The work was begun by Nathaniel Storrs, a school teacher in
Boston, who was descended from Samuel Storrs of Sutton, Notting-
hamshire, England. Nathaniel received his education at Dartmouth,
from which he graduated in 1796. He was principal of the Elliot
School in Boston from 1818 to 1826. While teaching school he came
to the conclusion that in teaching spelling it was first necessary to
determine the number of elementary sounds in our language and that
each sound should be represented by one letter only, and each letter
should invariably represent one sound. Soon after leaving the Elliot
School, Storrs determined the elementary sounds in our language and
fixed upon the letters to represent them. At this time he began
writing a phonetic dictionary of the English language. This occupied
his spare time for several years, and he completed more than a
thousand pages. He was convinced, after a careful analytical study
of the elements of the language, that he had not perfected his alphabet, but after making the desired improvements, his health prevented his rewriting the work. During his last illness he signed an
indenture for Smalley to prepare and publish a phonetic dictionary of
the English language, and directed that the expenses of writing it be
paid out of his estate. He died in Boston, June 16, 1851.[107]

Storrs' alphabet is based on the romanic, the letters of which
he employs in their most common signification, and makes the new
letters harmonize with the old in form and general appearance. He
rejects q, k, and x. According to his scheme there are thirteen
simple vowels, six of which are long and seven short. They are
arranged in pairs, the short vowels bearing a close resemblance in
quality to the long one, except u, which has no corresponding long
sound. He employs four diphthongs: i in mine, oi in noise, ow in
now, and ew in new. He also uses a symbol for the syllables ur,
er, ir, or, which he considers the same in their elements. Smalley
has aimed to present the phonetic scheme of Storrs as it was
developed by himself.[108]

Storrs' phonetic alphabet is too complicated to be given here. It is found in the Dictionary opposite page 1. The rules for syllabication and pronunciation are as follows:

1. When one consonant is found between two vowels, the consonant is to be taken with the first vowel when it has a final effect on it, and with the second vowel in other cases.
2. When several consonants come between two vowels, all those that have a final effect on the preceding vowel may be, and at least one of them must be, taken with it, while those which are left to be taken with the second vowel must be in all cases such as do or can exert an initial effect upon it. [109]

Words of two syllables are accented on the first; of three or more, on the third.

The work is an octavo of 776 pages, very elaborately made up. The copy at the New York Public Library, which was examined for this study, contains a paper pasted on the flyleaf with an inscription signed by Dan. S. Smalley, presenting the copy to Mrs. Ben Pitman as a reward for her services in correcting the final proofs of the work.

There are over fifty-eight thousand words in the Dictionary, arranged in two columns to a page. The words are respelled in the phonetic alphabet and are followed by short definitions written in the same manner. Following the words is a list of Greek, Latin, and Scripture Proper Names and a vocabulary of the most important geographical names. The pronunciation of these words is represented in phonotypy.

Krapp characterizes the American Phonetic Dictionary as follows:

... The phonetic alphabet used in the dictionary differs but slightly from the one devised by Isaac Pitman, but the changes, such as they were, are the only features of the book that can be called American. It is not a record of American speech, but merely a phonetic record of a generalized kind of English speech, published in America. It has now little present interest, neither has it been historically significant. To invent and illustrate a phonetic alphabet may be an interesting undertaking, but to carry the use of a phonetic alphabet through a whole dictionary, as the compiler of the American Phonetic Dictionary had done, has the ironic result of proving just the opposite of what the compiler intended. It proves that even a phonetic alphabet does not hold the mirror up to nature, but that after all it is only an approximate, therefore conventional, representation of real speech, like the traditional alphabet. [110]

In this chapter we have seen how the interest in the changes in the English language made by the American people culminated in the publication of three dictionaries of Americanisms, or lists of words the use of which was thought to be peculiar to the American people. Although these dictionaries are perhaps not as thorough and as scholarly as they might be, having been, in some cases, worked at as interesting pastimes, they are indicative of the fact that the English language is one of continuous growth and change. The life on the frontier was not that of the conventional English life; and the polished phrases common to the educated Englishman, or the perversions of the language which made up the daily speech of many provincial groups of the British Isles was found to be insufficient for expressing the thoughts and feelings and for describing the new situations that arose as a result of a new environment. The close contact with the elemental phases of life stripped life of its superficiality, destroyed many of the connotations of words that had been built up by conventional civilized society, and returned to many words their original descriptive power. There were added also many new and picturesque words and phrases, sometimes coarse and vulgar, it is true, but always exact and forceful.

The two phonetic dictionaries which have also been treated in this chapter are interesting mainly as experiments.

Notes

1. George H. McKnight, with the assistance of Bert Emsley. Modern English in the Making, New York: D. Appleton and Company, 1928, p. 468.
2. "Americanisms," National Quarterly Review, II (1860-61), 234.
3. Another writer says that perhaps the first reference to an Americanism is that of Gill, in 1621: "Sed et ab Americanis nonnulla mutuamur, ut Maiz et Kanos." "Reviews and Literary Notices," Atlantic Monthly, IV (1859), 638.
4. "The American Language," The Yale Review, XXV (Spring, 1936), 538.
5. John Witherspoon, Works, Edinburgh: J. Ogle, 1815, I, xii.
6. John Russell Bartlett. Dictionary of Americanisms, etc. New York: Bartlett and Welford, 1848, p. xxv.
7. "The Druid," Number V, John Witherspoon, Works, IX, 270.
8. Ibid., pp. 274-275.
9. The Marquis de Chastelleux in his notes on his travels in North America in 1782, when, finding that some of the people proposed to abandon their own language, says: "Nay, from their dislike of everything English, they seriously propose introducing a new language and some persons were desirous that the Hebrew should be substituted for the English. The proposal was that it should be taught in the schools and made use of in all public acts." Henry Pynchon Robinson, "Samuel Johnson Jr., of Guilford and His Dictionaries," The Connecticut Magazine, V (1899), 528-529.

10. "Inchiquen, the Jesuit's Letters, during a late Residence in the United States of America; being a Fragment of a Private Correspondence, accidentally discovered in Europe, containing a favourable View of the Manners, Literature, and State of Society, of the United States; and a Refutation of many of the Aspersions cast upon this Country, by former Residents and Tourists. By some Unknown Foreigner. - New York, 1810, " The Quarterly Review, X (1814), 528-529.
11. Preface, p. vi.
12. Essay, p. 18.
13. Ibid. , p. 19.
14. Ibid. , p. 18.
15. "The First Dictionary of Americanisms, " Harper's Monthly, CXXIX (1919), 103.
16. "Worcester's Universal Dictionary, " North American Review, LXIV (1847), 185.
17. Life of John Pickering. Boston: Printed for Private Distribution. University Press: John Wilson and Son, Cambridge, 1887, p. 256.
18. Ibid. , p. 258.
19. Pickering, op. cit. , footnote, p. 260.
20. Noah Webster, A Letter to the Honorable John Pickering, etc. , p. 59. See also Webster's letter to John Pickering, December, 1816, in Letters of Noah Webster. Edited with an Introduction by Harry R. Warfel. New York: Library Publishers, 1953, pp. 341-394.
21. Pickering, op. cit. , p. 270.
22. Ibid. , p. 305.
23. Ibid. , p. 431.
24. Op. cit. , p. 104.
25. Ibid. , p. 105.
26. Willard, op. cit. , pp. 184-185.
27. "American English, " Transactions of the Albany Institute, X (1883), 347.
28. T. Romeyn Beck, "Notes on Mr. Pickering's Vocabulary of Words and Phrases, Which Have Been Supposed to Be Peculiar to the United States, with Preliminary Observations, " Transactions of the Albany Institute, I (1830), 28.
29. Daniel Appleton White. Eulogy on John Pickering, delivered before the Academy, October 28, 1846. Cambridge: Metcalf and Company, printers, published by order of the Academy, 1847, p. 65.
30. H. L. Mencken. The American Language (First edition). New York: Alfred A. Knopf, 1919, p. 40.
31. Pickering, op. cit. , p. v.
32. Ibid. , p. vi.
33. Ibid. , p. 1.
34. Nation, XLV (1887), 255.
35. Pickering, op. cit. , p. 12.
36. Ibid. , p. 9.
37. Ibid. , p. 30.
38. White, op. cit. , p. 11.

39. Pickering, op. cit., pp. 37-38.
40. Ibid., p. 44.
41. Ibid., p. 45.
42. Ibid., p. 49.
43. Ibid., p. 92.
44. Ibid., p. 94.
45. Ibid., p. 220.
46. Ibid., p. 516.
47. Ibid., pp. 524-525.
48. Nation, XLV (1887), 255-256.
49. Ibid., p. 256.
50. Roorbach, op. cit., p. 43.
51. John Russell Bartlett. Memoranda; original manuscript in the John Carter Brown Library, pp. 43-45.
52. Introduction, p. iii.
53. Ibid., p. iv.
54. Ibid., pp. iv-v.
55. Ibid., pp. v-vi.
56. Ibid., p. vi.
57. Ibid., p. vii.
58. Duyckinck Collection, New York Public Library.
59. Introduction, p. viii.
60. Preface to the Second Edition, quoted in the Preface to the Fourth Edition, p. xi.
61. John Russell Bartlett. Genealogy of that Branch of the Russell Family which Comprises the Descendants of John Russell of Woburn, Massachusetts, 1640-1878. Providence: Privately Printed, 1879, p. 131.
62. Preface to the Second Edition, quoted in the Preface to the Fourth Edition, p. xi.
63. Quoted in Mencken, op. cit., p. 30.
64. Preface to the Fourth Edition.
65. "Reviews and Literary Notices," Atlantic Monthly, IV (1859), 638-639. The reviewer is evidently James Russell Lowell since he makes approximately the same statement about language in the Introduction to The Biglow Papers, Second Series, in Complete Writings. New York: AMS Press, Inc., 1966, XI, 11.
66. Ibid., pp. 641-642.
67. "A Glossary of Words and Phrases, etc.," Blackwood's Magazine, LXXXIX (1861), 421-423.
68. Op. cit., p. 376.
69. "Americanisms," Galaxy, XXIV (1877), 376-383.
70. Dictionary of American Biography, II, 7.
71. Evert A. Duyckinck and George L. Duyckinck, editors. Cyclopedia of American Literature. New York: Charles Scribner's, 1866, II, Part 2, 418.
72. Ibid.
73. Ibid.
74. Dictionary of American Biography, II, 7, and The Providence Journal, Saturday, May 29, 1886.
75. Duyckinck and Duyckinck, op. cit., p. 418.
76. Ibid.

77. The Providence Journal, Saturday, May 29, 1886.
78. Ibid.
79. William Gammell. Life and Services of The Honorable John Russell Bartlett. A Paper Read Before the Rhode Island Historical Society. Providence: Printed by the Providence Press Company, 1886, p. 9.
80. Preface, pp. iii-iv.
81. Ibid., p. xi.
82. Op. cit., p. 342.
83. J. Smith Futhey and Gilbert Cope. History of Chester County, Pennsylvania. Philadelphia: L. H. Everts, 1881, p. 530.
84. Henry Graham Ashmead. History of Delaware County, Pennsylvania. Philadelphia: L. H. Everts, 1884, p. 628.
85. Ibid.
86. Ibid.
87. Ibid.
88. Thomas William Herringshaw. Encyclopedia of American Biography. Chicago: American Publisher's Association, 1898, p. 339.
89. Ibid.
90. Roorbach, op. cit., p. 61.
91. Preface, p. iii.
92. Ibid.
93. Ibid., p. iv.
94. Ibid.
95. Ibid.
96. Ibid., p. vi.
97. Roorbach, op. cit., p. 61.
98. Advertisement at the close of Grimshaw's Etymological Dictionary, Third Edition, p. 8.
99. John A. Bolles. Genealogy of the Bolles Family in America. Boston: Henry W. Dutton and Son, 1865, p. 41.
100. Roorbach, op. cit., p. 61.
101. Preface, p. iii.
102. Ibid.
103. Ibid.
104. Ibid., p. iv.
105. Ibid.
106. Ibid., p. iv.
107. Memoir of Storrs, Introduction to the American Phonetic Dictionary, pp. ix-x.
108. Ibid., p. xi.
109. Ibid.
110. Op. cit., pp. 373-374.

PART TWO

WEBSTER AND WORCESTER
AND THEIR DICTIONARIES

NOAH WEBSTER

CHAPTER IV

NOAH WEBSTER AND HIS DICTIONARIES

Noah Webster, Junior, was born October 16, 1758, in the village of West Hartford, Connecticut, where he was baptized six days later by the young Rev. Nathaniel Hooker. [1] He was descended on his father's side from John Webster, one of the voluntary exiles from England who began the settlement of Hartford in 1635. [2] Tradition says that John Webster had formerly emigrated from Warwickshire and settled near Boston, Massachusetts, but later had joined the group which, on account of religious differences, migrated to Connecticut. [3] The fact that only four men took up more land than did John Webster, and but two an equal amount, shows that he was among the wealthier emigrants. [4] He also held several important positions in the administration of the government of the colony. [5]

Robert Webster, one of the four sons of John Webster, married Suzannah, a daughter of Richard Treat, Senior, of Wethersfield, one of the Patentees in the Royal Charter of Connecticut, and a sister of Governor Robert Treat. Their oldest son John married Sarah Mygatt of Hartford, whose maternal grandfather, William Whiting, was one of the first settlers of Hartford. Their youngest son, Daniel, married Miriam, daughter of Noah Cooke, of Northampton. [6] Of his ancestors Noah Webster, Junior writes:

> I remember the funeral of Daniel, my grandfather, (who in the Spanish War of 1745 commanded a military company). Noah Webster, my father, born March 20th, 1772 (O. S.), married Mercy Steele, [January 12, 1749] daughter of Eliphalet Steele of West Hartford and grand-daughter of Samuel Steele, who married Melatiah Bradford, daughter of William Bradford, Deputy Governor, and grand-daughter of William Bradford, Governor of the Plymouth Colony from 1621 until his death in 1651, excepting on five occasions, when by "importunity he got off. "[7]

Noah Webster, Senior, was a man of limited education but strong intellect, who spent his life on a farm of ninety acres which constituted the only means of support for his family of three sons and two daughters whom he trained to the same severe and unremitting labor. He was for many years justice of the peace in the town of Hartford, and a deacon of the church in the parish where he lived. [8]

The mother of Noah Webster, Junior, is spoken of by her daughter-in-law "as a woman of great intelligence and energy; a gentle loving mother, and care-taker, looking well to the ways of her household. She carried on the farm quite successfully while her husband and sons were in the War of the Revolution."[9]

As a family, the Websters were remarkable for longevity. "Noah Webster, Senior, died in his ninety-second year; Noah the son in his eighty-fifth; his two brothers lived for eighty years or more, and his two sisters for seventy."[10]

Until his fourteenth year, Webster worked on his father's farm and attended the district school where the principal books studied were Dilworth's Spelling Book, the Psalter, and the Testament.[11] Very little definite information is available about Webster's early years, but it is among the family traditions that

> ... even in those silent years upon the farm, and in the quiet of the household circle, words had a meaning in his apprehension, which they do not ordinarily have to children and youth. He weighed them one against another; he traced their resemblance and their differences, and sought to know their full and exact import.[12]

Webster early became interested in acquiring a college education. His daughter, Eliza Steeler Webster Jones, tells how he would take his Latin Grammar into the field and spend his rest periods in absorbing its contents. His father, finding his stretched on the grass thus, decided to let him follow his bent, and he was placed under the tuition of Rev. Nathan Perkins who fitted him for college.[13]

In September, 1774, Webster entered Yale College. His father was very much interested in his career, "for he mortgaged the farm to pay his college expenses, and more than once rode on horseback to New Haven to bring his boy home, once walking back and letting his son ride, saying that he was best able to walk."[14]

At the time when Webster entered Yale, the college could boast of only two small buildings and a chapel. The students were still under the care of tutors. English composition and oratory had just been admitted to the curriculum, which heretofore had included only classical languages, mathematics, philosophy, and polemic divinity.[15]

For the first three years at Yale, Webster was under the tutorship of Joseph Buckminster, who taught the freshmen "the Tongues and Logic" and tried to help them master "Virgillius, Ciceronis Orationes, Greek Testa, Wards Arithmetic."[16] He also took part in the meetings of the Brothers in Unity and delivered "Orations and Dialogues" along with Zephaniah Swift, Uriah Tracy, Joel Barlow, Alexander Wolcott, and Oliver Wolcott, Jr.[17] It was the custom with the undergraduates that

On Tuesdays and Fridays every Undergraduate in his
Turn, about eight at a Time, shall declaim in the English,
Latin, Greek or Hebrew Tongue, and in no other, without
special Liberty from the President, and shall presently
after deliver up his Declamation to his Tutor, fairly written with his name subscribed. [18]

As a sophomore, Webster read and delivered to Joseph Buckminster
a declamation in Latin, dated May 4, 1776, in which he attempted
to prove that a well-spent youth prepares for a happy old age. [19]
Webster was among the Yale men who in June, 1775, escorted
General Washington "out of town, " Webster furnishing the music. [20]

Webster was graduated with the Class of 1778 after under-
going the public examinations given the seniors by Ezra Stiles, who
only a short time before had been installed as the new president.
This event took place "about the Twentieth of July (on a day appointed by the President). " The seniors appeared then "in the Chapel,
to be examined by the President, Fellows, Tutors, or any other
Gentlemen of liberal Education, touching their Knowledge and Proficiency in the learned Languages, the liberal Arts and Sciencies,
and other Qualifications requisite for receiving a Bachelor's Degree. "[21]

As was also the custom, the seniors disputed forensically on
an academic question. President Stiles observed in regard to the
disputation of the Class of 1778: "They disputed inimitably well:
particularly Barlow, Swift, Webster, Gilbert, Meigs, Sage, &c.... "[22]

Among the forty members of the class were several men who
later distinguished themselves. In the list were Joel Barlow, poet
and American Ambassador to the Court of St. Cloud; Zephaniah
Swift, Chief Justice of the Supreme Court of Connecticut; Oliver
Wolcott, Secretary of the Treasury under the presidency of John
Adams; Josiah Meigs, Professor of Mathematics and Natural Philo-
sophy in Yale; and Uriah Tracy, who distinguished himself in the
Senate of the United States. [23]

After his graduation at the age of twenty, Webster remained
for a while at his father's home in West Hartford, not knowing what
to do. The country was in a wretched condition and there was little prospect of a change for the better. In one of his reminiscences,
Webster recalls the situation while he was in college.

So impoverished was the country at one time that the
steward of the college could not supply the necessary pro-
visions of the tables, and the students were compelled to
return to spend several months at home. At one time
goods were so scarce that the farmers cut corn-stalks and
crushed them in cider-mills, and then boiled the juice
down to a syrup as a substitute for sugar. [24]

The years which followed his graduation were still worse.

The country was impoverished by the war; there was no prospect of peace; and the outcome of the struggle was doubtful. One day Webster's father gave him an eight-dollar bill of Continental currency, worth only about four dollars in silver, and said to him: "Take this; you must now seek your living: I can do no more for you. "[25] Soon after this he left home, his brothers feeling that he should be assisted no further.

In order to make a living while he studied law, Webster took charge of a school in Glastonbury, Connecticut, for the winter only. In the summer of 1779 he taught in Hartford, living in the family of Oliver Ellsworth; in the winter of 1780, he taught in West Hartford, having lived during the summer with Jedediah Strong, register of deeds in Litchfield, Connecticut, and assisted him in the duties of his office. At this time he began the study of law under the Honorable Titus Hosmer of Middletown. He was admitted to the bar in Hartford in 1781. [26] In July, 1781, he established a private school at Sharon, Connecticut. [27] At the annual commencement of Yale College in September of that year, he was admitted to the degree of Master of Arts, having offered as his thesis a dissertation in English on the Universal Diffusion of Literature as Introduction to the Universal Diffusion of Christianity. [28]

One of the perplexities Webster had as a schoolmaster was in teaching his pupils how to spell. This difficulty induced him to project a book which should make the acquirement of orthography easier and also reduce the teacher's toil and trouble with pupils. The result was A Grammatical Institute of the English Language, comprising an Easy, Concise, and Systematic Method of Education, Designed for the Use of English Schools in America, in three parts, a spelling book, a grammar, and a reader. Joel Benton remarks that

> ... If this absolute and impressive need had not occurred, or if Webster's first pupils had been, by some unusual circumstance, spellers of phenomenal excellence, the line of authorship which Webster began might not have occurred to him. He did, as it was, drift backward at one time to his legal studies and practice, but the need and possibility of a successful spelling-book, which was followed by the grammar and dictionary, finally fixed his career as that of an author. [29]

Tarbox makes a similar observation:

> ... Had the condition of the country been peaceful and prosperous at the time he was admitted to the bar, he would probably have opened a law office, and the world might have lost him in his distinctive character as a lexicographer. But as the case stood, he turned aside to teaching and in the year 1782, only four years out of college, and only twenty-four years old, he entered upon a work which became a kind of turning-point and largely

helped to determine the subsequent course of his life. He conceived the plan of preparing and publishing a series of schoolbooks to aid in the better education of the children of America. [30]

In a letter published in New England Magazine, June 1, 1832, Noah Webster tells something about his speller and grammar, both of which led to the Dictionary. He says:

> My Spelling Book, in its first form, was compiled in 1782, at Goshen in Orange County, State of New York, where I then kept a classical school, and while the American Army lay at Newburg and New Windsor. In Autumn of that year I carried the first copy to Philadelphia, and showed it to several members of Congress.
>
> On my way, I called on Rev. Samuel S. Smith, then professor of theology in Nassau Hall, Princeton, who suggested to me the expedience of making an important alteration in the division of syllables. This was the union of tion instead of ti-on, according to Dilworth, and making these letters, one terminating syllable. I had my fears that such an alteration would not be received by the public, but he assured me it might be done with perfect safety. I followed his advice, and the event has answered his expectations. It is undoubtedly a great improvement, and has been one influential cause of that rapid progress which the children of this country have made in learning the language.
>
> Another improvement has, probably, been equally successful--that of uniting letters to the syllables to which they belong in pronunciation, as hab-it instead of ha-bit.
>
> The first copy of this book was published by Hudson and Goodwin, in Hartford, in 1783. But by the advice and recommendation of Pres. Stiles of Yale College, this book, with a "Grammar" and "Selections for Reading," were published under the title of "A Grammatical Institute of the English Language."
>
> The grammar was published the following year, 1784, and the selections soon followed, but the precise time of publication I do not recollect. This was, I believe, the first collection for reading published in this country.
>
> The Spelling Book, at subsequent intervals, was revised; and the last revision was published in 1804. Either at that time or at a former revision, it was published as a detached work, under the title of "The American Spelling Book."[31]

Although Webster's Spelling Book encountered opposition when it was first published,[32] it reached a popularity not attained by any other book in America except the Bible. It became not only a universal textbook in the schools and the master book on spelling everywhere, but a standard article of commerce and, like sugar and salt, was kept in the stores along with the gingham and calico.

More than five generations of Americans learned from
it. The first studied it before there was any United
States, as early as 1787; and it was still being used in
schools as late as the early 1900's. Boys learned from
the Blue-Back Speller, grew up, became Presidents of the
United States, died, and were relatively forgotten, while
the presses of D. Appleton & Company ground out new
editions for the second, third, and fourth generations. The
first edition was printed on a hand-press, the last on the
most modern Hoe; the first antedated the Presidency of
Washington, the last was contemporary with Roosevelt. [33]

There were approximately 209 publishers of the spelling
book. [34] On March 14, 1818, Webster made a contract with Hudson
and Company of Hartford, Connecticut, which gave that company the
exclusive right to publish the American Spelling Book for fourteen
years. [35] In a letter containing proposals to booksellers, November
20, 1815, Webster made an estimate of the value of the copyright
by giving the amount of the sales. According to his statement, the
average sales for the last eleven years, of which he had returns,
amounted to two hundred forty-one thousand, the real number being
much greater. The sales for the two years previous (1813-15) aver-
aged two hundred eighty-six thousand copies a year. The increase
in sales was about a third in ten years. [36]

On May 22, 1790, Hudson and Goodwin, who owned the copyright of the Spelling Book in the State of Connecticut, made the statement that the consumption of this book in that state was more than
eight thousand a year. They also stated that the price in New York
was thirteen shillings New York currency a dozen, or three-pence
lawful money less per dozen than in Connecticut. In Philadelphia the
price was fourteen shillings Pennsylvania currency, or eleven shillings and two-pence lawful money a dozen. In Boston the price was
eleven shillings. [37]

In the Preface to his Spelling Book (1790) Webster criticizes
the books then in use for their lack of a thorough investigation of
the sounds of the English language and the powers of the several
letters, the unnatural and arbitrary method of dividing syllables, and
the omission of a criterion by which the various sounds of the vowels may be distinguished. These defects Webster attempted to remedy. His plan was to simplify the problem of pronunciation, syllabication, and spelling by making a natural division of the syllables
and by giving specific directions for placing the accent. He also
arranged his spelling tables so as to show the manner of making
derivative words, and transformed the spelling of Indian geographical
names from the French to the English method.

The syllables of words are divided as they are pronounced, and for this obvious reason, that children learn the
language by the ear. Rules are of no consequence, but to
printers and adults. In Spelling Books, they embarrass
children, and double the labour of the teacher. [38]

In one of his early prefaces Webster says:

> One great advantage in using the book now offered, is
> the simplicity of the scheme of pronunciation, which exhi-
> bits the sounds of the letters with sufficient accuracy with-
> out a mark over each vowel. The multitude of characters
> in Perry's scheme renders it far too complex and perplex-
> ing to be useful to children, confusing the eye without en-
> lightening the understanding. [39]

More than a hundred years after the publication of the first
"Blue-Back Speller," Colton expressed the sentiment for it that still
lingered in the minds of those who had studied it.

> It lies before me - the genuine article; not the identical
> copy I used and was brought up on, long time ago, but of
> the same edition. It is nearly as old as I am, and has
> come spelling its way along down through two-thirds of a
> century, to these odd times. How long it has lain in the
> Boston Antiquarian bookstore where I found it thirty-five
> years ago, I cannot tell. It is an institution - yes, a
> university. It has trained and strained more heads than
> any other book of the kind ever did, or perhaps ever will.
> Later editions have been sent out; but give me the old
> wine, which to my liking is better. Very plain, even home-
> ly in outward appearance. Never mind. Homely people
> are generally the best. The back of the cover is of coarse
> linen cloth--very coarse--threads within sight of each
> other. The sides of cover are of layers of brown paper,
> with an over-all of thin blue paper. The paper and pages
> within look as if they might have come from a mill using
> bleached straw and slacked lime, with a little sulphur
> thrown in to give the tinting.
> And now as to the contents, the meat and marrow.
> Quite a book in size--one hundred and sixty-eight pages.
> The preface we did not have to read. But the next half-
> dozen pages, "Analysis of Sounds," we in our school had
> to commit to memory and recite. This amazed us, and
> does still. Just to think of a child eight or nine years
> old required to recite understandingly the opening sentence:
> "Language, in its more limited sense, is the expression
> of ideas by articulate sounds." You might about as well
> set a child to comprehending those vast themes, verities
> so important, but how profound, viz.: The wherefore of
> the why, the thingness of the this, and the thusness of
> the though. Makes one think of Horace Greeley, who,
> after reading a grandiloquent communication sent to him
> for the press, said of it, that it "obfuscated all his intel-
> lects, and circumgumfrigobrighisticated all his comprehen-
> sibilities."
> And come to the A B C page. In my times of old we
> children learned our A B C's at school, and not at home
> from lettered blocks and other knick-knacks as in these

latter days. Some of those first days at school were quite
impressive to the looker-on and listener. High day when
we advanced to table No. 2--bag, big, bog. But the almost dizzy elevation when we ascended and attained to--
baker, brier, cider, crazy. It is very observable this
placing crazy after cider. Here are fact and philosophy.
cause and effect; indeed, a temperance lecture entire....
In my ancient times the spelling lesson was studied column from the spelling-book, and spelled by the classes
old and young standing on the floor--the scholar taking
his place, and keeping it if he could the month in and out,
without having his head cut off every night, a rather dis-
couraging operation to an aspiring lad or lass. One winter
is remembered when a boy kept such headship all through
the term, and carried off the great prize--a punched and
pendent silver ninepence, tow-string and all. At a noted
spelling-match in a neighboring town, visitors were invited
to give in their names and take part in the contest. Sides
were chosen. Came out even at eight o'clock P.M. Another choosing up. Came out even again at nine. "Let us
have this out." One from each side must go upon the
floor and spell for the side. Against aforesaid boy was
placed an older person, a teacher who had taught school
four summers. Plied and pumped with the spelling-book
fore and aft, and aft and fore. "The combat deepens."
By and by the word apropos was put to the fairer and
gentler, and she spelled it "appropos," putting in too
many p's, and the boy getting it right carried off the glit-
ter.
    And what a day that was when we stood on the hilltop
of human greatness and grappled with our first reading
lesson! "No man may put off the law of God;" "my joy
is in the law all day." See that boy in his mighty wrest-
lings to spell out the words! Lips move vigorously; brow
knit; book turned this way and that, to give room for the
great idea to come in; his whole frame writhing and scre-
wed down hard and tight to the supreme task. Perhaps
he will "fetch it," perhaps not; but will come out of the
throes as an older boy did from the word picturesque--
pronouncing it picturesquee. But don't you give that small
boy up. There is promise for him in such energy and
bent as that.
    Then a succession of easy and familiar lessons. But
come to the fables and pictures. Here is richness. Putting on the spectacles of my ancientness, I have been
looking anew through the old spelling-book to see how, on
the whole, the old friend would appear to one in these latter days to which it and I have come down. Grandly, sir,
is my ready answer; never before handsomer than now--I
mean the book. And so will it appear to you, from the
glance or the scrutiny, if you be the sensible man I take
you for. [40]

After making a thorough study of the pronunciation as suggested by Webster in his early American spelling book, Joshua H.
Neumann comes to the following conclusions regarding Webster's
contribution to American pronunciation.

> In comparison with modern philological standards, Web-
> ster's linguistic equipment in the period under review does
> not, of course, appear at all satisfactory. But when one
> takes into consideration the general state of the science at
> that time and the fact that Webster was apparently working
> all by himself far away from the centers of linguistic
> study, and forming his opinions with but scanty material
> at his disposal, one cannot help feeling that his work was
> neither hopelessly wrong nor entirely trivial. The follow-
> ing remarks, therefore, in respect to Webster's orthoepi-
> cal theories and practices (as far as these concern the
> pronunciation of his earlier work) should be regarded in
> the light of these circumstances.
> Webster does not seem to have been aware at this early
> period of the nature of phonetic change. He apparently be-
> lieved that English pronunciation had remained stationary
> since the Middle English period....
> That Webster did not understand the working of phonetic
> laws may also be inferred from the criticism he directed
> against Sheridan and Walker for their failure to note and
> describe certain sounds. He believed, for example, that
> Sheridan wilfully refused to record the so-called "Italian
> a" in his Dictionary, when, as a matter of fact, it is
> entirely probable that that vowel did not exist in Sheridan's
> Irish pronunciation....
> Webster's ignorance of the nature of linguistic change
> led him to propound a theory in accordance with which he
> thought it possible that the English language in America
> might be mechanically "reduced" to a standard of pronun-
> ciation as immutable as he supposed to have been the case
> with Greek, Latin, and Arabic? These languages had not
> changed in thousands of years; why should English? Accor-
> dingly, the speller of 1783 was avowedly undertaken with
> this hope in mind. This idea also runs through the whole
> of the Dissertations. It was only later, in the light of his
> maturer linguistic experience, that he modified his views....
> Of one important principle in linguistic science, how-
> ever, Webster seems to have been keenly conscious; al-
> though his application of the principle was somewhat un-
> scientific. In case of doubt as to the pronunciation of a
> word, Webster usually appealed first to the principle of
> analogy.... As a general rule, he held every addition to
> the "anomalies" of language to be a corruption, and every
> elimination of them an improvement. (Speller, 1787, p.
> 78)[41]

Webster was not an accurate phonetician. He rarely
attempted to describe the origin of a sound. He was
generally content, as in the two early spellers and the

> Dissertation, to follow the older eighteenth century classi-
> fication and nomenclature.
>
> ...
>
> To sum up: Webster is unreliable when he attempts to
> theorize, or to account for the many points of difference
> between his pronunciation and what he conceived to be stan-
> dard British usage. This, of course, is a fault that may
> be ascribed to his time and to his lack of philological
> training. His early spellers and the Dissertations are,
> however, valuable to the student of language as a rather
> naive and trustworthy exposition of New England speech
> one hundred and forty years ago. [42]

As Webster worked on his spelling book, he became more
and more convinced of the need for a reformation of the English language in America. He wished to improve the English tongue, to
simplify English spelling and grammar, to destroy those dialectical
differences that distinguished the New Englander from other Americans,
and to establish the American language in the place of the speech of
England. John Bach McMaster describes his radicalism when he
says:

> ... Like most reformers, he [Webster] commenced by
> laying down a theory of perfection, which he carried out
> unswervingly to its logical extreme. Some words were to
> be proscribed; the spelling of others was to be materially
> altered; all silent vowels were to be cut out. But the
> most daring innovation was in the alphabet. The new lan-
> guage was to have every sound represented by a letter,
> and no letter was to be suffered to remain that did not
> stand for a distinct sound. Many new characters were
> therefore to be introduced, and many old ones cast aside.
> Such was his enthusiasm and conceit that he felt quite
> sure that letters familiar to hundreds of generations of
> men, and older than any other institution, human or di-
> vine, then existing, letters that had seen the rise of every
> language of Western Europe, that were old when the first
> Saxon set foot in Britain, when Christ came on earth,
> when Caesar invaded Gaul, when Rome was still a pretty
> hamlet on the banks of the Tiber, would at his suggestion
> be ruthlessly swept away.... [43]

On May 24, 1786, Webster wrote to Franklin and submitted a
plan for reducing to perfect regularity the orthography of the language and desired Franklin, should the plan be adopted, to lay the
matter before Congress. [44] Franklin was in favor of introducing a
new alphabet by which every sound in the language would be represented by a definite character, and since the twenty-six letters of
the Roman alphabet were insufficient to represent the elementary
sounds of the Anglo-Saxon, Franklin suggested that new letters be invented to supply the want. After several letters had been exchanged,

Webster seems to have rejected Franklin's scheme as too radical, for in the Preface to A Compendious Dictionary, page vi, in an attached note, he says that he declined Franklin's plan as too impractical, for the orthography could be rendered sufficiently regular without the addition of a single new character, "by means of a few trifling alterations of the present characters and retrenching a few superfluous letters, the most of which are corruptions of the original words. "

To bring his plan to the attention of the public, Webster wrote a series of lectures which he read during the winter of 1785 and the spring of 1786 at Annapolis, Baltimore, Philadelphia, Boston, and New York. He was well received at every place except Philadelphia, where in 1787, for about two months, practically ever number of the Independent Gazetteer contained some fling at Webster for his presuming to tell the Philadelphians about the right pronunciation and for daring to write after his name the word 'Squire. 45 But, in the main, the jests and sarcasms were directed against his book.

> ... In a mock address to the Federal Convention, that body was asked to see to it that the English tongue was properly established. One Webster, a New England man, had put out a book which he called an "Institute, " and which contained some new things. On the title-page was the word systematic. This strong propensity to clip off the al from systematical and like words was noticed with concern. It was an innovation. It was to be looked to, for was not the al essential to the language and the main pillar of the Federal Government? On another page he used need for needs, which every schoolboy knew was false. Could the States exist when a verb did not agree with its nominative case. The same Institutional Genius declared that all adjectives could be compared by more and most. What child did not know that one thing could not be more square or more cubical than another? Adjectives such as broad and long followed, he said, the nouns they qualified. It would therefore be proper to say hereafter that Chestnut was a street long and Market a street broad. Could a New England man be right? His attempt to introduce his "Institute" into the schools and displace Dilworth and Jonson [sic] was a Whig scheme. 46

The series of lectures served to direct public attention to Webster and his subject and to allow him to become acquainted with literary men and with different parts of the country. Many of Webster's ideas were set forth in the Dissertations on the English Language, published in 1789. In the Preface he states that he now agrees with Franklin that a reformation of our orthography is both "practicable and highly necessary. " In this opinion he has reversed himself since 1785. In the Appendix he gives the principal alterations, necessary to render our orthography sufficiently regular and easy.

1. The omission of all superfluous or silent letters; as a in bread.

2. A substitution of a character that has a certain definite sound, for one that is more vague and indeterminate. Thus by putting ee instead of ie or ea, the words mean, near, speak, grieve, zeal, would become meen, neer, speek, greev, zeel.

3. A trifling alteration in a character, or the addition of a point would distinguish different sounds, without the substitution of a new character. Thus a very small stroke across th would distinguish different sounds without the substitution of a new character.

These changes would facilitate the learning of the language, would render the pronunciation as uniform as the spelling in books, would diminish the number of letters about one-sixteenth or one-eighteenth, and, above all, make a difference between English and American orthography. However, there would be according to Webster, certain objections to these changes. They would oblige people to relearn the language; would render our present books useless; would injure the language by obscuring etymology; and would destroy the distinction between words of different meanings and similar sounds. Since pronunciation is continually changing, it is foolish to try to make orthography conform to it.

In his Essays and Fugitive Writings, published 1790, Webster attempted to carry out partially his idea of a reformed spelling, designated by some as the "deformed spelling." The following sentences, taken from the Preface, illustrate his reformed orthography.

... In the essays, ritten within the last yeer a considerable change of spelling iz introduced by way of experiment. This liberty waz taken by the writers before the age of queen Elizabeth, and to this we are indeted for the preference of modern spelling over that of Gower and Chaucer. The man who admits that the change of housbonde, mynde, ygone, moneth into husband, mind, gone, month iz an improvement must acknowledge also the riting of helth, breth, rong, tung, munth to be an improvement. There iz no alternativ. Every possible reezon that could ever be offered for altering the spelling of wurds, stil exists in full force; and if a gradual reform shoud not be made in our language, it will proov that we are less under the influence of reezon than our ancestors. [47]

Webster's First Dictionary

In 1806, Webster published A Compendious Dictionary of the English Language. As early as 1800 he had begun the preparation of

a school dictionary, but had abandoned it for the larger work. [48]
For many years, he had jotted down words which he met in reading
that he did not find in dictionaries. [49] His work on the spelling book
and grammar had also disclosed to him the deficiencies in current
dictionaries. The following letter contains the first suggestion that
Webster's philological labors might lead to a dictionary. [50]

W. MSS

From Daniel George   Portland, Sept 27th,
                                                        1790

Sir,

Permit a stranger to your person, but an admirer of
your writings to address you. For a long time have I
had it in contemplation to write to you; but an unhappy
want of acquaintance damped my ardor: however, stimu-
lated by gratitude for your highly serviceable writings, I
now venture upon your candor.

I was pleased with your useful and approved Institute:
I admired your learned Dissertations on the English Language; but with your late Collection of Essays and fugitiv
writings, I am pleasingly astonished. Go on, Sir, and
make a thoro reform in our orthography, the irregularity
of which, must give every American pain. Such is my
ambition on this head, that I cannot rest short of that
perfection, which the nature of the case is capable of.
Perhaps it is impossible to wipe away all anomalies; but
much may be done, and that without introducing any new
characters. In fine, the innovation may be natural, easy
and analogous, that an attentive reader may perfect himself in them in a day or two. As to illiterate persons,
they spell wrong now, and they will do no worse (but probably better) in the improved orthography. - But, Sir, we
must first have a Dictionary and to YOU we must look for
this necessary work. Until this shall be published, every
individual attempt to innovate, I apprehend, will contribute
to set the orthography afloat, and consequently discourage
many, who wish for a reform. I hope this work is already begun--I wish it were finished. [51]

That Webster was not averse to such a plan is shown in a
second letter from the same person. Perhaps it was his Philadelphia
experience that caused him to be "doubtful" of the public mind; however, as indicated in the letter, Webster had already thought of a
plan. [52] Webster gives the credit for the idea of the compilation of
his Dictionary to Dr. Goodrich.

On the first publication of my institute of the English
Language, more than twenty years ago, that eminent classical scholar and divine, the late Dr. Goodrich of Durham,
recommended to me to complete a system of elementary
principles, for the instruction of youth in the English

language, by compiling and publishing a dictionary. Whatever respect I was inclined to pay to that gentleman's opinion, I could not, at that time, believe myself qualified for such an undertaking; and private considerations afterwards interposed to retard its execution. My studies however have occasionally had reference to an ultimate accomplishment of such a work; and for a few years past, they have been directed immediately to that object. As I have advanced in my investigation, I have been, at every step, more and more impressed with the importance of this work; and an acquaintance with the Saxon language, the mother tongue of the English, has convinced me, that a careful revision of our present dictionaries is absolutely necessary to a correct knowledge of the language. [53]

The title of the first dictionary is a very imposing one for such a small book:

A Compendious Dictionary of the English Language in which Five Thousand Words are added to the number found in the Best English Compends. The Orthography is, in some instances, corrected; The Pronunciation marked by an Accent or other suitable directions; and the definitions of many words amended and improved, to which are added for the benefit of the merchant, the student and the traveller,

I. Tables of moneys of most of the commercial nations in the world, with the value expressed in sterling and cents.

II. Tables of weights and measures, ancient and modern, with the proportion between the several weights used in the principal cities of Europe.

III. The divisions of time among the Jews, Greeks, and Romans, with a table exhibiting the Roman manner of dating.

IV. An official list of the post-offices in the United States, with the States and counties in which they are respectively situated, and the distance to each from the seat of Government.

V. The number of inhabitants in the United States, with the amount of exports.

IV. [sic] New and interesting chronological tables of remarkable events and discoveries.

By Noah Webster, Esq.

From Sidney's Press, for Hudson and Goodwin, Book-sellers, Hartford, and Increase Cooke and Company. Book-Sellers, New Haven, 1806. [54]

The Dictionary is a 12mo. with 24 pages of introduction and 408 pages of subject matter. Three hundred fifty-six pages are devoted to the dictionary proper, the remainder to the items listed on the title-page; tables of moneys, weights and measures; list of post-offices, etc. There are approximately 40,600 words (counting 114 to a page) arranged in two columns on a page. It is an enlargement of Entick's Spelling Dictionary, with about five thousand words added, "collected from the best writers, during a course of several years reading."[55] Obsolete words have been included since the books in which they are found are still read. New words belonging to chemistry have been inserted, the words having been taken from Lavoisier, Fourcroy, Chaptal, Black, and Thompson, with a few old ones from Priestley, Scheele, and Stahl.[56] Words dealing with mineralogy have been taken chiefly from Kirwan, but Cronstedt and the various systems exhibited in Fourcroy and the Encyclopedia have been consulted. Since the spelling of these words has not been agreed upon by the writers, Webster has attempted to reduce the spelling to a system corresponding with the English analogues. Many new terms in botany, collected from the Linnean school, have been introduced. Proper adjectives have been included. In the alphabetical arrangement, the letter J has been separated from I, and V, from U, and I and U have been placed first in order.[57]

Although the appearance of the book would not compare favorably with almost any book printed at the present time, in reality it was an achievement. One critic says that as an example of printing it was monumental in character.

> ... Nothing equal to it had ever been done in America. The typography was excellent and the press work was well done. It evidently was printed four pages at a time on a 19x25 sheet, making eight pages to a sheet. There were no folios, or numbers, on the pages. But each signature, or sheet of eight pages, was numbered. That was about the only blunder in this dictionary--and Noah Webster may not have been to blame for that.[58]

In orthography Webster has resorted, in this dictionary, to a sort of middle ground. In the Preface, pages vi to vii, he says:

> ... The friends of a reform maintain that our alphabet should be rendered perfectly regular, by rejecting superfluous characters, and introducing new ones to supply defects; so that every sound may be represented by a distinct letter and no letter have more sounds than one. This scheme is impracticable and not at all necessary.
> The opposers of reform, on the other hand, contend that no alterations should be made in orthography, as they would not only occasion inconvenience, but tend to render old books, useless, and obscure etymology....

A
Compendious Dictionary

OF THE

English Language.

In which FIVE THOUSAND Words are added
to the number found in the BEST ENGLISH COMPENDS

The ORTHOGRAPHY is, in some instances, corrected ;

The PRONUNCIATION marked by an Accent or other suitable Direction ;

And the DEFINITIONS of many Words amended and improved.

TO WHICH ARE ADDED FOR THE BENEFIT OF THE

MERCHANT, the STUDENT and the TRAVELLER,

I.——TABLES of the MONEYS of most of the commercial Nations in the world, with the value expressed in Sterling and Cents.

II.——TABLES of WEIGHTS and MEASURES, ancient and modern, with the proportion between the several weights used in the principal cities of Europe.

III.——The DIVISIONS of TIME among the Jews, Greeks and Romans, with a Table exhibiting the Roman manner of dating.

IV.——An official List of the POST-OFFICES in the UNITED STATES, with the States and Counties in which they are respectively situated, and the distance of each from the seat of Government.

V.——The NUMBER of INHABITANTS in the United States, with the amount of EXPORTS.

IV.——New and interesting CHRONOLOGICAL TABLES of remarkable Events and Discoveries.

By NOAH WEBSTER, Esq.

From Sidney's Press.

FOR HUDSON & GOODWIN, BOOK-SELLERS, HARTFORD, AND INCREASE COOKE & CO.

BOOK-SELLERS, NEW-HAVEN.

1806.

The correct principle respecting changes in orthography seems to be between these extremes of opinion. No great changes should ever be made at once, nor should any change be made which violates established principles, creates great inconvenience, or obliterates the radicals of the language. But gradual changes to accommodate the written to the spoken language, when they occasion none of these evils, and especially when they purify words from corruptions, improve the regular analogies of a language and illustrate etymology, are not only proper, but indispensable.

The basis of the changes in orthography made by Webster in this dictionary, as in his spelling book and Dissertations is that of uniformity and analogy. He attempts to extend the changes made in a few words of certain groups, such as the omission of u in error, candor, superior, of k in public, music, etc., to include all words of those groups. The practice of uniformity, which "is the most convenient principle in the structure of language," would cause us "to write defense, pretense, offense, recompense, etc. with s instead of c; for we always use that letter in the derivatives, defensive, offensive, pretension, recompensing."[59] Instead of settling the question of doubtful spelling by reference to the practice of modern writers, as was the custom in Great Britain, Webster attempts to trace the real orthography by discovering the radical words and ascertaining the primitive spelling.

By pursuing this principle, we arrive at a point which cannot be disputed; thus gradually settling controversies and purifying our language from many corruptions introduced by ignorance or negligence, during the confusion of languages under the first Norman princes. Without recurring to the originals, in the manner here stated, it is impossible, I apprehend, to adjust the orthography of many words in the language, or to purify it from numerous barbarisms.[60]

It is because of the etymology that Webster would omit k after c, for both have the same original character. K is also omitted in the derivatives, musical, publication, republican. Most modern writers, he says, reject the k from words in which it is useless, and it is desirable that dictionaries should add their authority to the practice.[61]

Webster makes very few changes in orthography except to correct the most palpable errors.[62] In a few instances, as in scepter, sepulcher, he has followed Newton, Prideaux, Hook, Dryden, Whiton rather than Johnson, as being more analogical and purely English. "In omitting u in honor and a few words of that class," he says, "I have pursued a common practice in this country, authorized by the principles of uniformity and by etymology, as well as by Ash's dictionary."[63]

As shown in his first dictionary, Webster has modified his

views regarding pronunciation since he wrote the spelling book and
Dissertations, for in those he expounded the theory that the English
language in America could be reduced to an immutable standard.
He has decided that the living language admits of no fixed state and
that a standard of pronunciation cannot be set up by which even the
educated will consent to be governed. The primary principles regu-
lating accent are ease of pronunciation and melody of sounds, and
it is fruitless to oppose the natural accent by artificial rules.

> Real improvements in pronunciation arise from a popu-
> lar tendency to abridge words which are of difficult pro-
> nunciation; to soften or reject harsh letters and syllables;
> and to give to letters and syllables such sounds, and to
> words such a disposition of accent, as best suit the organs
> of utterance and of hearing. Any alteration in pronuncia-
> tion which is not recommended by these advantages, will
> never become general. [64]

The rules for pronunciation are given on page xxiv. When a
vowel has the accent over it, its sound is long. When the accent
is placed after the consonant, the preceding vowel is short. When
the accented syllable contains a diagraph or diphthongal sound, the
sound being indicated with sufficient clearness by the letters, the
accent is placed at the end of the syllable, as in renew.' When the
pronunciation of a word is very different from that which the letters
naturally indicate, it is expressed by a different orthography. Ch
has the English sound, as in church, unless a different pronunciation
is noted. G retains its soft sound like j, as in general, unless
the contrary is noted. The direction given concerning a radical
word is considered as extending to all the derivatives. A double
accent thus, lo'gic, denotes that the sound of the succeeding consonant belongs to the first syllable. Silent letters are italicized. Webster explains the meagerness of his directions for pronunciation by
saying that in regular words, which make up nine-tenths of the total
number, the accent alone is sufficient to teach the pronunciation.
"The accent being laid on the right syllable and letter, and the accented vowel correctly pronounced, the pronunciation of the unaccented vowel is extremely easy; so easy indeed, that it is more difficult
to be wrong than right. "[65] In the matter of representing pronunciation he makes two improvements. One is his departure from the
rule that in indicating the accent a single consonant between two
vowels must go with the latter syllable, and the other is the omission of diacritical marks on unaccented syllables. Definitions are
very brief and there is no attempt at etymology.

The Dictionary had a hard time making itself felt in the face
of the adherents to the English standards. In Boston the Monthly
Anthology and Boston Review, "Edited by a Society of Gentlemen, "
tried several times before it succeeded in getting someone to attempt
a review of the Dictionary. According to the Journal of the Proceedings of the Anthology Society, the Dictionary had been assigned
on April 11, 1806 to Mr. Buckminster for review. In July it was
assigned to Mr. Shaw "to write or procure to be written a review. "

The matter rested until October, when John Pickering was asked to do it, but refused, whereupon it was given to Rev. Samuel Willard. Six months later when the review was still not written, James Savage offered to attempt it and on October 10, 1809 it was read. Mr. Buckminster objected stoutly and Dr. Kirkland feebly to the first paragraph. After slight alteration, it was accepted. [66] A few selections from the review will illustrate its attitude.

> ... The English language is not indeed to be corrupted by a single writer, or undermined by a whole fraternity. It will continue in its present state as long as the rock-rooted seat of our forefathers is venerable for genius, learning, arts, liberty, religion, and law, and until these are forgotten by their descendants. But a temporary departure from the standard may be produced in a small part of our country by men, whose justification of the vulgar procure them adherents, and whose pride will be engaged to extol their exertions, since they have so long digged in the rubbish of antiquity, that everything discovered is thought to be a treasure. In fifty, or perhaps a hundred of our village schools this Compendious Dictionary of Mr. Webster is insinuating suspicions of the definitions of Johnson, justifying ridiculous violations of grammar, and spreading hurtful innovations in orthography.
>
> ...
>
> Over the orthography of our language Mr. Webster, in his twenty years warfare, has triumphed more frequently than the many millions who have written it for nearly a century and a half. If we may recur to his former heresies, we should declare him the wildest innovator of an age of revolutions; but we feel some pleasure in informing the public that he has abjured many of his first errours. Still his plan is injudicious and even impracticable; for who will follow him who declares that nobody should be followed, who forbids us to walk as the countless majority of our predecessors have walked? He says, that the orthography of our words ought not to be settled; ...
>
> ... We have, at every step, found Mr. Webster in pursuit of some novelty inconsistent with the settled grammar and orthography of our language, or carrying his correct principles too far to be useful. We are completely satisfied that he must change his original views before his work will be worth relying upon; and we believe that diffidence of the value of his own discoveries and a decent estimation of the knowledge of his predecessors is more necessary to his success, than the most laborious researches in etymology.
>
> ...

> ... We have marked with candour the most prominent
> faults in this work; and if it be asked why so little is
> said in commendation of it, we shall desire every one to
> compare it with Johnson. That some words of real value
> and importance are found in it, which are not found in the
> standard Lexicon of our language, is readily admitted; but
> so many dangerous novelties are inserted, that no man
> can safely consult it without comparisons with others.
> From the future labours of Mr. Webster we expect some
> amusement and some advantage in explaining our language,
> so far as its Saxon derivation is concerned; but he must
> remember that a volume of the Augustan age of our litera-
> ture is of more value than all the play-things of etymolo-
> gy. [67]

Josiah Quincy, whom Webster had asked to criticize the Dictionary, shows a more friendly interest than does the critic in the
Monthly Anthology. In a letter, written June 30, 1806, he expresses the belief that the new dictionary will be treated with indulgence
by men of literary inclination in the neighborhood but advises Webster not to invite newspaper notices of it until it has become better
known since some person of sarcastic temperament might be stimu-
lated to exercise himself upon it and thus give it a temporary unpo-
pularity. [68]

A letter from Thomas Dawes, Webster's brother-in-law,
August 14, 1806, reveals that Webster's Dictionary had been severely criticized in a newspaper and that Webster had answered the criticism, accusing the critic of malignity. This accusation Dawes
thinks is unjust. He is inclined to favor a "middle path between
yourselves and the players. Chooseday for Tuesday I cannot bear,
and as to keind, it sits worse on my stomach than Indian Root.
But I aint yet quite ripe for your Orthography. Still, I dare not
make up my judgment in a matter which has never been my study,
against a learned, laborious, ingenious, experienced investigator. "[69]

In a letter written in November of the same year, John
Quincy Adams discusses the three objections to the Dictionary made
by the newspaper critic as relating first to the peculiarities of
spelling, second to the principles of pronunciation, and third to the
introduction into the Dictionary of local vulgarisms. Adams offers
his opinion regarding the making of a larger dictionary which Webster was evidently contemplating and advises Webster to keep a
conservative position since spelling and pronunciation are dominated
by fashion and therefore not worth contending about. Regarding the
insertion of new words Adams thinks the Compendious Dictionary is
sufficiently liberal. [70]

The charge made against Webster by a writer in the Albany
Sentinel (probably the newspaper mentioned above), of introducing
too many local words into his Dictionary, was answered by Jeremiah
Atwater, of Middlebury College, Vermont, in a letter to Webster on

October 3, 1806. Atwater praised the Dictionary very highly and expressed the opinion that local words are always with propriety inserted in dictionaries, especially when marked as being local.[71]

In 1807 Timothy Dwight, president of Yale College, and nine members of his faculty wrote and signed the following statement for Noah Webster:

> The insertion of local terms in your small Dictionary, we approve. No good reason can be given, why a person who meets with words of this kind, should not be able to find their meaning in a Dictionary: the only place where it can usually be found at all. Nor can we see, why a Liberty granted to other Lexicographers, should be denied to you.[72]

It appears that Webster sent copies of his Dictionary to many of the colleges expecting in return letters recommending the book. Such a letter is one signed by the president and several professors of Williams College, December 10, 1806, containing the following postscript:

> P. S.
>
> Have you sent a copy of your dictionary to my brother in law, President Sanders of Burlington? If you have not, and will send one to me, I will forward it to him. In a letter which I wrote to him yesterday, I told him what the Colleges were doing to give circulation and celebrity to the work.[73]

Samuel Smith, of Princeton, although agreeing in the main with the plan of the Dictionary, thinks that the work will meet with more success if Webster does not "too strenuously attempt to maintain the peculiarities of what is called the New England pronunciation, particularly in those words in which it converts the sound of the long u into oo or e."[74] The long u, he thinks, will ultimately prevail in the American States.

Regarding Webster's orthography as exhibited in the Compendious Dictionary, a reviewer, writing a short time after the appearance of the Dictionary, acquiesces in Webster's preference of hainous to heinous; drouth and highth to drought and height; public to publick; scepter and theater to sceptre and theatre; but thinks that the omission of u from words originally Latin, which came into the English language through the French, such as honour, favour, etc., militates against the rule usually referred to in questionable cases, that of preferring the orthography of the language from which a word directly comes to ours. He also thinks that the omission of the final e in such words as determine, doctrine greatly lessens the utility of the Dictionary.[75]

The same reviewer agrees with Webster in blaming Sheridan

for sounding the a in father and in fat alike, but thinks that Webster goes too far in representing ti before a vowel as always equivalent to sh. On or ous, after ti, ci, si form but one syllable in pronunciation; but ingratiate, official, etc. are inadequately expressed by ingrashate, offishal.[76]

In the Preface to the first dictionary, which was "intended for a convenient portable book for gentlemen, and for the highest seminaries of learning, " Webster promises that an abridgment will be published at a reduced price for the use of Common English schools. This abridgment appeared the next year. In the Preface to the abridged edition the author says:

> The Compendious Dictionary which I published the last year, being intended to comprehend a complete vocabulary of English words now in use, with brief definitions, forms a convenient book for the definition of adults; but is rather too expensive for common schools; and contains many difficult terms of science, with which common readers of English have no concern. It is believed that an abridgment of that work containing all the words which common people have occasion to use, and sold at a less price, will be well received by the great body of farmers and mechanics in the United States. Every family and every child in school has occasion for such a Dictionary.
> In consulting the convenience of purchasers, I have not, however, proceeded so far in reducing the size and price, as to sacrifice the essential benefits of a dictionary, by omitting a great number of legitimate words of popular use. To retrench words of common use, with a view to render a book cheap, is not to consult the real interest of the purchaser; but rather to defraud him. A Dictionary ought not to be an imperfect vocabulary; nor can any work of this sort contain much less than thirty thousand words, without the omission of terms which are in daily use. I have endeavored by steering between extremes, to reconcile the interest of the purchaser's purse, with the advantage of a tolerably complete Dictionary.

Regarding the abridged edition of his dictionary, Webster wrote to Joel Barlow, October 19, 1807:

> ... I have in the press an abridgment of my Complete Dictionary for common schools, omitting obsolete, and technical terms, and reducing it to a dollar book. With the profits of these I hope to be able to finish my Complete Dictionary.... [77]

The Dictionary of the English Language; compiled for the Use of Common Schools in the United States contains 306 pages as compared with over four hundred pages in the first dictionary, and the pages of this dictionary are five lines shorter than in the early dictionary. In the second dictionary 303 pages are devoted to the

dictionary proper and 3 pages to a Chronological Table of Remarkable Events. The tables of weights, money, etc. included in the
Compendious Dictionary are omitted in the second one.

One of Webster's friends thinks that the School Dictionary
will supersede the numerous imperfect ones heretofore published.
He is especially pleased with it because it answers the purposes of
a dictionary as well as a larger edition, and is much less in price.
He says that he has used the Compendious Dictionary in the instruction of a class of young ladies, among whom were his own daughters,
and has found "none so useful, none so correct."[78]

Another person writes in April 13, 1853, that the feeling of
exultation with which he first looked over the pages of Webster's
school Dictionary several years previous had remained with him.
"In the language of a justly celebrated teacher of New Hampshire,"
he says, "there was no 'tshuing' then, but simple common sense,
founded on the use and derivation of the words, in spelling and pronunciation."[79]

An American Dictionary of the English Language

At the close of the Preface to A Compendious Dictionary,
Webster announces his intention of compiling and publishing a full
and comprehensive dictionary of the language. After answering the
objections which candid friends might raise, he expresses his contempt for and independence of those people "whose veneration for
transatlantic authors leads them to hold American writers in un-
merited contempt," and sets forth as his purpose, however arduous
the task, to make an effort to break this bond of attachment to
foreign writers.

The first dictionary had to create its own demand. Webster
tried to insure the success of his larger dictionary before he began
work on it. As early as February 17, 1806, he sent copies of his
first dictionary to the presidents of the colleges of the northern
states. Accompanying the Dictionary was a letter inviting the attention of the presidents to his dictionary and asking their opinion regarding the contemplated revision, for he felt that the labor of the
work would be so great that he would not be justified in prosecuting
it without the certainty of success. He concludes:

> ... If the Colleges and literary gentlemen of the north-
> ern states should generally approve of the Dictionary now
> published & receive it into use, I shall deem it safe to
> proceed with the great Work - if they should disapprove
> & neglect this, it will be imprudent for me to prosecute
> my design & I must abandon it - ... [80]

In 1807, Webster also began to inquire as to the possibility
of success in obtaining subscriptions to help him carry on his

philological studies. In this he was to find that he would receive
little encouragement. In May 1807, Rufus King wrote to Webster
from New York that he was able to discover but little probability
that he would receive adequate encouragement to continue to devote
his time and talents to his laborious investigation. Wealth and power, he said, seemed to be the ruling passions of the people, to the
neglect of learning; and even the best men could hardly be roused
from their intellectual torpor. [81] Thomas Dawes, Junior wrote to
Webster from Boston in August of the same year, that he was fear-
ful that Webster would lose money by his intended work. He also
says that Mr. Shaw had prevented several criticisms of Webster
from appearing in the Anthology because he thought Webster ill-
treated in them. [82] In September, 1807, Oliver Wolcott wrote to
Webster from New York that the size of the dictionary, the manner
in which it is to be published, and the sum required were causing
many people to object to his proposal. He concluded by saying that
he could not encourage Webster to expect success by means of popular subscription unless the public impressions elsewhere were different from those in New York. [83]

On February 25, 1807, Webster wrote a Circular Letter, entitled "To the Friends of Literature in the United States," in which
he made a plea for assistance in carrying on his chosen work. After giving a resumé of his philological labors, he said that the work
on the Dictionary had enlarged so much that the state of his property would not justify the prosecution of it entirely at his own expense.
The labor of eight or ten years was of itself a great sacrifice, to
which must be added the expenses of his family and the cost of
many books. Since similar undertakings in Great Britain had been
supported by contributions, he thought that the lovers of learning
in the United States would aid in like manner any design that promised to enlarge the sphere of knowledge. The two modes in which
friends of the undertaking might assist were by contributions in
money and by extending the use of his school books, which would
augment his own resources. [84]

Webster also wrote to many of his friends to ascertain their
opinions as to his contemplated undertaking. On October 19, 1807,
in a letter to Joel Barlow he expressed himself as very much pleased with Barlow's favorable opinion concerning his Dictionary, for
Barlow, he thought, belonged to the group of "classical scholars"
whose opinions were valuable. He also said that he hoped the profits from his dictionaries (1806-1807), would enable him to finish
his Complete Dictionary, a work which would require the incessant
labor of from three to five years. He felt that if he could get two
or three hundred subscribers to advance the price of the dictionary,
the amount thus obtained would be all he should need. His view,
he said, comprehended a whole system, intended to lay the foundation of a more correct practice of writing and speaking, as well as
a general system of instruction in other branches. He felt that
Great Britain was probably in her decline and that it was time for
the people of America to think for themselves. His plan was to
correct rather than to innovate. [85]

Another letter followed on November 12, 1807, in answer to Barlow's reply, in which Webster lamented the fact that America looked too much to Great Britain for opinions and facts regarding language, hence putting an end to inquiry and thereby checking improvement. Our literary men were so prone to accept, without question, anything that came from English authors of reputation that numerous errors, daily propagated from English presses, had become current in this country. In the same letter he mentioned the difficulties regarding his larger dictionary:

> The outline was drawn more than twenty years ago, but my circumstances compelled me to suspend the execution of it, for the purpose of getting bread by other business, until within a few years last past. Even now my resources are inadequate to the work; my income barely supports my family, and I want five hundred dollars' worth of books from Europe which I cannot obtain here, and which I cannot afford to purchase. I have made my wishes known to men of letters by a circular accompanied by certificates, and have issued a subscription paper, but I have not any encouragement that one cent will be advanced by the wealthy citizens of my country. I must therefore drudge on under all the embarassments which have usually attended like undertakings. [86]

In a letter to James Madison written a few days before Madison was to succeed to the presidency, Webster expressed his disappointment at the failure of his subscriptions and suggested that Madison appoint him to a government position abroad so that he might be able to continue the work on his dictionary. Whether or not Madison answered the letter is not known. [87] In July of the same year Webster wrote to Judge Dawes regarding his discoveries in language. He was not able to state when his dictionary would be completed, since new discoveries added daily to his problem. In true Websterian fashion he wrote at length of his discoveries and said that on the following points he had already obtained "most satisfactory evidence."

> 1. That the opinion of the descent of all nations from one pair, is well founded, and susceptible of new and satisfactory proof.
> 2. That whatever differences of dialect might have been introduced at Babel, languages entirely different were not formed, as the radical words in the principal languages of Asia, Africa and Europe are still the same.
> 3. That although the oldest writings extant are in the Hebrew language, yet the Hebrew language is not older than the Arabic, Celtic, and Teutonic.
> 4. As a consequence of the facts above stated, it is found necessary to recur, in some cases, to the languages of nations who migrated far to the west, south, and north, to find the radical signification of Hebrew words....
> 5. From a series of facts, it is demonstrable that the

> ancestors of the western nations of Europe inhabited Syria and Judea, anterior to the settlement of the Hebrews in that country; which the Jewish writers retained in the Celtic and Teutonic dialects; but which cannot be translated by Hebrew roots. ...

Webster, in this same letter, included a paragraph which by this time had become a sort of refrain to his letters.

> I have accumulated such a mass of materials for a Dictionary, materials which no other person could use to advantage, that I think it my duty, as it is my pleasure, to prosecute the work; provided I have health to sustain the labor, and property to defray the expenses, of the compilation. But I fear my pecuniary resources will not be adequate; and that the past labor of some years will be lost, from inability to prosecute the design. Were I a single man, I should probably leave my country, and seek patronage in a country where undertakings of this kind are never neglected, much less opposed.
> The labor requisite to accomplish the work upon my plan is certainly double to that which Dr. Johnson bestowed upon his dictionary. My etymological inquiries alone (a part of the subject on which Johnson bestowed no great pains, as he merely copied his etymologies from other authors) will probably incur as much labor as the whole execution of Johnson's works - But I am persuaded that the fruits of the investigation will repay the labor.

There was also a long discussion of the defects of English dictionaries. To supply these defects was a "very important part" of his design. He hastened to quiet the fears of those who were solicitous about the proposed orthography by assuring them that established orthography would not be disturbed, and only those changes would be administered which would correct the most palpable errors.

In April, 1808, Webster made a public profession of his faith. His "Reasons for Accepting the Christian and Calvinistic Scheme," published in The Panoplist, July, 1809, [88] aroused much interest in theological circles and was partly responsible for his ill-success in obtaining subscriptions to his Dictionary, as is seen in the following selection from a letter from Moses Stuart, March 16, 1810.

> The Anthology is outrageous against you. I believe it will do good, & promote the very cause, which it means to destroy. May the Lord turn their haughty & unfriendly designs into foolishness! Be assured, the object of their vengeance is more against your religion than against you; & be also assured, that your friends will view things, in their just light. [89]

The same idea was expressed by Thomas Dawes in a letter of January 12, 1811.

> Within a few days I shall converse with John West upon your subject. But what can be done, I know not. If I had any particular expectations or hopes, or any plan in my head for your succour, I would not now mention it, from a fear of your being again disappointed. It would be a useless task to say why your hopes were not realized before. But soon after your visit in this quarter I could perceive a sudden alteration in the intentions of some of the Bible Society to whom I believe some of your observations in some circles had been aggravated. Cabot who had taken up your case pretty zealously, as I thot, had dropped it. I tho't the same of a number of others. Your 'overweaning fondness for Morse and Griffin and that may be called Andover' was mentioned to me. I think I have the expressions. Now if I thought you could tell this, I should be afraid to write you again. But I believe many thought that your Dictionary would be tinged with the 'peculiar doctrines,' as Doctor Morse entitled your letter in the Panoplist. They thought your own sentiments would get into the work, as the true and only definition, as Johnson defined excise from his own politics, and Oats as bread for Scotsmen. I have now hinted only my suspicions of the cause of your disappointment about the help in these parts. I think there was another. Many men are loth to advance money for a book to be finished 12 years hence, when the author may be impaired or in his grave; tho' such men will not confess such motives; being unwilling to be thought niggardly. Another circumstance, I believe, diverted those who intended to subscribe only from charitable motives. I mean the story that you were so very dear to the Andoverians, you would certainly be one of their professors.... 90

In 1810, Webster published the "Prospectus of a New and Complete Dictionary of the English Language," in which he stated that in the forthcoming work he attempted the following objects.

> 1. To comprehend all the legitimate words, in the English Language, common and technical, with perspicuous and discriminating definitions, exemplified by authorities, in all cases in which authority is deemed necessary to vindicate the use of a word, or illustrate its signification. This article includes the new terms in chemistry, mineralogy, geology, botany and zoology.
> 2. To contract the size of the work within the smallest compass that is consistent with the comprehensiveness of its design; and by reducing the price considerably below that of Johnson's larger work, to render it more accessible to men of small property.
> 3. To exhibit the true orthography and pronunciation of words, according to the most approved English practice.

    4. To explain obsolete words, found in ancient English authors. These words will constitute a separate department of the work.

    5. To deduce words from their primitive roots, and exhibit the affinity of the English Language, with various other Languages. This part of the work will be new, and will offer results singularly novel and interesting; unfolding the connection between the languages of the principal races of men, consisting of the Assyrian stock in Asia and Africa; and of the Celtic and Teutonic, in Europe. [91]

Webster also stated in the <u>Prospectus</u> that the work would probably form three octavo volumes and could not be afforded for less than twelve or fifteen dollars. Since the execution of the work would probably occupy a large portion of the compiler's life, and cost about fifteen thousand dollars, he again invited subscriptions to the work to aid him in his task. He suggested that since the exact price could not be determined, the subscribers advance only a part of the price, the remainder to be paid when the book was delivered.

On February 12, 1811, Webster wrote to Josiah Quincy that he had, within the last two years, made discoveries in language which if ever published would interest the literati of all Europe and render it necessary to revise all the lexicons, Hebrew, Greek and Latin, now used as Classical Books. He said that his resources were almost exhausted and that in a few days he would sell his house to obtain bread for his children. All the aid that he had expected to receive from New York, Boston, etc. had failed and he would soon retire to a cottage in the country. [92] This was accomplished in September, 1812, when he moved from New Haven to Amherst, then only a small farming town. Here he not only was able to reduce his living expenses, but also was free of many distractions that interfered with his work.

    In the second story of his new home, in a large room, with windows looking to the south and east, Webster set up anew the large circular table which he had used for some years at New Haven. This table was about two feet wide, built in the form of a hollow circle. Dictionaries and grammars of all obtainable languages were laid in successive order upon its surface. Webster would take the word under investigation and standing at the right end of the lexicographer's table, look it up in the first dictionary which lay at the end. He made a note, examined a grammar, considered some kindred word, and then passed to the next dictionary of some other tongue. He took each word through the twenty or thirty dictionaries, making notes on his discoveries, and passing around his table many times in the course of a day's labor of minute and careful study. This was comparative philology which has given such great results to modern philologists. Not in the study of the roots of language--few in number and to be most closely scrutinized--but it was the same method applied in a lesser and more general way to the whole English language. 93

In a letter to Webster May 31, 1813, John Jay expresses the belief that the fear that Webster's dictionary would tend to impair the sameness of the English and its orthography in England and America had an unfavorable influence on the success of the subscriptions. 94 A letter from Jay, dated June 19, 1813, shows that Jay had come to the assistance of Webster in a financial way. 95 That Jay's interest in the dictionary did not disappear is shown by another letter to Webster written eight years later which contained an order for two copies of the dictionary for his two sons. 96 Later he ordered six other copies. 97

After Webster had carried his work through two letters of the alphabet, consciousness of his ignorance of the origin of words caused him to lay aside his work while he spent ten years making a comparison of words having the same or cognate radical letters, in about twenty different languages--the Chaldaic, Syriac, Arabic, Samaritan, Hebrew, Ethiopic, Persian, Irish, (Hyberne, Celtic), Armoric, Anglo-Saxon, German, Dutch, Swedish, Danish, Greek, Latin, Italian, Spanish, French, Prussian, with the English. The basis of comparing the primary elements was the consonants, the vowels having been found "so mutable as to be of no use." After completing the task, Webster says, "The result has been to open what are to me new views of language, and to unfold what appear to be the genuine principles on which these languages are constructed."98 Webster attempted to publish the work, which he called A Synopsis of Words in Twenty Languages, by private subscription, and failing in this, hoped to include it as an Appendix to his Dictionary, but there were not types in the United States to print it, and it has never been published. The manuscript is now in the New York Public Library.

That Webster intended seriously to publish the Synopsis is seen by the title page of his Dictionary which he sent to America while he was in England. It is as follows:

A Dictionary of the English Language Containing

    1.   The words used by the English nation and their dependents from the age of Gower to the present time, forming the most complete vocabulary of the language ever published.

    2.   A developement [sic] of the origin and primary sense of words, as far as these have been discovered; with a new exhibition of affinities between the English and other languages.

    3.   Definitions of words, more full, precise and technical, than those of preceding Lexicographers, illustrated by numerous examples.

    4.   The addition of new words, which the modern discoveries and improvements in the sciences and arts, have introduced into respectable use -

> To which is added, in a separate volume
>
> A Synopsis of the principal uncompounded or elementary
> words, in more than twenty different languages, alpha-
> betically arranged, with numerous references to their re-
> spectable affinities. By Noah Webster, LLD. [99]

In 1821 the work on the Dictionary had progressed as far as
the letter H. Webster at this time was sixty-three years of age.
He had spent about twenty-five thousand dollars on the work, and
all of it except about one thousand dollars had come from his own
income. At the same rate of progress, he calculated that it would
take him four more years to complete the work. His income at
this time was barely sufficient for his family expenses, and he still
needed many books to aid him in completing his task. He began to
think of visiting England and of attempting to sell the copy there
and revise the work at Oxford. [100]

Webster now gave almost his entire attention to the Dictionary.
His family became less expensive as his daughters married; and
his spelling book became more remunerative. In 1822 he resettled
in New Haven to keep his family nearer to communication during his
impending visit to European libraries. A letter from William Cranch,
March 1, 1824, to whom Webster had written for a letter of introduction to literary characters in Europe, contains the following paragraph, descriptive of the position that Webster held at this time.

> ... I have no doubt that your labours will be more
> justly estimated in England than they have been here. The
> greatest difficulty will be to make them believe it possible
> that any man but an Englishman can obtain knowledge of
> the English language. This country has not given you cred-
> it for one half your merit as a literary character, because
> you have been so unbending to the prejudices of our lit-
> erary men. If you should go to Europe, I shall most sin-
> cerely wish you success because I think you deserve it;
> for I doubt whether any other man in England or America
> has ever bestowed so much literary labour in analyzing the
> english [sic] language. [101]

Webster sailed for Europe in June, 1824, his son William
accompanying him to serve as copyist. [102] An offer from his daughter Harriet (Mrs. Cobb) of one thousand dollars was accepted as a
loan, the amount later being repaid. [103] The voyage required twenty-
five days. They landed at Havre and went directly to Paris, arriv-
ing there in July, 1824. S. G. Goodrich describes Webster as he
appeared to him in Paris during the summer of 1824.

> ... I knew him [Webster] well, and must mention an
> incident respecting him, still fresh in my memory. In
> the summer of 1824, I was in Paris, and staying at the
> Hotel Montmorency. One morning, at an early hour, I
> entered the court of the hotel, and on the opposite side,

I saw a tall, slender form, with a black coat, black small-
clothes, black silk stockings, moving back and forth, with
its hands behind it, and evidently in a state of meditation.
It was a curious, quaint, Connecticut looking apparition,
strangely in contrast to the prevailing forms and aspects
in this gay metropolis. I said to myself-- 'If it were
possible, I should say that was Noah Webster!' I went
up to him, and found it was indeed he. At the age of
sixty-six he had come to Europe to perfect his Dictionary!
It is interesting to know that such tenacity of purpose, such
persistency, such courage, were combined with all the re-
fined and amiable qualities which dignify and embellish
domestic and private life. [104]

On August 1, 1824, Webster wrote to his wife from Paris
that he was as hard at work as ever, that he had found some books
suited to his needs, but that he would probably go to England in
September. Again on August 27, he wrote:

... I expect to leave Paris about the middle of September, having gained substantially what I wanted here. My
intention is to seat myself down at Cambridge in England,
where Dr. Lee resides, who has written me, that he
will lend me all the aid in his power.... [105]

In another letter to his wife, written September 8, 1824, Webster said that he had finished the examination of such books as he
wanted to see except one in the King's Library which was closed
during the month of September, and that he had obtained a passport
to England, for which place he expected to start on the thirteenth. [106]
By September 24, Webster and his son were settled at Cambridge,
ready to begin work. While there Webster used the reading room
of John Miller. [107] The college buildings were in sharp contrast to
those Webster was accustomed to see in America, and he describes
them as

... mostly old stone buildings, which look very heavy,
cold & gloomy to an American accustomed to the new
public buildings in our country. I have not yet seen the
inside of any of them. [108]

However, he seems pleased with the prospects for obtaining the
necessary books.

I think I shall be well accommodated here. I have obtained some books from a booksellers library, for a small
quarterly payment, & others I am to obtain from the University Library, by means of Dr. Lee's kindness. I have
made an agreement with Mr. Emmerson which saves me
the trouble of procuring the necessaries & comforts of
life, & I have nothing to do but to attend to my duties &
my business.... [109]

On October 16, 1824, Webster wrote to Mrs. Webster that he hoped to finish the copy of his dictionary by the month of May, if not sooner. Since the work could not, he thought, be printed in the United States because of want of types, he was thinking of petitioning Congress to grant him the privilege of importing copies of the book into the United States, free of duty, for five years, until the character and success of the work should be ascertained. Arrangements could then be made for printing it in America.[110] Through the influence of Daniel Webster, a distant kinsman,[111] the petition was granted, but not used, for, as will be seen later, the Dictionary was published first in America.

On December 20, 1824, Webster wrote to Dr. Samuel Lee and suggested that a delegation from Oxford and Cambridge meet to consult on the question of adjusting the differences that existed in the English language regarding spelling, pronunciation, and construction. He added:

> ... I would meet them with pleasure, & lay before them such points of difference in the practice of the two Countries, England and the United States as it is desirable to adjust, & the Gentlemen would consider any other points that they might think it expedient to determine. I would also lay before them some thoughts on a plan for correcting the evils of our irregular orthography, without the use of any new letters.[112]

Lee did not reply.[113]

In a letter, December 26, 1824, Webster complained of the weakness of his right thumb, "the strength of which," he said, "is almost exhausted." It is to be remembered that Webster himself performed the greater part of the manual labor on his dictionary.

> Such also was the fact with the Synopsis of Words in Twenty Languages, and indeed with the whole series of his productions from the earliest years of his life. He never had the aid of an amanuensis in any of his literary labors, except in the proof-reading of his Dictionary--and later in its revision, when his eyes began to fail him, at the age of eighty.[114]

Webster lived very little known in Cambridge until the last three weeks, when he was invited to dine with the Officers and Fellows of Trinity College. Other invitations followed. He took occasion, he says,

> ... to lay before the Gentlemen a general statement of what I have done & am doing, & what I wish in regard to the publication of my MSS. The Gentlemen take a great interest in my work, and some of them offered to subscribe for it. They also express great regret that they had not been made acquainted with me at an earlier period.

From these Gentlemen & from several wealthy families in
Cambridge, I shall receive very warm support. How I
shall fare in London, remains to be determined.... [115]

Horace E. Scudder writes, concerning Webster's work at
Cambridge:

> There is something in the whole undertaking, and in the
> mode of its execution, which makes one by turns wonder
> at the splendid will and undaunted perseverance of this
> Yankee teacher, and feel a well-bred annoyance at his
> blindness to the incongruous position which he occupied.
> One is disposed to laugh sardonically over this self-taught
> dictionary-maker, encamped at Cambridge, coolly pursuing
> his work of an American Dictionary of the English Langua-
> ge in the midst of all that traditional scholarship.... [116]

On February 14, 1825, Webster left Cambridge for London to
try to obtain a publisher for his Dictionary. He remained there only
a short while, and in June of the same year returned to the United
States. He had failed to secure an English publisher, since those
who were competent to undertake such a work were already involved
in a new edition of Johnson and were unwilling to put on the market
another which might come into competition with their own. [117] He
had spent two months in Paris and eight in England, where he had
finished the Dictionary in January. In a letter to Dr. Thomas
Miner, written from New Haven, November 21, 1836, Webster describes his feelings when he reached the end of his work.

> When I finished my copy, I was sitting at my table in
> Cambridge, England, January, 1825. When I arrived at
> the last word, I was seized with a tremor, that made it
> difficult to finish the work, and then walking about the
> room, I soon recovered. [118]

Soon after Webster returned to this country, the necessary
arrangements were made for the publication of the Dictionary. Sherman Converse of New York undertook the publication of the work in
America, but he had to send to Germany for types of the oriental
languages. He was probably unable to obtain even in Germany types
for the Russian, Gothic, Swedish, and Saxon words, since these are
printed in common letter. Both Converse and Webster began immediately to acquaint the public with the forthcoming publication.
Converse issued proposals for publishing the work by subscription.
The Dictionary was to be entitled An American Dictionary of the
English Language, and was to present the following improvements:

> Additional words amounting to 20,000, upwards of 5,000
> of which are modern scientific terms; precise and technical
> definitions; additional significations omitted in most other
> works, and amounting to between thirty and fifty thousand;
> new etymological deductions, etc. [119]

The work was to appear in two quarto volumes and the price was to be twenty dollars. Two thousand two hundred subscribers were secured. [120]

Webster wrote a long letter to the public, announcing that his Dictionary, which had required twenty years of labor and thirty thousand dollars in money, was now completed. He stated that his visit to England, partly to ascertain the real state of the language, had convinced him that no book in that country was considered as a standard in orthoepy. All of the English dictionaries, according to his opinion, were half a century behind the state of science. There seems to be a sort of incongruity in his insistence on his dictionary's being an __American__ one and his statements comparing the merits of his own with those of Walker's dictionary:

> ... I affirm that my own pronunciation which was introduced into my book long before the name of Walker was known in this country, coincides more nearly with all the good practice which I witnessed in England, than Walker's --not that I agree in all respects with that practice, but the differences are few in number. [121]

He promises the public that "Whatever is well executed in the English Dictionaries I shall receive, and give due credit to the authors; ... Whatever is deficient, I shall supply, as far as I am able, and what is palpably wrong, I shall correct."[122] His method of advertising his dictionary seems to be to discredit other dictionaries and to show wherein his own remedies all defects. Since Walker's was the dictionary most favored in America, it seems to have been the one in which he found the greatest number of faults. In a publication (December, 1827) he asserts in very positive language that

> Walker's Dictionary is full of inconsistencies from beginning to end; and the attempt to make it a standard, has] done __more__ to __corrupt__ the __language__, than any event that has taken place for five hundred years past. No book is taken as the __ultimate__ __standard__ in England; and Walker's pronunciation __is__ __so__ __erroneous,__ that no less than three dictionaries have been published to correct it; all of them approaching much nearer to actual usage than Walker's. English gentlemen, with great unanimity declare, that Walker's is not their standard. Sheridan, Walker, Jones, Perry, and Jameson, all have their advocates; they all have their merits; but of all these __Walker__ __is__ __the__ __most__ __incorrect.__ [123]

The work of revising the manuscript and of reading the proof of the Dictionary was intrusted to James Gates Percival,[124] a poet and geologist who was also known for his linguistic attainments. Hezekiah Howe was chosen to superintend the printing. The material was put to press on May 8, 1827,[125] the work having been postponed because of delay in securing the types. To set it was an immense and tedious task. An insight into Percival's problem can be gained from his contract with Converse.

This Indenture witnesseth, That, whereas Sherman Converse proposes to publish an American Dictionary of the English Language by Noah Webster, LL. D. , and whereas said Converse has contracted with Hezekiah Howe, of New Haven, to superintend the printing of the same, it is mutually understood and agreed by and between said Converse and James G. Percival as follows, viz. : The said Howe is to read the first proof of said work, of each sheet as it comes from the press and by copy, to correct the same, and to furnish a clean proof; which clean proof the said Percival agrees to compare with the proof read by said Howe, to see whether the errors marked by the said Howe are corrected by the printer, and to mark such as are not; after which he is to read said proof with Mr. Webster by copy, which when read is to be corrected by the printer, and a clean proof taken for said Percival, and one for Mr. Webster; which clean proof said Percival is to compare with the one already corrected, and mark any errors previously marked, and not corrected by the printer. Said Percival is then to read the said proof, and Mr. Webster will also read his; which two proofs are to be corrected, and two clean proofs taken; which clean proofs said Percival is to compare with those already corrected, one of which Mr. Howe's printer is to read, and said Percival the other, and to revise both after they are corrected, by a clean proof, to stand by the form as it is going to press, to see that every error marked is corrected. Said Percival is to see that the last proof read is taken from the form after it is placed on the press for printing, in order to avoid errors by transferring it from the imposing-stone. All the above readings and revisions the said Percival is to give the said proofs promptly and faithfully, and at the time the said work requires, so as to facilitate as far as possible the progress of the work; and in no case is he to suffer any other engagement to interfere with a faithful execution of this contract. And if, in the judgment of said Percival, any additional reading or readings of any proof or proofs of said work shall be necessary, said Percival shall give it them. And the said Percival agrees to attend to the fulfilment of this contract, without interruption, from the commencement of the printing of said work to its completion, except prevented by sickness. And the said Converse agrees, on his part, to pay the said Percival eight hundred dollars for his said service, to be rendered as above, provided it takes not exceeding ten months to complete the work; and it is understood that one sheet of said work per day is to be executed. If it exceeds ten months to complete the work, then said Converse is to pay said Percival in proportion as for the ten months. Said Converse further agrees to pay said Percival one hundred dollars at the completion of each half volume, and the remainder at the completion of the entire work.

In witness whereof we have hereunto set out hands this
eleventh day of January, 1827, in New York. In presence
of Robert H. Davy, Henry S. Van Orden.

S. Converse
James G. Percival[126]

On July 4, 1827, a modification was made in the contract.
Percival was to receive two hundred and fifty dollars for extra service, which was to consist of a general inspection of the whole
manuscript and a particular inspection of all the scientific words, a
careful correction of errors which he might discover in such words,
and a careful attention to the alphabetical arrangement of the whole
vocabulary.[127] Percival later wrote that when fully employed on
the Dictionary, he received ninety-five dollars per month.[128]

Shortly after the work was begun Percival wrote:

The Dictionary is under way, but progresses slowly.
At the present rate of progression, it will be almost a
life-interest with me.[129] It obliges me to close and
lengthy application, but on the whole, it is not an unin-
teresting or uninstructive employment.[130]

In December, 1827, Percival wrote to George Hayward that
either he must give up his work on the Dictionary or it must be
essentially modified, since it was becoming too much for him to
endure. His demands were met by Converse, with whom his relation was always pleasant, although such cannot be said of his relations with Webster. One biographer attributes the friction between
Webster and Percival to the fact that both were independent and
firm, that when Percival thought he was right, nothing could change
him, and that he was probably a more thorough scholar in etymology
and the scientific bearings of words and was unwilling that any words
should pass through his hands unless they were correct in every particular. Webster did not feel that such accuracy was absolutely
necessary, and thought that his time was too valuable to be wasted
in controversies.[131] Some idea of the immensity of the task can be
gained from an account that Percival gives in a letter to George
Hayward, December 4, 1827, of the work required in getting out one
sheet.

... I begin (say Monday morning) at seven o'clock, A.
M., with reading the first proof from the manuscript, and
get it ready for the printer by five o'clock, P.M. I cannot
do it in less time. Then as soon as I can set about it, I
take up the manuscript for the next sheet, about which I
am often occupied till nine or ten o'clock. This depends
on the amount of revision. I am then quite exhausted
enough to go to bed. I take the manuscript next morning
early to the author and make revisions on his authorities,
and settle with him the corrections. This occupies till
ten o'clock, sometimes eleven or more. I immediately sit

down then to the second proof, which I complete by three
o'clock at least; after that I have to make two revisions, --
one at the press, --so that it is often seven o'clock before
all is finished. I have then an evening's laisure. This
has been my employment for most of six months; and I am
now done with it. I cannot, and will not go through twenty
months at least of such incessant labor; for it will take fully
that time to finish. The world may cry out what they choose;
but when I find myself bound by Gordian knots, I will
cut them. Some arrangement must be made to lighten my
task, or I shall resign it entirely. It is not necessary that
I should do all this; but my assistance, or that of someone
as competent, is absolutely necessary. Perhaps I have done
wrong in stating this to you, but I rely on your not betraying
me. My situation is therefore one of disgust and toil....
I regret that I have ever engaged in the thing. It will be
one of the miseries of my life to think of it; and I pray that
I may find a safe deliverance. As I find it, I appear to be
obliged to correct the blunders of ignorance. I feel like
the living tied to the dead.... [132]

Percival's work upon the Dictionary terminated in the early
autumn of 1828. Although Percival separated from it before it was
entirely finished, because of a misunderstanding between himself and
Webster, he was glad of the release. [133]

William C. Fowler, a son-in-law of Webster, says that during
the time the first edition of the large dictionary was in the press, he
was living with his wife and child in the home of his father-in-law,
and at Webster's request examined the sheets as they came into Webster's hands. In the course of nine months Webster read to Fowler
the Preface and Introduction, which he had shown to no one else, nor
expected to do so before publication. There were certain statements
in the Preface pertaining to the oppostion Webster had encountered,
and the ridicule he had experienced, which Fowler thought would be
injurious to him to publish, but which Webster was not willing to
omit. Fowler proposed to invite an advisory council composed of
President Day, Professors Silliman, Kingsley, Goodrich, Fitch, and
Olmstead, and others to decide the matter. This was done, and the
objectionable passages were erased. [134]

The Dictionary finally appeared, in 1828, in two large quarto
volumes. Volume I contains the words from A to I inclusive; Volume
II, those from J to Z inclusive. The pages are not numbered, but
there are approximately eight hundred pages in each volume. There
were over ten thousand pages of manuscript, the pages ranging from
two pages for the letter X to 1,346 for the letter S. [135] The title-
page is as follows:

An American Dictionary of the English Language: Intended to exhibit, I. The origin, affinities, and primary signification of English words, as far as they have been ascertained. II. The genuine orthography and pronunciation of

words according to General Usage, or to just principles
of analogy. III. Accurate and Discriminating definitions,
with numerous authorities and illustrations. To which are
prefixed, an introductory dissertation on the origin, history
and connection of the languages of Western Asia and of
Europe, and a Concise Grammar of the English Language.
By Noah Webster, LL. D. in two volumes. Vol. I. 'He
that wishes to be counted among the benefactors of posterity, must add, by his own toil, to the acquisitions of his
ancestors.' - Rambler. New York: Published by S. Converse, Printed by Hezekiah Howe, New Haven, 1828.

As stated in the Preface, the original design of Webster was
to limit his work "to the correcting of certain errors in the best
English Dictionaries, and to the supplying of words in which they
are deficient." This was later extended somewhat, and he restated
his purpose in the following language:

It has been my aim in this work, now offered to my
fellow citizens, to ascertain the true principles of the language, in its orthography and structure; to purify it from
some palpable errors, and reduce the number of its anomalies, thus giving it more regularity and consistency in
its forms, both of words and sentences; and in this manner, to furnish a standard of our vernacular tongue, which
we shall not be ashamed to bequeath to three hundred
millions of people, who are destined to occupy, and I hope,
to adorn the vast territory within our jurisdiction. 136

In the Preface Webster gives a summary of his philological
labors, beginning with the publication of his elementary spelling
book in 1783. He justifies the compilation of an American dictionary
on the ground that new and peculiar institutions in this country give
rise to new terms or to new applications of old terms unknown to the
people of England. "It is not only important," he says, "but, in a
degree necessary, that the people of this country, should have an
American Dictionary of the English Language; for, although the body
of the language is the same as in England, and it is desirable to
perpetuate that sameness, yet some differences must exist." He
asserts his pride in the fact that he can place as authorities such
Americans as Franklin, Washington, Adams, Jay, Madison, Marshall, Ramsay, Dwight, Smith, Trumbull, Hamilton, Belknap, Ames,
Mason, Kent, Hare, Silliman, Cleveland, Walsh, Irving, and many
others distinguished by their writings or science along with those
from England. After a life devoted to reading and to an investigation of the origin and principles of our vernacular language and to
an examination of the best American and English writers, he thinks
that the greatest English is as well preserved in this country as it
is in the best English writers.

... In this respect, Franklin and Washington, whose
language is their hereditary mother tongue, unsophisticated
by modern grammar, present as pure models of genuine

Two pages of Webster's manuscript of <u>An American Dictionary of the English Language,</u> 1828.

English, as Addison or Swift. But I may go further and
affirm, with truth, that our country has produced some
of the best models of composition. The style of President
Smith; of the authors of the Federalist; of Mr. Ames; of
Dr. Mason; of Mr. Harper; of Chancellor Kent; the prose
of Mr. Barlow; of the legal decisions of the Supreme
Court of the United States; of the reports of legal decisions
in some of the particular states; and many other writings;
in purity, in elegance and in technical precision, is equaled
only by that of the best British authors, and surpassed by
that of no English compositions of a similar kind. [137]

The American Dictionary was the culmination of Webster's
assertion of Americanisms In his American Spelling Book (1783) he
had said that "For America in her infancy to adopt the present maxims of the old world, would be to stamp the wrinkle of decrepit age
upon the bloom of youth, and to plant the seed of decay in a vigo-
rous constitution." [138] One of his six lectures delivered in Boston
in 1786 had for its subject, "Some Corruptions of language in England. Reasons Why the English Should not be our standard, either
in Language or Manners." [139] In a letter to Pickering the same
year he says:

I shall make one General effort to deliver literature and
my countrymen from the errors that fashion and ignorance
are palming upon Englishmen. The question will then be,
whether the Americans will give their opinions and principles as well as their purses to foreigners, and be the
dupes of a strolling party of players, who, educated in
the school of corruption, have no profession, but to make
people laugh, and who dependent on opinion for subsistence,
must conform to caprice, at the expense of every principle
of propriety.... Two circumstances will operate against
me. I am not a foreigner; I am a New Englandman. A
foreigner ushered in with titles and letters, with half my
abilities, would have the whole city in his train. [140]

In the Introduction to the American Dictionary Webster says,
speaking of orthoepy: "The time cannot be distant, when the population of this vast country will throw off their leading strings, and
walk in their own strength. "

That Webster was not entirely independent of English influences is shown by his writing to his friends about certain English pronunciation. William Samuel Johnson wrote to him from Stratford,
April 25, 1807, concerning the pronunciation in England of the word
nature. [141] Oliver Ellsworth wrote Webster in May, 1807:

In answer to your letter of the 11th, I can only say
that the standard sound of u in England or [as?] practiced
in the Universities & by the best-informed in London &
Bath, is yu; but that chu prevails among other classes,
so far as my very limited observations extended, as also

upon the Stage, of which I believe it to be an affectation. [142]

"Webster's American Dictionary of the English Language was a natural outcome of the prevailing tone of mind," says R. O. Williams, "and looking back upon its beginning we cannot help thinking that the undertaking was a very bold one. But the result is only one of the innumerable examples where success is reached by what seems inadequate means, if the times are favorable. "[143]

In an elaborate introduction of forty-three pages Webster presents his view as to the origin of language and the affinity or relationship of languages. He thinks that language, as well as the faculty of speech, was the immediate gift of God. His theory as to the affinity of language is that the languages of the East and West were originally the same, the variations having arisen from the dispersion of tribes and wandering groups into all parts of the world. Many words of the primary stock he supposes still to exist. To illustrate the affinity of the European and Oriental languages, he gives an extended discussion of the principal prepositions and prefixes. Regarding this division of the Introduction one critic made the following observation the next year after the publication of the Dictionary:

> ... In this part of the introduction, as well as in what he has said of the change of consonants and vowels, the change or loss of radical letters, and the change of the signification of words, with the various incidental topics discussed, the author will bear an advantageous comparison with any one who had before gone over any part of the same ground, and whose writings are known to us. We are not acquainted with the writer on these subjects, who is more entirely original, who has relied more on his own investigations, and who has been less swayed by mere authority; and we have seen no indication of a disposition to differ from others, from the mere love of singularity.... [144]

Charles Richardson, author of A New Dictionary of the English Language, says in a Prospectus to his Dictionary, regarding Webster's Introduction:

> ... There is a display of oriental reading in his Preliminary Essays, which, as introductory to a dictionary of the English Language, seems as appropriate and useful as a reference to the code of gentoo laws to decide a question of English inheritance. Dr. Webster was entirely unacquainted with our old authors; they must, too, be nearly inaccessible even to the literary classes of our American brethren; and it may be fairly anticipated that a Dictionary prepared upon a plan so totally different from that of their own countrymen, offering to their acceptance

such numerous specimen of sterling wealth, from the great
mine of their native English, will not be considered as a
superfluous addition to their libraries. [145]

In the Advertisement which precedes the Preface Webster
boasts of the fact that the American Dictionary contains twelve thousand more words than Todd's Johnson, which contains fifty-eight
thousand, the largest number in any dictionary up to that time; and
almost twice as many as those of Walker, Johnson, Sheridan, Jones,
and Perry, each of which contains approximately thirty-eight thousand. The words which according to Webster enlarged the vocabulary of this work are:

1. Words of common use such as grandjury, fracas, fire-
   warden, iceberg, parachute, repealable, revolutionize,
   oxydize, electioneer, savings-bank.

2. Participles of verbs, the omission of which in other
   dictionaries had resulted in much misspelling. The
   participles which had become mere adjectives needed
   a new definition to explain their meaning.

3. Terms of frequent occurrence in historical works,
   especially those derived from proper names, such as
   Shemitic, Punic, Augustan.

4. Legal terms, which are defined in this work with technical precision.

5. Terms in the arts and sciences. The exact number
   of these terms, now introduced for the first time is
   not short of four thousand. Assistance was given in
   this department by Olmstead and Silliman of Yale
   College, and James G. Percival.

Webster defends the introduction of newly coined words into
his Dictionary by saying that new terms are necessary for the progress in arts and sciences and it is the business of the lexicographer to insert and explain all words used by respectable speakers
and writers, whether the words are destined to be received into
general and permanent use or not. He has not gone as far as
Johnson and Todd have done in admitting vulgar words. [146]

Nearly the whole catalogue of obsolete words in Johnson
which was augmented by Mason and Todd have been inserted by Webster in his Dictionary. The list amounts to perhaps a thousand
words. Words local in England which occur in books read in the
United States are included, as well as law terms necessary to
gentlemen of the bar. A few Americanisms are admitted and noted
as peculiar to this country.

One critic who has carefully examined the vocabulary says
that the basis of Webster's vocabulary is that of Johnson, to which

Webster had added such new words as came his way.[147] For this use of Johnson Webster can hardly be blamed, since Johnson was entrenched in the public mind, but it led to his copying Johnson's bad points. Noah Porter says that Webster was not an indiscriminate collector of words, but was rather precise and fastidious on this point. If he discovered a word which did not suit his fancy or please his taste, he was rather slow to accept it even from the highest authority, or to yield it a place in his dictionary. But those words which had been long in use, especially in common life, and were a part of the speech of plain country folk, however homely and home-spun they were, he readily acknowledged to be English. His contribution of words that had been overlooked, and yet were neither new-fangled nor compounded, was not inconsiderable.[148]

It seems that a needless multiplication of the words in the Dictionary is the occurrence of the verbs twice, in the transitive and intransitive sense. Many Spenserian words, such as aby, adaw, certes, derring (daring), galage, gripple, rayne, housling, emper-ished, empight are included, as well as many Shakesperian words.

Webster says that nothing can be more disreputable to the literary character of a nation than the history of English orthography, unless it is that of orthoepy. The state of our written language is such that our citizens never become masters of orthography without great difficulty and labor, and a great part never learn to spell with correctness. The present orthography also leads to a false pronunciation.

Several attempts, he says, have been made to banish irregu-larities in spelling, the first of which was made by Sir Thomas Smith, Secretary of State to Queen Elizabeth, and the last by Ben-jamin Franklin, who compiled a dictionary on his scheme of reform and procured types to be cast, but never completed the publication. What course is a lexicographer to pursue in the face of so many irregularities? Shall he cite authorities in favor of each mode of spelling, with the result that so many names appear on one and so many on the other? Webster decided to conform the orthography to established English analogues. In many cases the old orthography is given in connection with the one prepared. His changes in spell-ing may be summarized under the following heads:

1. Words introduced from the Latin and Greek which our early ancestors spelled with both c and k, such as publick, musick, rhetorick, as a general rule, Web-ster spells without the k.

2. Words derived from the French all of which have not been Anglicized, such as metre, mitre, nitre, spectre, sceptre, theatre, Webster spells meter, miter, niter, specter, theater. The derivatives, centred, sceptred, sepulchred, he would also simplify.

3. A group of words, favor, honor, labor, candor, vigor,

inferior, ardor, terror, borrowed from the French
and Latin, from which Webster would eliminate the u
to make the analogy complete. He lays the blame for
establishing this error to Johnson who introduced these
words into the dictionary spelled with the u. Webster
says that in omitting the u he has followed the orthography of General Washington, of the Congress of the
United States, of Ash's Dictionary, and of Milford's
History of Greece.

4. Words such as defense, expense, offense, pretense,
   and recompense are written with the s instead of c,
   in comformity to their originals, and in correspondence
   with the derivatives, defensive, extensive, offensive,
   pretensive.

5. To preserve the proper pronunciation, the omission
   of the double l in befall, install, installment, recall,
   enthrall, etc. is not to be vindicated.

6. About eighty words which do not conform to the following rule Webster makes analogous. When a verb of
   two or more syllables ends in a single unaccented consonant preceded by a single vowel, the final consonant
   is not doubled in the derivatives. Also nouns from
   such verbs are written with a single consonant, as
   traveler, auditor, worshiper, laborer. In this Webster says he has followed one of the clearest analogies
   of the language, being also supported by the authority
   of Perry and Walker, as well as by the practice of
   distinguished writers.

Webster has a few words in the spelling of which he is at
least adventurous. Bridegoom is substituted for bridegroom, which
Webster says is a corrupted form that is a reproach to philology.
One critic states that this idea was not original with Webster, but
was put into his head by Horne Tooke.[149] Other words, the spelling of which was changed considerably are ieland, suveran, turnep,
and wo. For some words he gives two spellings, the first of which
indicates the preferred spelling. To this class belong the following
words: build, bild; group, groop; spread, spred; sepawn, sepon;
shamois, shammy; fat, vat; sheath, sheathe; turkey, turky; tongue,
tung; feather, fether; nuisance, nusance; thumb, thum; and neighbor,
nehbor. Acre and aker, deuce and duce, ranedeer and reindeer are
given in their respective places in the vocabulary. Molasses is given
as an incorrect spelling of melasses.

Webster thinks that since the language is the common property of the people, no individual has a right to change the established
orthography or pronunciation except to correct palpable errors and
to produce uniformity. "The man who perverts or changes the
established sound of a single letter, especially of a consonant, does
an injury to that language and to the community using it, which fifty

men of the same talents, can never repair. "[150] For this reason, he says, he has refrained from innovations as far as orthoepy is concerned. He feels that any attempt to indicate by characters the exact sound of vowels in unaccented syllables is calculated, in most cases, to mislead the speaker. The true pronunciation of words in a language cannot be completely expressed on paper, for it can only be caught by the ear and by practice. "It is for this reason that the notation of such vowels at all savors of hypercritical fastidious- ness, and by aiming at too much nicety and exactness, tends only to generate doubts and multiply differences of opinion. "[151] He says that no attempt has ever been made to mark the pronunciation of all the vowels in any other language, and in our language it is worse than useless. He thinks that in order to produce and preserve a tolerable degree of uniformity and the genuine purity of our language, two things are necessary: 1) To reject the practice of noting the sounds of the vowels in the unaccented syllables. 2) To banish from use all books which change the orthography of words to adopt the pronunciation of the fashion of the day. [152] The rule for syllabica- tion followed by the orthoepists by which "a single consonant between two vowels, must be joined to a latter syllable, " is arbitrary, ac- cording to Webster, and has for ages retarded and rendered difficult the acquisition of the language by children. The division of syllables should, as far as possible, be such as to lead the learner to a just pronunciation.

Webster thinks that the adoption of any scheme for removing the obstacles to English orthography must depend on public opinion. The plan that he has adopted for representing the sounds of letters by marks and points is intended to answer two purposes: to super- sede the necessity of writing and printing the words a second time in an orthography adopted to express their pronunciation, and to exhibit the outline of a scheme for removing the difficulties of our irregular orthography without the use of new characters. Under this scheme the visible characters of the language will present to the eye of a reader the true sound of words.

The standard Webster has used for determining the pronun- ciation of words in the American Dictionary has been that of respect- able English authorities, his own observations in both England and America, and the observations of American gentlemen of erudition who have visited England. [153] In general, the rules followed are these: 1) The usage of respectable people in England and the United States, when identical in the two countries, settled and undisputed. 2) When usage is unsettled or uncertain, the adjusting of the pronunciation to the regular established analogies of the language, as far as those can be definitely ascertained; with some regard for euphony, or the prosaic melody which proceeds from a due succession of accented and unaccent- ed syllables. [154]

In the case of some words, differently pronounced by respectable people, in which no decisive reasons appear for preferring one mode of pronouncing them to another, and either of which might be adopted with- out injury to melody or analogy, Webster has been guided by the rule of uniformity. In the instances where the common usage of a respectable portion of the people of this country accords with the analogies of the language, but not with the notation of English orthoepists, he has retained our own usage.

The key to the pronunciation is given in the "Directions for the Pronunciation of Words," which contains the basic statement that the "principal sounds of the vowels are the first or long, and the second or short." Examples of these two groups are given, followed by twenty-five rules for indicating the pronunciation of English words based on the accent and the sound of the vowel of the accented syllable. Rule I, which states that this mark, called an accent, designates the accented syllable, is typical of the list. A horizontal mark over a vowel indicates the long sound of the vowel. An accent placed after a consonant shows that vowel of that syllable if unpointed, is short; as in hab´it, ten´et. No diacritical marks are used except what Webster calls "pointed letters," as when a has the sound of aw in alter it is indicated by A. The grave accent is used before a vowel to indicate its Italian sound, as in àsk, b`ar, f`ather, m`ask. In words of two or more syllables, when no other accent is used, the grave accent designates the accented syllable. The pronunciation of derivatives follows the pronunciation of the radical or primitive in English. Before the letter r there is a slight sound of e between the vowel and the consonant, as bare, parent, pronounced baer, paerent. Words of anomalous pronunciation, not falling under the rules as given, are printed in an orthography which expresses their true pronunciation, as communion, communyon.

Regarding Webster's system of representing the pronunciation of words, Charles Richardson thinks that on the whole it is simpler and better than any before adopted, since the page is "not disfigured by the appearance of such ill-looking vocables as are sometimes made to represent the sounds in other dictionaries."[155]

Although to Webster the orthography of the English language is irregular and the pronunciation unsettled and corrupt, neither exhibits so strikingly the low state of philology as the etymological deductions of words, the history of their origin, affinities and primary signification. He says that a principal source of mistake on this subject is "a disregard of the identity of the radical consonants and a licentious blending and confounding of words, whose elementary letters are not commutable. Another source of error is an unwarrantable license in prefixing or inserting letters, for the purpose of producing an identity or resemblance of orthography."[156]

> ... first, the identity of radical letters, or a coincidence of cognates, in different languages; no affinity being admissible, except among words whose primary consonants are articulations of the same organs, as B, F, M, P, V, and W; or as D, T, Th, and S; or as G, C, hard, K and Q; R, L, and D. Some exceptions to this rule must be admitted, but not without collateral evidence of the change, or some evidence that is too clear to be reasonably rejected.

Second. Words in different languages are not to be considered as proceeding from the same radix, unless they
have the same signification, or one closely allied to it, or
naturally deducible from it. And on this point, much
knowledge of the primary sense of words, and of the manner in which collateral senses have sprung from one radical idea, is necessary to secure the inquirer from mis-
takes. [157]

In exhibiting the origin and affinities of English words the
corresponding word in the language from or through which it has
been received into the English language is given first; then the
corresponding words in the language of the same family or race;
and finally the corresponding word in the language of other families.
Thus of the word break taken from the Saxon, the Saxon word is
given first, then the same word in the other Teutonic and Gothic
languages, then the Celtic words, then the Latin, and lastly the Hebrew, Chaldaic, and Arabic. This order is not always followed, but
generally so. When there can be no rational doubt respecting the
radical identity of words, they have been inserted without any expression of uncertainty, otherwise the affinity is mentioned as a
probability. Words introduced into the English language in modern
times have been referred to the language from which the English
immediately received them.

It is generally conceded that Webster was at his best in the
making of definitions. Dr. James A. H. Murray called him "a
born definer of words."[158] Webster himself says that the great
and substantial merit of his dictionary for general use "must lie in
the copiousness of its vocabulary, and the accuracy and comprehen-
siveness of its definitions."[159] One critic says that "as a whole
Webster's definitions show a juster appreciation of values than those
of his predecessors, and often mark a medium between the extremes
of fullness and brevity of others."[160] His governing principles for
the manner of defining words is that of the primary sense which,
whenever it can be discovered, should stand first in order. Although this system is followed, there is nothing to indicate that the
secondary senses which follow proceed immediately from the root
sense or from senses themselves derivative. Webster says that he
has added between thirty and forty thousand definitions which are not
known to exist in any other work.[161] Regarding the use of illustrative citations Webster points out the principle that should govern
their use in a book: namely, to illustrate those definitions that are
not entirely evident in sense without the citations. In general, he
has illustrated the signification of words by a short passage from
one respectable author, often abridged from the whole passage cited
by Johnson. Only where the sense of a word is disputed does he
cite a number of authorities. Frequently the authorities are American writers. In many cases the brief illustrations are original; in
others, the names of the authors are omitted.

Noah Porter mentions among the defects of Webster as a
definer his not always exhibiting the various senses of words in the

order of their actual growth and historical development and his often
giving as a distinct meaning that which is simply a special application of a meaning already defined. Porter thinks that Webster's
numbered meanings are far too numerous, the attempted definitions
of which tend to confusion and embarrassment. He says that Webster often appends a string of words to a clear and well-announced
definition, an addition which tends to bewilder rather than to clarify.
Porter thinks Webster is sometimes over-diffuse and pedagogical,
but that he is also thorough, exact, painstaking, and precise. [162]

Webster was so desirous of giving information that he often
adds an item of special knowledge. Sometimes it is a little advice;
at other times it is a bit of homely wisdom, a practical or a moral
truth, or an interesting observation based on his New England environment. Examples of such definitions are as follows: "Dandy.
In modern usage, a male of the human species, who dresses himself like a doll, and who carries his character on his back. "
"Sauce. In New England culinary vegetables and roots eaten with
flesh. Sauce consisting of stewed apples is a great article in some
parts of New England: but cranberries make the most delicious
sauce. " "Sepawn, sepon. A species of food consisting of meal of
maiz boiled in water. It is in New York and Pennsylvania what
hasty-pudding is in New England. " "Stove. A small box, with an
iron pan, used for holding coals to warm the feet. It is a bad
practice for young persons to accustom themselves to sit with a
warm stove under the feet. " "Rail. In New England we never call
this series a rail, but by the general term railing. In a picket
fence, the poles or pickets rise above the rails; in a ballustrade, or
fence resembling it, the ballusters usually terminate in the rails. "
"Tackle. 2. To seize; to lay hold of; as, a wrestler tackles his
antagonist; a dog tackles the game. This is a common popular use
of the word in New England, though not elegant. But it retains the
primitive idea, to put on, to fall or throw on. " "Shaver. A boy
or young man. This word is still in common use in New England.
It must be numbered among our original words. " "Span. v. i. To
agree in color and size; as, the horses span well. New England. "
"Curfew. The ringing of a bell or bells at night, as a signal to
the inhabitants to rake up their fires and retire to rest. This
practice originated in England from an order of William the Con-
queror, who directed that at the ringing of the bell, at eight o'clock,
every one should put out his light and go to bed. This word is not
used in America; although the practice of ringing a bell at nine
o'clock continues in many places, and is considered in New England
as a signal for people to retire from company to their own abode;
and, in general, the signal is obeyed. " "Toast. Bread dried and
scorched by the fire. "

As was to be expected the Quarterly Review criticized the
Dictionary very severely. The following extract illustrates its
attitude:

We had seen Dr. Webster's work so highly praised,
particularly by his countrymen, that we were led to form

high expectations of its merit. These expectations have, in a great measure, been disappointed. We give the author credit for great industry--some of which is not unsuccessfully directed. He has added many words, and corrected many errors, especially in terms relating to natural history and other branches of modern science. But the general execution of his work is poor enough. It contains, indeed, the words in common use, with their ordinary acceptations, but conveys no luminous or correct views of the origin and structure of the language. Indeed, as an attempt to give the derivation and primary meaning of words it must be considered as a decided failure; and is throughout conducted on perverse and erroneous principles. The mere perusal of his Preface is sufficient to show that he is but slenderly qualified for the undertaking. There is everywhere a great parade of erudition, and a great lack of real knowledge; in short, we do not recollect ever to have witnessed in the same compass a greater number of crudities and errors, or more pains taken to so little purpose. In the sketch of languages, he describes Basque as a pure dialect of the old Celtic; it is neither allied to the Celtic nor to any other European family of tongues. He states further, that he 'has no particular knowledge of the Norwegian, Icelandic, and the dialects of languages spoken in Switzerland, further than that they belong to the Teutonic or Gothic family.' Could a man who professes to have spent half his life in comparing languages be ignorant that Icelandic is the venerable parent of the whole Scandinavian tribe; and, consequently, of first rate importance in tracing the origin of words? He discovers that the prefixed a in awake, ashamed, &c. is formed from the Anglo-Saxon ge - with which it has not the smallest connexion; and, moreover, that the same particle (ge) is retained in the Danish and in some German and Dutch words. It is notoriously of the most extensive use in Dutch and German--and the very few Danish words in which it occurs are one and all borrowed from the Lower Saxon. With equal felicity he asserts that the prefix be is of most extensive use in Danish and Swedish. Just as much as hyper and peri are in Latin; be like ge is in those two languages a borrowed particle, and from the same quarter. He thinks the negative prefix o in Swedish is probably a contracted word, being unable to perceive the German and English un. As might be supposed from these specimens--Dr. Webster's application of the northern tongues to English etymologies is often erroneous and perverse enough--it is, however, upon the whole, better than we should have anticipated from one so slenderly acquainted with their structure and peculiarities. He has taken great pains in collecting and comparing synonymes from different languages, and is often sufficiently happy in the explanation of individual terms. But the ambitious attempt to develope the radical import of words was an undertaking far beyond his strength and acquirements....

On the whole, Dr. Webster's quartos were hardly worthy of being reprinted in England.... [163]

Irrespective of the above remarks, the Dictionary was rather
well received in England, although it did not supersede Johnson except as to matter not included in Johnson. Of Webster's dictionary
the London Times says: "We can have no hesitation in giving it
our decided opinion that this is the most elaborate and successful
undertaking of the kind which has ever appeared;"[164] while the
English Journal of Education pronounces Webster "the greatest lexicographer that ever lived."[165] The Westminster Review characterizes this Dictionary as, to a large extent, an original work, abound-
ing in information adapted to the ordinary circumstances of life, and
in most curious philological observations. Although not sufficiently
historical or systematic to be the dictionary adapted to the feeling
and expectancy of the many enlightened and curious philologists of
the country, it is nevertheless a work of admirable practical utility,
and in the department of higher etymology provides much that will
enlighten and inform the most profound of our philologists.[166]

A. Roane says that, in his judgment, Webster's influence
upon our language has been most mischievous since, in the United
States, he has unsettled what before was fixed, and established an
additional rule where previously there was but one, that in attempting to carry out too far his principles of analogy, he sometimes
forgets that language itself is in part a thing of convention and usage,
and that uniformity in all cases is not so desirable as to be purchased at any sacrifice. He thinks, however, that Webster has
rendered a real service to English philology in the department of
etymology, and that his definitions are accurate and comprehensive,
but he protests against his radical innovations in orthography and
pronunciation. He says the merits of Webster may be thus described: "Derivations--capital, definitions--admirable, pronuncia-
tion--horrible, orthography--abominable."[167]

One critic summarizes the objections to Webster's writing
a dictionary under the following heads: 1) New dictionaries were
not wanted--the language was already embodied in Johnson. 2) To
enlarge the vocabulary would be to debase the pure sterling of
English speech. 3) The business of improving those already in use
belonged to the scholars of the parent country. 4) The introduction
of new words and new senses of words of American origin was de-
nounced as a project, the plain tendency of which was to corrupt
our speech by giving currency and show of legitimacy to local vulgarisms. 5) There was a general but not very accurately defined
apprehension in the public mind that in this dictionary some plot
was contriving against the purity of the language.[168]

Dr. Francis A. March, the Anglo-Saxon scholar, has charac-
terized Webster's researches in these words:

But Noah Webster had a genius for linguistic investigations which has not been surpassed by any English

lexicographer or grammarian. The dictionaries before
his time were in the first stage of philology, unorganized
accumulations of facts. Webster caught the spirit which
was beginning to move in France and Germany, and advanced from Horne Tooke to the second state. He grasped
the general principles of etymology; that certain root-sounds
have a definite sense which is the radical sense of all
words into which they enter; that the growth of words goes
on according to regular laws both of sense and sound; that
the various meanings of a word should be developed from
the radical meaning according to regular laws of philological suggestion; that all languages have like roots and laws,
so that a comparison of all should be made to throw light
on all, and on language in general; that letters of the same
organ interchange so that the recognizing of kindred words
is no guess-work. Noah Webster's life was nobly spent in
reorganizing English lexicography in view of these principles.... And he kept in mind the wants of the American
people. The merits and defects of his great work are
accordingly characteristic of America.

His independence is so--running sometimes into love of
innovation; any Englishman of that day would have simply
amended and enlarged Johnson and Walker. This is, on
the whole, a great merit. We have already said that it
advanced the philological stand-point a whole stadium. It
has also aided greatly in the improvement of the language....

Webster's Dictionary, then, is suited to the uses of the
American people, and well-deserves the popularity it has
attained. It is in its definitions, however, that its greatest worth is found. His attempt to deduce all of the
meanings of each word from one fundamental idea according to uniform laws of suggestion, naturally led him to
describe the ideas to be defined, and not to be content
with synonyms, and also led him to anticipate the changes
of meaning in individual words, and to be prepared with
distinctions carefully elaborated. His success has been universally acknowledged both in this country and abroad....

We have already said that the progress of modern philology has left Webster far behind....

The merit of Webster's definitions is such, that, until
another philological genius shall appear, with so superior a
method that it will be right for him to work into his book
the particular statements of Webster, we cannot hope to
have a popular dictionary which shall equal Webster as
a whole. [169]

The following comments are examples of extravagant praise
which the American Dictionary and its compiler received. The first
extract is from the Anniversary Address, delivered before the Connecticut chapter of the Phi Beta Kappa Society, by Chancellor James
Kent, of New York.

For nearly half a century, 'amidst obstacles and toils,

disappointments and infirmities,' he [Webster] has nobly
sustained his courage; and by means of his extraordinary
skill and industry in the investigation of languages, he
will transmit his name to the latest posterity. It will
dwell on the tongues of infants, as soon as they have
learned to lisp their earliest lessons. It will be stamped
on our American literature, and be carried with it over
every part of this mighty continent. It will be honored by
three hundred millions of people--for that is the number
which, it is computed, will, in some future age, occupy
the wide space of territory stretching from the Atlantic
to the Pacific Ocean, and from the torrid to the arctic
regions. The American Dictionary of the English Language
is a work of profound investigation, and does infinite honor
to the philological learning and general literature of this
country. Happy the man who can thus honorably identify
his name with the existence of our vernacular tongue.
There is no other way in which mortal man could more
effectively secure immortality beneath the skies. Obelisks,
arches, and triumphal monuments seem to be as transient
as the bubble of military reputation. No work of art can
withstand the incessant strokes of Time. The unrivaled
Parthenon, glowing in polished marble, and which, for
more than two thousand years, continued from the summit
of the citadel of Athens to cast its broad splendors across
the plains below, and along the coasts and head-lands of
Attica, is now crumbling to ruins, after being despoiled
of its most exquisite materials by savage war and heart-
less man. Even the Pyramids of Egypt, whose origin is
hidden in the deepest recesses of antiquity, and which have
always stood in awe-inspiring solitude and grandeur, are
now annoyed by the depredations of curiosity, and greatly
corroded by the elements, and gradually sinking under the
encroaching sands of the desert. This Dictionary, and the
language which it embodies, will also perish; but it will
not be with the gorgeous palaces. It will go with the
solemn temples, and the great globe itself! [170]

...

The scepter which the great lexicographer wields so un-
questionably, was most worthily won. It was not inherited;
it was achieved. It cost a life-struggle for an honest,
brave, unfaltering heart--a clear-serene intellect. No
propitious accidents favored his progress. The victory
was won after a steady trial of sixty years. Contemplate
the indices of his progress; for science, like machinery,
measures its revolutions. When the wheels of our ocean
steamers have moved round a million times, the dial hand
marks one. It was so with Galileo and Bacon--their books
marked their progress through the unexplored seas of
learning. It was so with Webster. When our republic
rose, he became its schoolmaster. There had never been

a great nation with a universal language without dialects.
The Yorkshireman can not now talk with a man from Corn-
wall. The peasant of the Ligurian Apennines, drives his
goats home at evening, over hills that look down on six
provinces, none of whose dialects he can speak. Here,
five thousand miles change not the sound of a word. A-
round every fireside, and from every tribune, in every
field of labor and every factory of toil, is heard the same
tongue. We owe it to Webster. He has done for us more
than Alfred did for England, or Cadmus for Greece. His
books have educated three generations. They are forever
multiplying his innumerable army of thinkers, who will
transmit his name from age to age. Only two men have
stood on the New World, whose fame is so sure to last--
Columbus, its discoverer, and Washington, its savior.
Webster is, and will be its great teacher; and those three
make our trinity of fame. [171]

That all was not smooth sailing for Webster after the publication of his Dictionary is shown by the attack made on him by Lyman Cobb who, in the years 1827 and 1828, a few years after he
himself had published a spelling book, began to publish in the Albany
Argus a series of papers, containing remarks on the American Spelling Book tending to show its imperfections. These papers were
signed "Examinator." In the following year they were published in
pamphlet form and were sent to various parts of the United States
by mail. Cobb's name was not signed as author, but on the back
of the title page was the following advertisement: "To Teachers,
School Committees or Inspectors, Clergymen, and to the Friends of
Correct Elementary Instruction. "

This critical review of Mr. Webster's Spelling Book is
submitted to your candid perusal and examination, with a
request that you will, after you shall have thoroughly and
impartially examined the defects of his book which are
pointed out in these numbers, and shall have become satisfied of their truth and importance, compare it carefully
with Cobb's Spelling Book, now before the 'publick,' in
which, it is believed, the defects contained in Mr. Webster's Spelling Book are remedied: You will thereby be
enabled to decide whether Mr. Webster's book, with all
its evident defects, should be longer retained in your
schools; and if not, whether Cobb's book ought to take its
place. It is also earnestly requested that each gentleman
who shall receive this review, will endeavor to procure
an examination of it by teachers and others of his acquaintance, who feels an interest in the cause of elementary
instruction. [172]

In the Evening Post of June 27, 1829, an article, nameless,
but later also shown to be by Cobb, entitled "Webster's Dictionary
and Spelling Book, " and addressed to the Editors, stated that the
Evening Post of May 28 gave the impression that the teachers in

New York had examined Webster's American Dictionary and were ready to adopt, as essential improvements, a series of smaller works which he was about to publish for the use of schools. In the same communication there also appeared an abstract of an unsigned report said to have been prepared by a committee appointed for the purpose and "read and accepted at a subsequent meeting." It also stated that between forty and fifty of the principal teachers in the city had manifested their approval of Webster's system of elementary instruction.

The author of the article thought it necessary that the public should be informed that Webster was present at the meeting for the purpose of forestalling public opinion relative to his forthcoming School Dictionary and Spelling Book. This, the author of the article considered as, to the highest degree, ingenuous and unfair, and said that no reliance could be placed upon the report of the committee since they had had it under examination only one week, with a view to a report, in which they mentioned its inadequacy, but that Webster gave only an abstract of the report and appended to it his own opinion of his new School Dictionary and Spelling Book. The course pursued by Webster, says the article, seems to be unjust. His spelling book, which has long been in use, is full of errors and defects. Many of the errors had been corrected only after they had been pointed out and exposed in the series of articles which had appeared in the Albany Argus. He says that in this revision Webster was assisted by Daniel H. Barnes, and that Aaron Ely, of New York, also aided in compiling the new spelling book, for which assistance he received one thousand dollars.[173]

This letter was answered in the issue of July 3, by A. M. Merchant, one of the three members of the committee which signed a report read at a meeting called at Public School No. 1, on May 25. Merchant says that the accusation made against Webster is a "most unjust and illiberal insinuation, and partakes too strongly of the effervescence of a jaundiced mind, deeply tinged with prejudice and jealousy." It is true, he says, that Webster was present at the meeting, as well as the author of Cobb's Spelling Book and Cobb's Walker, but that he [Webster] knew nothing of the sentiments of the language of the report before he came there. He says that Barnes did not assist in the compiling of the Elementary Spelling Book, although it was so intended, had he lived. However, it would not have mattered, since the making of the book was under Webster's supervision.

Another letter followed, in the Evening Post of July 7, 1829, signed by "A Schoolmaster." The author says that he knows nothing about the books, that he could not afford twenty dollars for the large dictionary, and the others were not yet ready for distribution, and that he thinks the majority of the teachers are no better off than he. He thinks it extraordinary that the few who had appeared to have judged both for themselves and for others should have hoped to do Webster a favor by publishing anonymously a report which could carry no more weight than their own signatures might have given it.

Deliberation, he says, was precluded by a vote taken against debate, and the number of those voting in favor of the report was evidently overrated.

In the Boston Courier of September 28, 1829, the publisher of Webster's Dictionary, in a communication addressed to the Editor, made the following appeal to the public relative to the criticisms recently published:

> Dear Sir, - Some twenty or thirty days since I believe, I was looking over a file of your paper, and fell upon a notice of some criticisms on Webster's Dictionary, which have appeared in the Morning Herald, in this city. As I am interested as Publisher of this work, any review which I might give of it, would be out of place. But while I leave others to review the work, it is but justice to the public, as well as to myself, to state the facts concerning these criticisms. They appeared under the signature of Inquirer. The author is a person by the name of Cobb, recently a schoolmaster, in one of our western villages, who has had the misfortune to compile a Spelling Book and a small Dictionary. [174]

Beginning July 4, 1829, a series of articles appeared in the New York Morning Herald signed by "Inquirer," who was again recognized as Lyman Cobb. He sets up as his thesis that justice to Webster and the importance of the subject required that the Dictionary be neither accepted nor rejected until it had been fully and candidly examined and compared with other works of the kind extant. This he takes upon himself to do. He says that any dictionary which is intended to be a standard of orthography must possess the following qualities in an eminent degree:

> 1. "Certain rules should be adopted and pursued through the several classes of words, and their orthography should be reduced to uniformity." 2. No innovation in orthography should be made, unless by the introduction of that innovation an "anomaly" is corrected and uniformity produced. 3. The orthography of the primitive and derivative words should be uniform and consistent. 4. The same words should not be differently spelled, either in the text, or in the definitions of other words; and want of decision in this particular alone, should be a paramount objection to the adoption of any dictionary as a "STANDARD OF ORTHOGRAPHY."

In the first six articles he shows that as far as the first three items are concerned, Webster has not, except in a very few instances, produced uniformity either in the rules he adopted or in the innovations which he has made.

In the first number (July 4) he states that it is his purpose to examine the work to ascertain whether Webster has "adopted certain rules or principles which he has pursued through the several classes of words, and reduced the orthography to uniformity"; or whether he has been under the "mischievous influence of innovation."

In the second number he examines the words coming under the rule laid down by Webster that k should be omitted in many words ending in ck, as publick, physick, garlick, etc., and that in all monosyllables in which a syllable beginning with e or i is added to the word, k should be used in the place of the Saxon c, as in licked, licking. He says that on examination he finds that Webster has retained the k in many words in which it is followed by e or i in forming derivatives, as lock, stock, attack, frolick, traffick, ransack, but has omitted it in physic and garlic from which physicking, physicked, and garlickeater are formed. Under the word unphysicked he has spelled physicked with k though he does not have k in physic. He has retained k in many words from which no derivatives are formed, and has omitted it in words of the same class, as almanack, bailiwick, barrack, bassock, bullock, frock, girrock, haddock, etc. He has inserted k after c in some derivative words, in which c is followed by a consonant, and omitted it in others, as frolickly, frolicksome, frolicksomeness, trackless, etc. and not in franticness, mimicry, publicly, publicness, and has inserted k after c in some compound words, and omitted it in others, as almanack-maker, barrack-master, and not in panic-grass, public-spirited.[175] Thus he shows to his own satisfaction that Webster is neither uniform nor consistent in this class of words.

The article next attempts to point out the difficulties that would arise if this class of words would end with c or k only. First, if k should be omitted in the primitive, it would necessitate the changing of the pronunciation of the derivatives since c is pronounced like s before e, i and y, and the sound of the primitive syllable or word would be lost in the derivative. Second, if c should be omitted in the primitive words, the k must be doubled in forming derivative words. He concludes that uniformity can be secured only by spelling all the words with ck in the primitives and k should be retained in the derivatives except when the k is followed by a, c, or u, unless the c be sounded like s in the derivative.

In the other articles he attacks with the same zeal the innovations of Webster with the purpose of proving that he has not been consistent and uniform. In the third article it is the discarding of u from such words as labour, rigour, vigour, inferiour, and words spelled with the terminations re that are discussed in detail; in Article 4 attack is made on Webster's spelling of words which end in ff, many of which Webster spelled with ff, and others with a single f; and the class of words which end in ence or ense, which Webster had changed to ense because of the derivatives. Mention is also made of the inconsistency and contradictions regarding the spelling of the word ache and its compounds as well as conscientious and analyze. Article V concerns the innovations regarding those words which usually end in l or ll, the spelling of which seems to vary according to the whim of Webster, as well as such words as traveler, counselor, which he spells with one l but includes two in chapelling, bordeller, medallist. In Article VI "Inquirer" shows in the class of words that end in mb Webster had not been consistent, spelling dumb, limb, and numb with b and crum without it; while thumb is spelled both ways with preference being given to thum. Attention is also called to the inclusion or dropping of final e, the use of y and i interchangeably, en and in as prefixes, and words ending in ough as ow or ough as the notion strikes.

In Article VII he attempts to show that Webster has exhibited a greater want of decision in giving the orthography of each word than has any of his predecessors. In the first place he has spelled many words two different ways without giving a preference, each of which he as defined precisely or nearly alike. Second, he has used the words thus differently spelled in the text to define other words, and has spelled them sometimes with one orthography and sometimes with the other. Third, he has spelled a word two ways and given a preference, but in his definitions has used the orthography which he has not preferred. Fourth, he has, in many instances, changed the orthography of a word, and inserted the former orthography, and has referred the reader to the new spelling, but he has changed the orthography of other words without having given the former orthography or any reference to it. Fifth, he has coupled some words spelled two different ways and has not coupled other words spelled two ways. Sixth, he has coupled many words which he has spelled two different ways, with one first in its alphabetical arrangement and in another place the other word first, matching the alphabetical arrangement of that word; in this manner he has alternately given each word thus coupled a preference by placing it first. Thus, he has croop and croup, croup and croop.

In Articles VIII, IX, X, XI, XII, and XIII Cobb illustrates the discrepancies mentioned in the items above, of which he says there are about twelve hundred in all. In Article XIII he says that the innovations and anomalies introduced by Webster in his several books have done more to introduce irregularity in orthography than all of the other works published in this country within fifty years. He concludes the article by giving the opinion of the late Daniel H. Barnes respecting the orthography of Webster's former and present publications.

Speaking of his dictionaries, and the variable words in them, Cobb quotes Barnes as saying:

> ... "These I have marked in that dictionary which Mr. Webster considers his best work, and such an appalling number I could not imagine or scarcely believe, had I not seen it and done it myself. " In speaking of his former works generally, he remarks, "Mr. Webster has no idea of the multitudinous errors in his works;" and finally, in alluding to the American Dictionary, he adds, "I have not seen any of the mammoth bones; the owner is afraid if they are exposed before the entire skeleton is

set up, that they will crumble to pieces. He said to me
'there must be no discussion of that kind while the work
is in press.' By and by the mountain will bring forth, I
hope not a mooncalf. - He cannot spell, what else he can,
remains to be seen. - Reading his dictionary, as I have
done, has taken away all hope that he will ever do more
than to aggregate materials for a good work."[176]

After the publication of the thirteenth number of these letters,
the octavo abridgment of Webster's dictionary made by Worcester
appeared. In a letter published in the Commercial Advertiser of
August 26, Webster states that "the errors in the quarto already
pointed out by Inquirer, are corrected in the octavo." In Articles
XIV, XV, XVI, and XVII "Inquirer" points out the variations in
orthography from the quarto, made in the octavo, and attempts to
show that part of the orthography objected to has been changed in
the text of the octavo, agreeably to the orthography of Johnson and
Walker, and that nearly all of the contradictions and inconsistencies
in the orthography of the text still remain in the octavo.

In the Morning Herald of August 27, 1829, an article appeared
signed by S. Converse, the publisher of Webster's American Dictionary, which answered the articles written by "Inquirer." Converse
says that Webster's dictionary must stand or fall on the basis of
sound criticism, that comparison must be the test of merit, and
that any person of moderate capacity can take Webster's Dictionary,
and place it by the side of any other, and decide for himself whether "for copiousness in his vocabulary, for learned research in the
etymologies, for fulness and accuracy in his definitions, and for
uniformity and consistency, (both with himself and good usage), in
his orthography, Mr. Webster has or has not, claims to superiority."
He excuses the inconsistencies in the dictionaries on the ground that
it was compiled over a period of several years with usage changing
constantly, that in a manuscript which comprised over ten thousand
pages it was impossible to detect all errors, and that with twelve
or fifteen proofreaders and printers, all accustomed to various spelling, he is surprised that more departures should not have been made
than actually occurred.

The main purpose in his writing, says Converse, is to per-
form an act of justice to the late Mr. Barnes, who was known as a
warm and decided advocate for the Quarto Dictionary. This fact,
he says, "Inquirer" knew, but only wanted to injure the memory of
Barnes by convicting him of duplicity.

Converse says that the public should know that the person
concealed under the name of "Inquirer" is a teacher from a village
in the interior of New York, who has compiled a spelling book and,
in order to secure a copyright, must vary it from Webster's. This
he has done by inserting the obsolete orthography of seventy years
ago. He also says that Cobb is the person who, two or three years
since, offered through the Albany Argus a reward of one hundred
dollars for the best criticisms of the spelling books of the country,

who labored industriously to mark the errors in Webster's spelling
for the benefit of Mr. Barnes, who undertook the examination for
the prize, and who when Mr. Barnes declared Webster's book the
most accurate of all, and his the most defective, in order to screen
his book and save his hundred dollars, disclosed himself as the
author, and shrank both from the public eye and the payment of the
prize. He also says that Barnes told him [Converse] that "Inquirer"
had mentioned to him that he approved of Webster's principles and
would adopt his dictionary with all his heart had he not a spelling
book to sustain.

In an article which appeared in the Morning Herald of September 5, "Inquirer" answered Converse by saying that either Converse
or Barnes was guilty of a falsehood, for he did not see the quarto
dictionary of Webster, nor was he acquainted with its principles of
orthography, until subsequent to the death of Barnes; and consequently had never had the conversation stated above. He also had never
heard Barnes express an opinion, either directly or indirectly, in
favor of the Dictionary.

Later Cobb published a new edition of his criticisms, making
the third publication of the remarks in the Argus, with considerable
additions which made up a fifty-six page pamphlet closely printed.
In this pamphlet he took up the old spelling book and dictionaries
which Webster had discarded and compared them with his new series
of books, to show that they did not agree in spelling. This pamphlet
was sent by mail to members of Congress, to judges of courts, and
to professors of sciences who had recommended Webster's books.
On the margin of the copies he pasted a printed note, which contained a very modest request, in the following words:

> Dear Sir - Having observed your certificate in a pam-
> phlet recently published, commending the dictionary and
> class book of Mr. Webster, for their uniformity in ortho-
> graphy and presuming, from their circumstance, that you
> are in possession of copies of these works, I hope you
> will do me the justice to compare the following structures
> with the publications to which they refer. [177]

Pages 47-54 inclusive of A Critical Review contain "Specimens of Webster's Orthography." There were approximately 720
words chosen to show the errors and inconsistencies in the various
publications. They are arranged under the headings indicated below.
The words marked with an asterisk were "evidently copied from
Dilworth's Spelling-Book, as they appeared the same in Dilworth's
Spelling Book contrary to all of Webster's Dictionaries and to the
Dictionaries of Johnson and Walker; and they have been thus contra-
dictory and erroneously spelled in Webster's old Spelling Book for
more than forty years!!!" Ten words were selected from the list
as samples (see p. 172).

That Cobb did not discontinue his attempts to injure the sale
of Webster's books is shown by letters written to Webster by his

Old Spelling Book	Dict. 1806	Dict. 1817	Quarto 1828	Octavo 1831	Duodecimo 1831	New S.B.
ache	ache, ake	do	do	do	do	ache
almanac*	almanack	do	do	almanac	almanack	do
fulfil	do	do	fulfill	do	do	do
hindrance	hinderance	do	do	do	do	do
empannel	impannel	do	empannel impannel	do	impannel	do
encumber	incumber	do	encumber incumber	do	do	encumber
neighbor	do	do	neighbor nahbor	do	do	neighbor
ocher	do	ocher oker	ocher	ochre ocher	ocher ochre	ocher
sovereign	do	do	suyeran sovereign(a) suveran sovereign(n)	sovereign suveran sovereign	do sovereign suveran	sovereign
specter	do	do	do	spectre specter		

son William G. Webster in December, 1835. In a letter of December 5, he says that he is confident that Cobb is still spreading reports to the injury of Webster, for recently he has received a paper from Madison, Indiana, which contains an extract from the Essays of Webster published forty years ago, in which comments of the writer are intended to impress upon the public that Webster still sanctions such orthography. In another letter of December 20 he writes his father that Webster's agent, Mr. White, had come into contact with Cobb's agents once or twice, and in Cleveland he had met one agent who was to deliver a lecture on "discrepancies on Dr. Webster's books" that evening. In order to prepare him better for the lecture, White put into the hands of Cobb's agent one of his pamphlets. In the evening White went to the lecture. After Cobb's agent had sat for half an hour in seeming uneasiness, he gave notice that he should defer the lecture on account of the few people present. The next moment he was off for Detroit. [178]

The American edition of the American Dictionary was followed by the publication of the work in England under the supervision of E. H. Barker, editor of the Thesaurus Graecae Linguae of Henry Stephens. Twenty-five hundred copies of the Dictionary had been printed in America;[179] the English edition included three thousand copies. [180] There are 71,323 words, 34,094 being in Volume I. [181] The title was changed to suit the English public and was very much abbreviated. It is as follows: Dictionary of the English Language; exhibiting the origin and affinity of every word, its orthography, pronunciation and accurate definition; to which are prefixed an Introductory Dissertation on the Origin, History and Connection of the Languages of Western Asia and Europe, and a philosophical and practical grammar. Edited by E. H. Barker, London: Black and Company, 1830-32, 4to. published in 12 parts, forming 2 vols.

A letter from Barker, written July 8, 1829, gives interesting information concerning this publication. [182] He said that his attention was first called to the American Dictionary by John Pickering, but that it was the North American Review and an article in the London Magazine for June, 1929 which convinced him that he would be doing a service to his countrymen if he reprinted the work. He stated that he was willing to give Webster one-sixth of the profits after the expenses were cleared, but that he wanted Webster to send material for an Appendix and copies of American magazines and reviews which contained notices of the Dictionary, as well as able reviews by "impartial and intelligent and eloquent Americans written in a free spirit, without any nationality, and calculated for insertion in our Quarterly Periodicals in England, and also one or two clever short notices for our magazines and monthly periodicals." He said that these would enable him to give extensive and early celebrity to the work and prevent the malignant attacks of the men interested in Todd's Johnson. He also asked for a deed of assignment of the property in the Dictionary, executed according to the forms of the American law, to protect him from depredation by piracy.

The Dictionary was advertised in 1830 as follows:

> Dr. Webster's Dictionary of the English Language.
> This work will appear in Twelve Parts, each consisting of
> Twenty sheets, price Nine Shillings, and will form Two
> Volumes, Quarto. Part V is just published. Part VI will
> appear on the First of December. London: Messrs.
> Black, Young and Young. Foreign Booksellers, 2, Tavi-
> stock Street, Covent Garden. List of Subscribers. Total
> Number 861, September 30, 1830. [183]

In a letter of March 29, 1832, Barker wrote to Webster that
the sale of the Dictionary was continuing, Mr. Black having sold
fifty complete copies since the commencement of the new year. The
original subscription price was £4. 5. 6 while the price at that
time was £5. 10. 0 in boards. He said that he thought that in less
than twelve months all the expenses would have been covered and
sharing in the profits would begin. The advertising alone, he said,
had cost £350, or nearer £400, because the duty on advertising was
so high. He also stated that he was making collections for a second
edition. [184] No record of another edition has been uncovered in this
study. The edition was sold to H. G. Bohn in 1835, when the price
was reduced to £2. 12s. 6d. [185]

In 1829 Sherman Converse published the first abridgment of
Webster's American Dictionary, arranged in octavo form by Joseph
E. Worcester. To it was added a "Synopsis of Words Differently
Pronounced by Different Orthoepists," and "Walker's Key to the
Classical Pronunciation of Greek, Latin, and Scripture Proper
Names."

Webster states in the Preface that he has been prevented by
the state of his health from attending personally to the abridgment,
and that although the work has been done by Worcester, he adheres
to the general principles laid down by the author. Cases of doubt
and such changes and modifications as seemed desirable were referred to Professor Goodrich of Yale College, who was requested
by the author to act as his representative. The "Synopsis of Words
Differently Pronounced by Different Orthoepists" was prepared by
Worcester, as was "Walker's Key," which also passed under the
revision of Goodrich. The most important principles on which the
abridgment has been conducted, as stated in the Preface, are as
follows: 1) The vocabulary is changed to embrace all the words
contained in the original work, and in Todd's edition of Johnson's
Dictionary, together with such additional words as appeared to the
author to be worthy of insertion. 2) The most important etymologies are retained. 3) The definitions remain unchanged, except by
an occasional compression in their statement. In some cases new
significations are added. The illustrations and authorities are generally omitted, except in doubtful cases, when they are retained.

The practice of introducing into the vocabulary the different
forms of words of disputed orthography is carried out in the

abridgment to a greater extent than in the Quarto. In most cases the old orthography takes the lead. The u and k are entirely omitted from such words as honor and music, "in accordance with the decided tendency of later usage, both in this country and in England." In derivative words, the final consonant of the primitive is doubled only when under the accent.

As a guide to pronunciation the words have been divided into syllables, which in most cases determine the regular sounds of the vowels; otherwise, a pointed letter is used to denote the sound. The regular long sound of the vowel, when under the accent, is indicated by a pointed letter. In cases of disputed pronunciation the different forms are often given. These are, however, exhibited fully for about eight hundred primitive words in the Synopsis prepared by Worcester, which gives the decisions of Sheridan, Walker, Perry, Jones, Fulton and Knight, and Jameson. A star is prefixed to the words in the list that appear as they do in the Dictionary.

The statement is made in the Preface that about sixteen thousand words and between thirty and forty thousand definitions are contained in the Dictionary, which are not to be found in any similar terms and significations relating to the various departments of science and arts, commerce, manufactures, merchandise, the liberal professions, and the ordinary concerns of life. There are approximately eighty-three thousand words arranged in two columns on the page. The dictionary proper contains 940 pages. The key to pronunciation is given at the bottom of each page.

The Dictionary sold at retail for six dollars; the retailer bought it for five. [186] Other issues of this dictionary followed, 1830-1842. [187] There was a revised edition in 1844, published at New York by Harper and Brothers. Other issues followed, 1845-1846.

It was Worcester's abridgment, under the supervision of Goodrich, which caused so much controversy, not only between Webster and Worcester (see Chapter VI), but also between Webster and Goodrich, and later between other members of Webster's family. It seems that at the time that Webster consented to Worcester's making the abridgment, he did so with the understanding that Goodrich would supervise it in accordance with the principles already laid down by Webster in the American Dictionary, but that instead of conforming to the principles of the original work, Goodrich departed so far from them as to make the two books inconsistent with each other. After Goodrich had annoyed Webster in conjunction with Converse, the publisher, [188] he persuaded Webster, who was then seventy-one years of age, to sell the work to him, at a very low price. Later, when Goodrich was in trouble because of the failure of the publisher, Webster consented not to stereotype in octavo form an edition of the original work which might come in conflict with Goodrich's work. Webster seems to have been very much displeased with the Abridgment. A little more than a month before his death he wrote to William Chauncey Fowler, another one of his sons-in-law, the following letter:

New Haven, April 11, 1843

Dear Sir: I have received your letter of the first, and note what you say on the subject of the Dictionary. It is much to be regretted that I suffered the American Dictionary to be abridged, not only as it [sic] regards profits, but as it regards its usefulness. The Octavo does not contain a History of the Language, and the important principles which I have adopted to correct its anomalies. The definitions are abridged, and in some cases are defective. The etymologies, also, are abridged, and many curious facts omitted. I found also that none of the corrections and improvements in the body of the work, which is stereotyped, are introduced into the last edition--I mean such as I have introduced into the large work. In a few instances the publishers or owners have deviated purposely from my decision, so that the work must not be considered as mine, though most of it is taken from mine.

Very affectionately yours,

N. Webster[189]

A revised edition of this same dictionary in royal octavo, edited by Chauncey A. Goodrich, appeared in 1847, with other issues following, 1848-1852. In this revision the additions and alterations which had heretofore been included in an Appendix were now carried into the body of the work. Much new matter was added to make it consistent with the larger dictionary published the same year, and it was "designed to present, on a reduced scale, a clear, accurate, and full exhibition of the American Dictionary in all its parts."[190]

As stated in the Preface the book is designed particularly for use in the higher classes of academies and other institutions of learning, in the counting house, and the family, and by those who need a book to aid them in composition and in pronunciation. The definitions have been prepared to fit the need of those who would be most likely to use the dictionary, and synonyms have been added to aid in developing variety of expression and in exact discrimination of synonymous terms.

It is also stated in the Preface that the pronunciation has received careful attention. Disputed pronunciations have been referred to the most important orthoepists of the country, and correspondence has been carried on with the most distinguished orthoepist of Great Britain, B. H. Smart, the information thus obtained being embodied in the "Principles of Pronunciation and Remarks on the Key," found in the Introduction.

In most cases the orthography in dispute is represented in both forms. Many of the innovations of Webster, as in his own revisions of his dictionaries, have been discarded. The Appendix includes Walker's Key to the Pronunciation of Classical Proper Names,

revised and improved by Professor Thatcher of Yale College;
Walker's Key to the Pronunciation of Proper Names, with additions
from other writers, such as Smart, Fulton, and Knight; A Vocabulary of Modern Geographical Names, mainly drawn from, or carefully collated with, the corresponding table in the American Dictionary; A Collection of Latin, French, Italian and Spanish Words translated; and other useful tables.

One critic says that the revision of 1847 "embraced, or ultimately affected, all the editions and sizes of Webster's Dictionary
and either had, or prepared the way for, the introductory and supplementary matter of the later revisions."[191]

Another edition of the abridged dictionary appeared in 1856,
with the title-page, A Pronouncing and Defining Dictionary of the
English Language, Abridged from Webster's American Dictionary,
with Numerous Synonyms, carefully Discriminated. By Chauncey A.
Goodrich, D. D., Professor in Yale College. To Which are Added,
Walker's Key to the Pronunciation of Classical and Scripture Proper
Names: A Vocabulary of Modern Geographical Names; Phrases and
Quotations from the Ancient and Modern Languages; Abbreviations
Used in Writing, Printing, etc. Philadelphia: J. B. Lippincott & Co.

As stated in the Preface, the specific aim of this dictionary
is to assist those who are cultivating English composition on a broad
scale and are desirous of gaining an exact knowledge of our language,
and a ready command of its varied forms of expression. Its vocabulary has been pruned of obsolete and useless words, and many
hundreds of new words belonging to various departments of science,
literature, and art have been added. The space gained by leaving
out useless material has been devoted to definitions, which are given
not "by a mere array of synonyms, but in short descriptive sentences or clauses, after the manner of the larger work." After the
words are thus defined, in many cases synonymous terms are added
to aid the writer in selecting the most appropriate word, thus acquiring a varied and expressive diction. About eighteen hundred of
the most important synonymous words in our language are carefully
discriminated in this dictionary. The distinctive meaning of each is
given; a comparison is made between them; and, in most cases,
brief illustrations are added. "More than six hundred distinct articles are devoted to discriminations of this kind, being a larger
number than is contained in any similar work in our language with
the exception of Crabbe."[192] Disputed cases of orthography are
given, to a great extent, both ways, the form preferred having been
sanctioned by distinguished English grammarians and orthoepists,
such as Lowth, Walker, and Perry. An Appendix is added which
contains: 1) Walker's Key to the Pronunciation of Classical and
Scripture Proper Names, revised and improved by Thacher, of Yale,
and others who have been thoroughly conversant with these subjects.
2) A Vocabulary of Modern Geographic Names, prepared expressly
for this work by Joseph Thomas. 3) Tables giving a full account
of the abbreviations used in writing and printing. 4) A collection of
Latin, French, and Italian words and phrases of frequent occurrence,

with their translations.   5) An account of the principal Deities and Heroes of Antiquity.

Webster himself made an abridgment of the American Dictionary entitled A Dictionary of the English Language: abridged from the American Dictionary for the use of Primary Schools and the Counting House.   It was published in New Haven by Hezekiah Howe, 1829, and is a 12mo. of 532 pages.   There were other issues between 1830 and 1842.   The copy examined for this study was published in New York by White, Gallagher and White, and stereotyped at E. White's Type and Stereotype Foundry, 1830.

As stated in its Preface, the purpose of the Dictionary is to furnish counting houses and primary schools with a vocabulary of the words which constitute the body of the English language, with a brief definition of each.   The orthography and pronunciation follow those in the Quarto Dictionary, with some corrections.   Words are divided into syllables and the syllable on which the stress is laid is marked with an accent, or with a point over the vowel.   The key to pronunciation is given at the top of the page.   Some of the difficult and uncommon technical words are omitted, as well as some participles of verbs.   Errors in orthography that appeared in the Quarto are corrected.

The words are arranged in two columns on the page.   There are approximately forty-seven thousand words.   A list of words and phrases of foreign origin, with their interpretation, and money tables are given.

Webster also prepared A Dictionary for Primary Schools, which was published in New York by N. and J. White and in New Haven by Durrie and Peck.   A stereotyped edition of this, by A. Chandler, New York, 1833, was examined for this study.   It contains 341 pages, in addition to six pages of introduction, and is 13 1/2 cm. in size.   Testimonials to the merit of Webster's books cover the copyright page and the last page.   One, signed by more than one hundred members of the previous Congress, is especially appreciative of the fact that Webster had improved the language by making the orthography more simple, regular, and uniform, and by removing difficulties arising from its anomalies.   It states that Webster's American Dictionary was becoming a standard in the United States, thereby preventing the formation of dialects in states remote from each other.   It was also beneficial in rendering the language easy to foreigners.   The last page contains the following statement signed by the Editors of Twelve Newspapers: "We make Dr. Webster's Dictionary our general standard of orthography, and would cordially recommend its adoption in schools and seminaries of learning. "

This same dictionary, with the name of William G. Webster as compiler, was published by Huntington and Savage, New York, 1835.   Another issue came out in 1841, with revised editions appearing in 1843, 1848, and 1857. [193]   New editions continued to be published from time to time.

The edition of 1848 by William G. Webster was for the purpose of making the Primary Dictionary coincide in orthography and
syllabication with those of the Quarto, Octavo, High School, and
Pocket editions, in which many changes had recently been made.
Various other changes are introduced to make it essentially a pronouncing dictionary. The words are divided into syllables, and diacritical marks are used. In some cases the words are respelled
to indicate the pronunciation. The rules of orthography laid down
by Webster in his earlier dictionaries are followed. The words are
arranged three columns to a page, with the key to pronunciation at
the bottom of each page. Introductory letters are placed at the top
of each column. "A Pronouncing Vocabulary of Geographical Names"
is attached, as well as lists of Greek and Latin Proper Names and
Scripture Proper Names, for which pronunciation is given.

Practically the same material was included in A High School
Pronouncing Dictionary of the English Language, abridged from the
American Dictionary of Noah Webster, with Accented vocabularies
of classical, scripture and modern geographical names - By William G. Webster. New York: Huntington & Savage, 1848. It is
a 12mo. with four pages of introduction and 360 pages of the dictionary proper. Other issues followed, 1849-1852. A revised edition
was published in 1857, and a new edition followed in 1868. Other
issues appeared later.

Letters from different retail businesses concerning the sale
of Webster's "School Dictionary" indicate that the price was entirely
too high to permit large sales. Bemis and Ward wrote from Canan-
daigua, January 16, 1833, that they were very much disappointed in
the sale of the dictionary, since they had hoped that it would go
along with the Spelling Book, but that they had sold only two hundred copies since the book was published. They advised a reduc-
tion in price, thinking that as much profit would result from large
sales at a moderate price as from a few sales at a high price.
They said that they were retailing Webster's book at 87 cents as
compared with Walker's at 50 cents. [194]

In June, 1833, Moses G. Atwood wrote to Webster from Concord that the price would keep it out of the schools in that quarter
for years. He said that if Webster could publish his dictionary so
that it could be sold to the trade for 6 dollars per dozen, it would
be introduced into the schools generally. [195]

The first edition of twenty-five hundred copies of the American Dictionary lasted thirteen years. Webster then published a
revised edition in two octavo volumes, at the price of fifteen dollars. [196] Before the new edition came out, there seems to have
been an unsatisfied demand for copies of the first edition. Webster's son, William G. Webster, wrote to his father in April, 1836,
urging him to arrange for the new publication and to inform the
public that the American Dictionary would be republished with extensive improvements. He says that there is no doubt of its being
wanted, that N. & J. White had told him that they did not know of
a single copy on the market, and several were wanted soon. [197]

The title of the new dictionary is as follows: An American Dictionary of the English Language; First Edition in Octavo, containing the whole vocabulary of the quarto, with corrections, improvements, and several thousand additional words: to which is prefixed An Introductory Dissertation on the origin, history and connection of the languages of western Asia and Europe, with an explanation of the principles on which languages are formed, by Noah Webster, LL. D.... General subjects of this work. 1. Etymologies of English words, deduced from an examination and comparison of words of corresponding elements in twenty languages of Asia and Europe. 2. The true orthography of words, as corrected by their etymologies. 3. Pronunciation exhibited and made obvious by the division of words into syllables, by accentuation, by marking the sounds of the accented vowels, when necessary, or by general rules. 4. Accurate and discriminating definitions, illustrated, when doubtful or obscure, by examples of their use, selected from respectable authors, or by familiar phrases of undisputed authority. In two volumes, New Haven: Published by the Author, Printed by B. L. Hamlen, 1841.

The number of words in the Dictionary has been increased. A smaller print is used and the pages are numbered. The first volume contains 944 pages and the second, 984 pages. A Philosophical and Practical Grammar, included in the first edition, is omitted and a section entitled "English Alphabet," merely an enlargement of the "Directions for the Pronunciation of Words," given in the original edition, is included. The list of pointed letters, or points or marks used with the letters to indicate the sound, is increased from twelve to fifteen.

The chief changes are the division of words into syllables, the addition of several thousand words to the vocabulary, and the correction of the definitions in several of the sciences, a task performed by Professor Tully of the Medical College of New Haven. Also added is the explanation that many phrases from foreign languages, frequently used by English authors and in conversation, have been added, as well as many foreign terms used in books of music.

The edition published in 1845 by George and Charles Merriam, Springfield--the first of the Webster dictionaries published by this company--contains a Supplement of over two thousand words, consisting of well authorized and useful words omitted in the body, a few obsolete words retained for the sake of readers of old books, and many new words that have appeared as a result of discoveries in the sciences. The list was prepared by Webster before his death,[198] but was entered for copyright by the executors of his estate, William W. Ellsworth and Henry White. There were other issues of this dictionary, 1848-1854.[199]

The new dictionary was advertised as follows:

In the Press, and in February next will be published,

Webster's American Dictionary
of the
English Language
A New Edition in Royal Octavo, Elegantly Printed

This edition will contain the whole of the contents of the
quarto edition, with several thousand additional words, and
with other valuable improvements, particularly in the sciences, in which the definitions are corrected by modern
discoveries.
The American Dictionary is now used in the courts of
law, in public offices and in seminaries of learning, in
all the United States. It is admitted, in Great Britain to
be the best etymological and defining dictionary in the
language; and indeed it is the only one which is tolerably
complete. It is in use among the literati on the continent
of Europe; and so highly are the definitions esteemed in
this country, that some gentlemen have read the volumes
in course from beginning to end.

New Haven, Conn., Act 1840

Price to subscribers handsomely bound in Calf and gilt
$14.00
Sheep
$13.00200

A letter included among Webster's MSS material is given below for what it is worth. No information bearing on the statement
contained in the letter has been found elsewhere.

Monday Morning Northampton June 24, 1842

Noah Webster, Esq.

Sir

Having endeavored to do justice to you in public, I feel
that it is a duty which I owe to you as well as to another,
to call upon you either publicly or privately for a public
avowal of your reasons for not acknowledging, nor giving
any intimation of your indebtedness to the Rev. Dr. William Allen formerly president of Bowdoin College, and now
resident in this place, for six or seven thousand new words
added to the last edition of your Dictionary--some of which
are inserted in the body of your dictionary but most of
them placed in the Apendix [sic]. These words with their
definitions and authorities were, with much care and labor
collected and encouraged by Dr. Allen in the course of his
literary pursuits extending over more than thirty years, and
generously forwarded to you to be inserted in the last edition of your Dictionary. That you should have entirely
omited [sic] to acknowledge your indebtedness to Dr. Allen

is a mystery to your friends who know that you are too
rich in well-earned reputation to grudge any man his pit-
tance of honor; and too honest to withold any man's dues.
The fact is as it is however; and <u>must</u> be explained by
somebody sooner or later, and if <u>not</u> done while you live,
will assuredly be attempted when you no longer remain to
correct any wrong view which may be taken of the matter.
I therefore, now call your attention to the subject: and I
do it in this private manner, that any public explanation
which you may give may seem to be entirely spontaneous
and therefore the more honorable. Permit me then respectfully to suggest the propriety of making a communication to the Hamshire Gazette, on the subject in question,
and leave nothing of this kind to be settled after your
death. For it must be obvious to you, Sir, that, if this
becomes a matter of public accusation instead of acknowledgment, it will be delicious food for your enemies, and
possibly an inexplicable ground of painful doubt to your
friends.

Very respectfully yours,
S

On the back is written, in Webster's handwriting: "Letter S Anonymous. Northampton Jany 24, 1842. "

That pirated and mutilated copies of Webster's dictionaries
began to appear on the market even before the author's death is
shown by the letter written to Webster by one of his agents (Mc-
Mahon) from Rahway, New Jersey, January 9, 1842. An extract
from the letter is given below:

According to your orders I commenced operations in
Newark last Monday, (for there was nothing to be done
on New Year's day). I found an unusual scarcity of
money, as well as bad copies of your Dictionary. Pur-
porting to be the <u>whole work,</u> but Proved to be the Hartford abridgment enlarged to more than a Thousand Pages.
Price $4.50. And one Gent. to whom I was recommended
tol [sic] me he has bot [sic] the 2 volumes in N. York of
your Publishers in Calf, Plain for $12.00--(it was W.
Chas. Aisdale) while a Lawyer from Morristown informed
me he had just Paid $14.00 in N. York for the Gilt in
Calf similar to those I offered. --But I had no idea of
being discouraged without a thorough Trial, and undertook
it in earnest. Prepared for the worst. [201]

A revised edition of the <u>American Dictionary</u> by Chauncey A.
Goodrich appeared in 1847, [202] with other issues following, 1848-
1852. The title-page of the dictionary, in part, is as follows: <u>An
American Dictionary of the English Language, ... Revised and</u>

Enlarged by Chauncey A. Goodrich, Professor in Yale College with
Pronouncing Vocabularies of Scripture, Classical, and Geographical
Names. Springfield, Massachusetts, published by George and Char-
les Merriam.

Goodrich states in the Preface that the demand for the American Dictionary had increased so rapidly within the last few years
that the publishers felt the necessity of its being stereotyped, for
the greater convenience of the public, in a single volume. They
also were desirous of thoroughly revising each department so that
it would represent the latest advances of science, literature, and
the arts of the present day. It was placed in the hands of Chauncey
A. Goodrich as one of the members of Dr. Webster's family, in
the expectation of his obtaining such additional aid as might be necessary for the accomplishment of the design. From time to time he
laid open the sheets to the inspection of other members of the family,
and no important alterations were made except with the concurrence
of Dr. Webster's legal representatives. [203]

Regarding orthography the principle laid down by Webster
that "The tendencies of our language to greater simplicity and
broader analogues, ought to be watched and cherished with the utmost care," has been followed in the main; but Goodrich has been
more heedful of the demand of established usage, and the old orthography has been restored to many of the words which were not
readily accepted by the American people in their new garb. The er
ending of such words as center, meter, scepter is preferred, but
the forms in re are given as optional. In words such as defense,
and offense, Webster's preference is followed in the s form, but
both spellings are given. Many of the other changes which Webster
made in orthography are given in this dictionary in both spellings.

More attention has been given to pronunciation. "A careful
comparison has been made with the latest authorities, and wherever
changes seemed desirable, and could be made in consistency with
the Author's principles, they have been here introduced." [204] The
key to pronunciation has been enlarged and placed at the bottom of
each page, and pointed letters have been used to a greater extent.
Many thousand words have been respelled.

In respect to etymologies, very few changes have been made,
the author not considering it within his province. The chief labor
on this part of the work has been on the task of giving with accuracy
the numerous words from Oriental and foreign languages which are
used in tracing the origin of the English words.

The revised Addenda to the 1840 edition, as well as later
improvements made by Webster down to the day of his death, have,
in this volume, been inserted under their proper heads. [205] New
matter to the amount of more than three hundred pages has been
added, but the use of a smaller type makes it possible to bring it
all within the compass of one volume of 1441 pages. The introductory material consists of the editor's Preface to the revised

edition, Webster's Preface and the Advertisement of the 1840 edition, Memoir of Webster, Webster's Dissertation on the Origin, History, and Connection of the Languages of Western Asia and Europe, a discussion of Webster's orthography as exhibited in the present edition, alphabets of various languages, and directions and explanations for pronunciation. The supplementary material consists of Tables of Scripture Names, Greek and Latin Proper Names and Modern Geographical Names, designed to exhibit the pronunciation of each, prepared under the direction of Noah Porter, Professor in Yale College.

Many other dictionaries were used in preparing this dictionary. Smart's English Dictionary, the unfinished dictionary by Gilbert, Richardson's Dictionary, the Analytical Dictionary by Booth, Brande's Encyclopedia of Science, Literature, and Art, the Penny Encyclopedia, and many other special dictionaries were consulted. [206]

James G. Percival was to revise the scientific articles, but completed the work through only a little more than two letters of the alphabet. [207] The task was finished by the editor's associates and by other gentlemen in various professional employments: law, Elizur Goodrich; ecclesiastical history and ancient philosphy, William Tully; oriental literature, Professor Gibbs of Yale; part of the articles on astronomy, meteorology, and natural philosphy, Professor Olmstead of Yale; mathematics, Professor Stanley of Yale; geology and mineralogy, and natural philosophy, Professor Olmstead of Yale; mathematics, Professor Stanley of Yale; geology and mineralogy, James D. Dana; practical astronomy and entomology, Edward C. Herrick; painting and fine arts, Nathaniel Jocelyn. [208]

Regarding the Dictionary Goodrich says:

> After a diligent study of the subject for the last thirty years, after visiting England with a view to satisfy my own mind by inquiries on the spot, after a correspondence with distinguished English scholars continued down to the present time, I feel authorized to say, that the Revised Edition of Dr. Webster's Dictionary does exhibit the actual pronunciation of our language in England, as accurately and completely as any single Dictionary which has ever been published. In the same edition important modifications have been likewise made, as the result of extensive correspondence with distinguished scholars in England and this country, bringing down the work to the year 1847. [209]

During the year 1850 about three thousand copies of the dictionary edited by Goodrich, in conformity with an act of the legislature, were purchased and distributed among the School Districts of Massachusetts. [210] The legislature of New Jersey also furnished a copy to each school. [211] Many copies were sold in various parts of the world. An order for twelve copies was received from Ceylon. [212] The G. & C. Merriam Company prepared a copy as a present to Queen Victoria. The volume was bound by J. B. Lippincott and Company of Philadelphia, and was presented to the Queen through

George Bancroft, the American minister. It was given to the Queen through Prince Albert, and its receipt was acknowledged by his secretary. The acknowledgment, directed to the American minister, is as follows:

> Sir, - I have the honor to inform your excellency, that her majesty the queen has accepted with great pleasure, the copy of the last edition of Webster's English Dictionary, which, according to the directions you gave me, was laid by me before his royal highness Prince Albert, and was presented afterwards by the prince to her majesty, on the part of the publishers, Messrs. Merriam; and I have been commanded to express to your excellency, and to beg of you to transmit to Messrs. Merriam, her majesty's gracious thanks for this beautiful present, which her majesty highly values, not only on account of the great merits of the work itself, but still more as a sign of those feelings towards her royal person on the part of a large portion of the Anglo-American nation, which, after the political disunion which has taken place between the United Kingdom and the United States, could not indeed have found a more appropriate way of expressing themselves than the presentation to her majesty of a work of the English language, which directly refers to that powerful and indissoluble band by which the two cognate nations on the eastern and western side of the Atlantic will forever remain united. Your excellency, as well as Messrs. Merriam, will, no doubt, feel great pleasure in learning that her majesty has placed the work, presented through your excellency, amongst the few selected volumes which compose her own private library. [213]

The London <u>Literary Gazette</u> speaks of the dictionary in the following terms:

> The original edition of the American Dictionary is too well known and appreciated in England to require us to dwell at length on its plan and execution. In the present edition, Professor Goodrich has been ably assisted by several eminent men, each distinguished in his own sphere of inquiry; and the result is in the highest degree satisfactory. The work is a noble monument of erudition and indefatigable research; and the style and accuracy of its typography would do honor to the press of any country in Europe. This volume must find its way into all our public and good private libraries, for it provides the English student with a mass of the most valuable information, which he would in vain seek for elsewhere. [214]

In 1856 J. B. Lippincott and Company of Philadelphia published <u>A Pronouncing and Defining Dictionary of the English Language</u>, <u>abridged from Webster's American Dictionary, with numerous Synonyms carefully discriminated, by Chauncy A. Goodrich, D. D.</u>

Professor in Yale College. To Which are added Walker's Key to the Pronunciation of Classical and Scripture Proper Names; A Vocabulary of Modern Geographical Names; Phrases and Quotations from the Ancient and Modern Languages; Abbreviations used in Writing, Printing, etc. This dictionary became known as the University and Family Pronouncing Dictionary.

In the same year, 1856, G. & C. Merriam and Mason Brothers of New York published substantially the same work, entitled An Explanatory and Pronouncing Dictionary of the English Language, with Synonyms, abridged from the American Dictionary of Noah Webster, LL. D. By William G. Webster, assisted by Chauncey A. Goodrich, D. D., with numerous Useful Tables. This dictionary became known as the Counting House Edition, and contained, besides the Tables appended to the University Edition, various tables important for commercial uses, such as tables of money, weights, and measures of the principal commercial countries in the world; the currency, rates of interest, penalties for usury, and laws in regard to collection of debts, etc. in the United States. The same dictionary was published in London, in 1848, by H. G. Bohn and reprinted in 1851 and 1856 by Bogue, and by Kent and Company, 1859, at £1. 11s. 6d. [215]

It was Goodrich's securing the editorship of Webster's American Dictionary that precipitated a quarrel between Goodrich and William Chauncey Fowler, sons-in-law of Webster. Both had planned to become Webster's successor and when Goodrich was successful, Fowler became angry and accused Goodrich of filial rudeness. In an article entitled "Webster's Dictionary, Booksellers Edition, published by George and Charles Merriam, Springfield, 1848,"[216] Fowler calls attention to the radical departures made by Goodrich in the 1847 edition. The ideas are, for the most part, those already set forth in a pamphlet entitled Printed, But Not Published, also by Fowler, which, he states at the close, was not for the public but for the family of Dr. Webster and such others as Goodrich had conversed with on the subject. Whether or not it was published has not been determined in this study.

In the first article Fowler compliments the dictionary on its external appearance, but says that Webster has been deserted by his family; for examination of the vocabulary reveals that hundreds of words have been changed in spelling and pronunciation from the usage of Webster, without any notice of the change. "These changes many of them are made, not only in opposition to his Dictionary but also in opposition to his practice, to his disclosed preferences, to his Lectures delivered in different places, to his controversial papers and to the public defense of his principles, which he encourages his Friends to make." These changes were made even though a short time after Webster's death the family published a pamphlet defending his principles and literary character. "Either," he says, "he [Webster] was unqualified for the work which he undertook--and incompetent to its performance, or they have been guilty of arrogance and filial rudeness to his memory."

The article states that besides being at variance with Webster, his family are at variance among themselves, as shown in the points of difference between the pamphlet published in reply to an attack by a minority of the convention at Newark, New Jersey, and the Dictionary under consideration; and between the different editions of the "University" dictionary, all of which differ from the Quarto. "That those members of the family who are named in the Preface should be willing to be responsible for both editions differing from each other, shows a high degree of courage, and but little part of that valor which is discretion. In both editions they deserted Dr. Webster; in one of them they desert themselves. Only a slight inspection is necessary to show that this is ridiculously true. In the pamphlet, in the edition of the University and in the Quarto, taking them altogether, they stand in such an awkward position before the public, that they are in danger of being shown up by some American or English Punch."

Fowler gives two suggestions to explain the changes. One is that Goodrich was at variance with Webster in regard to Worcester's abridgment, which was executed under the direction of Goodrich, and that he took advantage of Webster's death to bring his works into harmony with his own and Worcester's views. The other answer is that the publishers became alarmed, thinking that they were in danger because of prejudices aroused by Webster's orthography and pronunciation, and at a meeting of the publishers and the family of Webster decided to revolutionize Webster's works.

Fowler says that the American public will refuse to accept the alterations of a "philological tinker" and will continue to follow Webster, or will accept Worcester. He feels that the course taken by the family of Webster is an outrage upon Webster's opinions and fame, since it has proceeded from a commercial motive.

In the pamphlet Printed, But Not Published, Fowler says that Webster, when he first began to think of preparing a new edition of his great work, proposed that he (Fowler) become joint editor in preparing the Dictionary for publication. Later, in 1837-1838, Webster repeatedly proposed that Fowler become editor with him and be so mentioned on the title-page. Fowler says that he entertained the proposals so far as to say to Webster that if he could buy off the lien that Goodrich and White had on the quarto, so as to prevent its being published in a form that might injure the sale of the abridged octavo, and that if they could obtain a publisher on favorable terms, he would become joint editor and owner (see page 175). But Goodrich was unwilling to make any concessions, and the matter was dropped. Goodrich also persuaded Webster not to alter the title-page of his revised edition, and in so doing changed the time during which Webster's heirs would own the copyright of his great work, and also kept Webster in the power of Goodrich and White.

On the death of Webster in 1843, it was found that Goodrich and his wife had been cut off from a share in the estate on the grounds that, by the purchase of the abridged octavo at a price below its value, they would receive as much from Webster as would the other heirs. [217]

The year after Webster's death, Fowler says that he was requested by some members of Webster's family to visit New Jersey, where there was a school convention at which it was expected there would be an attack upon Webster's dictionaries, chiefly on the ground of orthography. It had been suggested, he says, that he should be employed in getting out new editions of Webster's works, and promoting their use in the community. At the convention held at Newark, a vote was passed recommending the use of Webster's dictionary, but a minority published a "Dissent," which contained the substance of what was said in the convention in opposition to his works.

Fowler decided to write a reply to the attacks contained in the "Dissent," and as Goodrich was owner of the abridged octavo, he asked him to assist in the reply. In the pamphlet there was a statement, supplied by Goodrich, that the family would make changes in the orthography on the same principles that Webster had done. Fowler says that after the publication of the pamphlet, he was given, through the authority of William W. Ellsworth, son-in-law of Webster and executor of his estate, the right to make the changes necessary in the University abridgment of the dictionary which he was preparing. About this time the large dictionary was sold to the Merriams. [218] Fowler says that he received a letter from Goodrich stating that he was going to edit the large work for the Merriams, and requested Fowler to authorize him [Goodrich] to make the alterations without consulting anyone. To this Fowler and Ellsworth would not agree, and Goodrich said that he would have nothing to do with the editing, but the next day changed his mind and asked Fowler to go with him to Hartford to consult Ellsworth. After a scene in Ellsworth's office, Goodrich agreed to the arrangements proposed in a letter from Ellsworth to Goodrich, January 14, 1845, to the effect that it would not be proper to make any alterations that would be subject to a copyright, thereby allowing another person a distinct interest in the dictionary. Goodrich and Fowler then made the necessary alterations in the letter a in the dictionary, and the alterations agreed upon were printed. But a few weeks later Goodrich insisted that if Fowler refused to give him full authority to make alterations it would produce a public quarrel between the two.

Goodrich then consented to let Ellsworth act as umpire between Fowler and himself with respect to alterations. Matters worked harmoniously for a while. The University edition, of which Fowler was editor, was to be printed first, and the large dictionary was to conform to it. Finally, the last corrections were made; the Preface, Memoir, and Rules prefixed to the work were printed, and a thousand copies were struck off, when Fowler received a letter from Ellsworth which enclosed a letter Ellsworth had received from William Webster proposing a meeting of all the family of Webster, and of the publishers, Merriams and Huntington. Fowler wrote to Ellsworth that he did not think such a meeting was proper; and having heard nothing more about the proposed meeting, supposed that it was given up until some weeks afterwards, when he accidentally heard that there had been a meeting to which he had not been invited and of which he had had no notice.

At this meeting changes were hastily made in subservience to Goodrich, who, as Fowler believed, contrived to get into his hands the University edition of the dictionary and to insert into the Preface the following sentence; "The changes in orthography and pronunciation have been made under the direction of Rev. CHAUNCEY GOOD-RICH, formerly professor of Rhetoric and Oratory in Yale College, Rev. WILLIAM C. FOWLER, lately professor of Rhetoric and Oratory in Amherst College, WILLIAM G. WEBSTER, Esq., member of the family of Dr. Webster, who was acquainted with his views and his principles. "

A new edition of Webster's Unabridged Dictionary, known as the Pictorial Edition, was published in 1859 by George and Charles Merriam under the supervision of Chauncey A. Goodrich. About the only additions are some fifteen hundred pictorial illustrations given in a section before the main body of the dictionary and arranged in twenty-two groups according to the subject, as architecture, botany, carpentry, machinery, music, etc. Appended to the engraving is the number of the page where the verbal definition can be found under the appropriate word in the vocabulary, while in the body of the work a star is appended to the words which are illustrated in the pictorial department. The engraving was done by John Andrew, of Boston, and the electrotyping by Thomas B. Smith and Son of New York. The designs, to a large degree, are based on those of the Imperial Dictionary. [219]

A Table of Synonyms prepared by Goodrich has been enlarged. The Appendix, immediately following the general vocabulary, contains more than nine thousand new words and meanings collected by the Editor since the edition of 1847. In this collection he was aided by men familiar with various special departments of science.

Only Webster's contribution to the field of lexicography has been stressed in this chapter. Born during the stormy period preceding the Revolution, he managed to exist through the lean years and to finish the regular course at Yale. With only an eight dollar bill of Continental currency as his financial asset, he began to earn his living by teaching school. Here he found his life work-- that of trying to improve the language and of making it an integral part of the new nation. He was one of the first to emphasize the spirit of nationalism and to preach the doctrine of intellectual and linguistic independence. With his elementary textbooks, one of which--the spelling book--became the standard American text for more than one hundred years and enjoyed a sale surpassed only by the Bible, he began a career which ended with his name becoming synonymous with that of dictionary. He had practically everything against him--scant philological knowledge, scholars ready with adverse criticisms, very little money at his command and a large family to support, and insufficient libraries. He worked for more than twenty years and spent thirty thousand dollars before the completion of his American Dictionary which became the basis of all the later works that bear the name of Webster.

Notes

1. Increase N. Tarbox, "Noah Webster," Congregational Quarterly, VII (January, 1865), 1; and Emily Ellsworth Fowler Ford. Notes on the Life of Noah Webster, edited by Emily Ellsworth Ford Skeel, New York: Privately Printed, 1912, I, 12. Hereafter referred to as Ford and Skeel.
2. Ibid., p. 1.
3. Ibid.
4. Ibid., p. 2.
5. Ibid., p. 3.
6. Ibid., p. 6.
7. Ibid., p. 7.
8. Ibid., p. 9.
9. Eliza Steele Webster Jones. Reminiscences, not published, quoted in Ford and Skeel, op. cit., I, 9.
10. Horace E. Scudder. Noah Webster. Boston: Houghton Mifflin Company, 1889. p. 3.
11. "Schools As They Were Sixty Years Ago," The American Journal of Education, XIV (1863), 123.
12. Tarbox, op. cit., p. 1.
13. Ford and Skeel, op. cit., I, 15.
14. Ibid., p. 16.
15. Charles Burr Todd. Life and Letters of Joel Barlow. New York: G. P. Putnam, 1886, pp. 3-4.
16. The Literary Diary of Ezra Stiles, IX, 120, in Theodore Albert Zunder. The Early Days of Joel Barlow. New Haven: Yale University Press, 1934, p. 27.
17. Ibid., p. 28.
18. Quoted by Theodore Albert Zunder, "Noah Webster as a Student Orator," The Yale Alumni Weekly, XXXVI, No. 9 (November 19, 1926), 225.
19. Ibid.
20. Webster's MSS, New York Public Library.
21. Laws of Yale College, pp. 8-9, quoted by Zunder, The Early Days of Joel Barlow, p. 51.
22. Literary Diary, edited by Franklin Bowditch Dexter. New York: Charles Scribner's Sons, 1901, II, 284.
23. Tarbox, op. cit., p. 2.
24. Scudder, op. cit., p. 8.
25. Ford and Skeel, op. cit., I, 38.
26. F. Sturgess Allen. Noah Webster's Place Among English Lexicographers. Springfield: G. and C. Merriam, 1909, p. 2.
27. Ford and Skeel, op. cit., I, 42.
28. Stiles, op. cit., p. 554.
29. "The Webster Spelling Book," Magazine of American History, X (July-December, 1893), 299.

30. Tarbox, op. cit., p. 3.
31. Quoted in A. J. Philpott, "A Pioneer Publishing Romance," p. 4., reprinted from the Boston Globe by G. and C. Merriam, Springfield, Massachusetts, date not given.
32. Tarbox, op. cit., p. 4.
33. Mark Sullivan. America Finding Herself. New York: Charles Scribner's Sons, 1927, pp. 125-126.
34. Webster's MSS, New York Public Library.
35. Webster's MSS, New York Public Library.
36. Ibid.
37. The Connecticut Courant, Monday, May 24, 1790, Number 1322.
38. Preface, p. ix.
39. Quoted by Joel Benton, op. cit., p. 301.
40. A. M. Colton, "Our Old Webster Spelling-Book," Magazine of American History, XXIV (1890), 465-466.
41. Cf. this statement: "The two points, therefore, which I conceive to be the basis of a standard in speaking, are these: universal undisputed practice, and the principle of analogy. Universal practice is generally, perhaps always, a rule of propriety; and in disputed points, where people differ in opinion and practice, analogy should always decide the controversy." Noah Webster. Dissertations on the English Language: with Notes, Historical and Critical. Boston: Isaiah Thomas and Company, 1789, p. 2.
42. Joshua H. Neumann. American Pronunciation According to Noah Webster (1783). Doctoral Dissertation, Copyright 1924, Columbia University Press (mimeographed), pp. 115-120.
43. History of the People of the United States. New York: D. Appleton and Company, 1888, I, 428-429.
44. Ford and Skeel, op. cit., II, 455-456.
45. McMaster, op. cit., p. 431.
46. Ibid., p. 429.
47. Quoted by Ford and Skeel, op. cit., I, 296.
48. Ford and Skeel, op. cit., II, I.
49. Scudder, op. cit., p. 216.
50. Ford and Skeel, op. cit., I, 289.
51. Ibid., p. 290.
52. Ibid., p. 292.
53. Webster's MSS, New York Public Library.
54. The price was one dollar and fifty cents. Harry R. Warfel. Noah Webster, Schoolmaster to America. New York: The Macmillan Company, 1936, p. 309.
55. Preface, p. xix.
56. Ibid., p. xx.
57. The failure to separate these letters was one of the faults that Webster found later with Richardson's Dictionary (1836-7), and other English dictionaries. It was a practice which, according to Webster, originated before the separation of the letters in pronunciation and shape. Letter to Charles Richardson, undated, Webster's MSS, New York Public Library.
58. Philpott, op. cit., p. 5.

59. Preface, p. ix.
60. Ibid., p. v.
61. Ibid., p. viii.
62. Ibid., p. xix.
63. Ibid.
64. Ibid., p. xvi.
65. Ibid., p. xxiv.
66. Ford and Skeel, op. cit., II, 491-492.
67. The Monthly Anthology and Boston Review, VII (1809), 247-264.
68. Webster's MSS, New York Public Library.
69. Ibid.
70. Webster's MSS, New York Public Library.
71. Ibid.
72. Quoted by Allen Walker Read, "The Development of Faith in the Dictionary in America," a paper read before the Modern Language Association, Present-Day English Research Section, December 29, 1934, p. 4.
73. Webster's MSS, New York Public Library.
74. Letter to Webster, August 8, 1806, Webster's MSS, New York Public Library.
75. The Panoplist, III (July, 1807), 80.
76. Ibid.
77. Ford and Skeel, op. cit., II, 30.
78. Letter from Fred W. Hotchkiss, January 23, 1808, Webster's MSS, New York Public Library.
79. Quoted by William Draper Swan. A Reply to Messrs G. & C. Merriam's Attack Upon the Character of Dr. Worcester and His Dictionaries. Boston: Jenks, Hickling and Swan, 1854, p. 4.
80.
80. Copy of a letter inserted in a copy of A Compendious Dictionary, 1806, in the New York Public Library.
81. Webster's MSS, New York Public Library.
82. Ibid.
83. Ibid.
84. Ibid.
85. Todd, op. cit., pp. 244-246.
86. Ibid., p. 247.
87. Madison Papers, Library of Congress, XXXIII, 98, quoted by Ford and Skeel, op. cit., II, 60.
88. Ford and Skeel, op. cit., II, 48.
89. Ibid., p. 77.
90. Webster's MSS, New York Public Library.
91. The Panoplist, II (n. s.)(1810), 430.
92. Webster's MSS, New York Public Library.
93. Ford and Skeel, op. cit., II, 116.
94. Webster's MSS, New York Public Library.
95. Ibid.
96. Ibid.
97. Ford and Skeel, op. cit., II, 296.
98. Preface to An American Dictionary of the English Language, 1828, p. 1. (not numbered)
99. Webster's MSS, New York Public Library.
100. Letter to John Jay, November, 1821, Ibid.

101. Ibid.
102. Ford and Skeel, op. cit., II, 198.
103. Ibid.
104. Recollections of a Lifetime. New York: Miller, Orton and Company, 1857, II, footnote, pp. 18-19.
105. Webster's MSS, New York Public Library.
106. Ibid.
107. Ibid.
108. Letter to his wife, September 24, 1824, Webster's MSS, New York Public Library.
109. Ibid.
110. Letter to his wife, October 16, 1824, Ibid.
111. Ford and Skeel, op. cit., II, footnote, p. 297. Warfel, op. cit., p. 2, says that Daniel Webster was not even his kinsman.
112. Webster's MSS, New York Public Library.
113. Philpott, op. cit., p. 5.
114. Ford and Skeel, op. cit.
115. Letter to Mrs. Webster, February 15, 1825, Webster's MSS, New York Public Library.
116. Noah Webster, p. 238.
117. Quoted in "Noah Webster," The New Englander, I, No. IV (October, 1843), 565.
118. Quoted in Ford and Skeel, op. cit., I, 293.
119. "Mr. Webster's Dictionary," The American Journal of Education, I (1826), 379-380.
120. Charles Richardson, "An American Dictionary of the English Language," Westminster Review, XIV (1831), 56.
121. "Mr. Noah Webster's Proposed Dictionary," The American Journal of Education, I (1826), 315.
122. Ibid., p. 316.
123. Quoted in American Quarterly Review, IV (1828), 204.
124. There were twelve or fifteen proofreaders and printers. S. Converse, "Webster's Dictionary," New York Morning Herald, August 27, 1829.
125. Webster's MSS, New York Public Library.
126. Julius H. Ward. The Life and Letters of James Gates Percival. Boston: Ticknor and Fields, 1866, pp. 264-266.
127. Ibid., p. 266.
128. Ibid., p. 290.
129. After the work was under way, it was found that the proofreaders could examine only three sheets per week. Ibid., p. 266.
130. Ibid., p. 275.
131. Ibid., p. 285.
132. Ibid., pp. 286-287.
133. Ibid., p. 292.
134. Printed, But Not Published. New York Public Library, p. 1.
135. S. Converse, "Webster's Dictionary," New York Morning Herald, August 27, 1829. Also Webster's MSS, New York Public Library.
136. Preface.
137. Ibid. Richard M. Rollins says that although several historians

believe that Webster wrote the American Dictionary of the
English Language as a nationalistic tract, his own opinion
is that Webster's main motive was "to counteract social
disruption and reestablish the deferential world order that
he believed was disintegrating." "Words as Social Control:
Noah Webster and the Creation of the American Dictionary,"
American Quarterly, XXVIII(1976), 415-430.

138. Quoted in George H. McKnight. Modern English in the Making.
New York: D. Appleton and Co., 1928, pp. 482-483.
139. Ibid., p. 484.
140. Ibid., pp. 484-485.
141. Webster's MSS, New York Public Library.
142. Ford and Skeel, op. cit., II, 17.
143. Our Dictionaries and Other Language Topics. New York:
Henry Holt and Company, 1890, p. 30.
144. North American Review, XXVIII (April, 1829), 451.
145. Webster's MSS, New York Public Library.
146. Introduction.
147. "An American Dictionary of the English Language, etc.,"
Westminster Review, XXVII (1831), 70.
148. "English Lexicography," Bibliotheca Sacra, XX (1863), 93.
149. "An American Dictionary of the English Language, etc.
1859," Atlantic Monthly, V (1860), 633.
150. Introduction.
151. Ibid.
152. Ibid.
153. Ibid.
154. Ibid.
155. "An American Dictionary of the English Language, etc.,"
Westminster Review, XXVII (1831), 82.
156. Ibid.
157. Ibid.
158. Quoted by Louis Dyer, "A Lexicographer on Lexicography,"
Nation, LXXI (1900), 29.
159. Advertisement to An American Dictionary. New York: Sherman Converse, 1828, I.
160. Allen, op. cit., p. 15.
161. Advertisement to An American Dictionary.
162. Op. cit., p. 103.
163. Richard Garnett, "English Lexicography," The Quarterly
Review, LIV (1835), 305-309.
164. Quoted by Nicolas Trubner. Bibliographical Guide to American
Literature. London: Trubner and Company, 1859, p. lxiv.
165. Ibid.
166. The Westminster Review, XXVII (1831), 67.
167. "English Dictionaries, with Remarks upon the English Language," Southern Literary Messenger, XXII (1856), 172.
168. "An American Dictionary of the English Language, etc., by
Noah Webster, 1828," North American Review, XXVIII
(1829), 433.
169. "English Lexicography." The American Theological Review,
II (1860), 446, 448, and 449, quoted by Ford and Skeel,
op. cit., II, footnote, pp. 386-387.

170. Quoted in "An American Dictionary of the English Language by
Noah Webster. Revised by Goodrich, 1848," <u>Literary</u>
<u>World</u>, (N. Y.), II (1847-48), 454.

171. <u>Dictionaries in the Boston Mercantile Library and Boston</u>
<u>Atheneum.</u> Springfield: G. & C. Merriam, 1856, p. 2.

172. Noah Webster. "To the Friends of American Literature."
Bound with other pamphlets in a volume entitled <u>English</u>
<u>Language</u>, New York Public Library.

173. Barnes had been employed to edit the spelling book to make
it conform to the <u>American Dictionary</u>, but he died from
an accident before he completed the task and the work was
given to Aaron Ely, also of New York. Ely worked only
as a collaborator of Webster. Warfel, <u>op</u>. <u>cit</u>., pp. 390-
391.

174. Quoted by Lyman Cobb. <u>A Critical Review of the Orthography</u>
<u>of Dr. Webster's Series of Books for Systematick Instruc-</u>
<u>tion in the English Language, etc.</u> New York: Collins and
Hannay, 1831, footnote, p. iii.

175. In a "Review of Webster's Quarto Dictionary," p. 7, in <u>A</u>
<u>Critical Review</u>, Cobb points out that in this class of
words there are in our language and acknowledged by Webster in his dictionaries about five hundred. Of these,
Webster has terminated about three hundred and twenty
with <u>c</u> only, and about one hundred and eighty with the <u>c</u>
and <u>k</u> both.

176. Daniel Barnes said to Webster in 1827: "Your Dictionary, Sir, is
the best book of the kind that has been published since
the flood. As soon as it is published, I will lay it on my
table, and tell my pupils, 'That is your canon; follow
that, and no other book.'" Quoted by Allen Walker Read,
<u>op</u>. <u>cit</u>., p. 7.

177. Quoted in Webster. <u>To the Friends of American Literature</u>,
p. 3.

178. Webster's MSS, New York Public Library.

179. Philpott, <u>op</u>. <u>cit</u>., p. 5.

180. Trubner, <u>op</u>. <u>cit</u>., p. lxiii.

181. Notation made by Webster on a small slip of paper, Webster's
MSS, New York Public Library.

182. Webster's MSS, New York Public Library.

183. <u>Ibid</u>. Barker wrote a letter to Webster January 9, 1831, on
the back of the advertisement. At the bottom of the advertisement is written in Barker's hand, "Now 916."

184. Webster's MSS, New York Public Library.

185. Allibone, <u>op</u>. <u>cit</u>., III, 2628.

186. Websterls <u>MSS</u>, New York Public Library.

187. Ford and Skeel, <u>op</u>. <u>cit</u>., II, 538.

188. Converse became deeply embarrassed in his circumstances
and was unable to proceed with the publication. The stereotype plates and right of publication were mortgaged to
D. & J. Ames, by whom they were offered to G. & C.
Merriam about the year 1833 or 1834. They were bought
by N. & J. White of New York. <u>A Gross Literary Fraud</u>
<u>Exposed: Relating to the Publication of Worcester's</u>

Dictionary in London, as Webster's Dictionary. Springfield: G. & C. Merriam, 1854, p. 9.

189. W. C. F. [William Chauncey Fowler]. Printed, But Not Published. pp. 6-7. New York Public Library.

190. Preface.

191. "Webster's International Dictionary--Especially Its Pronunciation," New Englander, LIII (1890), 423.

192. Preface.

193. Ford and Skeel, op. cit., II, 540.

194. Webster's MSS, New York Public Library. It is not indicated which one of the dictionaries is meant.

195. Ibid.

196. An announcement prepared by Webster stated that the price would be twelve dollars. Webster's Miscellaneous MSS, New York Public Library. In Webster's manuscript material in the New York Public Library there is a note signed by Webster, dated October, 1841, to the effect that booksellers taking subscriptions and paying for the books on delivery should have them at a price which will give them a profit of at least three dollars a copy, either bound or folded.

197. Webster's MSS, New York Public Library.

198. A note signed by Webster is given at the close of the Supplement, page 1041, but there is a statement in Ford and Skeel, op. cit., II, 361, with reference to the Yale Biographies by Dexter that in the spring of 1843 he revised an Appendix prepared by his son.

199. Ford and Skeel, op. cit., II, 538.

200. Webster's MSS, New York Public Library.

201. Webster's MSS, New York Public Library.

202. The copy examined for this study was the edition of 1848.

203. Preface to the Revised Edition, p. iii.

204. Ibid., p. x.

205. Ibid., p. iii.

206. Preface, p. iv.

207. A writer in Putnam's Monthly gives the reason for the engagement's being broken off.

"He [Percival] could only work in his own time and way. Nothing could be passed over until thoroughly finished; and the consequence was, that he would sometime spend days upon some single insignificant word, whose history, if attainable, was of no importance. In the meantime, printers, compositors, and proof-readers must be paid for standing idle; so, after a short trial, they were reluctantly compelled to give up, and go on without his aid. During the time he was occupied in the work, I occasionally saw him at Professor Goodrich's rooms. He pursued his investigations standing by the side of the book-shelves; generally holding two or three books in his hands, having a pile of others collected at his feet, wearing on his head his ragged leather cap, usually keeping his back turned toward any persons in the room, and never, while I was

present, speaking or raising his eyes from the work. "
Quoted in Ward, op. cit., pp. 474-475.
208. Preface, p. vi.
209. Quoted in Have We a National Standard, etc. ? p. 9.
210. Fly-leaf to the 1853 edition.
211. "Webster's Unabridged Dictionary," The American Journal of
Education, II (1856), 517.
212. Fly-leaf to the 1853 edition, quoted from the New York Tribune, August, 1848.
213. Ibid.
214. Ibid.
215. Lowndes, op. cit., p. 2864.
216. Webster's MSS, New York Public Library.
217. The items appear as follows in Webster's will:
    4. Having given to my daughter Julia & her husband
       Chauncey A. Goodrich, the sum of thirty seven cents
       on every copy of my Octavo dictionary, which shall be
       printed & sold, during twenty eight years from its
       first publication, which will probably include a full
       share or more than an equal share of my property,
       when divided among my children; I therefore give &
       bequeath to my other children, Emily, Harriet, Wil-
       liam & Eliza, & to my granddaughter Mary W. Trow-
       bridge, & to their legal representatives, all my other
       property, including real and personal estate, & copy-
       rights now vested in me and not otherwise bequeathed
       nor assigned to my son William, by an agreement for
       the publication of my comprehensive dictionary, all
       which property is to be equally divided among my
       said children & grandchild according to law.
    9. If in the course of events it shall appear that my
       daughter Julia & her husband, Chauncey A. Goodrich,
       shall not receive from the copyright of my dictionary
       as stated above, an equal share of my property, my
       will is that her share shall be made equal from my
       other property.
    Webster's MSS, New York Public Library.
218. "A really important publishing house was that of J. S. & C.
    Adams in Amherst. This house bought the copyright of
    'Webster's Dictionary' from Webster's executors, and for
    a time the dictionary was printed in Amherst itself. Later
    the copyright was sold to G. & C. Merriam and the work
    of publication was removed to Springfield. " Edwin D.
    Mead, 'Noah Webster: Massachusetts, Dictionary Made at
    Amherst, " Springfield Sunday Republican, October 18,
    1908. Cf. also J. C. Derby. Fifty Years Among Authors,
    Books, and Publishers. New York: G. W. Carleton and
    Company, 1884, p. 377: "It was there I learned for the
    first time that they [Merriams] had just purchased from
    J. S. & C. Adams, publishers at Amherst, the copyright
    of Noah Webster's Dictionary, which had been sold them

by Governor Ellsworth, a son-in-law and executor of Dr. Webster. "
219. Publisher's Preface, p. lxxxi.

CHAPTER V

WORCESTER AND HIS DICTIONARIES

Of the American lexicographers who belong to the period studied, the one who ranks second in importance to Webster is Joseph Emerson Worcester, a school teacher and author of several textbooks in geography and history in addition to his dictionaries. A native of New Hampshire, he established himself in Cambridge and became the leader of the conservative language group that claimed Boston as its center. In this chapter the discussion centers around Worcester's dictionaries, beginning with his abridgment of Johnson's Dictionary as Improved by Todd, and abridged by Chalmers, with Walker's Pronouncing Dictionary Combined, 1828, and extending through his large quarto, A Dictionary of the English Language, published in 1860.

Joseph Emerson Worcester was a descendant of one of the early New England ministers, Reverend William Worcester, who came to Massachusetts from England and was settled as the first minister of the Congregational society in Salisbury, between the years 1638 and 1640. [1] Although William Worcester left nothing to posterity to indicate his intellectual achievements, Cotton Mather considered him of sufficient importance to include in his "List of the Reverend Learned and Holy Divines Coming from Europe to America, by whose Evangelical Ministry the Churches in America have been illuminated. "[2]

The Reverend Francis Worcester, third in line of descent from William Worcester, moved in 1750 to Hollis, New Hampshire, where he remained until his death in 1783. [3] The youngest son of Francis Worcester was Noah Worcester, who came to Hollis with his father at the age of fifteen, and who married Lydia Taylor of Hollis, February 22, 1757, and settled with his father upon the paternal homestead. [4] He held many important offices and was much respected for his intelligence, vigor of mind, and integrity. He was twice married and had sixteen children. His second son was Jesse Worcester, the father of Joseph Emerson. In June 1782, Jesse Worcester, at the age of twenty-one, was married to Sarah Parker, daughter of Josiah Parker, of Hollis, by whom he had nine sons and six daughters, all of whom lived to maturity and the majority to an advanced age. [5]

Joseph Emerson Worcester, the second son, was born at Bedford, not far from Manchester, New Hampshire, on August 24, 1784. Ten years later his father moved to Hollis where the Worcester home remained for many decades. Jesse Worcester was of the hard-working, thrifty, shrewd Yankee type, who required every child to have his routine duties on the farm, and who allowed the older ones to leave only after they had become twenty-one. [6]

The children were brought up in the severe doctrines of the Calvinist faith and with little opportunity for education, but they probably inherited from their father his repressed longing for knowledge, for fourteen out of the fifteen children became teachers in New England schools or academies. [7] The father was for many years a teacher in the public schools both in Bedford and Hollis, held various public offices, was an occasional contributor to the public journals of his time, and was the author of an unpublished work entitled The Chronicles of Nissitissit. [8] It is related that after the toils of the day, Joseph Emerson used to sit until midnight, in company with his elder brother Jesse, reading Rollin's Ancient History, Josephus, and similar works by the light of pitchpine knots. [9] He gained possession of a grammar, which he mastered by himself. [10] The two oldest boys ploughed the soil, milked the cows, did other farming chores, and spent a few odd terms at the district school when work was slack.

When Joseph Emerson reached twenty-one, he persuaded Jesse that the time had come for them to secure an education, and in the autumn of 1805 the two registered at Phillips Academy. [11] With them in the same recitation were boys of eight or nine. Both Jesse and Joseph remained in Phillips Academy for four years and graduated with distinction. Joseph also helped to prepare himself for college at Boscamen and Salisbury, New Hampshire, and at Salem, Massachusetts, where he spent two or more years in teaching. [12] In 1809 he entered the Sophomore Class in Yale College. Here he won a reputation as a thorough and enterprising scholar. His particular interest was in linguistic studies, but he was also interested in debating and was President of Linonia. He was elected to Phi Beta Kappa, as one of the four highest men in the class. He had nothing to do with the many riots of the period and took his degree uneventfully in 1811. [13]

After leaving college, Worcester was employed for five years as the teacher of a private academy at Salem. [14] It was while teaching at Salem that he had as his pupil Nathaniel Hawthorne, whose first school master he was. The story is told of Hawthorne's being made lame in ball-playing, and of Worcester's coming to the house to carry on the lessons. [15]

It was in Salem, also, that Worcester began the preparation of his first work, a Geographical Dictionary or Universal Gazetteer, Ancient and Modern, which was published at Andover in 1817, in two octavo volumes of near one thousand pages each. [16] This was followed by a Gazetteer of the United States, published in 1818. [17]

In 1816 Worcester had moved to Andover and, in 1819, in order to obtain greater literary advantages, he established himself permanently in Cambridge. [18]

The remaining years of his life were filled with indefatigable labor, with no outstanding events except the appearance of volumes of his writings from time to time. In 1847, when he was nearly sixty, he married Amy Elizabeth McKean, daughter of the Reverend Joseph McKean, Professor of Rhetoric and Oratory in Harvard College. Mrs. Worcester was a lady of culture and accomplishment and was in full sympathy with her husband's work. They had no children. [19]

For one year Worcester lived in Craigie House with Longfellow. In a letter to his father, dated May 3, 1841, Longfellow writes:

> ... For the last week this house has been a scene of confusion and desolation, such as I hope never to see again. The sale of Mrs. Craigie's furniture began and continued two days; and the delivery after the sale, and clearing the house, continued till Saturday. But at length all is quiet again. Mr. Worcester takes the house for one year, and I keep my rooms. I should dislike to move. Had it come to that, I should have gone into College; an arrangement which, on the whole, I should not be very well satisfied with. [20]

Thomas Wentworth Higginson says that Worcester shared Craigie House with Longfellow for a time, that he bought the house, and ultimately sold it to Nathan Appleton, father of the second Mrs. Longfellow, to whom Appleton presented it. [21]

Longfellow wrote in his Journal, October 18, 1854,

> My morning walk at sunrise is delightful in this delicious weather. Meet Mr. Worcester, the lexicographer, jogging along on his black horse. He says, with a jolt after each word, "Why - don'tyou - get a - horse and - ride as - I do?"[22]

In 1819 was published Worcester's Elements of Geography, Ancient and Modern, for the use of public schools and academies, accompanied with an ancient and modern atlas. It became so popular that it passed through several editions, and was used as a textbook in many of the public schools and academies of New England. [23] In 1824 two other works in geography appeared.

In 1825 Worcester was elected a member of the American Academy of Arts and Sciences, before which he read an essay entitled "Remarks on Longevity and the Expectation of Life in the United States, relating particularly to the State of New Hampshire, with some Comparative Views in Relation to Foreign Countries."[24]

Within the next few years Worcester published several other textbooks in history and geography.

Worcester's first work in lexicography was an edition of
Johnson's Dictionary, as improved by Todd, and abridged by Chalmers with Walker's Pronouncing Dictionary Combined, which was
published in Boston in 1828. It was a large octavo volume of 1,155
closely printed pages, [25] based on Walker's fourth edition. [26] The
sales in 1858 and before were about twelve thousand per annum. [27]

In 1830 was published the first of Worcester's own dictionaries, A Comprehensive, Pronouncing and Explanatory Dictionary of
the English Language, a 12mo., pp. xx, 400, Boston. A second
edition was published in Boston, 1831. [28] It was revised and enlarged in 1835, 1860, and 1864. The number of copies printed from
1856 to September 1865 was fifty-seven thousand, or an average of
over eight thousand per annum. [29] The edition of 1835 was examined
for this study. It was published at Boston, 1843, by Jenks and
Palmer, and sold for ninety cents a copy. [30]

The author states in the Preface that he formed the plan for
the work while engaged in editing Johnson's Dictionary, as Improved
by Todd, and abridged by Chalmers, with Walker's Pronouncing Dictionary Combined. The small dictionaries in use seemed to be too
defective, with respect to the number of words they contained and
also with regard to definition and pronunciation, to supply the need
of schools and for other uses for which the large octavo would be
too expensive. The execution of the work was delayed by Worcester's abridgment of Webster's American Dictionary of the English
Language, 1829 (see Chapter IV), to which Worcester prefixed A
Synopsis of Words Differently Pronounced by Different Orthoepists,
which he had originally designed for his own work and which he inserted in this dictionary in alphabetical order. [31]

In preparing the work the author says that he made much
use of Jameson's Dictionary, which is chiefly a combination of Johnson and Walker. Many other dictionaries were consulted. A list
of twenty-seven lexicographers and orthoepists considered as authorities are given in the Introduction. The English authorities most
frequently cited are Sheridan, Walker, Perry, Jones, Enfield, Fulton
and Knight, and Jameson, all of whom are authors of pronouncing
dictionaries. [32]

The vocabulary consists of 343 pages with approximately
43,000 words arranged two columns to a page, the key to letters to
each column appearing above each column. This number of words
is six thousand more than are contained in Walker's Critical Pronouncing Dictionary. [33] An Appendix of eight pages contains about
seven hundred words, some of which are English words which have
been long in use, but which were omitted by oversight; some are
technical terms; and some are words which are of recent introduction
into the language, but which have had the sanction of respectable
usage. [34] Authorities are given for most of these.

The Appendix is followed by four pages of remarks on orthography which precede A Vocabulary of Words of Doubtful or Various Orthography. "These Remarks and Rules, together with the Vocabulary, embrace nearly or quite all the difficulties and doubtful cases that are often met with in English orthography."[35] The words of doubtful orthography are arranged in two columns, the orthography of the left-hand column deemed to be well authorized, while in that on the right there is great diversity. There are over eleven hundred of these words. In many cases the difference consists in the first syllable being em or im, en or in, or in the commutation of c or s, s and z, e and o, etc. Pronouncing vocabularies of Greek, Latin, and Scripture proper names, as well as Geographic names, embracing about three thousand words, with remarks on their pronunciation, are added, the last as a special addition to the revised edition.

The author states that with respect to those words for the orthography, pronunciation, or definition of which an intelligent English reader has most frequent occasion to consult a dictionary, this is one of the most complete vocabularies extant, and that words in other dictionaries not contained in this are either obsolete, not in good use, or are participles or compounds.[36] Obsolete words are included in this dictionary when they were found in works not obsolete. Numerous technical terms in the various arts and sciences as well as words and phrases from foreign languages are included. The foreign words, if not anglicized, are printed in italics, and the languages to which they belong are indicated in parenthesis after the word. Some of these words seem to be useless, such as "Jannizereffendi, an officer among the Turks, whose duties are similar to those of the provost-marshal in the European armies." The imperfect tenses and the perfect participles of all the irregular verbs are given, as well as the plural forms of irregular nouns. The imperfect forms and the perfect participles of the irregular verbs are inserted separately in their alphabetical places. Words used as different parts of speech are repeated for each part of speech; even transitive and intransitive verbs are listed separately, as break, v. a.; break, v. n.; break, n. Words of recent or doubtful authority are noted as such. Abolitionist and emphasize are marked as modern words.

According to a statement in the Preface, pronunciation has received particular attention in this dictionary. Words of various or doubtful, or disputed pronunciation are exhibited, in brackets, in the modes in which they are pronounced by all the most eminent English orthoepists. An example of this is the word ĕp´och, or ē´poch [ĕp´ok, S. J. E. & Ja; ē´pok, P. Wb.; ĕp´ok or ē´pok, W.] The number of primitive words respecting which authorities are presented amounts to about thirteen hundred. An elaborate system of notation is employed. In the "Key to the Sounds of the Marked Letters," page iii, the vowel a is distinguished by seven separate sounds, e with five, o with six, u with six, y with four, while the diphthongs oi and oy, ou and ow, and eu are noted. Many of the sounds of the letters are exhibited at the bottom of each page. The

asterisk is prefixed in many instances to two or more words of the
same class or family to show that their pronunciation is governed
by the same rule.

The marks are applied to the letters in the words in their
proper orthography, thus avoiding the necessity of respelling most
of the words. The secondary and primary accents of the vowels
are distinguished. The Preface discusses the way in which Sheridan, Walker, Jones, and Jameson mark the different sounds of the
vowels. Worcester says that since the pronunciation of the English
language is in a great measure arbitrary, varying more or less
according to the caprices of fashion and taste, the ultimate standard
is not the authority of any dictionary or any orthoepist but the usage
of literary and well-bred society; it is the duty of the orthoepist
merely to record what the pronunciation actually is, rather than
what it should be. [37] Yet he clings to the usage of London as the
best standard.

> ... Although it is not to be questioned that with respect
> to the many millions who speak the English language, the
> usage of London is entitled to far more weight than that
> of any other city, yet this is not the only thing to be ob-
> served. The usage of the best society in the place or dis-
> trict where one resides, is not to be disregarded. If our
> pronunciation is agreeable to the analogy of the language,
> and conformed to the practice of the best society with
> which we have intercourse, we may have not sufficient
> reason to change it, though it should deviate more or less
> from the existing usages of London. [38]

Two modes of pronouncing a word are, in many instances,
given, independent of the forms included within the brackets, the
compiler being usually inclined to the pronunciation most conformable
to analogy or orthography. In some cases where the mode of pronunciation indicated by the orthography and other modes deviating
from it seem to be equally worthy of approbation, the compiler has
presented, on his own authority, the former only. An example of
this is the word lieutenant. The pronunciation of lieu tĕn´ant is
supported by respectable authority, and is given first outside the
brackets, yet, the other forms lif tĕn´ant, liv tĕn´ant, lū tĕn´ant
are also given with the authorities for the pronunciation attached.

The definitions are short, usually consisting of synonymous
words or phrases. In many instances, technical, provincial, and
American usage of words is explained or pointed out, such as
"agitator, n. one who agitates: in English history persons chosen by
the army, in 1647, to watch over its interests"; "aground, ad.
stranded: applied to a ship. "

According to the author, much care has been given to orthography, and in order to determine the spelling of many words written differently, several of the best English dictionaries were used
and regard was paid to usage and analogy. With respect to the

words which end in ic or ick, Worcester says that the general usage, both in England and America, is now so strongly in favor of the omission of the k, that "it is high time it was excluded from the dictionaries."39 He, however, retains it in monosyllables, such as stick, brick, and in words ending in ock; as, hemlock, hillock. The verbs frolic, mimic, and traffic, which Webster excepts from the general rule and writes with the k, are here given without it, but in the past tenses and participles it is retained.

The question of omitting or including the letter u in words ending in or or our required more consideration since there was so much diversity among the dictionaries and in general usage. Worcester decided that since the omission had become the established practice in many words, he would extend it to all the words in question.

There are several other classes of words that should be noticed: 1) Certain verbs derived from the Greek are written with the termination ize and not ise. 2) Derivative adjectives ending in able are written with the e before a, except those which end in ce or ge. 3) Words ending in the syllable al or all, with the full sound of broad a, have the l double; as befall, downfall, miscall. 4) A class of compound words retains the final double l, which is found in the simple words; as, foretell, down-hill. 5) Words of one syllable ending with a single consonant, preceded by a single vowel, and words of two or more syllables ending in the same manner and having the accent on the last syllable, double the final consonant on adding the additional syllable, unless a diphthong precedes the last consonant or the accent is not on the last syllable. There is an exception to this rule in most of the verbs ending in the letter l, which double the consonant even though the accent is not on the last syllable. In this dictionary these words are given both with the double l and single l, except parallel which does not double the last l. 40

The words kidnap and worship always double the p on assuming an additional syllable. Several other verbs which end in p, s, and t are sometimes allowed to double the final consonant when another syllable is added, but Worcester says the more correct and regular mode is to write them without doubling the final consonant, as bias, biased, biasing; gossip, gossiped, gossiping; benefit, benefited, benefiting.

Two ways for spelling several words are given: jelly, gelly; joust, just; julap, julep; kale, kail; kalendar, calendar; ottar, otter; nosle, nozle; kaw, caw; keg, cag; bourse, burse; brocage, brokage; mannikin, manikin. In the spelling of words ending in tre, as centre, metre, Worcester follows the English lexicographers. Other words of doubtful or various orthography are given in the list on pages 357-362, the authorized spelling being given in the left hand column.

Worcester calls attention to the fact that the orthography of flour instead of flower denoting the edible part of grain, and of dye instead of die, in the sense of color, are now well-established. Johnson did not recognize flour and Webster in his American Dictionary, 1828, page 350, gives the meaning as an edible part of corn under flower, but calls attention to the fact that it is now written flour.

The Comprehensive Dictionary came rapidly into favor.   Krapp calls it a "discriminating and scholarly piece of work. "[41]   The Common School Journal complimented the Dictionary on the number of words, on the inclusion of the imperfect and past participle forms of the verbs, on its lists of words of doubtful orthography, and on its pronouncing vocabularies of proper names. [42]   Sidney Willard says of it: "No English dictionary since its publication has, we believe, been so extensively used as a manual or so much relied upon as an authority. "[43]   An English classical scholar, Professor Dunglison, of the University of Virginia, said of it, soon after its appearance: 'I can, without hesitation, award to this Dictionary the merit of being best adapted to the end in view of any I have examined. It is, in other words, the best portable pronouncing and explanatory Dictionary that I have seen and as such is deserving of very extensive circulation. "[44]

In 1835 Worcester published his Elementary Dictionary with a pronouncing vocabulary of classical, scripture and geographical proper names, for the use of public schools.   Many editions followed. It is a duodecimo of 360 pages, containing over 44, 000 words, which sold for sixty cents.   It was published by Jenks, Palmer and Company, Boston. [45]

After the publication of the Universal and Critical Dictionary in 1846, the Comprehensive Dictionary was revised and considerably enlarged and made substantially an abridgment of the larger work. It is a duodecimo of 491 pages.   The "Principles of Pronunciation" was inserted, the several vocabularies were considerably increased, and all parts of the work materially improved.   In all its vocabularies it contains about sixty-seven hundred words.   Again, in 1849, further additions were made, comprising "Abbreviations used in Writing and Printing, " "A Collection of Phrases and Quotations from the Latin, French, Italian, and Spanish Languages, " and the "Principal Deities, Heroes, etc. in Greek and Roman Fabulous History. "

In 1855 Hickling, Swan, and Brown published the work entitled A Pronouncing, Explanatory, and Synonymous Dictionary of the English Language, a duodecimo volume of 565 pages, by Joseph E. Worcester, for the use of high schools and academies.   This work is substantially an enlargement of the Comprehensive Dictionary. The vocabularies are increased, nearly three thousand words having been added to the dictionary proper, and fuller definitions having been given to many of the words.   The Vocabulary of Greek and Latin Proper Names has about forty-five hundred names added to the list found in Walker's Key, most of these having been taken from the works relating to this subject by Carr, Sharpe, and Trollope. [46]   A list of common Christian names with their signification has been added.

The main new feature of this dictionary is the discrimination of the principal synonyms of the language. In the preparation of these synonyms use was made of the works on this subject by Crabb, Taylor, Platts, and Graham, and of a small work revised by Archbishop Whately. [47] The synonyms are illustrated by sentences.

In 1860, the Comprehensive Dictionary was again revised and published in Boston by Swan, Brewer, and Tileston, and in Cleveland by Ingham and Bragg. This edition is a combination of the Comprehensive Dictionary of 1849 and the Synonymous Dictionary of 1855, and contains 612 pages, duodecimo.

In November, 1831, Worcester made a voyage to Europe for his health, and to extend his linguistic researches. He spent about seven months, visiting many of the chief places of interest in England, Scotland, France, Holland, and Germany, and in collecting books in the departments of geography, history, philology, and lexicography. [48] After his return from Europe he became editor of the American Almanac and Repository of Useful Knowledge, a statistical annual of from three hundred to three hundred seventy-five pages containing information about each of the separate states, and of several nations of Europe. He continued as editor for eleven years. [49] O. W. B. Peabody wrote in 1835 that Worcester had prepared all of the contents of the Almanac except the astronomical department. This, he adds, was no mean title to distinction since "There are very few works, in which so much information, of a kind not easily accessible, is presented with so much authenticity." [50] Thomas Wentworth Higginson gives the following picture of Worcester in connection with a discussion of the literary publications of Cambridge:

> Nor must be forgotten another important publication always edited in Cambridge, --The American Almanac. Its main founder was another of those eccentric characters of whom the university town was then prolific. Among the various academic guests who used to gather in my mother's hospitable parlor on Sunday evenings, no figure is more vivid in my memory than one whom Lowell in his "Fireside Travels" has omitted to sketch. This was Dr. Joseph E. Worcester, whose "Elements of History, Ancient and Modern," I had faithfully studied at school; and who was wont to sit silent, literally by the hour, a slumbering volcano of facts and statistics, while others talked. He was tall, stiff, gentle, and benignant, wearing blue spectacles, and with his head as if it were engulfed in the high collar of other days. He rocked to and fro, placidly listening to what was said, and might perhaps have been suspected of a gentle slumber, when the casual mention of some city in the West, then dimly known, would rouse him to action. He would then cease rocking, would lean forward, and say in his peaceful voice: "Chillicothe?" What is the present population of Chillicothe?" or "Columbus? What is the pupulation of Columbus?" and then,

putting away the item in some appropriate pigeonhole of
his vast memory, would relapse into his rocking chair
once more.... [51]

In 1846 appeared A Universal and Critical Dictionary of the
English Language; to which are added Walker's Key to the Pronunciation of Classical and Scripture Proper Names, much enlarged
and improved; and a pronouncing Vocabulary of Modern Geographical
Names, Boston: Wilkins, Carter and Company, octavo, pp. lxxxvi,
956, at the price of three and one-half dollars for the regular edition, and five dollars for the library edition. [52] The compiler states
in the Preface that after beginning the preparation of his Comprehensive Dictionary he adopted the practice of recording all the English words which he met that were used by respectable authors and
were not found in Todd's edition of Johnson's Dictionary. This
practice was continued with the purpose of providing the means of
improving the Comprehensive Dictionary, but he found the words so
numerous that he decided to make a new and a larger dictionary
that would contain as complete a vocabulary as he should be able to
make. [53] Todd's edition of Johnson's Dictionary and Walker's Critical Pronouncing Dictionary were used as the basis of the work,
but their words were revised in relation to orthography, pronunciation, etymology, definition, etc., and many that relate to the arts
and sciences were defined anew. [54] Words in Todd's Johnson which
are in common use, and of the correctness of which there can be
no doubt, are for the most part left without cited authority. As in
the Comprehensive Dictionary the definitions are very brief.

To the words in Todd's Johnson nearly twenty-seven hundred
were added, making a total of over eighty-three thousand words. An
asterisk is annexed to words that have been included which were not
found in Todd's Johnson. These new words were taken from English
dictionaries, particularly those of Ash, Richardson, and Smart. The
technical words were taken from the best written scientific works,
or from dictionaries and encyclopedias. Between fourteen and fifteen hundred words were contributed by William Allen. [55] For the
new words authorities are cited. Most of these authorities are
English because the author thinks that it is satisfactory to many
readers to know that a new or doubtful word is not peculiar to American writers. [56] Regarding his indebtedness to Webster, Worcester
makes the following statement: "With respect to Webster's Dictionary, which the compiler several years since abridged, he is not
aware of having taken a single word, or the definition of a word,
from that work, in the preparation of this; but in relation to words
of various or disputed pronunciation, Webster's authority is often
cited in connection with that of English orthoepists."[57]

The compiler states that much care has been taken to note
such words as are technical, foreign, obsolete or antiquated, local
or provincial, low or exceptional. Many rare or disputed words
are given with the authors cited. "The grammatical forms and inflections of words have been given more fully than ever before in
any English dictionary; and brief critical notes on the orthography,

the pronunciation, the grammatical form and construction, and the peculiar, technical, local, provincial, and American uses of words, are scattered throughout the volume.... The design has been to give the greatest quantity of useful matter in the most condensed form, and to specify, as far as practicable, authorities in doubtful or disputed cases. "[58]

The Introduction is very full, and is divided into six parts or sections. The first, on principles of pronunciation, contains the same elaborate key to the sounds of marked letters as is given in the Comprehensive Dictionary. So elaborate was this system that it caused many comments. One critic says that he considers "the attempt to distinguish and indicate every slight and doubtful change of sound not merely useless, but positively hurtful--likely to mislead natives, and still more likely to mislead foreigners. "[59] A detailed discussion of the principles of pronunciation is given. In the section of "Orthoepy and Orthoepists" Worcester again expresses his preference for the usage of London as the standard of pronunciation, but he also thinks that the usage of society in the place or district where one resides and the analogy of the language should be considered.

The second section of the Introduction is on orthography, but little material not included in the Comprehensive Dictionary is given. The list of words of doubtful or various orthography has been increased by a few hundred words. The third section contains an outline of English grammar for the purpose of facilitating the use of the Dictionary. A list of words with the proper prepositions attached is included. One of the combinations is that of independent on. Worcester objects to "a strange and awkward neologism" which had recently been introduced by which the present passive participle has been substituted for the participle ending in ing.

The fourth section deals with the origin, formation, and etymology of the English language. In Part V there is given a brief essay on archaisms, provincialisms, and Americanisms. Worcester says that there is more uniformity of the language in this country than in England, due to the frequent removals of the inhabitants from one place to another, their free intercourse with one another, and to the fact that elementary education is more generally diffused among the middle and lower classes here than in England. The people are also more in the habit of having recourse to a dictionary for the pronunciation and use of words.[60] He lists a few words which owe their origin or peculiar use to American institutions; words that relate to the political and civil institutions of England, that are rarely used in this country except with reference to England; terms that are used with different meanings in England and America; some words in America that are regarded as of Indian origin; English provincialisms often used in the United States; words of disputed propriety used in both England and America; and words which have senses affixed to them in the United States which are different from the senses in which they are commonly used in England. The last group comprises the following words: baggage, balance, clever, cob, corn, creek, fall, lumber, merchant, quite, spell, stage, store, and a few verbs. 61

Part VI is a history of English lexicography. In this discussion Worcester pays tribute to the contribution of Webster in these words: "It [An American Dictionary] is a work of great learning and research, comprising a much more full vocabulary of the language than Johnson's Dictionary, and containing many and great improvements with respect to the etymology and definition of words; but the taste and judgment of the author are not generally esteemed equal to his industry and erudition."62 A discussion is given of English orthoepists and a catalogue of English dictionaires is included. There are eighteen American dictionaries in the list.

Walker's Key to the Classical Pronunciation of Greek, Latin, and Scripture Proper Names" is added to the Dictionary. It was enlarged and improved by Worcester's adding about three thousand other Greek and Latin names, of which about twenty-four hundred have been taken from the Classical Pronunciation of Proper Names, established by Citations from the Greek and Latin Poets, Greek Historians, Geographers and Scholiasts, by Thomas Swinburne; between five and six hundred are words which were added by W. Trollope to his editions of Walker's Key, and some were taken from Scheller's Latin and German Lexicon. 63 The words to which initials of the authors from which additions were taken are not annexed, are words found in Walker's Key. A Pronouncing Vocabulary of Geographical Names completes the book. Observations on the topic concerned are prefixed to both these divisions.

In respect to etymology the general rule followed is that of giving the etymons of such words as are derived from foreign languages, especially the Greek, Latin, French, Spanish, Italian, Dutch, German, Danish, and Swedish. Since the greater part of English words of frequent occurrence were derived from Anglo-Saxon, the etymology of these words have been, for the most part, omitted. The number of primitive words respecting which authorities are presented amounts to about two thousand.

It was this dictionary that Bohn, an English bookseller, published in England with a false title page and a mutilated Preface. For a discussion of the consequences see Chapter VI.

Sidney Willard estimates Worcester's ability as a lexicographer, as exhibited in this dictionary, as follows:

> While Mr. Worcester has included in his vocabulary most of the words he has found in the productions of respectable writers, on some of which, however, he sets a discountenancing mark, we do not find that he has excluded any which have heretofore been admitted into dictionaries, and are entitled to respect. He does not belong to the corps of militant etymologists, who war against custom, which establishes the laws of language. On the

contrary, he pays due fealty to these laws, and gives no countenance to a revolutionary spirit. We have discovered no instance in which he has changed the orthography of a word to make it conform to an assumed theory. In these respects, he has, wherever we have traced him, shown that fidelity to our language as we found it, which makes him worthy of entire confidence. [64]

In 1847-49 Worcester was threatened with loss of sight. Both of his eyes were almost wholly useless for nearly two years. During this period three operations for cataracts were performed on the right eye, and two on the left. Eventually the right eye became nearly blind, but the left eye was saved. [65]

After the partial recovery of his sight he continued his lexical work. In 1850 his <u>Primary Dictionary</u> for public schools, an 18mo. containing 384 pages, was published in Boston. [66] Other editions appeared in 1857 and 1861. The number of copies printed from 1856 to September 1863 was forty-five thousand. [67] The number of copies of it sold, as reported by its publishers, for the five years next prior to 1877, was nearly fifty thousand, or a little less than ten thousand per annum. [68]

The most important and elaborate of all of Worcester's literary labors in the department of lexicography is his large quarto, <u>A Dictionary of the English Language,</u> published in Boston by Swan, Brewer and Tileston, 1860, when Worcester was seventy-five years of age.

This dictionary, electrotyped at the Boston Stereotype Foundry and printed by H. O. Houghton and Company at Cambridge, is formed on a plan similar to the <u>Universal and Critical Dictionary,</u> but it is much larger and more comprehensive. It is an octavo of 1796 pages with 1696 pages in the main part. The number of copies printed to September, 1863, was twenty-seven thousand. [69] It sold for seven dollars and fifty cents to subscribers, nearly one thousand of which were obtained in New York City. [70] The work contains about one hundred and four thousand words, or nineteen thousand more than are contained in the <u>Universal and Critical Dictionary,</u> 1847. These are arranged three columns to a page, in a different print and better spaced than in the smaller dictionary. Of printer's ems it contains 14,944,572. [71] The words, the definitions, and the synonyms are set in different types, thereby making it easier to acquire the desired information. Authorities are given for most of the words inserted. Technical, obsolete, antiquated, rare, provincial, local, colloquial words, and those of recent introduction or of doubtful propriety are generally noted as such and proper authorities cited. In preparing the technical words use has been made of a large number of dictionaries and encyclopedias, a list of which is given in the Introduction. Several other dictionaries and glossaries were also used. When Webster is cited as an authority, the edition of his dictionary is that of 1841. In the preparation of this work Worcester was assisted by Richard Soule, William Wheeler, Loomis J.

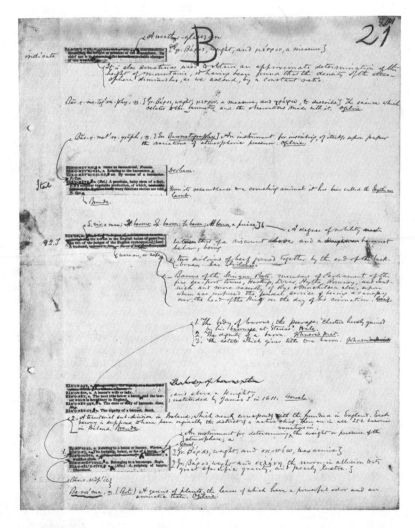

The printer's copy of column 3, page 116 of Worcester's A Dictionary of the English Language, 1860. There are slight variations between this page and the final copy. The original is in the Public Library of the City of Boston.

Campbell, William P. Drew, Joseph Hale Abbot, and John S. Dwight.
A letter to William D. Swan, the publisher of the Dictionary,
dated Boston, October 9, 1857, and signed by Charles Folsom,
Richard Soule, and William Wheeler, gives some idea of the arrangement made to prepare the manuscript for publication.

> Wm. D. Swan, Esq.
> Dear Sir,
>   Understanding from you, that the matter of organi-
> zing the best system for publishing the Quarto Dictionary
> in the shortest time and at the least expense is left en-
> tirely to your direction, and having been called on by you
> for our opinion in this regards, we beg leave to submit
> the following suggestions for your consideration.
>   I.   That, in a room properly arranged, warmed, and
> lighted, and furnished with a complete apparatus of the
> books directly used in the work of the Dictionary, all the
> collaborators labor, separately indeed, but in such prox-
> imity as will afford the opportunity of brief consultation,
> each with each, without engaging the attention of the rest;
> - and of all together at stated times, to settle reserved
> points and do up definitely and finally the work of each
> and all, according to their best light at the time.
>   II. That the person whose duty it is to pass upon the
> copy, furnish it to the printer, and revise the proofs,
> have the assistance, as he now has, of a competent per-
> son especially addicted to his department.
>   III. It is believed by us, that by the above arrangement,
> the value of the services of all would be very much en-
> hanced, and the progress of the work very materially faci-
> litated.
>   1. By saving much time now necessarily spent in
> research to justify what, though it may be sound, can-
> not be admitted without reexamination, but where often
> a single word from the person who prepared the arti-
> cle, would dispel the doubt and stamp the word as
> right, or lead to an unhesitating correction of the error,
> if one existed.
>   2. By the greater uniformity it would secure in the
> preparation of the copy.
>   3. By the greater animation it would give to the
> labors of all, from the feeling that each possessed the
> views of all, as founded on the authorities which pur-
> port to be followed, & which would thus all be at hand.
>   IV. That, in commencing this proposed new arrange-
> ment, Mr. Soule and Mr. Wheeler co-operate with Mr.
> Folson for the present, so far as may be useful in urging
> through the press the MS. already prepared, so as to in-
> sure as rapid a progress, in this respect, as the publi-
> shers desire. In regard to the copy not yet written, it
> is believed that Mr. Soule and Mr. Wheeler, though their
> time for the present would be much occupied in expediting
> the work of printing, would be able before long, under this

arrangement, to devote considerable time to the preparation of new MS.   But in order to insure the preparation
of the MS. so as to keep in advance of the printing, we
suppose it will be necessary to employ additional collabo-
rators.   The objections to employing additional help hitherto have been, first, that the slow progress of the work
through the press did not seem to justify it, and, secondly,
that there would be great difficulty in providing the additional apparatus, that would be required.   By the change
above suggested, both objections may be obviated.

                                    Charles Folsom
                                    Richard Soule, Jr.
Boston, 9 Oct. 1857.   William A. Wheeler. [72]

     About five thousand words have their synonyms exhibited both
by definitions and by illustrative sentences.   In the preparation of
these words use was made of the works on English synonyms by
Crabb, Taylor, Platts, Graham, and Whately. [73]

     In treating the etymology of words the derivations of nearly
all of the primitive words, as far as they have been ascertained,
are given.   In disputed or uncertain etymologies, the authorities are
generally specified.   This is shown in the etymology of the word
abash, v. a.

          Fr. esbahir, to affrighten.   Bailey - "Perhaps from
          abaisser, Fr. " Johnson. - Richardson says, "The past
          tense and past part of abase was anciently written abaisit,
          abayschid; whence the word abash appears to be formed. "
          - Probably from Old Fr. esbahir.   The following is from
          Cotgrave: "Esbahir, to be astonished, esbahi, abashed. "
          Chaucer has abawed in the sense of abashed.

     The compiler states in the Preface that in the treating of the
etymology of words the Teutonic, or Gothic, languages, especially
the Anglo-Saxon; and the Graeco-Gothic languages, especially the
Latin through the French, are kept distinct.   He also says that besides the strict etymons of English words derived from the Latin,
the parallel words of several sister languages of Latin origin have
been in many cases inserted, and with regard to words of northern
origin parallels of cognate words of the different languages of the
Teutonic or Gothic family have also been generally given.   These
regulations, in the main, have been followed, but in some cases,
the cognate words are taken from both groups.   Examples, Barbacan, n. [A.S. barbacan, an outwork; It. barbacane; Sp. barbacana;
Fr. barbacane;] ; fan [A.S. fan; Dut. wan; Ger. wanne. - L. vannus,
a winnowing fan; It. vanni, wings; Port. & Sp. abanico; Fr. van.]

     The definitions as given in the Universal and Critical Diction-
ary have been lenghtened both in the definitions themselves and in
the number of different definitions given to each word.   The different
definitions are numbered and separately paragraphed.   They are often
accompanied with illustrative passages from good authors.

In orthography and pronunciation this dictionary follows the
Universal Dictionary. The section on the Pronunciation of Greek
and Latin, and also of Scripture Proper Names, has been much enlarged and greatly improved by Ezra Abbot. Although based originally on Walker, the list of Greek and Latin Proper Names has
been so revised as to constitute almost a new work. Many unnecessary words have been omitted, others added, and many errors corrected. Of Walker's initial vocabulary of 10,480 names, 2,200 were
rejected as useless or as mere typographical errors; in about 500
his pronunciation was corrected, and about 6,580 names have been
added. [74] In the list of 3,950 Scripture Proper Names contained
in Walker, about 500 have been rejected and 746 have been added. [75]
The Pronunciation of Modern Geographical Names has been enlarged
by the examination of new authorities, especially Baldwin's Universal
Pronouncing Gazetteer, Lippincott's Pronouncing Gazetteer of the
World, and Muller's Wörterbuch der auslandicher Eigennamen. [76]

An addition to this dictionary is the one thousand illustrative
cuts which are inserted upon the page and at the word which they
illustrate.

From distinguished literary friends and authors, to whom
Worcester sent copies of the English Dictionary he received flat-
tering replies. In a letter of January 20, 1860, Charles Folsom
wrote to Worcester that he felt that the Dictionary would be found
to be more useful to the whole public than any dictionary of our
language that had yet appeared, or was known to be projected either
in this country or in England. "I cannot doubt," he says, "that its
general utility will commend it to the mass, and that its special
excellencies will gain for it the suffrages of those whose opinions
will stamp it with authority." [77] Thomas Carlyle wrote to him in
his note of acknowledgment:

> So far as I yet examine, it is a most lucid, exact, com-
> prehensive, altogether useful-looking dictionary; the defini-
> tions of meaning are precise, brief, correct, --the wood-
> cuts occasionally a great help, --new fields are opened with
> success, everything is calculated for carrying information
> by the directest road. Samuel Johnson said of his work,
> "Careful diligence will at last prevail"; you too I believe I
> can congratulate on a great mass of heavy and hard work
> faithfully done, --a good victory, probably the only real
> victory possible to us in this world. [78]

William Makepeace Thackeray writes:

> I have had no dictionary all my life but an old (abridged)
> Johnson of my father's, and whenever I have consulted it I
> have been aware of its countless short-comings. Let me
> thank you for giving me this useful and splendid book, and
> for thinking it would be acceptable to an English man of
> letters who holds Boston and the States in very cordial and
> grateful remembrance. [79]

Charles Dickens ends his note of thanks by saying that the Dictionary is a most remarkable work of which America will be proud and for which all who study the English language will be grateful. [80] Josiah Quincy, then in his eighty-seventh year concludes his acknowledgment with these words: "Without putting on any wing of fancy, assuming no airy stand on Parnassus, but resting on a deeply laid rock of useful labor, you have a right as much as any poet to exclaim, 'Exegi monumentum sere perennius. '"[81]

Ezra Abbot characterizes the contribution of Worcester in the following words:

> All the works of Dr. Worcester give evidence of sound judgment and good taste, combined with indefatigable industry and a conscientious solicitude for accuracy in the statement of facts. The tendency of his mind was practical rather than speculative. As a lexicographer, he did not undertake to reform long-established anomalies in the English language; his aim was rather to preserve it from corruption; and his works have certainly contributed much to that end. In respect both to orthography and pronunciation, he took great pains to ascertain the best usage; and perhaps there is no lexicographer whose judgment respecting these matters in doubtful cases deserves higher consideration. In the mazy paths of etymology, if he cannot claim the merit of an original explorer, his good sense preserved him from the wild aberrations and extravagances into which many have been mislead. His definitions, for neatness and precision, will not suffer, perhaps, in comparison with those of any of his predecessors; but it must be confessed that all our English dictionaries too often mistake a special application of a word for an essential change of meaning, and hide its precise signification in a cloud of undiscriminated synonymes. [82]

George S. Hilliard says of Worcester:

> His long and busy life was passed in unbroken literary toil; though his manners were reserved and his habits retiring, his affections were strong, and benevolence was an ever-active principle in his nature.... He was a stranger to the impulses of passion and the sting of ambition. His life was tranquil, happy and useful. A love of truth and a strong sense of duty were leading traits of his character. Little known to the public, except by name and his literary works, he was honored and loved by that small circle of relatives and friends who had constant opportunities of learning the warmth of his affections, and the strength of his virtues. [83]

Conservative in his views, Worcester accepted the ideas of the English dictionary makers and followed, in the main, their spelling and pronunciation. He believed that the duty of a lexicographer was to record the language rather than to make innovations, and we are not surprised that he became the champion of the group that opposed Webster. The controversy that arose between these two men is treated in the next chapter.

Notes

1. Samuel T. Worcester, "Joseph E. Worcester," The Granite Monthly, III (April, 1880), 245.
2. Ibid.
3. Ibid.
4. Ibid., pp. 245-246.
5. Claude M. Fuess, "Joseph Emerson Worcester (1784-1856)," The Phillips Bulletin, XIC (1925), 6.
6. Ibid.
7. Ibid.
8. Worcester, Samuel T., op. cit., p. 246.
9. Ezra Abbot, "Joseph Emerson Worcester," Proceedings of the American Academy of Arts and Sciences, VII (1865-68), 112.
10. National Cyclopedia of American Biography, VI, 50.
11. Fuess, op. cit., p. 6.
12. Abbot, op. cit., p. 112.
13. Fuess, op. cit., p. 8.
14. Ibid.
15. George E. Woodberry. Nathaniel Hawthorne. Boston: Houghton Mifflin Company, 1902, p. 5; also Julian Hawthorne. Nathaniel Hawthorne and His Wife. Fifth Edition. Boston: Ticknor and Company, 1884, I, 100.
16. Worcester, op. cit., p. 247.
17. Abbot, op. cit., p. 112.
18. Ibid.
19. Fuess, op. cit., p. 10.
20. Samuel Longfellow, editor. Life of Henry Wadsworth Longfellow. Boston: Houghton, Mifflin Company, 1891, I, 391.
21. Henry Wadsworth Longfellow. Boston: The Riverside Press, 1902, p. 121.
22. Samuel Longfellow, op. cit., p. 277.
23. Worcester, op. cit., p. 247.
24. Abbot, op. cit., p. 113.
25. Worcester, Samuel T., op. cit., p. 248.
26. American Quarterly Review, IV (1828), 192.
27. Allibone, op. cit., III, 2839.
28. Dexter, op. cit., VI, 437.
29. Allibone, op. cit., III, 2839.
30. Roorbach, op. cit., p. 595.
31. Preface, pp. vii-viii.
32. Preface, p. viii.
33. Ibid., p. vii.
34. Advertisement, p. vi.
35. Ibid.
36. Preface, pp. vii-viii.

37. Ibid., p. viii.
38. Ibid., pp. viii-ix.
39. Preface, p. xvi.
40. Preface, pp. xvi-xvii.
41. George Philip Krapp. The English Language in America. New York: The Century Company, 1925, I, 371.
42. "Words Often Mispronounced," The Common School Journal, I (1839), 361.
43. The North American Review, LXIV (1847), 190.
44. Quoted in The American Monthly Review, I (1832), 101-102.
45. Roorbach, op. cit., p. 595.
46. Preface, pp. 3-4.
47. Ibid., p. 4.
48. Worcester, Samuel T., op. cit., p. 249.
49. Ibid.
50. The North American Review, XLI (1835), 484.
51. Old Cambridge. New York: The Macmillan Company, 1899, pp. 51-52.
52. Roorbach, op. cit., p. 595.
53. Preface, p. iv.
54. Ibid.
55. Ibid., p. v. [Note the accusation made against Webster in 1842 for failing to acknowledge his indebtedness to William Allen (see page 181-82).]
56. Ibid.
57. Ibid.
58. Ibid.
59. The Literary World, II (1847-1848), 529.
60. Introduction, p. lvii.
61. Ibid., pp. lvii-lviii.
62. Ibid., p. lxv.
63. The Editor's Preface, p. 841.
64. The North American Review, LXIV (1847), 194-195.
65. Worcester, Samuel T., op. cit., pp. 249-250.
66. Ibid., p. 250.
67. Allibone, op. cit., III, 2838.
68. Worcester, Samuel T., op. cit., p. 250.
69. Allibone, op. cit., III, 2839.
70. Advertisement of the Dictionary, Webster's MSS, New York Public Library.
71. Allibone, op. cit., III, 2839.
72. Manuscript Letter in the Folsom Collection, Boston Public Library.
73. Preface, p. v.
74. Preface to "Key to the Classical Pronunciation of Greek, Latin, and Scripture Proper Names," p. 1701.
75. Preface to "Pronunciation of Scripture Proper Names," p. 1737.
76. "Pronunciation of Modern Geographical Names," p. 1751.
77. Manuscript Letter in the Folsom Collection, Boston Public Library.
78. William Newell, "Memoir of J. E. Worcester, LL.D.," Proceedings of The Massachusetts Historical Society, XIV (1880), 173.

79. Ibid.
80. Ibid.
81. Ibid.
82. Op. cit., p. 115.
83. Quoted in Worcester, Samuel T., op. cit., p. 252.

CHAPTER VI

"THE WAR OF THE DICTIONARIES"

This chapter presents the conflict that arose between Webster and Worcester, and between their publishers and friends, over the merits of their respective dictionaries. As the first American to consider the business of dictionary making seriously enough to spend several years and thousands of dollars in the preparation of an unabridged dictionary, Webster was chagrined when the field in which he felt that he had more or less a monopoly was invaded by a rival. Since Worcester represented the conservative language group, the struggle is another example of the difficulty of introducing new ideas and of trying to force an unwilling public to put such ideas into practice.

The material for this chapter has been found in newspaper and magazine articles, and in pamphlets published by the contending parties.

The controversy was hotly contested. Many prominent people were drawn into the bitter struggle. One reviewer says that "since the famous Battle of the Books in St. James's Library, no literary controversy has been more sharply waged."[1] According to Harry R. Warfel, author of Noah Webster, Schoolmaster to America, the War was probably of more vital significance than the Civil War. Every important person in the United States was drawn into the conflict.[2] Oliver Wendell Holmes says that "... the war of the dictionaries is only a disguised rivalry of cities, colleges, and especially of publishers. After all, it is likely that the language will shape itself by larger forces than phonography and dictionary-making."[3]

The controversy extended over a period of about thirty years, with epidemics of it appearing at intervals. The attack was begun soon after the publication of Worcester's Comprehensive Dictionary in 1830. It was renewed after the publication of his Universal and Critical Dictionary in 1846, and, with occasional skirmishes in the meantime, was brought to a crisis after the appearance of Worcester's enlarged work in 1860. The controversy was an outgrowth of the attack made by Cobb on the orthography of Webster immediately after the publication of the American Dictionary and was another implication of the fact that even the literary men of our country had not yet become convinced that any good could come out of America, intellectually and linguistically speaking, and that we must still look to England for our standards. To the Tory language group headed by Worcester, Webster's innovations were entirely too revolutionary. Even as late as the last decade of the nineteenth century, Harvard University specified Worcester's dictionary as the authority in spelling. [4] Aside from all the advertising propaganda of which the linguistic battle was at times merely a concomitant, the belief on the part of many of the literary men of the time that we should abide by English literary dictates provided sufficient incentive for continuing the struggle.

As far as has been determined in this study, the beginning of the Webster-Worcester controversy was an article published on the editorial page of the Worcester Palladium, November 26, 1834, entitled "Webster's Dictionary," in which the author accuses Worcester, who had been employed in abridging Webster's American Dictionary and had afterwards published a dictionary of his own, of appropriating in his own work the result of long years of labor on the part of Webster. The accusation is made in no veiled language.

> A gross plagiarism has been committed by Mr. J. E. Worcester on the literary property of Noah Webster, Esq. It is well known that Mr. Webster has spent a life, which is now somewhat advanced, [Webster was at this time seventy-six years of age] in writing a dictionary of the English language, which he published in 1828 in two quarto volumes. Three abridgements have since been made; one in octavo form--and two still smaller, for families and primary schools. To aid in the drudgery of providing these abridgements, Mr. Webster employed Mr. Worcester, who after becoming acquainted with Mr. Webster's plan, immediately set about appropriating to his own benefit the valuable labors, acquisitions, and productions of Mr. Webster. He has since published a dictionary, which is a very close imitation of Webster's; and which, we regret to learn, has since been introduced into many of the primary schools of the country. We regret this, because the public, inadvertently, do an act of great injustice to a man who has rendered the country an invaluable service, and ought to receive the full benefit of his labors. If we had a statute which could fix its grasp on those who pilfer the products of the mind, as readily as our laws embrace the common thief, Mr. Worcester would hardly escape with a light mulct. At all events before people buy his wares, they would do well to inquire how he came by them.

This "ferocious assault" is followed by an evaluation of Webster's works that calls attention to the fact that they had been produced only by great labor, expense, and personal sacrifice; that his dictionary is much superior to those of Walker and Johnson, containing more words than either and having both its spelling and pronunciation modernized, and that it is now printed in a cheap form for schools--a fact which should make it worthy the consideration of those who "have charge of the mental improvement of youth." The article is an excellent example of advertising propaganda, and the chief cause for complaint on the part of the author seems to be the introduction of Worcester's dictionary into "many" of the primary schools of the country.

Sidney Willard, the editor of the Christian Register, published in Boston, answered the attack made on Worcester even before Worcester himself had learned that such an attack had been made.[5] Worcester wrote a letter to the Editor of the Palladium, December 3, 1834, in which he states that he believed the Editor was not aware that he had been publishing a statement that was grossly false, but that he had merely been misinformed. In order to make his position clear he makes the following statement concerning his relation to Webster's dictionary.

> ... The design of my "Comprehensive Pronouncing and Explanatory Dictionary" was formed in 1827, while editing "Johnson's Dictionary as Improved by Todd, and abridged by Chalmers, with Walker's Pronouncing Dictionary Combined," and before the appearance of Dr. Webster's quarto dictionary. But before my Dictionary was prepared for the press, the publisher of Dr. Webster's Dictionary made repeated applications to me by letter, to form for him an abridgment of it, which I promptly declined. He then made a journey expressly for the purpose of engaging me to undertake the work. I mentioned to him that I was preparing a small Dictionary of my own; but at his urgent solicitation I was induced to undertake it, and to suspend the preparation of my own till it was completed. I also consented to insert the "synopsis of words differently pronounced," which I was preparing for my own use, with an express stipulation, in the contract, that I should use the Synopsis as I pleased, in my own Dictionary. This subject is mentioned, as you may see, at the beginning of the Preface to my Dictionary.
> After having finished the abridgment, I proceeded in the preparation of my own work; but so far from appropriating the labors of Mr. Webster to my own use, I challenge any one to enumerate a dozen words in my Dictionary for which I cannot readily give other authorities than Dr. Webster, or to show that with respect to the rise, orthography or pronunciation of a dozen words, I have been governed solely by his authority.[6]

Worcester also says that his and Webster's dictionaries differ widely in plan, in the selection of words, in notation, pronunciation, and in the orthography of a considerable number of words. The dictionaries with which his is supposed to be in competition are the two smaller forms for families and primary schools, neither of which, he says, he had seen until after his own dictionary was prepared for the press, and the smallest one he had not seen at all except in a book store.

Both Willard and Worcester were answered in a scathing article in the Palladium, December 10, 1834. Willard was accused
not of trying to defend Worcester, but of using the opportunity to
gratify his "passion for pedantic exhibitions." After dismissing
Willard as being unable to "convey instruction in the tone and temper
of a gentleman," the author of the editorial makes an explanation to
Worcester by saying that his information concerning the part that
Worcester had taken in the abridgment of Webster's book had been
derived from a person who he had believed was familiar with the
facts, but he adds that the fact that Worcester had been thus employed by Webster or his publisher, that his dictionary was made
shortly after the publication of Webster's first abridgment, and that
there were many strong points of resemblance between them was
sufficient justification for the conclusion that "Mr. Worcester had
appropriated to his own benefit the labors of a gentleman, who had
rendered a more essential service to American literature, than all
the lexicographers, or dealers in roots, American, or Hebrew,
which the country has ever produced."7 Worcester's letter was
published at the close of the article.

The following number of the Worcester Palladium, December
17, 1834, contained a letter from Webster, preceded by an editorial
comment that Worcester, it appears, had "some little occasion to
be indebted to Dr. Webster," notwithstanding his denial of the fact.
The letter follows:

New Haven, (Conn.) Dec. 11, 1834

To the Editor of the Worcester Palladium.

Sir - I see in your paper some remarks made on the
plagiarisms committed on my Dictionary by J. E. Worcester, and Mr. Worcester's denial of the fact. I wrote
to Mr. Worcester, March 22, 1831, inquiring whether he
had borrowed many words and definitions from my books.
He replied, by letter, dated March 25, and wrote, --"No,
not many." That he borrowed some words and definitions,
I suppose to be proved by the fact that they are found in
no British Dictionary; at least in none that I have seen.
How many he took, I know not, and shall not take the
trouble to examine. Had he taken more, his works would
have been less defective, and more correct. Of his plagiarisms of another kind, you will hear more hereafter.

Respectfully yours,

N. Webster

Another letter appeared in the Worcester Palladium, January
28, 1835, dated January 25, addressed by Webster to Worcester and
containing a list of one hundred and twenty-one words, "which prima
facie would seem to have been taken from my Webster's dictionary."
Webster asks Worcester to state in what other dictionary except his

he had found these words and how many or which he had borrowed
from him. Worcester's answer appeared in a letter dated February
6, 1835, and published in the Worcester Palladium of February 11.
It is sufficiently sarcastic.

> Of the one hundred and twenty-one words in your list,
> eighteen are found in an edition of Bailey's Dictionary,
> published more than a century ago, and twenty-one in a
> later edition; thirty-five, in Ash's Dictionary, published
> in 1775; thirty-seven, in Todd's Johnson's Dictionary com-
> bined with Walker's, edited by J. E. Worcester, and pub-
> lished before the appearance of yours; twenty-one, in
> Mr. Pickering's Vocabulary, published in 1816; not less
> than thirty in the Encyclopaedia Americana, and nearly as
> many in Brewster's New Edinburgh Encyclopedia; - and in
> these several works upwards of ninety of the words are
> found, and many of them several times repeated. I have,
> in addition to the works mentioned, about fifty English
> Dictionaries and Glossaries, in a majority of which I have
> ascertained that more or less of the words in question
> are to be found, but I have not leisure, at present, to go
> through a minute examination of them.
> Of your hundred and twenty-one words, six or seven
> are not to be found, as far as I can discover in your
> Quarto Dictionary, and one of them is one of those three
> thousand words which are contained in Todd's Johnson's
> Dictionary, but are not to be found in your great work,
> and which were inserted by me in the octavo abridgment
> of your Dictionary. Whether any of the others are among
> the words which were inserted in the abridgment at my
> suggestion, I cannot say with certainty.

In the same letter Worcester calls attention to the fact that
all the words in Webster's dictionaries, except those recently coined
or stamped, were either to be found in earlier dictionaries or had
been previously used by other persons. Such words coined by Webster as ammony, bridegoom, canail, ieland, nightmar, proropopy,
etc., he had scrupulously avoided, not even inserting them in his
"Vocabulary of Words of Various Orthography."

Worcester's letter was answered by Webster in the Worcester
Palladium for February 18, 1835. The points of contention were
that Worcester had added Webster's definitions to some words and
had borrowed his rules of orthography. However, it seems that
what bothered Webster most was the fact that Worcester's dictionaries were interfering with the sales of his own. One imagines
that it is almost with tears in his eyes that Webster writes:

> ... My Quarto Dictionary cost me about twenty years
> of labor and 20,000 dollars. For this labor and such an
> expense I could never receive remuneration had the
> market been left open. --How unkind then was it, for you,
> who had been intrusted with the task of making an

> abridgment, and had been well rewarded for it, to sit
> down and introduce some of my improvements into a book
> of your own compilation, and to put into operation several
> sets of stereotype plates; for such I am informed is the
> fact. Now, Sir, rather than treat you in this manner, I
> would beg my bread.

This letter was answered by Worcester in the Worcester
Palladium, March 11, Webster's answer following on March 25, and
the accusations were disposed of for a time.

In 1846, Worcester completed his Universal and Critical Dictionary of the English Language, and, in 1847, G. & C. Merriam published
the quarto edition of Webster's dictionary edited by Chauncey A.
Goodrich. Since these were rival publications, the controversy was
renewed. An article published in the American Review, the reputed
author of which was Noah Porter, exerted an unfavorable influence
upon the sale of Worcester's book, [8] which was not as full as Webster's in definitions and etymologies--a fact which caused such
glaring phrases as "Get the Best," "Get Webster," "Get the Quarto
Unabridged," to be emphasized. When it was rumored that Worcester had regained the use of his eyes, and was engaged in the
preparation of his Royal Quarto Dictionary, the attack was continued
by the Webster publishers with increased energy. [9] According to one
of Worcester's publishers:

> ... The grossest misrepresentations were put forth
> through the press, in the form of advertisements, and
> sometimes of communications, while their travelling agents
> have unscrupulously done little else but to vilify, traduce,
> and slander both Dr. Worcester and ourselves.... The
> newspapers and magazine offices were besieged and weighty
> arguments used for the adoption of Webster's orthography,
> while the publishers of school books were threatened with
> the combined opposition of the most influential publishing
> houses in the United States unless they would "show their
> flag" in favor of Webster's Dictionaries. [10]

As indicating the limit to which the Webster publishers went
in their attempt to suppress the Worcester publications, one of the
Worcester pamphlets (The Critic Criticised) tells the following story.
Mason Brothers, of New York, were publishers of some of Webster's school dictionaries, under a lease from the Messrs. Merriam.
Presuming that the "one of the firm" of H. Cowperthwait & Co., the
publishers of Warren's Geography, was not cooperating with them in
making a "National Standard" they addressed to them the following
letter:

> Messrs. Cowperthwait & Co., Philadelphia

> Gentlemen: If you are interested in Worcester's Diction-
> aries, or are using influence for them, we, and the
> other publishers of Webster, would be glad to know it.

We have often heard that such was the case, but have
paid no attention to it. The matter now comes to us in
such a shape, however, that one of your firm appears to
be acting as an agent for the Worcester publishers.
    We of course do not question your right to work for
these books or any others, but would like a clear understanding in the matter, as we are disposed to reciprocate
favors in these book matters. Please to show your flag.

                                    Very truly yours,

New York, June 19, 1858   Mason Bros.

    Among the publishers now having important pecuniary
interest in the success of Webster, are: W. B. Smith &
Co., Cincinnati; Sanborn & Carter, Boston; Ivison & Phin-
ney, New York; A. S. Barnes & Co., New York; Apple-
tons, New York; G. & C. Merriam; Morton & Griswold,
Louisville; Phillips, Sampson & Co., Boston.
    If you have joined hands with the Worcester interest,
we should like to have these parties know it, as their
agents are able incidently to do something in geography
matters without much trouble. [11]

To the above letter the following reply was made:

Messrs. Mason & Bros.

    Gents: We should have great pleasure in defining our
position with reference to Worcester's Dictionaries, were
it not for the implied threat which accompanies your letter.
As it is, a decent self-respect prevents our replying to
it.
    We do not believe you are authorized to speak for the
firms, whose names you use. We expect our competitors
in business will do what they can honorably to secure the
introduction and sale of the books they publish; but we do
not believe those of them who do not publish geographical
works will instruct their agents adversely to our geogra-
phies, as you intimate will be the case, whatever may be
our course with reference to "joining hands with the Worcester interest."

                                    Yours truly,

                                    H. Cowperthwait & Co. [12]

    In accordance with the threat contained in the letter an attempt
was made by the agent of Webster's Dictionaries to displace Warren's
Geography in the Boston schools. An attack was made upon the book
in the press, and the book was discussed at several meetings of the
school committee of that city, until the correspondence was revealed
and the conspiracy disclosed. It was shown that the firms of W. B.

Smith & Co. and the Merriams were the only ones implicated, and that the Mason Brothers was not authorized to use the names of the other firms in the correspondence. [13] The Boston Daily Advertiser says of the transactions:

> We doubt if the history of mercantile morality contains a blacker page than is here disclosed. The closing sentence of the postscript of the first letter, if it means anything, means that the hostility of the publishers named therein will be invoked against the geography published by the Messrs. Cowperthwait, unless they "show their flag" in favor of Webster's Dictionary. We have now the key to the extraordinary popularity which it is pretended that Webster's Dictionaries have attained. It appears that a number of leading publishers have, or are said to have "important pecuniary interest in the success of Webster;" --and this fact, or alleged fact, is secretly used as a lever, in a manner which the public would not have been likely to have suspected had not the correspondence happened to be disclosed. The precise connection between a dictionary and a geography does not appear on the surface; but it seems that a man who refuses the abominations of Noah Webster's spelling cannot be allowed to publish a geography without incurring the persecution of parties who have important pecuniary interest in the success of Webster. [14]

The lack of an international copyright between England and America brought about one of the most serious conflicts between the Webster and Worcester groups. Henry G. Bohn, an English publisher, after purchasing in Boston a set of the stereotype plates of Worcester's Universal and Critical Dictionary of the English Language, published an edition of it in London, 1853, under the title of A Universal, Critical, and Pronouncing Dictionary of the English Language; including Scientific Terms, compiled from the Materials of Noah Webster, LL. D., by Joseph E. Worcester. New Edition, to which are added Walker's Key to the Pronunciation of Classical and Scripture Proper Names, enlarged and improved; A Pronouncing Vocabulary of Modern Geographical Names: and an English Grammar. The statement made by Worcester in the Preface to his Universal and Critical Dictionary, published in 1846, that "with respect to Webster's Dictionary, which the compiler several years since abridged, he is not aware of having taken a single word, or the definition of a word, from that work, in the preparation of this" was omitted. On the title page Webster was placed first, in large type, and Worcester in another line, in another type, and the book was lettered on the back Webster's and Worcester's Dictionary. [15] This publication was the signal for the renewal of the attack.

On July 29, 1853, there appeared on the editorial page of the Daily Advertiser, Boston, an article entitled "Noah Webster's Dictionary," which stated that the paper had received the day before two copies of a pamphlet of forty-eight pages issued by G. & C. Merriam, which was devoted to recommending and defending Webster's Dictionary. To the excellence of Webster's Dictionary, especially as far as its orthography is concerned, the writer of the editorial does not agree. The orthography he regards as a fatal deficiency, which makes the Dictionary wholly unfit for use by young persons or those who have not learned to spell so perfectly as to be beyond all danger of being misled. The article calls attention to the fact that a statement made by Washington Irving concerning Webster's Dictionary had been published by the Merriam Company in such a way as to present a false idea. A letter from Washington Irving was inserted to explain the affair.

"Sunnyside, June 25, 1851

"Dear Sir: Several months since, I received from G. & C. Merriam a copy of their quarto edition of Webster's Dictionary. In acknowledging the receipt of it, I expressly informed them that I did not make it my standard of orthography, and gave them my reasons for doing so, and for considering it an unsafe standard for American writers to adopt. At the same time I observed the work had so much merit in many respects, that I had made it quite a vade mecum.
"They had the disingenuousness to extract merely the part of my opinion which I have underlined, and to insert it among their puffs and advertisements, as if I had given a general and unqualified approbation of the work. I have hitherto suffered this bookseller's trick to pass unnoticed; but your letter obliges me to point it out, and to express my decided opinion that Webster's Dictionary is not a work advisable to be introduced 'by authority' into our schools as a standard of orthography.
'I am, sir, with great respect,
"Your obedient servant,
"Washington Irving.
"To Hon. James W. Beckman,
Chairman of the Senate Committee of Literature. "

The article points out that many of the gentlemen who have written recommendations of the Dictionary do not follow its authority in their own writings. Prominent among these are William H. Prescott, the historian, and Daniel Webster. It also states that the new edition of Webster's Dictionary was so extensively sold as to allow the Messrs. Merriam to withdraw from the publishing business except for the Dictionary.

In the next number of the Daily Advertiser (August 5, 1853) an article appeared as an advertisement, signed by G. & C. Merriam, in answer to the preceding article. Regarding the letter written by Irving the following statement is made:

In a letter to us from Mr. Irving, he writes:--
"I consider this Dictionary in many respects the best

in our language, and find it an invaluable vade mecum. "
He added, "I must frankly tell you, however, that I do
not make it my standard for orthography, in the publication of my works. My reason simply is, that it differs
occasionally from the orthography in use among the best
London publishers. Now, however much we of the United
States may refine and improve the language of our own
country, yet the world will look to London as the standard
of pure English, as they will to Paris for pure French,
and to Madrid for pure Castilian. Any deviation on our
part from the best London usage, will be liable to be considered as a provincialism, " &c. He adds, "I do not pre-
tend to take any part in the controversy which is going
on in the periodical press on the subject, the Macaulay
controversy, and indeed I am apt to be somewhat negligent
in matters of the kind, " &c.

The article says the sentence quoted as published by the Merriams was not published at all; what was published was the following
phrase, "I find it an invaluable vade mecum, "--a statement which
did not commit Mr. Irving to an unqualified approval of everything
the work might contain. However, upon examination it had been
disclosed that Mr. Irving, in Putnam's authorized edition of his
works, issued under his own supervision, makes Webster his standard of orthography so far that it would be safe to say that in any
given chapter of the Alhambra nine cases could be pointed out in
which the orthography conforms to Webster as opposed to London
usage, to one where the latter differs from the former. "Had we,
therefore, given Mr. Irving's theory, and then stated his practice,
of orthography, we should have made him a party to the controversy
going on, to our advantage, perhaps, but in opposition to his intimated wishes. " This being true, "notoriously interested parties, to
subserve private ends of their own, wormed from him the letter
you [The Daily Advertiser] publish. "

To show the extent to which the orthography of Webster had
attained, the article affirms that at the present time, the Daily
Advertiser in nine cases uses Webster's orthography to one where
it departs from it as compared to its usage in 1827, and that Eng-
ligh usage is gradually approximating the Websterian system, their
recent lexicons presenting a mixture--now retaining the u, now
omitting it. As indicative of the estimate placed upon Webster's
work in England, attention was called to the publication there recently of Worcester's Dictionary with the name of Webster attached.
The story of Worcester's supposed plagiarism of an earlier date
was reiterated. The statement that the Merriam Company had discontinued all publications except the Dictionary was denied.

The following paragraph from the same article indicates one
angle that the controversy had taken.

While, however, cherishing a high regard for the
memory of Dr. Webster or his family, the purity of his

character, and the intelligence and industry displayed in
his works, we must yet confess that he committed one un-
pardonable sin--he did not graduate at Cambridge University. As, however, it may be supposed his parent was
at least partially responsible for this, unless it should be
thought that he "sinned in him and fell with him in his
first transgression," we should hope this might not be
deemed a perpetual casus belli upon him, in his memory
and his literary progeny.

An editorial in the same issue of the Daily Advertiser attempted to refute the Merriam article by saying that the assertion of the
Merriams, that Irving in his letter stated that he did not make Webster's Dictionary his standard of orthography and yet exhibited it in
his published works, was an insult to Irving. Further insult was
provided in the statement that the letter printed in the Daily Advertiser had been "wormed from him" by interested parties for their
own ends. Another article, signed by "S" and printed on the same
page, contained a scathing denunciation of Webster's system of orthography.

In a pamphlet entitled Gross Literary Fraud Exposed: Relating to the Publication of Worcester's Dictionary in London, 1853,
Worcester attempted to make clear his position concerning the London publication. The pamphlet contains a letter from Worcester to
John Wilkins, of the late firm of Wilkins, Carter and Company, the
original publishers of Worcester's Dictionary, telling him about the
publication and asking his explanation and advice. The letter of
Wilkins in reply, dated August 31, 1853, helps to explain what had
happened. An extract from the letter is given here.

Early in 1847, Mr. James Brown, of the firm of Little,
Brown, & Co., of this city, was about to visit Europe;
and we (Wilkins, Carter, & Co.) authorized him to nego-
tiate for the publication of your Dictionary in England if
he had opportunity, and particularly with Mr. Bohn, from
whom we had received an application for the privilege.
Subsequently Mr. Brown informed us of an offer he had
received from Mr. Bohn, and furnished us with the letter
from Mr. Bohn to him; to the proposals in which we
acceded, and in October of that year shipped the plates
to London.
I remember perfectly well that we felt some doubt in
regard to the validity of a contract made on paper not
bearing a stamp; but we supposed Mr. Bohn was an honorable man, and would not repudiate it.
After shipping the plates we heard nothing from Mr.
Bohn until the next year, when we became somewhat im-
patient of the delay, and we wrote him urging him to go
on in fulfilment of his agreement. We received an answer
stating that he was sorry the plates had been sent. And
we learned that he had become interested in the sale of
Webster's Dictionary. Several letters passed between

him and us, but we were unable to induce him to fulfil
his agreement.

In the autumn of 1849, more than two years after the
plates were sent, Mr. Carter went to Europe for his
health, --intending to see Mr. Bohn and come to some
arrangement with him. But his health did not allow of
this. In the summer or autumn of 1850, Mr. Bohn wrote
us asking our lowest terms to sell the plates, which I
named, --never dreaming that any other use would be made
of them than that of publishing your Dictionary under your
name. He accepted my offer, and the transfer of the
plates was effected.

On Mr. Carter's return from Italy, in the summer of
1851, he brought home a copy of his (Mr. Bohn's) bare-
faced publication. You can judge of our surprise, I might
say amazement, at the audacity of this literary fraud. We
felt very uncomfortable about it, but did not see that anything could be done to remedy the evil. Mr. Carter was
never afterwards able to attend to business, and the subject of this publication was never further considered between us.

You may well think it strange that I did not at the time
call your attention to the subject of this literary imposition;
but as I did not see any means of remedying the evil, and
knowing that the condition of your eyes was such that you
could make but little if any use of them, I did not feel in
haste to trouble you with a knowledge of it. I have, however, never seen any notice of this spurious publication in
this country, until you called my attention to one. Had
any such notice met my eye, I should certainly have
deemed it my duty to call your attention to the volume
brought home by Mr. Carter.

Had I leisure to narrate the details of our business trans-
action with Mr. Bohn, I think it would appear to be, on
his part, as commercially dishonorable, as this literary
enterprise is fraudulent and disgraceful. 16

Mr. Bohn makes the following explanation of his participation in the affair:

Mr. Worcester has protested against any associating
his name with Webster in the afore-named Dictionary,
[Universal, Critical and Pronouncing Dictionary of the English Language] which he declares to be exclusively his
own. I can only say, that when I engaged to purchase the
book in 1846, on a sample of the sheets, I understood it
to be an enlarged and Anglicized edition of the Abridgment
which had previously been compiled by him under the name
of Webster. After having extensively announced it as a
joint production, I could not alter my advertisements without great inconvenience. Nor did it seem to me to sig-
nify. The jealousy, however, of the American copyright-
holders of Webster, against what seems to be the rival

publication of Worcester, appears to render this explanation necessary. [17]

 In the same pamphlet, Worcester says that the statement made by the publishers of Webster's Dictionary in their communication to the Boston Daily Advertiser (August 5, 1853) noted above, that Worcester had been employed by Dr. Webster or his family to abridge the American Dictionary, is "void of truth," but that he was employed by Sherman Converse, the original publisher of Webster's Dictionary. [18] So far, he says, was the task not one of his own seeking that he declined two applications that were made to him to undertake it because of the fear that it would bring him into some difficulty or embarrassment in relation to his Comprehensive Dictionary, which he was then preparing. After seeing the notice referred to in the Daily Advertiser, Worcester sent a copy of it to Sherman Converse, whom he had seen only once in more than fifteen years, and asked him to make a brief statement of the facts in the case. [19] He received a letter from him dated August 31, 1853, from which the following extract is taken:

> The simple history of the whole matter is this. I had published Mr. Webster's great Dictionary, and presented it to the public. The labor had cost from two to three years of the best portion of my business life, without any adequate remuneration. For this I looked to an Abridgement and such future editions of the larger as the demand might authorize. But if I published an Abridgement I wished to stereotype it, and, as a business man, I desired, it to be made by an able hand, and with some variations, of minor importance, from the original. On conferring with Mr. Webster upon the subject, he stated two objections to my views. He felt that he had not the physical power left to perform the labor in a reasonable time, and that he could not preserve his literary consistency and be responsible for the variations which I desired. Yet, as I had published the great work after it had been declined, and that not very graciously, by all the principal booksellers on both sides of the Atlantic, he was willing that I should derive any remuneration I might anticipate from an octavo abridgement. With these views and feelings, he consented to commit the subject to the mutual discretion of Professor Goodrich and myself; setting a limit, however, beyond which variations should not be made; and that he might not incur the least responsibility for such variations as the abridgment might contain, I understood him to say he should give the copyright to another.
> As soon as Mr. Webster had made his decision, which was probably a sacrifice of feeling on his part to do me a favor, I applied to you to undertake the labor. You declined, and so decidedly that I made a visit to Cambridge for the sole purpose of urging your compliance with my request. You assured me that you could not undertake to abridge Mr. Webster's Dictionary, for the very good

reason that you had then already made considerable progress in preparing a Dictionary of your own. At the same time, you showed me a Synopsis of Words of disputed pronunciation, with the respective authorities. But the results of our interview was an agreement on your part to abridge the Dictionary for me, and to allow me to use your Synopsis, with the express reservation of the right to use it as your own, for your own Dictionary. And I must say that my persuasive powers were very severely taxed in securing the desired results.

I returned to New Haven, and subsequently called on you in company with Mr. Goodrich, when the matter of variations was settled, and you entered upon the labor; and I am free to say you performed it to my entire satisfaction, and I believe to that of Professor Goodrich also, for I never heard an intimation to the contrary.

I am very faithfully yours,

S. Converse[20]

Worcester also includes in his pamphlet some brief extracts from letters which he received from Webster and Goodrich soon after they had been informed that he would undertake the abridgment. The following is an extract from a letter of Dr. Webster, dated New Haven, July 27, 1828:

Sir, - Mr. Converse has engaged you to abridge my Dictionary, and has requested me to forward you the copy of the first volume. This was unexpected to me; but under the circumstances, I have consented to it, and shall send the copy. [21]

The other is from a letter of Goodrich to Worcester, dated Yale College, July, 1828:

My dear Sir, - Mr. Converse, who was here on Saturday, informed us that you had consented to undertake the abridgment of Mr. Webster's Dictionary. This gives me and Mr. Webster's other friends the highest satisfaction; for there is no man in the United States, as you know from conversation with me, who would be equally acceptable. [22]

Worcester refutes the accusation made by the Merriams that as American editor of Todd's Johnson, published in 1827, and having entire control of the matter, Worcester retained the k in words terminating in c, as musick, physick, almanack, and the u in honour, favour, authour, but that when Worcester's own dictionaries appeared, the spelling followed Webster's in that they omitted the k and u, by saying that in editing Johnson's English Dictionary, as improved by Todd, his work was done on principles fixed upon by the publishers and some literary gentlemen who were their counselors, the counselor who did the most in the business being John Pickering.

> ... It was made my duty to conform to the principles
> established for my guidance; and I had "no control of the
> matter." The Dictionary was to contain Johnson's ortho-
> graphy, and Walker's pronunciation. I was so far from
> defending the use of the final k in music, physic, & c.,
> that I said in relation to it, in my Preface to the Diction-
> ary: "The general usage, both in England and America,
> is at present so strongly in favor of its omission, that
> the retaining of it seems now to savor of affectation or
> singularity."[23]

Worcester also says that the omission of k in such words as
those mentioned above is found in Martin's English Dictionary, published in 1749 and by many other later dictionaries. The omission
of u was countenanced in the dictionaries of Ash and Entick, published long before that of Webster.[24]

The first twenty-four pages of this pamphlet (Gross Literary
Fraud Exposed) were issued from the press in October, 1853. Soon
after, the Merriams published a second pamphlet. This was followed
by Worcester's publication of a Second Appendix of four pages in
January, 1854, in which was inserted an extract of a letter he had
written to Goodrich as well as an extract from Goodrich's reply
dated November 2, 1853. The latter extract is given below.

> It is perfectly true, as you say, that I was entirely
> satisfied with respect to your management in abridging
> the American Dictionary. I have always spoken, in high
> terms of the exactness and delicacy with which you con-
> ducted that difficult concern. I have always felt and said,
> that I knew of no ground whatever for any imputation upon
> you, as though you had made use of Dr. Webster's Diction-
> ary in the production of your own. On the contrary, I
> have uniformly stated, that you had acted, in my view,
> with great delicacy on this subject, and that if any coinci-
> dences should be discovered between the two works, I
> had no belief they were intentional or conscious ones on
> your part.[25]

This letter is followed in the pamphlet by Webster's reply to
Goodrich. Early in December, Worcester says he received from the
Merriams a copy of a new pamphlet, in which they had added to the
"falsehood and wrong," in attempting to defend what they had published. Soon after receiving the pamphlet, Worcester wrote to Converse asking him to state whether or not his statement that he was
employed by Dr. Webster or his family to abridge the American
Dictionary was "void of truth." Converse's answer, dated December
19, 1853, is given below.

> To Mr. Worcester: - Dear Sir, You request me to say
> whether, in negotiating with you to abridge Mr. Webster's

Quarto Dictionary, I acted as <u>agent</u> either of Dr. Webster
or his family. My answer is <u>that</u> I acted as <u>agent of no</u>
<u>man.</u> My arrangement with Mr. Webster and <u>his family,</u>
<u>was</u> permission to make and publish an octavo abridgment
of the large work with liberty to include some slight alterations from the original. The alterations were left to the
mutual discretion of Professor Goodrich and myself, carefully restricted within a limit, dictated by Mr. Webster.
This point settled, I determined to stereotype the work;
and as the whole responsibility of the undertaking rested
on <u>me alone,</u> I could think of but <u>one man</u>[26] to whom I
felt willing to confide the important trust of making an
abridgment which involved a risk so great. Your attainments and pursuits had eminently qualified you for the
task, and I decided at once to engage your services if
possible. Either before or directly after my correspondence with you upon the subject, I intimated my preference
and purpose to Professor Goodrich, and received his cordial approval. The risk and expense both of abridging
and stereotyping the Octavo Dictionary were exclusively my
own. The family of Mr. Webster had no share in either,
and I do not know that I ever disclosed to any member of
it the terms of my contract, either with yourself or the
type founders. Yours, &c., S. Converse[27]

Soon after the second Appendix was issued, the Merriams
published a third pamphlet, "A Gross Literary Fraud Exposed; Relating to the Publication of Worcester's Dictionary in London," as
Webster's Dictionary, in which an explanation is made of their position. The pamphlet relates that during the summer of 1853 one of
the firm, being in Great Britain, happened in at a bookseller's shop
in Almwick, Northumberland, and inquired what English dictionary
was sold there. "Webster's" was the reply. Upon requesting to
see a copy he was presented with a "transatlantic acquaintance, viz.,
Worcester's Dictionary, a perfect fac simile of the work published
on this side the water; indeed, (as since appears) from a duplicate
set of the Plates from which the volume is printed here;--excepting
that so much of the Preface as disavows having used Webster at all,
was stricken out, with a slight modification as to that point; while
the Title-page read, ... Compiled from the Materials of NOAH
WEBSTER, LL.D., by Joseph E. Worcester."[28]

The pamphlet expresses the feeling that Worcester should not
have felt at liberty to charge the Merriam Company with attributing
to Worcester a participation in the fraud when it had not so charged
him; that when in replying to Worcester's published statements, the
company had expressly avowed its disbelief in his having had any
connection with the London affair, Worcester should have accepted
the statement; that when the Appendix to his pamphlet was published,
Worcester had in his possession proofs, in the form of a letter
from Professor Goodrich, which sufficiently ignored such beliefs on
the part of the Merriams. An extract from the same letter from
Professor Goodrich to Worcester, November 2, 1853, which Webster

had quoted earlier to show that Goodrich had been satisfied with his
abridgment of the <u>American Dictionary</u>, is included in this pamphlet
to show the unprejudiced attitude of the Merriam Company. Goodrich says, speaking as one of the firm:

> I saw him [Charles Merriam] for a short time, early
> in August last, as I was passing through Springfield, and
> he then spoke to me of the London Title page and Preface,
> which had been sent him by his brother who was in Europe.
> He spoke of them in a way which showed that he had not
> the least suspicion of your being concerned in that trans-
> action. He alluded to the discrepancy between your state-
> ment and the new Title page only as showing the extent
> to which Mr. Bohn had felt himself to be driven, since he
> was compelled to alter the Title page, and suppress your
> statement, that you had made no use of Dr. Webster's
> labors. The whole tenor of his conversation showed me,
> that he had no intention whatever to cast any personal re-
> flections on you.... I ought also to say, in justice to the
> Messrs. Merriams, that they have uniformly deprecated,
> in their conversations with me, any collision with your
> publishers, &c. [29]

In the same pamphlet the Merriams explain the presence of
the same errors in Worcester's dictionaries as were found in earlier
editions of Webster as probably having been copied from Knowles,
Smart, and other English lexicographers who had borrowed largely
from Webster. [30] Regarding Worcester's statement that the charge
that he had been hired by Webster's family to make the Abridgment
was "void of truth," the pamphlet says that it was preposterous to
suppose that Webster ever gave such an unqualified license to any
person to make and publish an abridgment of his work, independently
of his own control, as Converse's letter implied. Every circumstance disproves such a position. The extract published by Worcester of a letter to him from Webster in which he says, "Under the
circumstances I have consented to it," shows that his assent was
necessary. Worcester, likewise, disclaims having any control over
the orthography, etc. when he said that they "were decided upon by
his [Dr. Webster's] representative, and over which I had no control."
Goodrich in the Preface to the Revised Edition of Webster's Octavo,
published in 1847, speaks of the original abridgment as "made under
the author's direction" by Worcester. An extract of the contract
made by Webster with Converse is given as evidence of the fact that
Worcester was hired by Webster.

> The said Webster, on his part, having the fullest confidence
> in the ability and judgment of Joseph E. Worcester, Esq.,
> of Cambridge, Massachusetts, he doth <u>authorize</u> the said
> Converse to <u>commit</u> to said Worcester the work of abridg-
> ing said Dictionary into an octavo volume as aforesaid, on
> the following principles. "The pronunciation, as marked
> and indicated by characters in said Dictionary, shall be re-
> tained, and such other words ... shall have their pronun-

ciation indicated ... by the use of the above mentioned
characters and such additional ones as said Webster
shall furnish and point out." "Should said Worcester
doubt at any time as to the pronunciation intended by
said Webster, the words in question shall be referred
to said Webster for his decision." "Any suggestions
made by said Webster as to alterations and improvements, shall be attended to." "And the said Webster
doth hereby agree that the said Converse may retain
five hundred dollars, from the first payments due
said Webster on the proceeds of the said Octavo edition, as his the said Webster's share of a recompense
to said Worcester for his services in abridging the
Dictionary aforesaid. 31

Worcester received two thousand dollars for his services. 32

The pamphlet also explains the relation to the Dictionary of
Professor Porter, of Yale College, whom Worcester had referred
to as "employed by the publishers of Dr. Webster's Dictionary as
a public advocate of that work." The story is as follows:

... The Joint Committee on Education of the Massachusetts Legislature, at the session of 1850, considered the
question of introducing a Bill providing for placing a copy
of an English Dictionary (we believe Webster's Unabridged
the only one they originally contemplated,) in each District School in the State. Mr. Jenks, of Boston, a graduate of Cambridge, we believe, appeared before that
Committee, employed, as the public understood, by Mr.
Worcester's publishers, and in an elaborate argument
violently assailed the work of Dr. Webster and lauded that
of Mr. Worcester. While that argument was yet in progress, being in Boston, we [Merriams] telegraphed to Professor Porter, then in New Haven, begging of him the
favor to come down and meet these statements before the
Committee. At very great personal inconvenience, in mid-
winter, with hardly an hour for preparation, leaving New
Haven at 5 or 6 P. M., reaching Boston at midnight, and
hearing the next morning the remainder of Mr. Jenk's
speech, Professor P. replied to his address, or more
properly assault, in the able Argument we have since published. This, as far as we are aware, was his first and
only "public advocacy" of our work--and this the original
and unprovoked attack which made it necessary. If Mr.
Worcester "knew the facts in the case," and designs to
represent Professor P. as a mercenary, hired "public
advocate of our work," he does what "no honorable or
honest man would do." We feel sure that he did not know,
as in other particulars he certainly has not known, "the
facts in the case." 33

In a letter to Webster, dated Camden, N. J., April, 1854,

Converse says that he is sending an answer to the attack made on him by the Merriams, which he wishes to have published as a third Appendix to Worcester's pamphlet. Worcester complied with his request. [34]

In his Answer Converse gives the history of the origin and progress of his connection with Webster and his dictionaries. He says that when Webster returned from Europe with his Manuscript, greatly disheartened because he had not obtained a publisher, he (Converse) agreed to undertake the publication. In order to obtain subscribers sufficient in number to allow the publication he had to break down the prejudice that had arisen in this country against Webster as a lexicographer because of his earlier attempt to spell each word as it was pronounced. The contact that he (Converse) had with the principal literary and influential men throughout the nation in obtaining the subscriptions enabled him to form an estimate of what would be popular or unpopular in a new dictionary. This led him to decide to undertake the Octavo Abridgment at once if Webster would consent to certain alterations and variations from the original. Webster had already agreed to give Converse the right of an Octavo Abridgment, but he was expected to make it himself, or procure it to be made at his own expense. Converse hints at a strained relation that arose between himself and Webster when he says, "This brings me to a passage in my intercourse with Dr. Webster, from the history of which I shall not lift the veil. He has gone to his rest, and no man was witness to our interviews. Were he here, he would answer for himself, and would confirm my statements."[35]

Webster's health was not good and he felt that he could not undertake the work himself, but he gave Converse permission to employ a suitable person to do the work. Permission was also given to introduce modifications from the original, within such limits as Webster should prescribe. In conclusion, he says, Webster added with emphasis: "I shall submit the modifications to the discretion of Professor Goodrich and yourself, and that I may not be responsible for them as author, I shall give the copyright to another," naming the person.[36] This same feeling, he states, is evident in the Preface to the Octavo Abridgment. "As the author of the original work has intrusted the superintendence of the abridgment to another person, he is not to be considered as responsible for any of the modifications already alluded to."

Converse continues his story by saying that after twice writing to Worcester and receiving a negative reply, he visited him at Cambridge, whereupon Worcester consented to make the abridgment. The contract was made to include both the "Synopsis of Words Differently Pronounced" which Worcester had prepared for his own dictionary, and a number of extra words from Todd's Johnson not found in Webster's Dictionary. The contract was dated July 11, 1828.

After returning to New Haven, Converse says that he called on

Webster and asked him to draw up a contract securing him the right
to abridge and publish. This contract was made on July 26, 1828.
It shows that Worcester had been employed by Converse and not by
Webster, for he had authorized Converse to do for himself what
Webster under pressure of circumstance could not do for him.

Converse accuses the Merriams of suppressing a passage
from his letter to Worcester in order to make the letter imply exactly the opposite to what it declares. He emphatically states that
Webster did not make him his agent to employ Worcester to do the
work of abridging, but took special care that he should not be so in
fact, or to be held so in law.

That Converse was probably not in sympathy with Webster
and that he was interested only in pushing the sale of the Dictionary
over which he had control is revealed in letters from Webster to
his wife written while he was in Washington trying to get a copyright law passed. Goodrich also leaned toward Worcester's plan.
For the relation of Goodrich to the Dictionary see page 175. The
letters from Webster follow.

Washington, Jan. 26, 1831

My Dear Becca,

. . . .

Mr. Goodrich writes that Mr. Converse came here at
his suggestion to aid the copy-right bill. Fortunately the
bill had passed the House of Representatives before he
arrived. A more unpopular man could not be selected;
and if any opposer of the bill had stated to the house how
Mr. Converse had used or abused his monopoly (as it is
called) of my dictionary, he probably would have defeated
the bill. I hope no knowledge of it will reach the Senate.
Two days ago a Gentleman from Boston asked me where
he could get a copy of my Quarto. He said he could not
get it at the booksellers and knew not where to find it. I
will not trouble myself to write what I know, nor express
my feelings on this subject; and I hope Mr. Goodrich will
not write to me on the subject any more. The truth is
not one fifth part of the United States are supplied with
the books. [37]

The second letter was dated February 3, 1831.

When I was in New York, Dr. Ives told me that an
agent of Mr. Converse had told him most palpable false-
hoods, stating that I had sent him to him. I have forgotten the particulars but will endeavor to obtain them,
on my return. I paid not much attention to this information, until the other day. Mr. Evans, a member of Congress from Maine, a fellow-lodger in our family, informed

me that an agent of Mr. Converse, probably the same
man, applied to him to purchase one of my dictionaries,
and told him that I desired to call on him, representing
that I was acquainted with him, Mr. Evans, and would be
glad to see him at my house. This was last winter, when
I never heard of such a man as Mr. Evans.

This information astonishes me, --it is possible that the
same thing may have happened in other cases. It had the
effect with Mr. Evans to disgust him, and he would not
buy a book. On being informed of the truth and becoming
acquainted with me, he says he will buy a copy of the
Quarto. It is very possible that this lying agent has done
me injury in other places. 38

Jenks, Hickling & Swan published a defense of Worcester and
his dictionaries in A Reply to the Messrs. G. & C. Merriam's
Attack upon the Character of Dr. Worcester and His Dictionaries,
1854. The reputed author was William Draper Swan, one of the
firm.

The letter from Converse to Webster, dated August 31, 1853,
insists Swan, is sufficient proof of the fact that Worcester was not
"employed by Mr. Webster or his family to prepare an abridgment
of the American Dictionary," but that he undertook the task solely
for Converse, and only upon his earnest solicitations. It states
that Worcester inserted nearly three thousand words into this dictionary (Webster's Abridged) which were not contained in Dr. Webster's
Quarto Dictionary and which, it may be presumed, were unknown to
Webster at the time he made it. 39 The pamphlet also says that
this was the only connection Worcester had with Webster or his
family, although G. & C. Merriam, nearly a quarter of a century
later, published to the world "that Worcester was at once the pupil
and assistant of Webster, and seeing that he, Webster, had taken a
step in advance of the age, etc., --treacherously went to work,
catering to the Walkerian taste of the day, and produced this [his
own] 'bastard dictionary.'"40 Worcester answers this argument by
saying that so far from having been 'a pupil and assistant of Webster," he never saw him to speak with him more than three or
four times during his life. 41

Swan objects only to the orthography and pronunciation of
Webster and feels that Webster overstepped the province of a lexicographer, whose business is to record the language as used by the
best speakers and writers, in introducing innovations which the
public refused to sanction. He answers the statement made by the
Merriams that the spelling and pronunciation of a few words were
becoming more nearly Websterian, by listing words that show that
Webster had followed Worcester in his orthography. "By comparing
the words with each other, as found in his first Spelling Book, his
Dictionaries of 1806, of 1817, of 1828, of 1840 and in his New
Spelling Book, the reader would be led to infer that he actually
labored to see how inconsistent he could be with himself."42 He
calls attention to the fact that many prominent persons who had

spoken of Webster's Dictionary in complimentary terms as a book of reference used Worcester's orthography in their own writings. A-mong these were Daniel Webster, Everett, Irving, Bancroft, Prescott, Longfellow, Sparks, Hillard, Ticknor, Hawthorne, and Bryant. Even the Merriams, in their publications, <u>Chitty on Contracts</u>, <u>Chitty on Pleadings</u>, <u>Chitty on Bills</u>, follow Worcester's orthography in every line. [43]

Swan gives an extract from an advertisement of Webster's Dictionary which says that in Massachusetts, where the legislature had offered to each school district its choice without cost, of a copy of Webster or Worcester, three thousand and thirty-five of the districts within the first few months ordered Webster, and but one hundred and five took Worcester, or the ratio of thirty to one selecting Webster. [44]

Swan explains this popularity of Webster's Dictionary by saying that many of the committees selected Webster because their schools were already supplied with Worcester's; that others took Webster's from the State and voted to purchase Worcester's; some selected Webster's because they valued a present of <u>four</u> dollars more than one which cost only two; while others voted to receive Webster's Dictionary from the State, but did not adopt it "as their standard work." As evidence of this, he inserts a list of names from twenty schools. He objects to Webster's Quarto Dictionary as a book for children because of its size, since "good order cannot be maintained in a large school where children are constantly leaving their seats to consult a Dictionary." He thinks they should be provided with a smaller work as a handbook and, in support of his opinion, quotes an extract from the Annual Report of the School Committee of Boston for 1851:

> Instances of mispronunciation also occurred; and, on calling for a Dictionary, none was at hand. A fine edition of Webster's large work lay on the master's table in another story, but, for all practical uses, where it was then wanted, it might as well have been in Texas. It is recommended that all the teachers be required to have Dictionaries in their several rooms. It is also proposed that all the younger pupils be required to have Worcester's Primary Dictionary and the more advanced pupils his Comprehensive Pronouncing and Explanatory Dictionary. These books are very cheap, and for the price are the most valuable school books in the English language. [45]

Swan gives an extract from the Report of the Annual Visiting Committee for 1853 in Boston as indicative of the success with which Worcester's dictionaries were being used. The pupils of the first and second classes of all the grammar schools in Boston were required by a vote of the School Committee to have a copy of Worcester's Dictionary as a handbook for daily use.

In some schools, Worcester's Comprehensive Dictionary

was upon every pupil's desk, and the prompt replies showed the good use that had been made of it. We found in
one school a practice which we would recommend our
teachers to pursue. In every reading lesson a sentence
was given out for definition, and every word was defined
in course by the class; and thus, all those little common
words, such as if, with, in, as, etc., of which we all
think we know the meaning, till we are called to define
them, were considered by the pupils, their origin sought
out, the manner shown in which, from being first verbs
or nouns, they came to be employed as connectives, their
appropriate uses taught, and also the relation which they
sustain to other words in the language.... [46]

To refute letters published by the Merriams to show that
more of Webster's than Worcester's dictionaries were sold in "Western Massachusetts, " Swan includes a statement taken from an article
in the Boston Transcript of October 12, 1850, to the effect that according to the abstract of the school returns at the office of the
Secretary of the Board of Education, only the poorest schools in the
Commonwealth from the standpoint of appropriations use Webster's
books. An extract is given from a report from James W. Beekman, Chairman of the Committee on Literature, of the New York
Legislature, who was unable to agree with other members of the
committee in recommending Webster's Dictionary as suitable to be
purchased by school districts throughout the State, to show that the
Merriams were not justified in publishing the statement that in the
state of New York Worcester was almost wholly unknown. Mr.
Beekman quotes statements by prominent men to prove the faults in
Webster. One is by Edward W. Gould, who says that Webster's
career as a lexicographer was a mistake. Assuming that the language needed reforming, says Gould, Webster set about attempting
it, but finding by criticism that he had gone too far he began to
modify to suit the critics, and in a course of years published five
different dictionaries, all in retreat from his original ground.

The sum of the matter is, that Webster was a vain,
weak, plodding Yankee, ambitious to be an American Johnson, without one substantial qualification for the undertaking, and the American public have ignored his pretensions. One publisher of note has adopted his orthography,
because he publishes his Dictionary, and one newspaper
editor of note has done the same thing; but beyond these
two establishments, neither of which can claim any authority as umpire in a literary question, Webster's orthography
is as unpopular as it is abominable; and I hardly know how
our Legislature could do a greater wrong to popular education than by inflicting Webster's radicalism on the rising
generation. [47]

A statement is given from William Cullen Bryant to the effect
that not ten scholars in a hundred accept Webster's Dictionary as a
standard of language. [48] Another reason why Webster's Dictionary

should not be used in the schools is that the foreigners who are
learning the English language, recognizing words and phrases of
their own on every page, will not fail to add others, and thus hast-
en the corruption of our tongue. For all the above reasons, the
Chairman of the Committee on Literature reports that in his judgment the introduction of Webster's Dictionary in the manner proposed
by the Legislature would be unwise because it is neither an English
Dictionary nor a standard of authority.

The same year, the Merriams published another pamphlet in
which they proposed to summarize the charges, together with their
refutations, made by Worcester, Converse, and Jenks, Hickling, and
Swan, on Webster, his dictionaries, and his publishers. No new
arguments are presented, but attention is called to the fact that since
the contract between Converse and Worcester was dated July 11,
1828, and the American Dictionary did not appear until the December
following, lack of success in publishing the Quarto could not be given
as cause for the Abridgment. 49

In the Traveller of March 7, 1855, there appeared a communication from the publishers of Worcester's Dictionaries denouncing
the remarks made by Professor Stowe in a letter to a Boston publishing house, concerning the merits of Webster's Dictionaries. 50
The communication was answered by G. & C. Merriam in the Boston
Post of March 22, 1855 in an article which quoted the reasons as
given by Stowe for favoring Webster's Dictionary. His reasons are
as follows:

1. Webster is the most uniformly analogical and self-
consistent.
2. His system falls in most completely with the tendencies
of the language; and if in anything he goes beyond present usage, it is in the right direction, and the usage
will soon overtake him.
3. He has present possession of the ground more than
any one. In the United States he is the authority
everywhere except in Boston; and even there, more
than any other one. In England he has more authority
than any other one, and is continually gaining.
4. He is the great American philologist, the most learned
and devoted scholar in his special department, that the
English language knows; and for this reason, other
things being equal, he deserves the preference.
5. If we would have uniformity, we must adopt Webster,
for he cannot be displaced; but others may be. 51

Following the article by G. & C. Merriam was another copied
from the current number of the Boston Mercantile Library Reporter,
with the signature "P," supposed to be a Mr. Poole, the librarian
of the Association. The burden of the article is to dispel the idea
made current by the Boston publishing houses in the contest waged

with the Springfield publishers, that Worcester was the standard
authority in Boston. As proof to the contrary, the comparative use
of the two dictionaries in the Mercantile Library is cited. Although
the best editions of both dictionaries were equally available to the
readers, the copy of Worcester which was placed in the library in
May, 1848 still had on its edges the original polish of the binder's
knife, and only the stamp of the Association kept it from being
taken for a new copy. Webster's Unabridged, which had been in
the library since October, 1849, was in constant use, being asked
for as often as twenty times a day. The same was true of the
dictionaries in the Boston Atheneum. Mention is made of the popularity of Webster in foreign countries--a popularity due to his
success in reforming the absurd philological anomalies in our
language.

In the battle of the dictionaries reference is frequently made
by the Worcester adherents to the orthography of Webster as compared with the excellence of Worcester's orthography. Poole asserts
that most people refer to a dictionary not so much for spelling as
for definition and etymology, and that as far as orthography is concerned, Webster has tried to record the changes while Worcester
would delight in an "absolute and complete petrefaction of the orthography of our language as he gives it."

In another pamphlet, 52 the Merriams attempt to show that as
far as vocabulary, pronunciation, orthography, and definitions were
concerned, Webster, and not Worcester, was accepted as the standard in this country. Regarding the extensiveness of the vocabulary
of Worcester, the pamphlet insists that many of the words which
increase the number are either useless compounds or are words
which any intelligent man would refuse to incorporate into the English language. Among the seventy-seven words of this type listed
in the pamphlet are dandyize, cookee (a female cook), coxcomicality,
fiddle-fiddler, unleisuredness, wegotism, weism, pish-pash, poi-
soneress, jig-gumbob, and thundery. Worcester is criticized for
marking the letters to indicate pronunciation, since the exact sound
cannot be represented and the marks only perplex instead of en-
lightening the reader. Mention is also made of the fact that Worcester is not consistent in his pronunciation. Concerning orthography, the author of the pamphlet says that there are only two
methods for a lexicographer to pursue. One is to watch the tendencies of the language to simplicity and broader analogies and to carry
forward changes that have begun, and the other is to attempt, regard-
less of system or principles, to follow existing usage. Webster, he
says, has adopted the first method; Worcester, the last. But Worcester, in spelling the words fervor, honor, neighbor, etc. without
the u, as does Webster, departs from English usage, and since he
follows Webster only partially, does not conform to American usage.
A list of words is given to show that Worcester had adopted Webster's method of spelling. 53

Todd's Johnson's by Worcester, 1827	Worcester, 1854, following Webster
almanack	almanac
acoustick	acoustic
achromatick	achromatic
acrostick	acrostic
academick	academic
acknowledgement	acknowledgment
abridgement	abridgment
adespotick	adespotic
agonistick	agonistic
agonothetick	agonothetic
agrestick	agrestic
alchymist	alchemist
alchymy	alchemy
alembick	alembic
alexipharmick	alexipharmic
algebraick	algebraic
aloetick	aloetic
amasment	amassment
ambassadour	ambassador
ambrosiack	ambrosiac
anabaptistick	anabaptistic
anacamptick	anacamptic
angelick	angelic
antarctick	antarctic
antick	antic
antiphlogistick	antiphlogistic
apopletick	apoplectic
ardour	ardor
arithmetick	arithmetic
armour	armor
Atlantick	Atlantic
attick	attic
authentick	authentic
behaviour	behavior
Catholick	Catholic
clamour	clamor
clamourer	clamorer
colick	colic
colour	color
colourably	colorably
endeavour	endeavor
arrour	error
favour	favor
honour	honor
inferiour	inferior
labour	labor
rigour	rigor
superior	superior

As far as definitions are concerned the pamphlet stresses the superiority of Webster's over Worcester's by quoting testimonials to that effect and by giving the definitions of the same word as found in the two dictionaries. An Appendix is added which gives the relative sales of the two dictionaries by booksellers throughout the United States. These are given in Table I (see Appendix).

An elaborate essay on Webster's orthography was published in the Democratic Review, a New York monthly magazine, in March, 1856. It is a long article, but it was copied into several of the daily and weekly papers of New York, Boston, and Philadelphia. The editor of the New York Evening Post made the following comment on it.

> We do not remember to have seen elsewhere such full justice done to Noah Webster's System of Orthography, under which the English language has been corrupting for the last quarter of a century, as in an article which we find in the last number of the Democratic Review. We have copied it at length in our columns, and would gladly contribute toward the expense of having it read twice a year in every school-house in the United States, until every trace of Websterian spelling disappears from the land. It is a melancholy evidence of the amount of mischief one man of learning can do to society, that Webster's System of Orthography is adopted and propagated by the largest publishing house; through the columns of the most widely circulated monthly magazine, and through one of the ablest and most widely circulated newspapers in the United States.
>
> The article is attributed to the pen of Edward S. Gould, of this city. [54]

An answer was made to the review by Epes Sargent, who attempts to show that the innovations for which the reviewer had criticized Webster so severely were not original with Webster. He says that in his great folio dictionary, printed in 1617, entitled The Guide to Tongues, John Minsheu spells with the er ending the words cited by the reviewer, as was also done in a number of dictionaries of foreign languages about the same period. Phillips, the nephew of Milton, did the same in New World of English Words, in 1658. Sepulcher, theater, miter, was the general spelling of the dictionaries of the day. He calls attention to the fact that the word scepter came into our language from the first with the spelling ter, that in Wycliffe's Bible it was spelled cepter, and it retained its termination in er through all the versions to that of King James inclusive; nor was it altered therein until a comparatively late period. Even Bailey gives scepter as the only proper spelling. [55]

In the editorial columns of the New York Home Journal of March 19, 1859, an anonymous article appeared under the title of "Webster's Dictionary," known to have been written by Edward S. Gould. [56] The author sanctions the Dictionary as far as vocabulary and definitions are concerned, but disagrees with Webster's system

of orthography. The Orthographical Hobgoblin, signed by "Philorthos" (probably William F. Poole),[57] was offered to the Journal as
an answer, and upon its being declined was published by G. & C.
Merriam Company. A publisher's notice at the beginning of the
pamphlet emphasizes the number of school books and periodicals
using Webster's orthography. A summary of the annual sale is
given in Table III (see Appendix). The article states that five-
sixths of all the school books published in this country, so far as
they follow any standard, follow Webster; that twenty of his dictionaries are sold to one of other authors; and that the orthography of
Webster differs only slightly from that of Worcester, whose publishers are the instigators of the controversy. He concludes:

> ... If Webster is not the standard of orthography in
> America, there is no standard. Worcester's orthography
> is neither American nor English, but is a mongrel, va-
> cillating compilation, without purpose or system other than
> assumed usage. Each succeeding edition improves and
> conforms more and more to Webster. Worcester sets up
> no such claim as is assumed by his publishers; but he
> gives a list of 1575 "Words of Doubtful and Various Ortho-
> graphy," spelled in two, three, and four different ways,
> the number of forms amounting to nearly 4000.... The
> changes he has made in words under the first four letters
> of the alphabet, in different editions, are more in number
> than the entire differences between his latest edition and
> Webster's Unabridged.[58]

In 1859 was published the Pictorial Quarto Unabridged edition
of Webster's Dictionary edited by Chauncey A. Goodrich. It was
followed the next year by Worcester's Quarto Dictionary. These
publications caused the controversy to be continued with renewed
zeal.

The New York World of June 15, 1860 contained a critical
notice of the two dictionaries signed by "G. P. M." (George P.
Marsh). Objections were raised to the Webster Dictionary because
of its failure to contain a sufficient number of obsolete words and
its outmoded etymology, and because of the form and orthography of
its words. The plan of Worcester, according to this reviewer, is
more comprehensive and judicious, and, in most respects, more
satisfactorily executed and better suited to the wants of a generation
which is no longer content to limit its study of the literature of its
native tongue to the production of this and the last century. The
two dictionaries are compared on the basis of completeness in vocabulary, fullness and certainty in etymological history, accuracy in
the forms of words, pronunciation, and definition. Regarding vocabulary the article states that Worcester not only embraces more
words numerically, but offers a wider sphere of language, both as
to the time of its employment and the subjects with which it is conversant; his dictionary is therefore a truer and fuller embodiment
of the speech of English and Anglo-American humanity than that of
Webster. Most of Webster's orthographical innovations have been

discarded in later editions, but there still remains so much arbitrary violation of established usage that those who use his dictionary can never be sure whether he is following generally recognized authority or setting up his own. Worcester conforms more strictly to English usage. His orthoepy also exhibits the actual pronunciation of the most cultivated circles in English and American society. Although Webster's definitions are the strongest point of his dictionary, they are sometimes erroneous, and confuse by attempting to convey by description that which can be understood only by exemplification. "As an etymologicon, ... except with respect to words whose source is almost too well known to need to be given at all, Webster's dictionary is unscholarlike and unsound."59 The reviewer concludes that while great merit must be awarded to Webster, Worcester must be regarded as the best existing standard of orthography and orthoepy and as the completest repertory of the English tongue.

This review was answered in the same journal by an article, "The Two Dictionaries, or the Reviewer Reviewed," signed by "Equal Justice," later published in pamphlet form by the publishers of Webster. After comparing the two dictionaries as to the obsolete words, etymology, orthography, pronunciation, and definition--all to the advantage of Webster--the author sums up the differences in the two dictionaries as follows:

> ... In the vocabulary there is not much to choose. In pronunciation and orthography, not stuff enough to make an argument. In etymology, Webster is an original with the errors of his time, still instructive and inspiring, often sagacious, and always full. Worcester is meager, un-scholarlike, and of little worth, and altogether behind the means at command. In definitions, Webster maintains his unquestioned supremacy, as also in the synonyms and pic-torial illustrations.
> In some respects, Worcester and Webster supplement each other, and every literary man who can, will choose to have the two. 60

In this pamphlet, attention is called to the fact that someone curious about the number of words in the two dictionaries, in order to determine the claims put forth by the publishers of Worcester, had the words in the vocabularies of the two counted, and the ems in each measured, with the following result:

> ... The vocabulary proper of Webster contains 99,780 words, the appendices 40,276, making a total of 140,056; that of Worcester 103,855, the appendices, 28,551; total 132,406, making 7,650 more in Webster than in Worcester. The number of ems in Webster is 14,747,352; in Worces-ter, 13,273,532, leaving a balance of 1,473,820 ems of printed matter in favor of Webster. 61

On January 27, 1860 there appeared in the Congregationalist, a religious newspaper published in Boston, an article printed as an editorial, in which the writer warns the public against the purchase of Worcester's Dictionary. A large number of the papers were purchased by the publishers of Webster's Dictionary, or their agents, for distribution, and the article was inserted as an advertisement in the Boston Journal and into other papers in different sections of the Union. 62 The assertion made in a previous pamphlet that five-sixths of all the school books published in this country follow Webster as their standard is answered in this article by saying that of three hundred and twenty-six different school books published in Boston, only ten were printed in Webster's orthography, while the proportion was still less in New York and Philadelphia. 63 The article was answered in a pamphlet from Worcester's publishers, entitled The Critic Criticised, etc. in which an attempt was made to point out the misrepresentations and inaccuracies of the article. Another pamphlet was issued by the publishers of Webster's Unabridged Dictionary called Webster's and Worcester's Dictionaries Compared, which contains reviews of the two works from the Congregationalist, Zion's Herald, and other publications, and many testimonials as to the merits of the Webster publication. This was followed by a Worcester pamphlet, A Comparison of Worcester's and Webster's Quarto Dictionaries, which consists mainly of extracts from reviews and testimonials showing the greater value of the Worcester diction- ary. Reference is again made to the fact that many prominent writers, among whom are Edward Everett, Daniel Webster, Ban- croft, Bryant, Hawthorne, Prescott, Hillard, Longfellow, refuse to use the Webster innovations in spelling; and quotations are given to call attention to the uselessness of the illustrations included in the Pictorial edition of Webster, referred to by the Atlantic Monthly as "primer-pictures," more "fitted for a child's scrap-book than for a volume intended to go into a student's library." An interesting discussion of the illustrations is taken from the Christian Advocate.

> Dr. Webster has four pages devoted to mythology, wherein we have pictures of Apollo, Bacchus, Cupid, Juno, Mars, Neptune, Pluto, and some forty others, all of which, for aught we know, may be lifelike representations of the originals; but we could not help asking, why are many others omitted? Where is the lovely Hebe, and the beauti- ful Venus, and the jolly Vulcan, her husband? Surely their pictures were quite as important as the others, and until better informed, we must believe that genuine likenesses were equally accessible....
> The picture of a "lady attired in hooped dress" was intended doubtless for posterity, so that our descendants may see what was the fashion in this year of grace 1860. We are bound to say, however, that the thing is a vile caricature. The publishers ought to be ashamed of thus slandering the sex.
> A cut presenting a gentleman and lady in rather ridicu- lous posture--in fact, we suppose him to be a little boozy --is entitled "Fandago," meaning that they are going through the saltatory performance thus designated. There is, un- fortunately, no representation of a waltz, a jig, or a horn-

pipe, so that we cannot decide which is the most graceful variety of the dance....
     Does the reader know what a furbelow is? Walker says
it is a "fur or fringe sewed on the lower part of the gar-
ment. " But, bless you, that is but a vague definition
compared with Webster's. He tells us that a furbelow is
"a piece of stuff plaited and puckered on a gown or petticoat"; and then, with a laudable determination to make so
important a matter as clear as possible, he says, "See
pictorial illustrations. " Of course we hunt through the
pictorial illustrations, and under the word Furbelow we find
a picture of a dubious-looking female in a dress such as
our grandmothers used to wear, and really there does
seem to be something on her petticoat which we are bound
to believe must be a furbelow. There are a great many
other articles of feminine apparel of which we are pro-
foundly ignorant, and we marvel why furbelow should be
the only one selected for a picture. So, too, the necessity of illustrating by wood-engravings a balloon, a harp,
a harpoon, an ear of Indian corn, and a pumpkin, is not
apparent. A witch, we are told, is "a woman who, by
compact with the devil, practices sorcery or enchantment";
and for a representation of one we are referred to the
pictorial illustrations, among which we find the picture of
an old woman astride of a broomstick! Silliness can go
no further. We are told indeed that in late copies this
ridiculous picture is omitted, but the asterisk directing
the reader to look for it is still retained. [64]

     The last seven pages of the pamphlet are taken up with sixty-
seven recommendations from presidents and professors of universities and colleges, forty-two from other distinguished scholars and
literary men, nine from representatives of government publications,
eleven foreign testimonials, and thirty from leading periodicals.
The list includes such names as Oliver Wendell Holmes, Horace
Mann, Henry W. Longfellow, Napoleon, Thomas Carlyle, and Charles Dickens.

     In DeBow's Review for May, 1860 a review of Webster's
Dictionary appeared which called forth another article in reply which
was published in a later number. The second article contains a
letter signed by D. Appleton & Company, Charles Scribner, and
George P. Putnam, answering the statement as to whether they
"especially eschew Webster and have adopted Worcester" as their
standard in orthography. The answer is that they leave the matter
to the authors of their books, but that the authors of educational
textbooks and other works in reference to which the question of
orthography is carefully considered, usually follow Webster as their
standard. Another letter signed by J. B. Lippincott & Company
states that they sell over one hundred thousand copies of Webster's
dictionaries per annum, which is sufficient evidence of the preference of the public. Other letters, similar to those mentioned above,
and in some instances more emphatic, from Butler and Company;

Crosby, Nicholas, Lee and Company; Little, Brown and Company;
Crocker and Brewster; T. R. Murvin; Bosin and Ellsworth; Henry
Hoyt; Chase, Nicholas, and Hill; and J. E. Tilton and Company are
inserted.

Answer is also made to the statement in the preceding review
about Macaulay's not wanting his book published in Websterian orthography.   Reference is made to an article in the Boston Mercantile
Reporter of March, 1855, which quotes the reply of Macaulay on
the subject, "that it was a matter of supreme indifference to him
how they (the Messrs. Harpers) spelled his writings, provided they
made him state just what he intended." He hoped they would make
the orthography of his history conform to the best usage in America;
and he complimented the appearance of the New York edition.   But,
says the article, had Macaulay made such protest, it would have
been as much against Worcester as against Webster, since Worcester had done his best to perpetuate the blunders of Webster.   The
following comparison is given of the two dictionaries.

> The etymology of Webster, admirable for his time, is
> not in accordance with the improved method of the new
> philology, that of "Worcester" is simply a crude accumu-
> lation of vocables on the old, unscientific plan of Webster,
> with even less of historical etymology, and entirely want-
> ing in the fertility of suggestion which makes "Webster's"
> valuable even now.
> The pictorial illustrations and the incorporation of sy-
> nonyms are both valuable features in a dictionary; but in
> "Worcester's" the former are mainly cuts of birds' heads
> and leaves of plants, sparsely scattered along the pages
> to the number of eight or nine hundred, with a dozen or
> two of illustrations, and most of which, are only reduced
> patterns of cuts to be found in any elementary work on
> Natural History.   The illustrations in "Webster" are much
> larger and more finely executed, and better selected, but
> still not, to our apprehension, exactly what is wanted.
> The synonyms of "Worcester" are largely taken, verbatim,
> from Platt's little work on English Synonyms, and are
> not to be compared with the admirable table of synonyms
> in "Webster," the last literary labor of the lamented
> Goodrich.   In scientific terms we hardly know which is
> the worse.   Many in "Webster" need revision, and the
> vocabulary of these terms is inadequate.   But the fault
> in "Worcester" is, that there seems to have been no prin-
> ciples of selection.   The most unusual terms of classifi-
> cation are included, and the words in most frequent use
> omitted.   But even in this, the selection is entirely ar-
> bitrary and inconsistent; terms being included or rejected
> for no apparent reason.   Again, in the definition of such
> terms, it seems to be forgotten, that what is wanted in
> a general dictionary, is a definition of the word and not
> a description of the thing, which is only appropriate in
> a cyclopedia or strictly scientific hand-book. [65]

The following lines from one of the Webster pamphlets concerning the Worcester method of warfare is descriptive of the controversy as waged by both sides.

> Various motives, it may be supposed, have prompted
> the one class and the other of those strictures. Pecuniary
> interest, a desire for the notoriety supposed to result from
> attacking a distinguished man, or work; display of lore; an
> aversion to changes, even if salutary, and an inordinate
> attachment to old forms, and scholarly criticism, have all,
> at one time or another, been apparent. [66]

* * *

The work of dictionary making in America had its beginning
in the publication of A School Dictionary by Samuel Johnson, Jr.
of Guilford, Connecticut, in 1798. Within the next two years Johnson collaborated with John Elliott in the making of another dictionary.
Before the publication of Webster's first dictionary in 1806 three
other school dictionaries had been published. These were the work
of Caleb Alexander, William Woodbridge, Henry Priest, and Daniel
Jaudon, Thomas Watson, and Stephen Addington, the last three
having worked on one dictionary.

During the first half of the nineteenth century many other
school and pocket dictionaries were published. They were prepared
for use as textbooks and as handy reference books and "parlour
companions." The school dictionary became a substitute for the
spelling book as a school text and filled conveniently the gap between
the spelling book and the larger and more expensive dictionary.
Along with the list of useful words other information came to be
included. With the publication of A Compendious Dictionary by Noah
Webster in 1806 began the practice of adding such material as tables
of money, weights, and measures, lists of distinguished people of
antiquity, and mythological data. Brief grammars of the English
language were also added, and where these were omitted much of
the grammatical material was inserted with the vocabulary. It
came to be thought necessary that the child know something of the
derivation of words he studied, and etymological information was
included.

Almost with the beginning of colonial history the difference
between the use of words by the English people and the American
colonists became apparent. Interest in this fact continued and
caused much comment especially by Englishmen, who regarded the
use of the language by Americans as barbarous. Among those who
called attention to such changes was John Witherspoon, a Scotch
clergyman who became the sixth president of the College of New
Jersey. In a series of essays, first published in 1761, Witherspoon
devotes about twenty pages to Americanisms, perversions of language
in the United States, and cant phrases. He made a collection of
errors he heard in public speeches and noticed in articles from the
press. This collection probably constitutes the first published list
of expressions peculiar to this country.

The first attempt to make a collection of all such words as were supposed to be American peculiarities was that of John Pickering, who, in 1814, communicated to the American Academy of Arts and Sciences his Memoir on the Present State of the English Language in America, with a Vocabulary. The Vocabulary was published the next year in the Collections of the Academy, and in 1816, it was reprinted as A Vocabulary, or Collection of Words and Phrases Which Have Been Supposed to Be Peculiar to the United States of America. To Which Is Prefixed An Essay on the Present State of the English Language in the United States. The decided pro-English attitude expressed by Pickering provoked the hostile criticism of his more nationally-minded American friends.

In 1848 was published A Dictionary of Americanisms. A Glossary of Phrases, Usually Regarded as Peculiar to the United States by John Russell Bartlett. Bartlett contends that the colloquial peculiarities of New England were derived directly from Great Britain. Another collection of Americanisms, made by Alfred L. Elwyn, appeared in 1859.

Two of the American dictionaries are devoted almost entirely to the problem of pronunciation. These are: An Explanatory and Phonographic Pronouncing Dictionary by William Bolles, published in 1845, and The American Phonetic Dictionary of the English Language, published in 1855 and compiled by Daniel S. Smalley. The latter was designed by Nathaniel Storrs and it attempts to represent pronunciation by means of a phonetic alphabet.

It remained for Noah Webster and Joseph Emerson Worcester so to raise the quality of dictionary making that their works came to be recognized as standard in England. Webster began his philological career by the publication of his spelling book in 1783. His Compendious Dictionary, published in 1806, was followed by an abridged edition for common schools in 1807, but it was the American Dictionary of the English Language, published in two quarto volumes in 1828, that established Webster's reputation as a lexicographer.

Worcester began his lexical work by abridging Johnson's Dictionary as improved by Todd, and abridged by Chalmers, with Walker's Pronouncing Dictionary Combined, 1828, and Webster's American Dictionary, 1829, but A Comprehensive Pronouncing and Explanatory Dictionary, 1830, was his own work. Other dictionaries by Worcester followed: Elementary Dictionary, 1835; A Universal and Critical Dictionary of the English Language, 1846; Primary Dictionary, 1850; A Pronouncing, Explanatory and Synonymous Dictionary of the English Language, 1860.

After the publication of Worcester's first original work in 1830 a controversy arose between Webster and Worcester and their publishers and friends as to the merits of their respective dictionaries. Although the War began with the accusation made by Webster that Worcester had copied his materials, in reality it was

Webster's attempt to prevent a rival publication from entering the field in which he considered that he had more or less a monopoly. The publishers of both Webster and Worcester, seeing in the controversy an opportunity for good advertisement, took up the struggle. The conflict continued until after 1860, with epidemics flaring up at intervals as rival publications came from the press.

Notes

1. Atlantic Monthly, V (1860), 631.
2. Personal letter, June 30, 1935.
3. The Professor at the Breakfast Table. Boston: Houghton, Mifflin and Company, 1893, p. 44.
4. McKnight, op. cit., p. 484.
5. J. E. Worcester. A Gross Literary Fraud Exposed; Relating to the Publication of Worcester's Dictionary in London. Boston: Jenks, Hickling, and Swan, 1853, Appendix, p. 19.
6. Worcester Palladium, December 10, 1834.
7. Editorial, Worcester Palladium, December 10, 1834, p. 2.
8. The Critic Criticised and Worcester Vindicated: Consisting of a Review of an Article in the "Congregationalist" upon the Comparative Merits of Worcester's and Webster's Quarto Dictionaries. Boston: Swan, Brewer, and Tileston, March, 1860, p. 64.
9. Ibid.
10. Ibid., pp. 64-65.
11. Ibid., p. 65.
12. Ibid., p. 66.
13. Ibid., p. 66.
14. Ibid., pp. 66-67.
15. G. & C. Merriam. "A Gross Literary Fraud Exposed; Relating to the Publication of Worcester's Dictionary in London," as Webster's Dictionary. Springfield, Mass.: Geo. & Chas. Merriam, 1854, p. 4.
16. Ibid., pp. 8-9.
17. William Thomas Lowndes. The Bibliographer's Manual of English Literature, revised by Henry G. Bohn. London: George Bell and Sons, 1864, IV, 2965.
18. Worcester, Gross Literary Fraud, etc., p. 11.
19. Ibid.
20. Ibid., pp. 12-13.
21. Ibid., p. 13.
22. Ibid., pp. 13-14.
23. Ibid., p. 14.
24. Ibid., p. 15.
25. Ibid., Appendix, p. 25.
26. Note a statement made by James G. Percival in a letter to George Hayward, August 27, 1829: 'I was offered the abridgment of Webster's Dictionary, and for this I should have been paid $1,500, but I could not at that time engage, on account of this engagement [Geography].

It was offered me winter before last, when I had prepared only three volumes of the Geography. That sum has been paid for it; and I have no hesitation in saying, it would have been an easier task than the Geography...." Ward, op. cit., p. 297.

27. Worcester, Samuel T., op. cit., p. 27.

28. G. & C. Merriam. "A Gross Literary Fraud Exposed; Relating to the Publication of Worcester's Dictionary in London," as Webster's Dictionary. Springfield: G. & C. Merriam, 1854, p. 4.

29. Ibid., p. 5.

30. Ibid., p. 7.

31. Ibid., pp. 8-9.

32. A Reply to Messrs. G. & C. Merriam's Attack Upon the Character of Dr. Worcester and His Dictionaries. Boston: Jenks, Hickling and Swan, 1854, p. 1.

33. Geo. & Chas. Merriam, op. cit., p. 10.

34. Mr. Converse's Answer to an Attack on Him by Messrs. G. & C. Merriam, p. 1, attached to Worcester, A Gross Literary Fraud Exposed.

35. Ibid., p. 5.

36. Ibid., p. 6.

37. Webster's MSS, New York Public Library.

38. Ibid.

39. Reply to Messrs. G. & C. Merriam's Attack, p. 8.

40. Ibid.

41. Ibid., p. 9.

42. Ibid., p. 19.

43. Ibid., p. 21.

44. Ibid., p. 23.

45. Ibid., p. 25.

46. Ibid.

47. Ibid., p. 31.

48. Ibid.

49. A Summary Summing of the Charges with Their Refutations, in Attacks Upon Noah Webster, LL.D., His Dictionaries, or His Publishers, Made by Mr. Joseph Worcester, Mr. Sherman Converse, Messrs. Jenks, Hickling, and Swan. Springfield: Geo. & Chas. Merriam, 1834, p. 13.

50. G. & C. Merriam, "Webster's Dictionaries," Boston Post, March 22, 1855.

51. Ibid.

52. Have We a National Standard of English Lexicography? or, Some Comparisons of the Claims of Webster's Dictionaries, and Worcester's Dictionaries. Springfield: Geo. & Chas. Merriam, 1855.

53. Ibid., p. 12.

54. Quoted in Recommendations of Worcester's Dictionaries; to Which Is Prefixed a Review of Webster's System of Orthography from the United States Democratic Review, for March, 1856. Boston: Hickling, Swan and Brown, 1856, p. 2.

55. Epes Sargent. The Critic Criticised: A Reply to a Review

of Webster's System in the Democratic Review for March, 1856. From the Democratic Review for June, 1856. Springfield: G. & C. Merriam, 1856, p. 14.

56. Philorthos. The Orthographical Hobgoblin. Springfield: G. & C. Merriam, 1856. p. 3.

57. An unsigned statement written on a slip of paper inserted at the front of a copy of The Orthographical Hobgoblin owned by the American Antiquarian Society, Worcester, Mass.

58. Philorthos, op. cit., pp. 5-6.

59. "The Two Dictionaries," The New York World, June 15, 1860.

60. The Two Dictionaries or the Reviewer Reviewed, A Reply to a Correspondent of the New York World. Springfield: G. & C. Merriam, 1860, p. 15.

61. Ibid., footnote, p. 8.

62. William Draper Swan. The Critic Criticised and Worcester Vindicated; Consisting of a Review in the "Congregationalist," upon the Comparative Merits of Worcester's and Webster's Quarto Dictionaries, Together with a Reply to the Attacks of Messrs. G. & C. Merriam upon the Character of Dr. Worcester and His Dictionaries. Boston: Swan, Brewer and Tileston, March, 1860. p. 4.

63. Ibid., footnote, pp. 64-65.

64. A Comparison of Worcester's and Webster's Quarto Dictionaries, also Specimen Pages of Worcester's Quarto Dictionary, Recommendations from Eminent Scholars, and Reviews from Leading Periodicals, American and Foreign. Boston: Swan, Brewer, and Tileston. Date not given, p. 7.

65. "The English Language," DeBow's Review, XXX (1861), 331.

66. "Equal Justice," op. cit., p. 1.

APPENDIX

Included in the Appendix are a list of the dictionaries of the English language compiled by Americans before 1861, and four tables pertaining to the comparative popularity of the dictionaries of Webster and Worcester. Two of the tables show the sales of the Webster dictionaries during the years 1854 and 1860 as compared with those of Worcester. The other two tables emphasize the number of school books that use the orthography established by Webster. These tables were compiled from data contained in pamphlets published by the Merriam Company. They are included here to illustrate the type of advertising propaganda indulged in by the publishers of the rival dictionaries, and to show the extent to which the dictionary fever had spread over the country

A LIST OF AMERICAN DICTIONARIES OF
THE ENGLISH LANGUAGE BEFORE 1861
ARRANGED IN CHRONOLOGICAL ORDER

Only the principal editions of Webster are included. The asterisks indicate that the dictionaries were not located and therefore were not included in the study.

Samuel Johnson, Jun'r, A School Dictionary	1798
Samuel Johnson, Jun'r and John Elliott, A Selected Pronouncing and Accented Dictionary	1800
Caleb Alexander, The Columbian Dictionary	1800
William Woodbridge, A Key to the English Language	1801
Henry Priest, The Young Ladies' Pocket Companion	1801
Daniel Jaudon, Thomas Watson, and Stephen Addington, An English Orthographical Expositor	1804
Abel Flint, A Spelling, Pronouncing, and Parsing Dictionary	1806
Noah Webster, A Compendious Dictionary of the English Language	1806
Susanna Rowson, A Spelling Dictionary	1807
Noah Webster, A Dictionary of the English Language; compiled for the Use of Common Schools in the United States	1807
Richard Wiggins, The New York Expositor	1811
Richard S. Coxe, A New Critical Pronouncing Dictionary	1813
Burgess Allison, The American Standard of Orthography	1815
John Pickering, A Vocabulary of Words and Phrases Which Have Been Supposed to Be Peculiar to the United States	1816
William Grimshaw, An Etymological Dictionary	1821

J. Kingsbury, A New Improved Dictionary for Children   1822

Hezekiah Burhans, The Nomenclature and Expositor of the
English Language ... according to John Walker's
Pronouncing Dictionary.   1826

Lyman Cobb, an abridged edition of Walker's Critical Pronouncing Dictionary   1828

Eliza Robbins, Primary Dictionary   1828

Noah Webster, An American Dictionary of the English
Language   1828

Joseph Emerson Worcester, abridgment of Johnson's
Dictionary, as improved by Todd, and abridged
by Chalmers, with Walker's Pronouncing Dictionary Combined   1828

Joseph Emerson Worcester, abridgment of Webster's
American Dictionary of the English Language   1829

Noah Webster, A Dictionary of the English Language for Primary Schools and the Counting
House   1829

Edward Hazen, The Speller and Definer   1829

William W. Turner, The School Dictionary   1829

William Grimshaw, The Gentleman's Lexicon   1829

William Grimshaw, The Ladies' Lexicon   1829

Joseph Emerson Worcester, A Comprehensive, Pronouncing and Explanatory Dictionary of the
English Language   1830

Noah Webster, A Dictionary of the English Language;
Edited by E. H. Barker   1830-32

Noah J. T. George, The Gentlemen and Ladies' Pocket
Companion   1831

D. J. Browne, The Etymological Encyclopedia of Technical Words and Phrases   1832

Lyman Cobb, A New Dictionary of the English Language   1832

Lyman Cobb, Expositor or Sequel to the Spelling Book   1833

Lyman Cobb, The Ladies' Reticule Companion, or Little
Lexicon of the English Language   1834

Joseph Emerson Worcester, <u>Elementary Dictionary</u>   1835

Rufus Claggett, <u>The American Expositor, or Intellectual Definer</u>   1836

T. H. Gallaudet and Horace Hooker, <u>The School and Family Dictionary</u>   1841

Noah Webster, <u>An American Dictionary of the English Language.</u>   First Edition in Octavo.   1841

William Bolles, <u>An Explanatory and Phonographic Pronouncing Dictionary of the English Language</u>   1845

William Bolles, <u>A Phonographic Pronouncing Dictionary.</u> Abridged edition.   1846

Joseph Emerson Worcester, <u>A Universal and Critical Dictionary of the English Language</u>   1846

Noah Webster, <u>An American Dictionary of the English Language.</u>   Revised by Chauncey A. Goodrich.   1847

John Russell Bartlett, <u>A Dictionary of Americanisms</u>   1848

*William Grimshaw, <u>A Primary Pronouncing Dictionary</u>   1850

Joseph Emerson Worcester, <u>Primary Dictionary</u>   1850

*B. H. Hall, <u>A Collection of College Words and Customs</u>   1851

James H. Martin, <u>The Orthoepist</u>   1851

Edward Hazen, <u>The New Speller and Definer</u>   1851

"A Public School Teacher," <u>The Public School Dictionary</u>   1855

Daniel S. Smalley, <u>The American Phonetic Dictionary of the English Language</u>   1855

Joseph Emerson Worcester, <u>A Pronoucing, Explanatory and Synonymous Dictionary of the English Language</u>   1855

Chauncey A. Goodrich, <u>A Pronouncing and Defining Dictionary of the English Language.</u>   Abridged from Webster's <u>American Dictionary</u>   1856

Alfred L. Elwyn, <u>A Glossary of Supposed Americanisms</u>   1859

Alexander H. Laidlaw, <u>An American Pronouncing Dictionary of the English Language</u>   1859

Joseph Emerson Worcester, <u>A Dictionary of the English
Language</u>   1860

*Anonymous, <u>A New Pocket Dictionary</u>   1860

TABLE I

SALES MADE OF WEBSTER'S AND WORCESTER'S DICTIONARIES AS REPORTED IN MARCH, APRIL, MAY, 1854*

DEALER	PLACE	WEBSTER'S	SALES REPORTED WORCESTER'S	ALL DICT. EXCEPT WEBSTER'S
1. A. S. Barnes & Co.	New York	Small - as many as all others large - 9	to	1
2. Ivison & Phinney	"	20	to	1
3. Pratt, Woodford & Co.	"	6	to	1
4. D. Burgess & Co.	"	3	to	1
5. Clark, Austin & Smith	"	2,317	421	1,275
6. Robert B. Collins	"	3	1	
7. S. S. & W. Wood	"	Sell more Webster's than all others		
8. Leavitt & Allen	"	5	to 1	scarcely any
9. Kiggins & Kellog	"	50	to 1	
10. W. K. Cornwell	"	5 4	to 1	1

| | | SALES REPORTED | | | ALL DICT. EXCEPT WEBSTER'S |
DEALER	PLACE	WEBSTER'S		WORCESTER'S	
11. B. B. Mussey & Co.	Boston	1 (small) 8vo 3-4to two 8vo	to equal	2 (Comprehensive) 8vo	
12. Tappan & Whittemore	"	4 (large) (small)	to equal	1	
13. John Philbrick	"	1,000 (4to 7 8vo) 5	to	50 (large) to	1
14. Sanborn & Carter	Portland	100 (4to) 10 (com. sch.)	to to	1 (8vo) 1 (elem.)	
15. John Keith & Co.	Worcester	100 (small) 50 (8vo) 140 (unabr.)	to to to	150 (elem.) 3 (8vo) 150 (Comp.)	
16. Edward Livermore	Worcester	4to 8vo 1 (school) 2	to to	none 10 (Comp. &elem.)	1
17. J. S. & C. Adams	Amherst	100	to	1	
18. L. & E. Edwards	Norwich	9	to	1	
19. W. J. Hamersley	Hartford	Sell only Webster's except few Worcester's			

20.	Durrie & Peck	New Haven	hundreds to half dozen of others			|
21.	Joseph Steen	Brattleboro	Sell only Webster in large form			1
22.	Clark & Hesser	Philadelphia	40 (whole series)	to	1 equal	
23.	Smith & English	"	20 / 10	to	1 to	
24.	H. C. Peck & Theo Bliss	"	50 (8vo & 4to)	to	1 equal	|
25.	Uriah Hunt & Son	"	3 more than all others	to	1	
26.	Kay & Co.	Pittsburgh	2		to	1
27.	Jas. S. Waters	Baltimore	sell only Webster			
28.	Geo. M. West	Richmond, Va.	50 (unabridged)		to	1
29.	James Woodhouse	Richmond, Va.	5		to	1
30.	Frank Taylor	Washington City	12		to	1 equal
31.	Morton & Griswold	Louisville	5		to	1 |
32.	Henry C. Morton	Louisville	4to has no rival / 10 (8vo) / 25 (Hi sch.)	to / to	1 / 1	

	DEALER	PLACE	WEBSTER'S	SALES REPORTED WORCESTER'S	ALL DICT. EXCEPT WEBSTER'S
33.	W. L. Pomroy	Raleigh, N. C.	4 to	1	
34.	H. Crittenden	St. Louis	9	to	1
35.	J. B. Steel	New Orleans	6	to	1
36.	Burnett & Bostwick	New Orleans	In favor of Webster by a large proportion		
37.	Keith & Woods	St. Louis	19	to	10
38.	J. H. Riley & Co.	Columbus, Ohio	Webster to almost exclusion of others		
39.	W. B. Smith & Co.	Cincinnati	20	to	1
40.	Jobbing House	Cincinnati	9	to	1
41.	Truman & Spafford	Cincinnati	5	to	1
42.	Applegate & Co.	Cincinnati	4	to	3
43.	Wests & Stewart	Indianapolis	25 to	4	
44.	Werden & Chamberlain	Indianapolis	20	to	1
45.	L. F. Chaflin & Co.	Dayton	Sell only Webster's		
46.	Payne & Wheaton	Dayton	12 8	1 to	1

No.	Firm	Location			
47.	Knight, King & Co.	Cleveland	450 (sch. ed.) 200 (Hi. sch.) 150 (academic) 300 (university) 40 (Harper's 8vo) 50 (unabridged)	9 0 0 2 (8vo) 0	12 of all
48.	J. B. Cobb & Co.	Cleveland	5	to	3
49.	Murry & Stock	Lancaster, Pa.	12 to	1	
50.	Wm. H. Young	Troy, N. Y.	Webster almost exclusively		
51.	Merriam, Moor & Co.	Troy, N. Y.	500		0
52.	Fist & Little	Albany	500		very few
53.	Hopkins, Bridgman & Co.	Northampton	50	to	1
54.	F. Hall	Elmiron	Webster exclusively except occasionally a copy of Cobb		
55.	E. H. Babcock & Co.	Syracuse	50 (sch. ed.) to	1	
56.	Alden, Beardsley & Co.	Auburn, N. Y.	Sales confined to Webster's and Walker's		
57.	D. M. Dewey	Rochester	Sell only Webster's		
58.	E. Darrow & Bro.	"	10 100	1 to	33

	DEALER	PLACE	WEBSTER'S	SALES REPORTED WORCESTER'S	ALL DICT. EXCEPT WEBSTER'S
59.	Wm. Alling	Rochester	"Webster's only one that sells."		
60.	William N. Sage	"	99	to	1
61.	Phinney & Co.	Buffalo	10	to	1
62.	Miller, Orton & Mulligan	Buffalo	500-600 to	15-20	
63.	S. C. Griggs & Co.	Chicago	400 (16mo) 300 (University) 50 (Harper's ed.) 500 (High School) 50 (pocket) 150 (unabridged)		25 in all
64.	Keen, Bro. & Co.	"	950	80	30
65.	A. H. & C. Burley	"	720	5	40
66.	A. Whittemore & Co.	Milwaukee	550-600		25-30
67.	C. Morse	Detroit	50	to	1
68.	S. D. Elwood & Co.	Detroit	50	to	1
69.	Cushings & Bailey	Baltimore	larger than Worcester less than all others		

70.	Thomas L. White	N. Orleans	3	to		1
71.	E. Smith	Burlington, Vt.	3	to	1	1
			4		to	
72.	F. A. Brown	Hartford	sells Webster's almost exclusively			
73.	O. V. Woodmore & Co.	Vicksburg, Miss.	50	to	1	1
			5		to	
74.	J. S. Taft	Houston, Texas	10		(not used)	1

*Compiled from Appendix to Have We a National Standard of Lexicography? etc., pp. 17-20.

TABLE II

SCHOOL BOOKS BASED ON WEBSTER*

Name	Number Sold Annually
Webster's Elementary Spelling Book	1,000,000
Town's Speller	200,000
Eclectic Series of School Books said to have an annual sale of about 1,500,000, probably	2,000,000
Sanders' Series of School Books over	1,000,000
Town's Series, Parker's Series, Denman's Series, Webb's Readers all follow Webster	
Price's Spelling Books	
Total annual sales can hardly be less than	6,000,000

*Have We A National Standard of English Lexicography? or, Some Comparison of the Claims of Webster's and Worcester's Dictionaries, Springfield: G. & C. Merriam, 1855, pp. 3-4.

TABLE III

SALES OF SCHOOL BOOKS USING WEBSTER'S ORTHOGRAPHY*

DEALER	TIME AND PLACE	NAME OF BOOKS	YEARLY SALES REPORTED
W. B. Smith & Co.	Cincinnati May 2, 1859	Eclectic Educational Series, and all other works published	2,000,000
Ivison & Phinney	New York 1858	Sanders' Series of Readers and Spellers	900,000
		Other Common School Books	200,000
		Scientific books, including music books	175,000
D. Appleton & Co.	New York May 2, 1859	Webster's Elementary Speller and other educational works	1,500,000
A. S. Barnes & Burr	New York May 2, 1859	Parker & Watson's Series of Readers	500,000
Pratt, Oakley & Co.		National Series of Standard School Books	200,000
		Total	5,475,000

*Compiled from data given in Philorthos, The Orthographical Hobgoblin, Springfield: G. & C. Merriam, 1859, p. 4.

TABLE IV

SALES MADE
OF WEBSTER'S AND WORCESTER'S DICTIONARIES
AUGUST AND SEPTEMBER, 1860*

DEALER	PLACE	SALES REPORTED	
		WEB. 'S PICT.	WORCESTER'S
Applegate & Co.	Cinn.	372	8
A. S. Barnes & Burr	N. Y.	813	110
Sheldon & Co.	N. Y.	5 to 1	
E. H. Butler & Co.	Phila.	10 to 1	
Ivison, Phinney & Co.	N. Y.	206	50 (all the sales made within a few weeks after publication)
D. Appleton & Co.	N. Y.	686	200
Pratt, Oakley & Co.	N. Y.	633	40
Collins & Brother	N. Y.	4 to 1	
Clark, Austin, Maynard & Co.	N. Y.	462	12
E. P. & R. J. Judd	N. Haven	292	5
Moore, Wilstock, Keyd & Co.	Cinn.	20 to 1	
L. Bushnell	St. Louis	93	7
Keith & Woods	St. Louis	15 to 1	
The Largest Boston Jobbing House		1, 301	229
Another Boston Bookseller		113	2
Randall & Aston	Columbus, O.	8 to 1	
Anderson & Fuller	Toledo	92 to 1	
J. H. Baumgardner & Co.	Wooster, O.	50	0
W. B. Smith & Co.	Cinn.	100	3
George Blanchard	Cinn.	25 to 1	
_____	Masillon, O.	12	1
_____	Portland, Me.	10 to 1	
_____	Amenia, N. Y.	30-40	0
_____	Chicago	324	12

*Compiled from data given in the advertisement on the last page of
a pamphlet The Two Dictionaries, or the Reviewer Reviewed, Spring
field: G. & C. Merriam, date not given, penciled date, May 22,
1861.

BIBLIOGRAPHY

Dictionaries

Alexander, Caleb. The Columbian Dictionary of the English Language.... Boston: Isaiah Thomas and Ebenezer T. Andrews, ..., 1800.

Allison, Burgess. The American Standard of Orthography and Pronunciation.... Burlington: Printed by John S. Meehan, for David Allinson; et al., 1815.

Bartlett, John Russell. A Dictionary of Americanisms. A Glossary of Phrases, usually regarded as peculiar to the United States.... New York: Bartlett and Welford, 1848; also Fourth Edition, Boston: Little Brown and Company, 1877.

Bolles, William. An Explanatory and Phonographic Pronouncing Dictionary of the English Language.... New London: Bolles and Williams, 1845.

Burhans, Hezekiah. The Nomenclature and Expositor of the English Language.... Philadelphia: Uriah Hunt, 1826.

Claggett, Rufus. The American Expositor or Intellectual Definer.... Boston: Perkins and Marvin, ..., 1836.

Cobb, Lyman. Expositor or Sequel to the Spelling-Book.... New York: Collins and Hannay, 1833.

Cobb, Lyman. A New Dictionary of the English Language, in the Treasury of Knowledge, Vol. I, pp. 77-444 (Sixth Edition), New York: Conner and Cook, 1836.

[Coxe, Richard S.]. A New Critical Pronouncing Dictionary of the English Language, compiled ... by An American Gentleman. Burlington: D. Allinson and Company, 1813.

Elliott, John, and Johnson, Samuel, Jun'r. A Selected, Pronouncing, and Accented Dictionary. Suffield: Printed by Edward Gray, for Oliver D. and Increase Cook, 1800.

Elwyn, Alfred L. A Glossary of Supposed Americanisms. Philadelphia: J. B. Lippincott and Company, 1859.

Flint, Abel. A Spelling, Pronouncing, and Parsing Dictionary. Hartford: Hudson and Goodwin, 1806.

George, Noah J. T. The Gentlemen and Ladies' Pocket Dictionary.... Concord: Luther Roley, 1831.

Grimshaw, William. An Etymological Dictionary of the English Language.... Philadelphia: Lydia R. Bailey, 1821.

Grimshaw, William. The Ladies' Lexicon.... Philadelphia: Grigg, Elliott and Company, 1829.

Jaudon, Daniel, Watson, Thomas, and Addington, Stephen. An English Orthographical Expositor:.... Philadelphia: D. Hagan, [1804].

Johnson, Samuel, Jun'r. A School Dictionary. New Haven: Edward O'Brien [1798].

Laidlaw, Alexander. An American Pronouncing Dictionary of the English Language.... Philadelphia: Grissy and Markley; et al., 1859.

Pickering, John. A Vocabulary, or Collection of Words and Phrases which have been supposed to be peculiar to the United States of America.... Boston: Cummings and Hilliard, 1816.

Priest, Henry. The Young Ladies' Pocket Companion.... New York: Isaac Collins, 1801.

Robbins, Eliza. Primary Dictionary or Rational Vocabulary.... Third Edition, New York: Roe Lockwood, 1842.

Smalley, Daniel S. The American Phonetic Dictionary of the English Language.... Designed by Nathaniel Storrs, ..., with a general introduction by A. J. Ellis, Cincinnati: Longley Brothers, 1856.

Turner, William W. The School Dictionary.... Hartford: H. and F. T. Huntington, 1829.

Webster, Noah. An American Dictionary of the English Language:.... In Two Volumes, New York: S. Converse. Printed by Hezekiah Howe, New Haven, 1828.

Webster, Noah. An American Dictionary of the English Language ... Revised and Enlarged by Chauncey A. Goodrich.... Springfield: George and Charles Merriam, 1847, reprinted 1848, 1853. Pictorial Edition, 1859.

Webster, Noah. A Compendious Dictionary of the English Language.... Hartford: Hudson and Goodwin, 1806.

Webster, Noah. A Pronouncing and Defining Dictionary of the English Language, Abridged from Webster's American Dictionary, ..., by Chauncey A. Goodrich. Philadelphia: J. B. Lippincott and Company, 1856.

Woodbridge, William. A Key to the English Language, or a Spelling, Parsing, Derivative, and Defining Dictionary: .... Middletown, T. & J. B. Dunning, 1801.

Worcester, Joseph Emerson. A Dictionary of the English Language. Boston: Swan, Brewer and Tileston, 1860.

Worcester, Joseph Emerson. A Pronouncing, Explanatory, and Synonymous Dictionary of the English Language. Boston: Hickling, Swan, and Brown, 1855.

Worcester, Joseph Emerson. A Universal and Critical Dictionary of the English Language;.... Boston: Wilkins, Carter and Company, 1846.

Manuscript Material

Letters:

John Russell Bartlett to E. A. Duyckinck, December 20, 1934, and January 7, 1837. Originals in Duyckinck Collection, New York Public Library.

Charles Folsom to J. E. Worcester, January 20, 1860. Original in the Folsom Collection, Boston Public Library.

Charles Folsom, Richard Soule, Jr. and William A. Wheeler, Jr. to William D. Swan, October 9, 1857. Original in Folsom Collection, Boston Public Library.

A. H. Grimshaw to Childs and Peterson, not dated. Original in the library of the Historical Society of Pennsylvania.

Noah Webster to Presidents of Colleges, February 17, 1806. Inserted in a copy of A Compendious Dictionary, in the New York Public Library.

Communications to the Present Author:

Elizabeth G. Davis, Guilford, Connecticut, September 5, 1935, and September 16, 1935.

Frederick Calvin Morton, Guilford, Connecticut, June 22, 1935.

Harry R. Warfel, June 30, 1935.

Material concerning Samuel Johnson, Jr. on fly-leaves of a New Testament, formerly owned by Samuel Johnson, Jr. and now in the possession of Mrs. George S. Davis, Guilford, Connecticut.

Memoranda of John Russell Bartlett. Original in the John Carter Brown Library.

Noah Webster's Papers in the New York Public Library. These include many of Webster's letters and many letters to Webster, papers, the manuscript of the Synopsis, and the diaries.

Pamphlets

Allen, Sturgess. Noah Webster's Place Among English Lexicographers. Springfield: G. & C. Merriam, 1909.

Cobb, Lyman. A Critical Review of the Orthography of Dr. Webster's Series of Books for Systematick Instruction in the English Language. New York: Collins and Hannay, 1831.

A Comparison of Worcester's and Webster's Quarto Dictionaries, also Specimen Pages of Worcester's Quarto Dictionary, Recommendations from Eminent Scholars, and Reviews from Leading Periodicals, American and Foreign. Boston: Swan, Brewer, and Tileston. Date not given.

The Critic Criticised and Worcester Vindicated: Consisting of a Review of an Article in the "Congregationalist" upon the Comparative Merits of Worcester's and Webster's Quarto Dictionaries. Boston: Swan, Brewer, and Tileston, March, 1860.

Dictionaries in the Boston Mercantile Library and Boston Atheneum. Springfield: G. & C. Merriam, 1856.

"Equal Justice," The Two Dictionaries or the Reviewer Reviewed, A Reply to a Correspondent of the New York World. Springfield: G. & C. Merriam, 1860.

F., W. C. [Fowler, William Chauncey]. Printed, But Not Published. [1854?] New York Public Library.

Have We a National Standard of English Lexicography? or Some Comparisons of the Claims of Webster's Dictionaries, and Worcester's Dictionaries. Springfield: G. & C. Merriam, 1855.

Merriam, G. & C. "A Gross Literary Fraud Exposed; Relating to the Publication of Worcester's Dictionaries in London," as Webster's Dictionary. Springfield: G. & C. Merriam, 1854.

Philorthos. The Orthographical Hobgoblin. Springfield: G. & C. Merriam, 1859.

Philpott, A. J. "A Pioneer Publishing Romance," reprinted from the Boston Globe. Springfield: G. & C. Merriam. Date not given.

Read, Allen Walker. The Development of Faith in the Dictionary. A paper read before the Modern Language Association, December 29, 1934.

Recommendations of Worcester's Dictionaries: to Which is Prefixed a Review of Webster's System of Orthography from the United States Democratic Review, for March, 1856. Boston: Hickling, Swan and Brown, 1856.

A Reply to Messrs. G. & C. Merriam's Attack Upon the Character of Dr. Worcester and His Dictionaries. Boston: Jenks, Hickling and Swan, 1854.

Sargent, Epes. The Critic Criticised: A Reply to a Review of Webster's System in the Democratic Review for March, 1856. From the Democratic Review for June, 1856. Springfield: G. & C. Merriam, 1856.

A Summary Summing of the Charges, with Their Refutations, in Attacks Upon Noah Webster, LL. D., His Dictionaries, or His Publishers, Made by Mr. Joseph Worcester, Mr. Sherman Converse, Messrs. Jenks, Hickling, and Swan. Springfield: G. & C. Merriam, 1834.

Swan, William Draper. The Critic Criticised and Worcester Vindicated; Consisting of a Review in the "Congregationalist," upon the Comparative Merits of Worcester's and Webster's Quarto Dictionaries, Together with a Reply to the Attacks of Messrs. G. & C. Merriam upon the Character of Dr. Worcester and His Dictionaries. Boston: Swan, Brewer, and Tileston, March, 1860.

Swan, William Draper. A Reply to Messrs. G. & C. Merriam's Attack Upon the Character of Dr. Worcester and His Dictionaries. Boston: Jenks, Hickling, and Swan, 1854.

The Two Dictionaries or the Reviewer Reviewed, A Reply to a Correspondent of The New York World. Springfield: G. & C. Merriam, 1860.

Webster, Noah. Dissertations on the English Language; With Notes, Historical and Critical. To which is added, by way of Appendix, an Essay on a Reformed Mode of Spelling, with Dr. Franklin's Arguments on that Subject. Boston: Isaiah Thomas and Company, 1789.

Webster, Noah. A Letter to the Honorable John Pickering, on the Subject of His Vocabulary; or, Collection of Words and Phrases, Supposed to Be Peculiar to the United States of America. Boston: West and Richardson, 1817.

Webster, Noah. To the Friends of American Literature [1831].
Bound with other Pamphlets in a volume entitled English Language. New York Public Library.

Webster, Noah. To the Friends of Literature in the United States.
A printed circular in Webster's MSS, New York Public Library.

Worcester, Joseph Emerson. A Gross Literary Fraud Exposed;
Relating to the Publication of Worcester's Dictionary in London.
Boston: Jenks, Hickling, and Swan, 1853.

Magazine and Newspaper Articles

Abbot, Ezra. "Joseph Emerson Worcester," Proceedings of the
American Academy of Arts and Sciences, VII (1865-1868),
112-116.

"An American Dictionary of the English Language by Noah Webster,
Revised by Chauncey A. Goodrich, 1848," The Literary World.
(N. Y.), II (1847-1848), 451-454.

"Americanisms," The National Quarterly Review, II (1860-1861),
230-240.

Beck, T. Romeyn, "Notes on Mr. Pickering's Vocabulary of Words
and Phrases Which Have Been Supposed to Be Peculiar to the
United States, with Preliminary Observations," Transactions of
the Albany Institute, I (1830), 25-31.

Benton, Joel, "The Webster Spelling Book," Magazine of American
History, X (July-December, 1893), 299-306.

Colton, A. M., "Our Old Webster Spelling Book," Magazine of
American History, XXIV (1890), 465-466.

"The Columbian Dictionary of the English Language, ...," American
Review and Literary Journal, I (1801), 217-228.

"A Compendious Dictionary of the English Language ... by Noah
Webster ...," The Panoplist, III (1807), 78-84.

"A Comprehensive, Pronouncing and Explanatory Dictionary of the
English Language ... by Joseph Emerson Worcester ...,"
American Monthly Review, I (1832), 93-104.

Connecticut Courant, Monday, May 24, 1790.

Converse, Sherman. "Webster's Dictionary," The New York Morning Herald, August 27, 1829.

"Domestic Occurrences," The Portfolio, I (1801), 247-325.

Dyer, Louis, "A Lexicographer on Lexicography," Nation, LXXI (1900), 28-30.

Editorial, Worcester Palladium, December 10, 1834.

"The English Language," DeBow's Review, XXX (1861), 323-325.

Fuess, Claude M., "Joseph Emerson Worcester," Phillips Bulletin, XIC (1925), 6-11.

Garnett, Richard. "English Lexicography," Quarterly Review, LIV (1835), 295-330.

Gibson, Martha Jane. "America's First Lexicographer, Samuel Johnson, Jr., 1757-1836," American Speech, XI (December, 1936), 283-292; American Speech, XII (February, 1937), 19-30.

"A Glossary of Words and Phrases usually regarded as peculiar to the United States. By John Russell Bartlett," Blackwood's Magazine, LXXXIX (1861), 421-439.

"Inchiquen, the Jesuit's Letters, during a late Residence in the United States of America, being a Fragment of a Private Correspondence, accidentally discovered in Europe, containing a favourable View of the Manners, Literature, and State of Society, of the United States; and a Refutation of many of the Aspersions cast upon this Country, by Former Residents and Tourists, By Some Unknown Foreigner, New York, 1810," Quarterly Review, X (1814), 494-539.

"John Pickering," Nation, XLV (1887), 255-256.

"Johnson's Dictionary," New York Times Saturday Review, October 15, 1898.

"Johnson's English Dictionary, as improved by Todd, and abridged by Chalmers; with Walker's Pronouncing Dictionary Combined: ... Edited by Joseph E. Worcester, ...," American Quarterly Review, IV (1828), 191-214.

"A Key to the English Language ... by William Woodbridge....," American Review and Literary Journal, II (1802), 226.

Kingsley, J. L., "An American Dictionary of the English Language, ... by Noah Webster ... 1828," North American Review, XXVIII (April, 1829), 433-480.

"The Life and Labors of Rev. T. H. Gallaudet, by Rev. Heman Humphrey....," North American Review, LXXXVII (1858), 517-532.

Lounsbury, Thomas R. "The First Dictionary of Americanisms," Harper's Monthly, CXXIX (1919), 103-110.

Lowell, James Russell. Introduction to The Biglow Papers, Second Series in Complete Writings. New York: AMS Press, Inc., 1966.

Mead, Edwin D. "Noah Webster: Massachusetts, Dictionary Made at Amherst," Springfield Sunday Republican, October 18, 1908.

Mencken, H. L. "The American Language," Yale Review (Spring, 1936), 538-552.

Merriam, G. & C. "Webster's Dictionaries," Boston Post, March 22, 1855.

"Mr. Noah Webster's Proposed Dictionary," The American Journal of Education, I (1826), 315-316.

"Mr. Webster's Dictionary," The American Journal of Education, I (1826), 379-380.

Newell, William, "Memoir of J. E. Worcester, LL. D. ," Proceedings of the Massachusetts Historical Society, XIV (1880), 169-173.

"Noah Webster," The New Englander, I, No. IV (October, 1843), 565.

Obituary, Hon. John Russell Bartlett, The Providence Journal, May 29, 1886.

Obituary, Lyman Cobb, The Ithaca Journal and Advertiser, Wednesday, March 1, 1865.

Peabody, O. W. B. "A Comprehensive, Pronouncing and Explanatory Dictionary of the English Language, Revised and Enlarged, Boston, 1835," North American Review, XLI (1835), 482-488.

Pickering, John. "Johnson's English Dictionary, as improved by Todd, and abridged by Chalmers, edited by Joseph E. Worcester ...," American Quarterly Review, IV (1828), 191-214.

Porter, Noah. "English Lexicography," Bibliotheca Sacra, XX (1863), 78-124.

Read, Allen Walker. "An Obscenity Symbol," American Speech, IX (1934), 264-278.

"Reviews and Literary Notices," Atlantic Monthly, IV (1859), 638-651; V (May, 1960), 631-637.

Richardson, Charles. "An American Dictionary of the English Language ... By Noah Webster ... 1828....," Westminster Review, XXVII (1831), 56-93.

Roane, A. "English Dictionaries, with Remarks Upon the English Language," Southern Literary Messenger, XXII (1856), 168-173.

Robinson, Henry Pynchon. 'Country Sketches,' No. 10, New Haven (weekly) Palladium, January 15, 1880, in Levermore, Charles H., "Two Centuries and a Half in Connecticut," New England Magazine, I (n. s.), (December, 1889), 421.

Robinson, Henry Pynchon. "Samuel Johnson, Jr., of Guilford and His Dictionaries," The Connecticut Magazine, V (October, 1899), 526-531.

Rollins, Richard M. "Words as Social Control: Noah Webster and the Creation of the American Dictionary," American Quarterly, XXVIII (1976), 415-430.

Sargent, Mary E. "Susanna Rowson," The Medford Historical Register, VII (April, 1904), 26-40.

Savage, James. "A Compendious Dictionary ...," The Monthly Anthology and Boston Review, VI (1809), 246-264.

"Schools As They Were Sixty Years Ago," The American Journal of Education, XIV (1863), 123-144.

"A Selected, Pronouncing and Accented Dictionary ... by John Elliott ... and Samuel Johnson, jun ...," American Review and Literary Journal, I (1801), 210-217.

Tarbox, Increase N. "Noah Webster," The Congregational Quarterly, VII, No. 1 (1865), 1-16.

Tucker, Gilbert M. "American English," Transactions of the Albany Institute, X (1883), 334-360.

"The Two Dictionaries," The New York World, June 15, 1860.

"A Universal and Critical Dictionary of the English Language ... by J. E. Worcester ...," The Literary World, II (1847-1848), 529.

Webster, Noah. "Prospectus of a New and Complete Dictionary of the English Language," The Panoplist, II (n. s.) (1810), 430.

"Webster's Dictionary," Worcester Palladium, December 10, 1834.

"Webster's International Dictionary--Especially Its Pronunciation," New Englander, LIII (1890), 421-440.

"Webster's Unabridged Dictionary," The American Journal of Education, II (1856), 517.

White, Richard Grant. "Americanisms," Galaxy, XXIV (1877), 376-383.

Willard, Sidney. "A New Critical Pronouncing Dictionary of the English Language ...," The General Repository and Review, IV (1813), 150-174.

[Willard, Sidney]. "A Universal and Critical Dictionary of the English Language ... by Joseph E. Worcester ...," North American Review, LXIV (1847), 179-208.

Worcester, Samuel T. "Joseph E. Worcester," The Granite Monthly, III (April, 1880), 245-252.

"Words Often Mispronounced," The Common School Journal, I (1839), 361-363.

Yale University Gazette, III (1929), 65.

Zunder, Theodore Albert. "Noah Webster as a Student Orator," The Yale Alumni Weekly, XXXVI, No. 9 (November 19, 1926), 225.

Books (General)

Ashmead, Henry Graham. History of Delaware County, Pennsylvania. Philadelphia: L. H. Everts and Company, 1884.

Atkins, Nelson Frederick. Fitz-Greene Halleck. New Haven: Yale University Press, 1930.

Barnard, Henry. Tribute to Gallaudet, A Discourse in Commemoration of the Life, Character and Services, of the Rev. Thomas H. Gallaudet, LL. D. Delivered before the Citizens of Hartford, January 7, 1852, Hartford: Brockett and Hutchinson, 1852.

Bartlett, John Russell. Genealogy of That Branch of the Russell Family Which Comprises the Descendants of John Russell of Woburn, Massachusetts, 1640-1878. Providence: Privately Printed, 1879.

Bolles, John A. Genealogy of the Bolles Family in America. Boston: Henry W. Dutton and Son, 1865.

Browne, Eliza Southgate. A Girl's Life Eighty Years Ago. New York: Charles Scribner's Sons, 1887.

Bruce, Dwight H., editor. Onondaga's Centennial. Boston: The Boston Huston Company, I, 1894.

Cambridge History of American Literature, The. Edited by William Peterfield Trent, John Erskine, Stuart P. Sherman, and Carl Van Doren. New York: G. P. Putnam's Sons, IV, 1921.

Clement, John. Sketches of the First Emigrant Settlers in Newtonship. Old Gloucester County, West New Jersey. Camden: Printed by Sinnickson Chew, 1877.

Critical Dictionary of English Literature and British and American Authors. Edited by S. Austin Allibone, Philadelphia: J. B. Lippincott and Company, I, III, 1882.

Crosbie, Lawrence M. The Phillips Exeter Academy, A History. Norwood, Massachusetts: The Plimpton Press, 1924.

Cyclopedia of American Literature, The. Edited by Evert A. and George L. Duyckinck. New York: Charles Scribner's Sons, II, Part 2, 1866.

Derby, J. G. Fifty Years Among Authors, Books, and Publishers. New York: G. W. Carleton and Company, 1884.

Dexter, Franklin Bowditch. Biographical Sketches of the Graduates of Yale College with Annals of the College History, 1701-1815. New Haven: Yale University Press, III, IV, V, VI, 1903-1913.

Dictionary of American Biography. Edited by Francis S. Drake. Boston: Houghton, Osgood and Company, 1879.

Dictionary of American Biography, The. Edited by Allen Johnson et al., New York: Charles Scribner's Sons, II, 1929; III, 1929; IV, 1930; X, 1933.

Encyclopedia of American Biography. Edited by Thomas William Herringshaw. Chicago: American Publishers' Association, 1898.

Fitch, Eleazar T. A Sermon Preached at the Funeral of the Reverend John Elliott, D.D., Late Pastor of the Church in East Guilford. New Haven: Printed by Nathan Whiting, 1825.

Flint, John, and Stone, John H. Flint Genealogy. Andover: W. F. Draper, 1860.

Ford, Emily Ellsworth Fowler. Notes on the Life of Noah Webster. Edited by Emily Ellsworth Ford Skeel. New York: Privately Printed, 2 Vols., 1912.

Futhey, J. Smith, and Cope, Gilbert. History of Chester County, Pennsylvania. Philadelphia: L. H. Everts, 1881.

Gallaudet, Edward Miner. Life of Thomas Hopkins Gallaudet. New York: Henry Holt and Company, 1889.

Gallup, James A. "Historical Discourse," Proceedings at the Celebration of the 250th Anniversary of the Settlement of Guilford, Connecticut. New Haven: The Stafford Printing Company, 1889.

Gammell, William. Life and Services of the Honorable John Russell Bartlett. Providence: Printed by the Providence Press, 1886.

Genealogy of the Descendants of John Eliot, "Apostle to the Indians," 1598-1905, A New Edition, 1905. Prepared and published by the Committee appointed at the Meeting of His Descendants, at South Natick, Massachusetts, June 3, 1901.

Goodrich, Samuel G. Recollections of a Lifetime. New York: Miller, Orton and Company, II, 1857.

Goodwin, Harley. "History of the Town of New Marlborough," in History of the County of Berkshire. Edited by David D. Field. Pittsfield: S. W. Bush, 1829.

Griswold, Rufus Wilmot. Female Poets of America. New York: James Miller, 1873.

Hawthorne, Julian. Nathaniel Hawthorne and His Wife, (Fifth Edition). Boston: Ticknor and Company, I, 1884.

Higginson, Thomas Wentworth. Henry Wadsworth Longfellow. Boston: The Riverside Press, 1902.

Higginson, Thomas Wentworth. Old Cambridge. New York: The Macmillan Company, 1899.

Holmes, Oliver Wendell. The Professor at the Breakfast Table. Boston: Houghton Mifflin and Company, 1893.

Humphrey, Heman. The Life and Labors of the Rev. T. H. Gallaudet. New York: Robert Carter and Brothers, 1857.

Knight, Edgar W. Reports on European Education. New York: McGraw-Hill Book Company, 1930.

Krapp, George Philip. English Language in America. New York: The Century Company, I, 1925.

Lawrence, Thomas. Historical Genealogy of the Lawrence Family. New York: E. O. Lawrence, 1858.

Livingston, John. Portraints of Eminent Americans Now Living. New York: Cornish, Lamport and Company, I, 1853.

Longfellow, Samuel, editor. Life of Henry Wadsworth Longfellow. Boston: Houghton, Mifflin Company, I, 1891.

Lowndes, William Thomas. The Bibliographer's Manual of English Literature, revised by Henry G. Bohn. London: George Bell and Sons, IV, 1864.

McKnight, George H. Modern English in the Making. New York: D. Appleton and Company, 1928.

McMaster, John Bach. History of the People of the United States. New York: D. Appleton and Company, I, 1888.

Mencken, H. L. The American Language (First Edition). New York: Alfred A. Knopf, 1919.

Monroe, W. S. "Samuel Johnson," in Cyclopedia of Education, The, edited by Paul Monroe. New York: Macmillan, III, 1914.

Nason, Elias. A Memoir of Mrs. Susanna Rowson. Albany: Joel Munsell, 1870.

National Cyclopedia of American Biography, The. New York: James T. White and Company, VI, 1896; X, 1900; XII, 1904.

Neumann, Joshua H. American Pronunciation According to Noah Webster (1783), Doctoral Dissertation. New York: Columbia University Press (mimeographed), 1924.

Pickering, Mary Orne. Life of John Pickering. Boston: University Press, John Wilson and Son, 1887.

Robinson, Henry Pynchon. Guilford Portraits. New Haven: The Pease-Lewis Company, 1907.

Roorbach, O. A. Bibliotheca Americana, Catalogue of American Publications, including Reprints and Original Works, from 1820 to 1852, inclusive. New York: Orville A. Roorbach, 1852.

Savage, James. Genealogical Dictionary of the First Settlers of New England. Boston: Little, Brown and Company, II, 1860.

Scharf, I. Thomas. History of Westchester County. Philadelphia: L. E. Preston and Company, I, Part 2, 1886.

Schneider, Herbert and Carol. Samuel Johnson, President of King's College, His Career and Writings. New York: Columbia University Press, I, 1929.

Scudder, Horace E. Noah Webster. Boston: Houghton Mifflin Company, 1889.

Sellers, Edwin Jaquett. An Account of the Jaudon Family. Philadelphia: J. B. Lippincott, 1890.

Smith, Ralph D. The History of Guilford, Connecticut, from Its First Settlement in 1639. Albany: J. Munsell, 1877.

Sprague, William B. Annals of the American Pulpit. New York: Robert Carter and Brothers, II, 1866; III, 1868; VI, 1865.

Steger, Stewart Archer. American Dictionaries. Baltimore: J. H. Furst, 1913.

Stiles, Ezra. Literary Diary, Edited by Franklin Bowditch Dexter. New York: Charles Scribner's Sons, II, 1901.

Sullivan, Mark. America Finding Herself. New York: Charles Scribner's Sons, 1927.

Todd, Charles Burr. Life and Letters of Joel Barlow. New York: G. P. Putnam, 1886.

Todd, John. John Todd, The Story of His Life, Told Mainly by Himself. New York: Harper and Brothers, 1877.

Trubner, Nicolas. Bibliographical Guide to American Literature. London: Trubner and Company, 1859.

Vail, R. W. G. Susanna Rowson, the Author of Charlotte Temple, A Bibliographical Study. Worcester: The American Antiquarian Society, 1933.

Ward, Julius H. The Life and Letters of James Gates Percival. Boston: Ticknor and Fields, 1866.

Warfel, Harry R. Noah Webster, Schoolmaster to America. New York: The Macmillan Company, 1936.

Webster, Noah. The American Spelling Book: Containing an Easy Standard of Pronunciation. Being the First Part of a Grammatical Institute of the English Language (Second Edition). Boston: Isaiah Thomas and Ebenezer T. Andrews, 1790.

Webster, Noah. Letters of Noah Webster. Edited with an Introduction by Harry R. Warfel. New York: Library Publishers, 1953.

Wheeler, Edmund. History of Newport, New Hampshire. Concord: Republican Press Association, 1879.

White, Daniel Appleton. Eulogy on John Pickering. Cambridge: Metcalf and Company, 1847.

Williams, R. O. Our Dictionaries and Other Language Topics. New York: Henry Holt and Company, 1890.

Wilson, James Grant. The Life and Letters of Fitz-Greene Halleck. New York: D. Appleton and Company, 1869.

Witherspoon, John. Works. Edinburgh: J. Ogle, II, IX, 1815.

Woodberry, George E. Nathaniel Hawthorne. Boston: Houghton, Mifflin Company, 1902.

Woodward, E. M., and Hageman, John F. History of Burlington and Mercer Counties, New Jersey, with Biographical Sketches of Many of the Pioneers and Prominent Men. Philadelphia: Everts and Peck, 1883.

Woody, Thomas. A History of Women's Education in the United States. New York: The Science Press, I, 1929.

Zunder, Theodore Albert. The Early Days of Joel Barlow. New Haven: Yale University Press, 1934.

INDEX OF AUTHORS

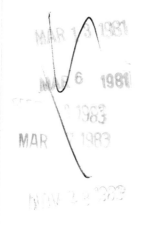